ARUNABHA KUNDU

SOME PAGES OF LIFE

I am a Kolkata and Howrah based street photographer. As a photographer, my aim persists on to explore street photography as a key to reach the common people and their lives. I like to tell their stories through my lens. Kolkata, earlier known as Calcutta, is the capital of west Bengal and the most densely populated cities of India. Kolkata became a British trading post in the last part of the 17th century. Kolkata once served as the capital of British power in India is known for its colonial buildings including the grand Victoria memorial. Other important sights include the Howrah Bridge, an engineering marvel over the river Hooghly, Howrah station and the Indian museum and many more. Apart from these, one can find stories in the streets of Kolkata. The streets are sometimes glorified with different festivals, rituals, parades and rallies. As it is the place of cultural harmony, one can enjoy the flavor of different festivals of different cultures.

The places I visit vary from the narrow alleys of North Kolkata to the huge mosque as Nakhoda, from the far away Sagar island to the small villages of Howrah district. I smelled the essence of winter maidan, when it turns into an ocean of dense fog. I followed the trail of light and shadow at Mallick Ghat situated near the extremely beautiful Howrah Bridge and tried to capture the candid moments of street lives over there. When I got the opportunity to show my works printed in a book, it was very tough for me to select the pictures from the huge pile of my clicks. Every frame tells a story as I tried to tell stories within a frame.

A huge thanks to the people who have encouraged and helped me a lot to bring out this book. I am grateful to the different web sites providing the required information. Thanks to all, who look at the stories that I wanted to tell through my lens.

I am Arunabha Kundu, an amateur photographer, live in Howran, West Bengal. I had a keen interest towards creative works from my childhood. I liked to draw and paint. I never thought about photography. But i liked to watch photographs. Slowly, after a long time, I grew interest in photography. After completing my studies, I bought a camera. My first camera was Nikon Coolpix L 100. I tried to click some pictures using that. I carefully observed other people's photography. In this way I started to work on my passion. Then, in the year 2013, I bought my first dslr Nikon D5200. Till now I am using that camera. All of my pictures are shot with this camera. My favourite subject is Street. Other than that, I love to click anything except wildlife.

In that sense, I never gone through any formal photography learning course. But learned about how to edit a picture. All the ideas I got about photography is due to my engagement in social media. Each day I see new pictures and try to learn from them. But, here I should mention someone. He is Mr. Tapas Basu sir. He is the only tutor of my photography. He taught me how to edit a picture. I love to experiment with photography. I never follow any rules. I click the ones which are beautiful in my eyes.

My first award came in 2014 when I won the grand prize from Shenzhen International Photography Contest (China). I got many prizes and some of my shots were published in national and international magazines. But, to me, the first award was the most special one.

Every year on the occasion of Makar Sankranti, the largest fair of West Bengal held at Sagar Island. Millions of pilgrims, mostly from Uttar Pradesh, Bihar, Odisha, Rajasthan and from other parts of India, gather to celebrate this three days festival.

Before going to the Sagar Island, all the pilgrims congregate at the Babu Ghat transit camp area. The whole area turns into a beautiful and colorful place while people, especially when the women dry their clothing. The spectacular scenes can amaze anyone with the variety of colors and reflects some glimpses of their lives

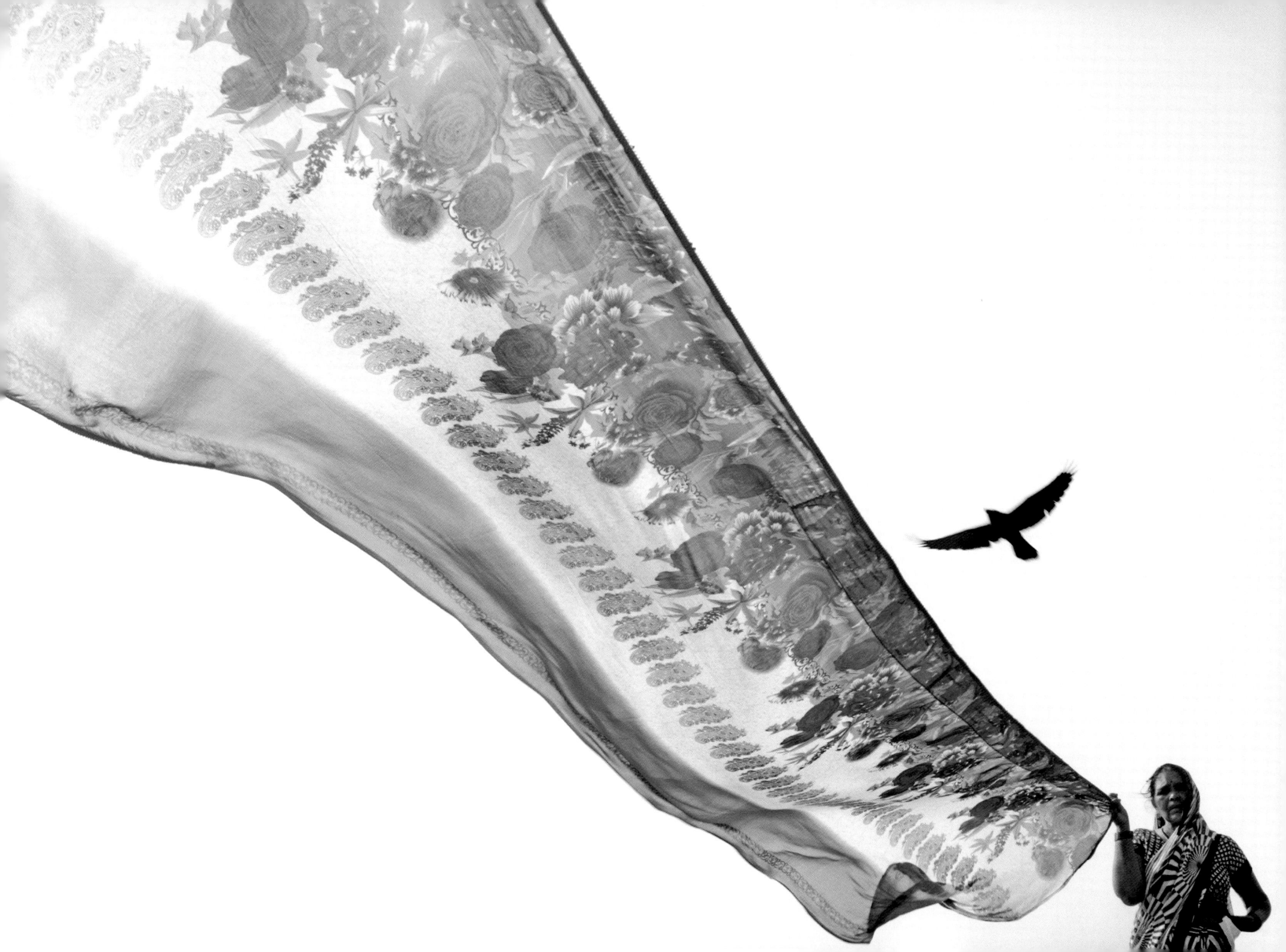

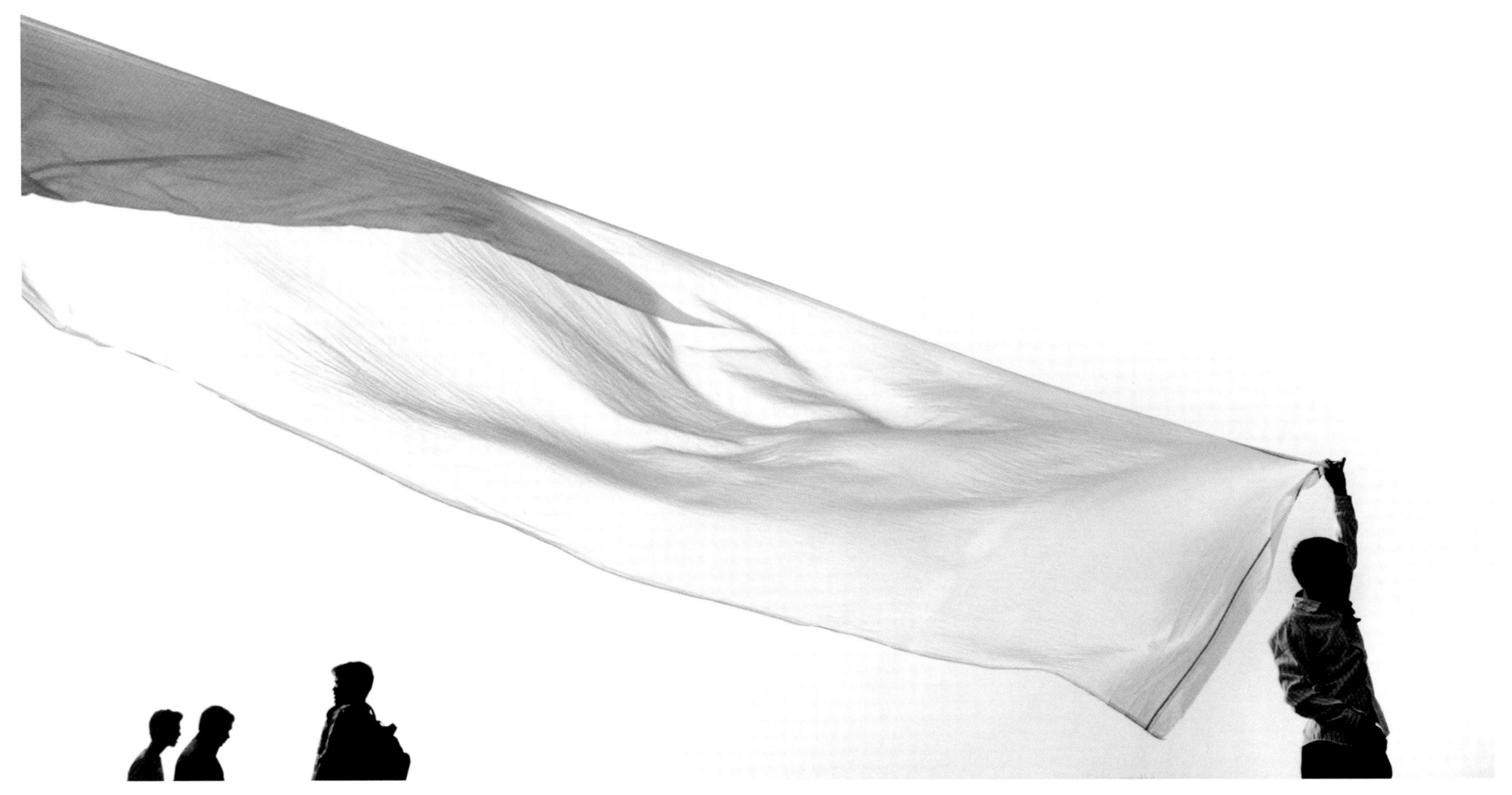

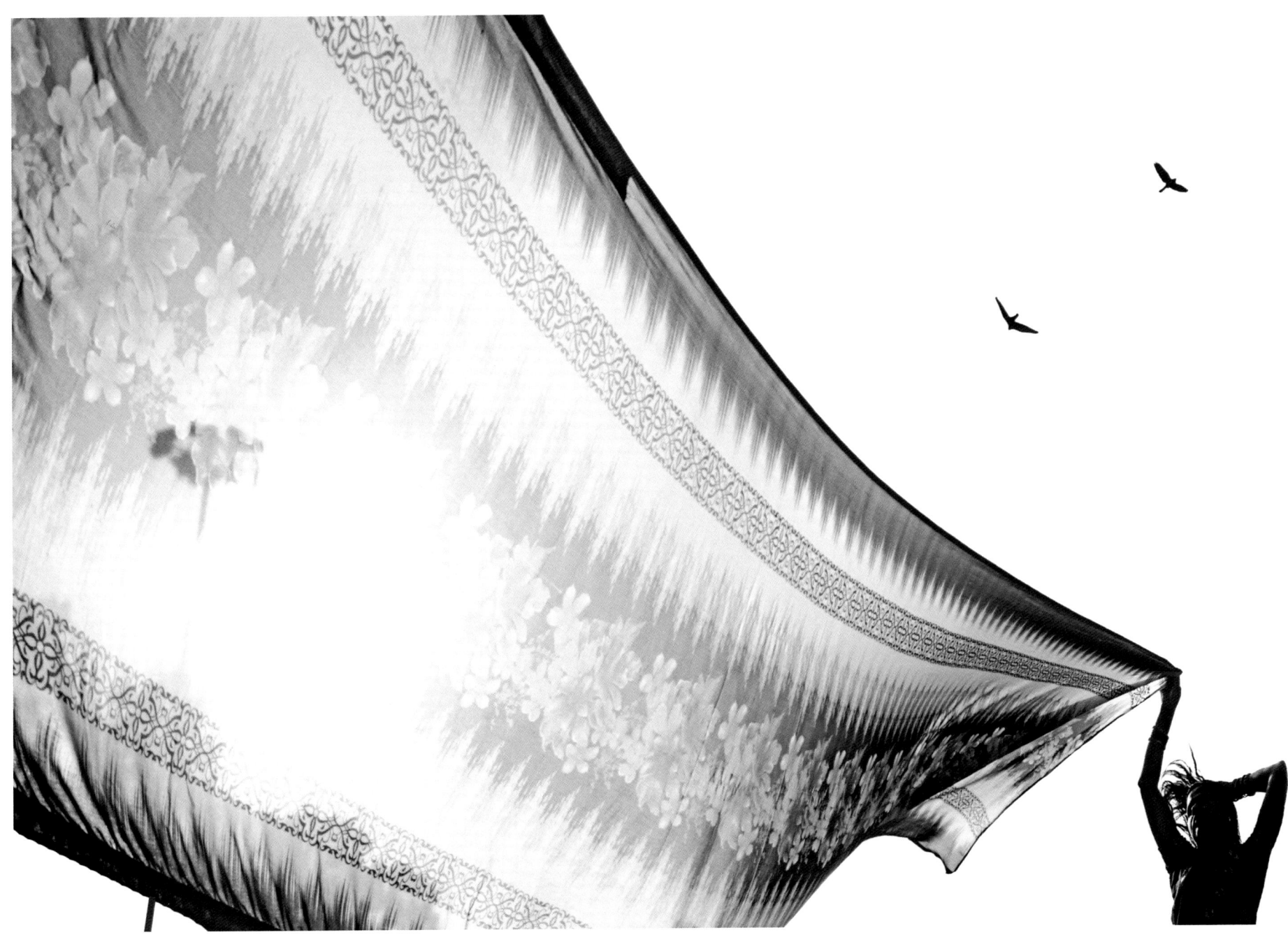

Durga puja is the most famous and gorgeous festival in India, especially in West Bengal. The vibrant festival that is witnessed all over West Bengal and especially in Kolkata it is magnificent. And this festival is incomplete without the iconic 'Dhunuchi Naach'. Besides worshipping the Durga idol, the most famous is the 'Dhunuchi Naach'.

'Naach' is the term used to denote dance and 'Dhunuchi' is nothing but an earthen pot filled with coconut husks, burning charcoal and incense. It is a devotional and traditional dance performed during the evening Durga aarti, when dancers are decked up in colorful clothes, balance clay pots in both hands and mouth. The sight is spectacular as the dancers dance to the beats of the dhak (Bengal drum, a musical instrument). This dance was previously only a men affair, but now women participate actively in it.

On the last day of Durga Puja, Dhunuchi Naach is performed in front of the idol, before going for immersion. I took these pictures to capture the beauty and essence of this dance form. The atmosphere became superb and everyone gathered around the dancers, with the Durga idol as a backdrop. The whole place turned smoky but smelled divine.

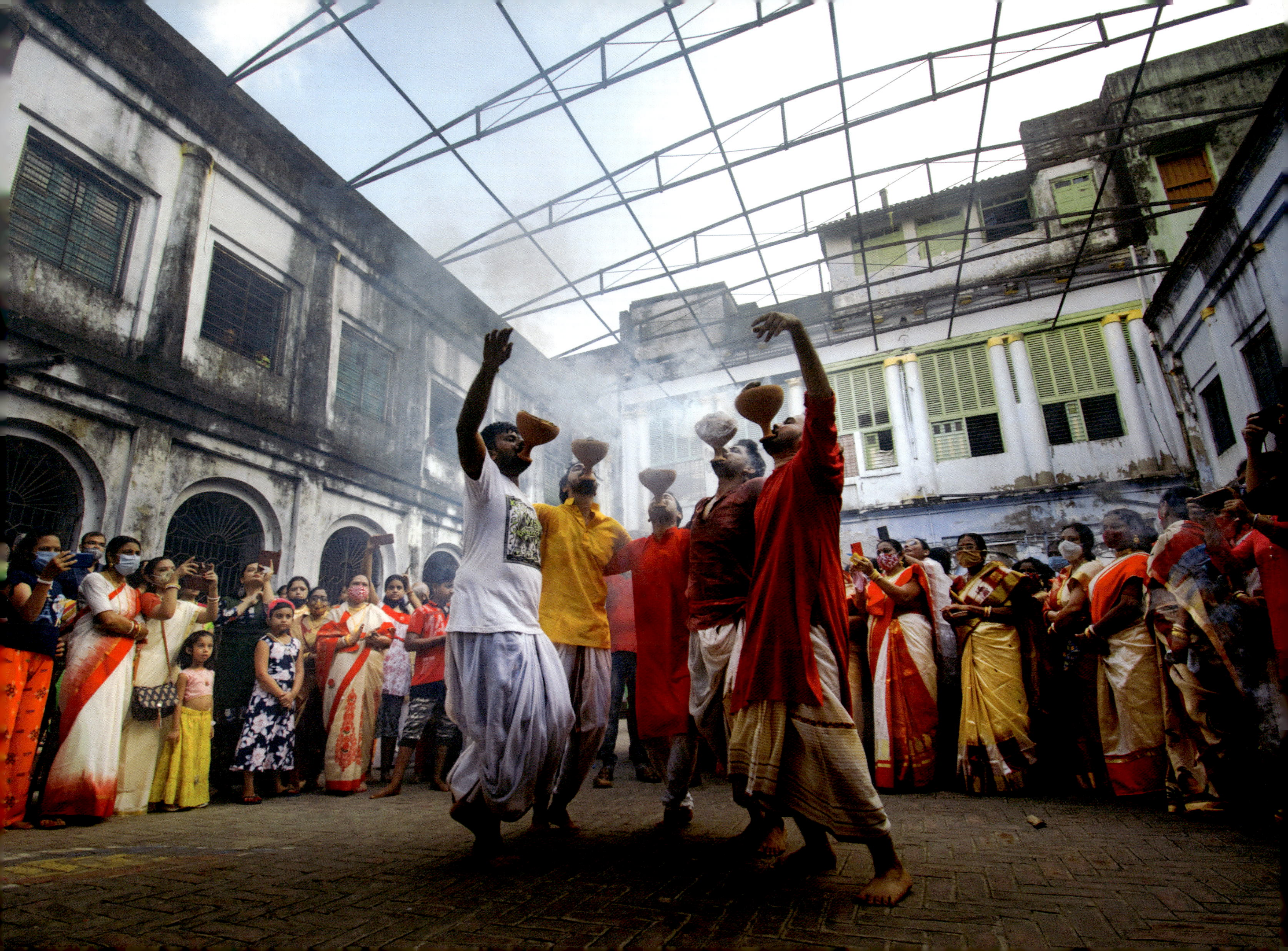

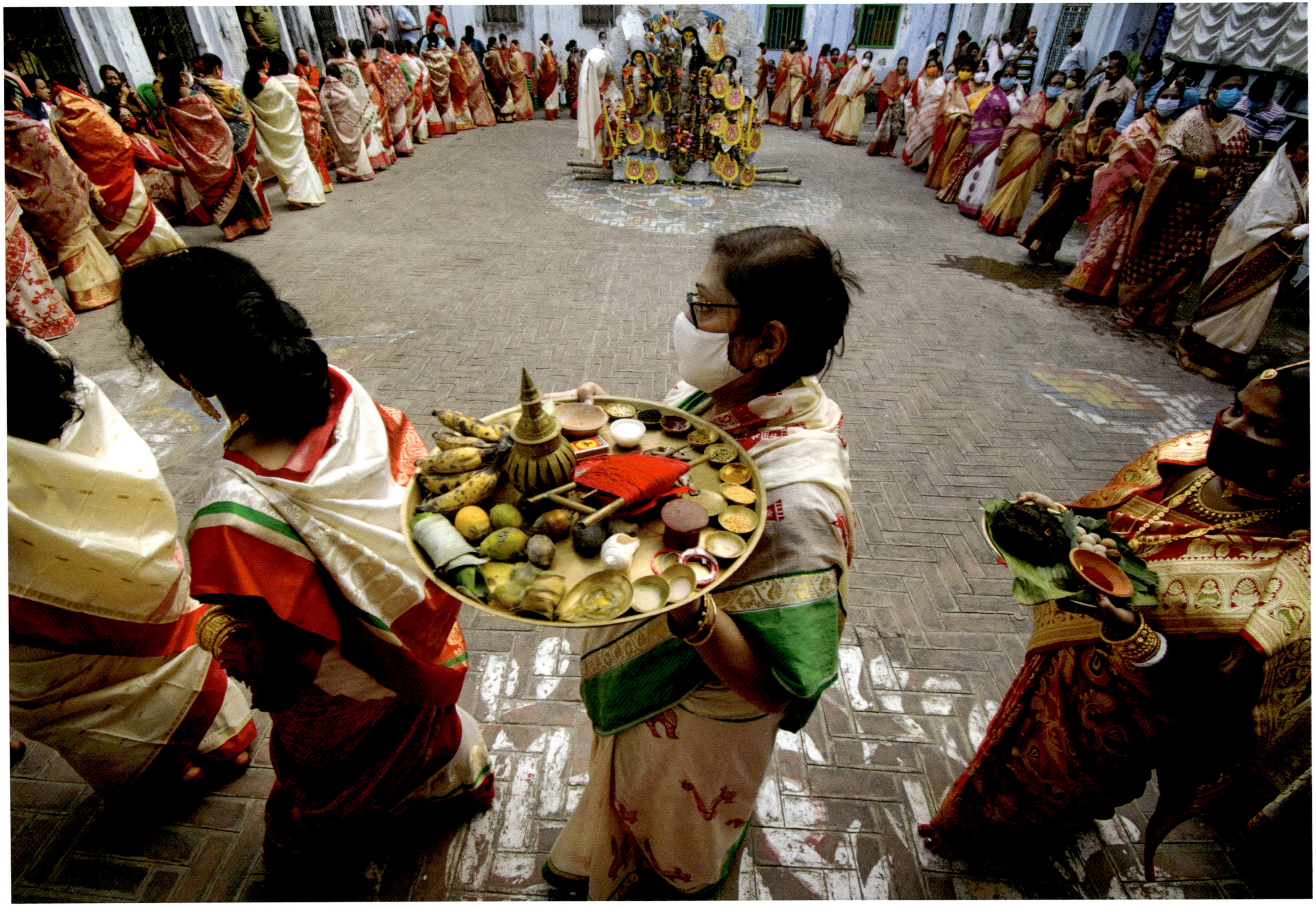

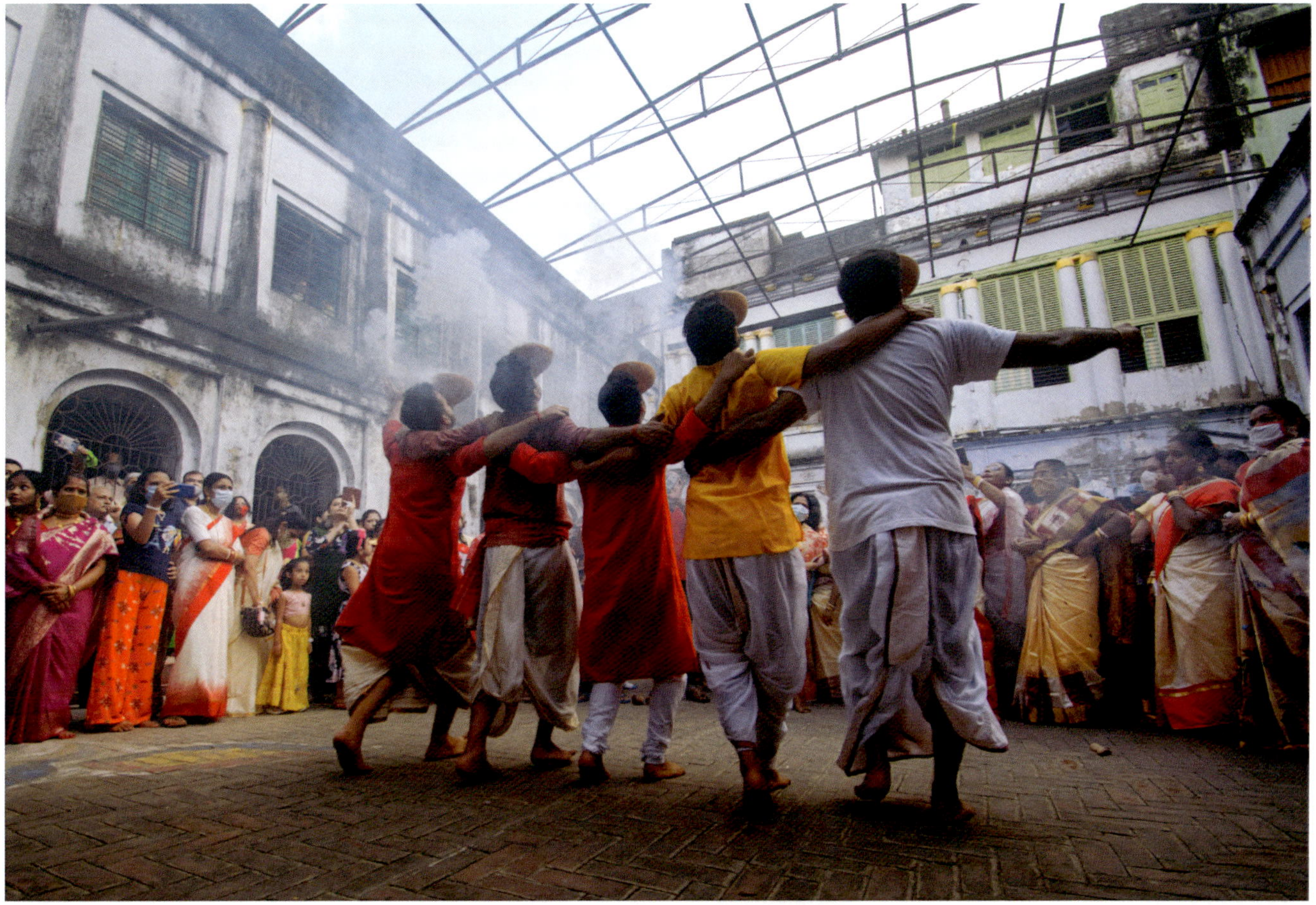
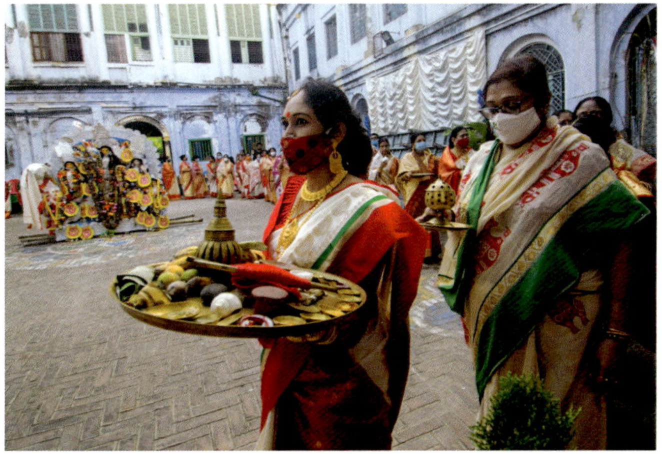
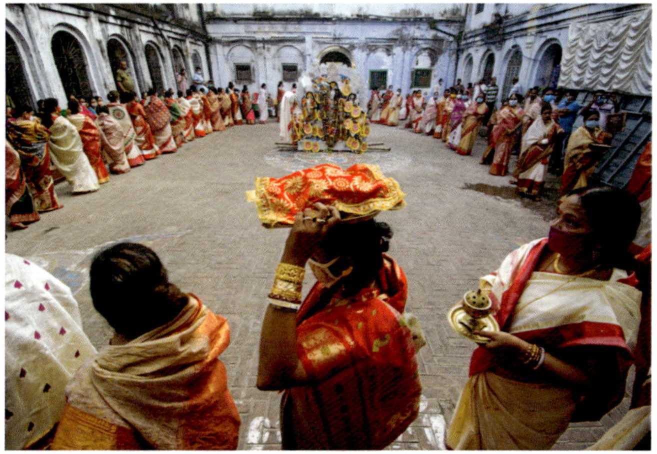

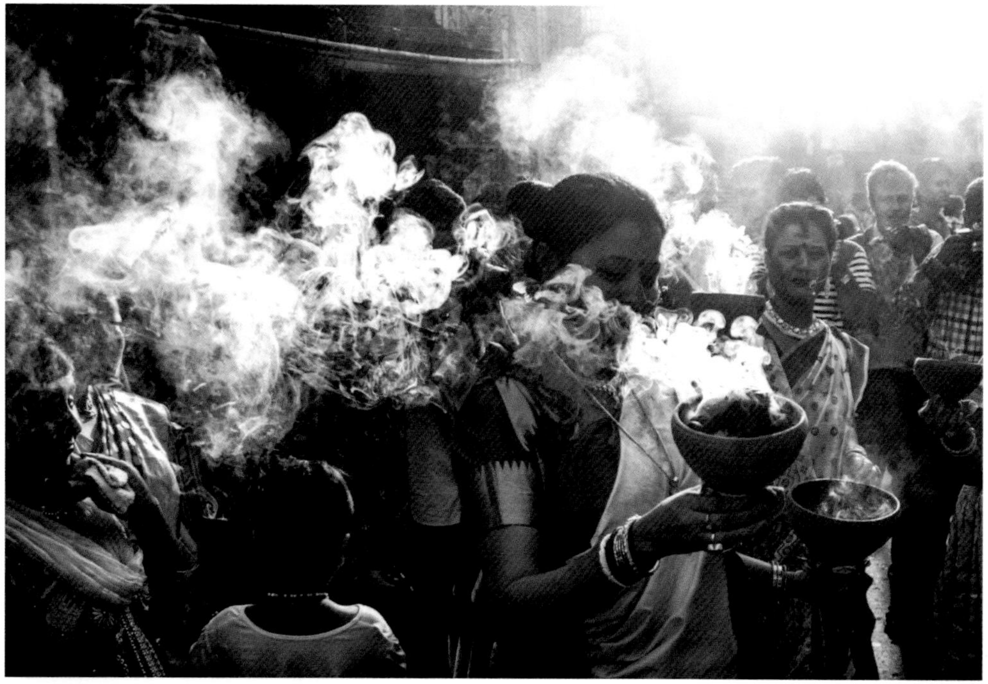
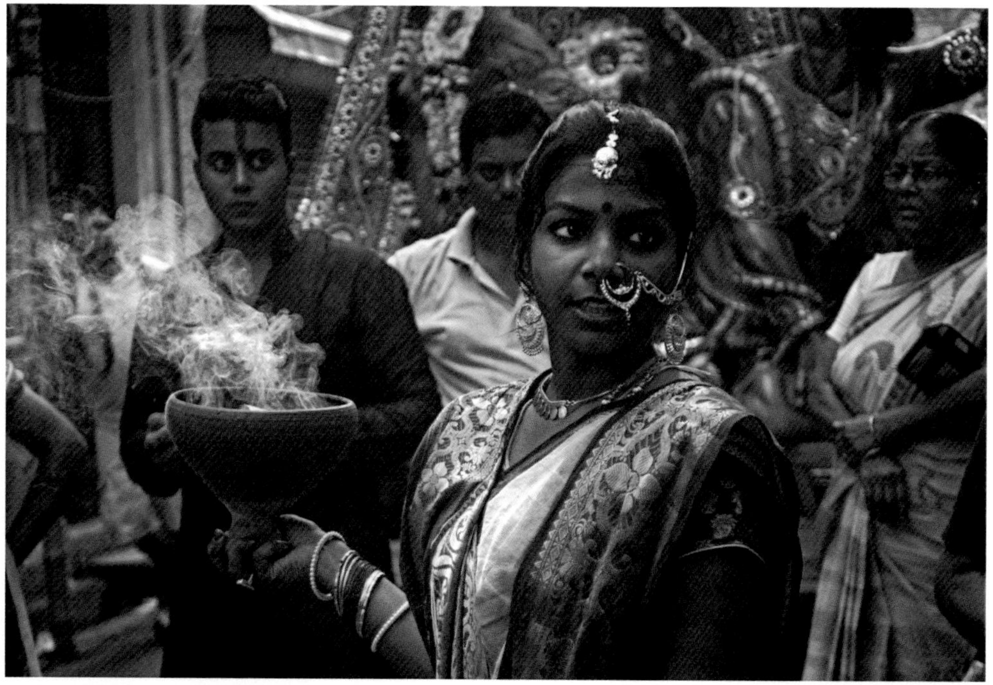
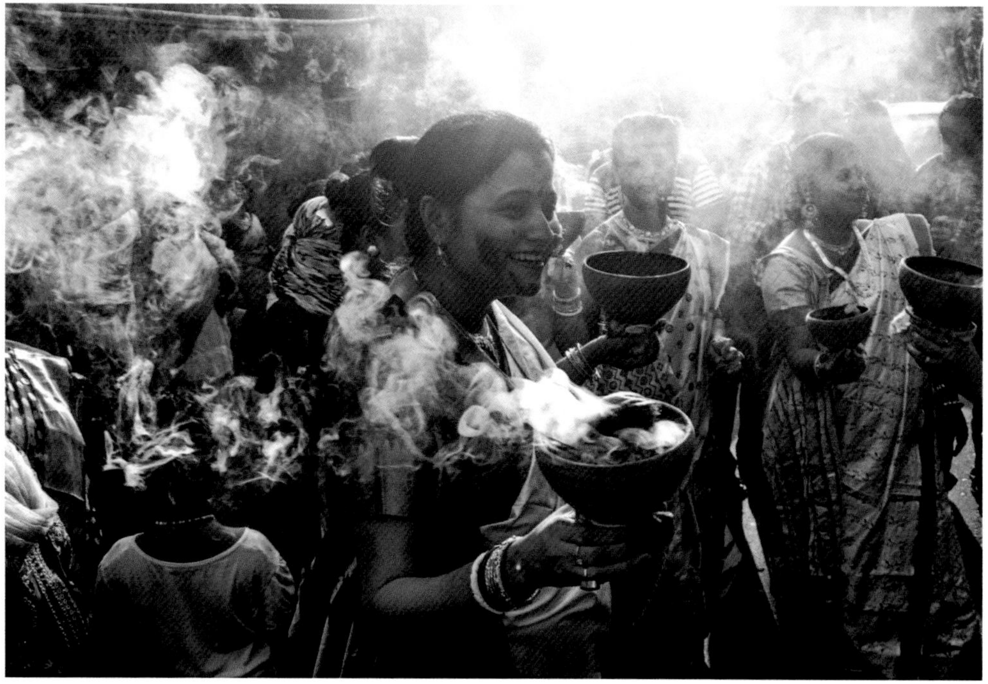
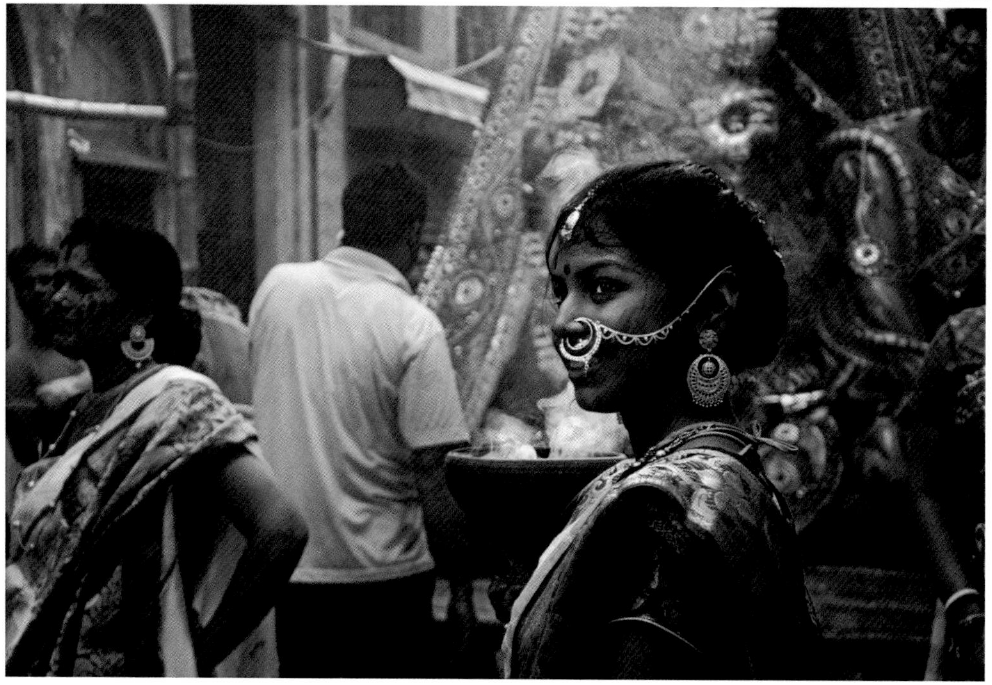

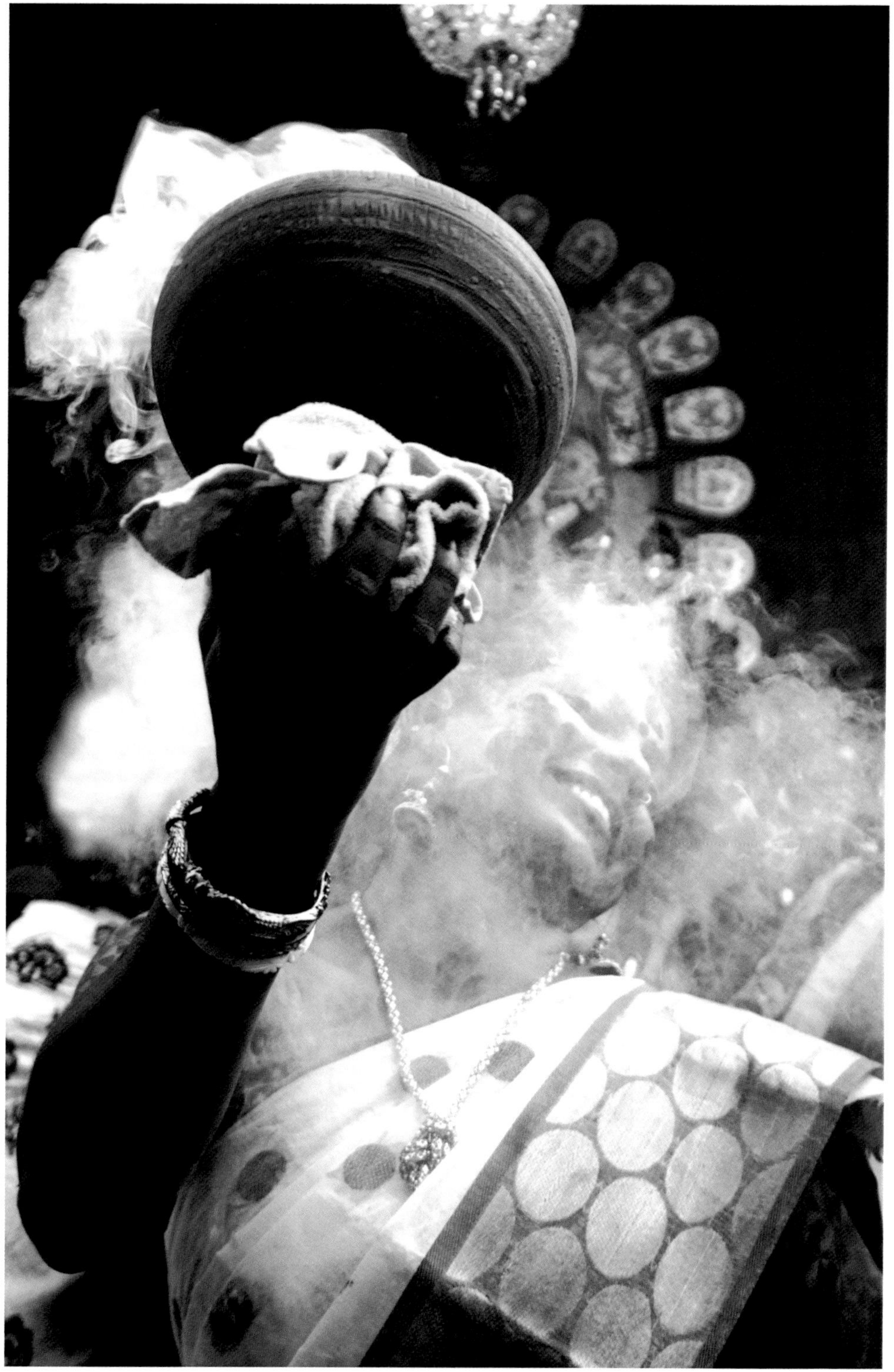

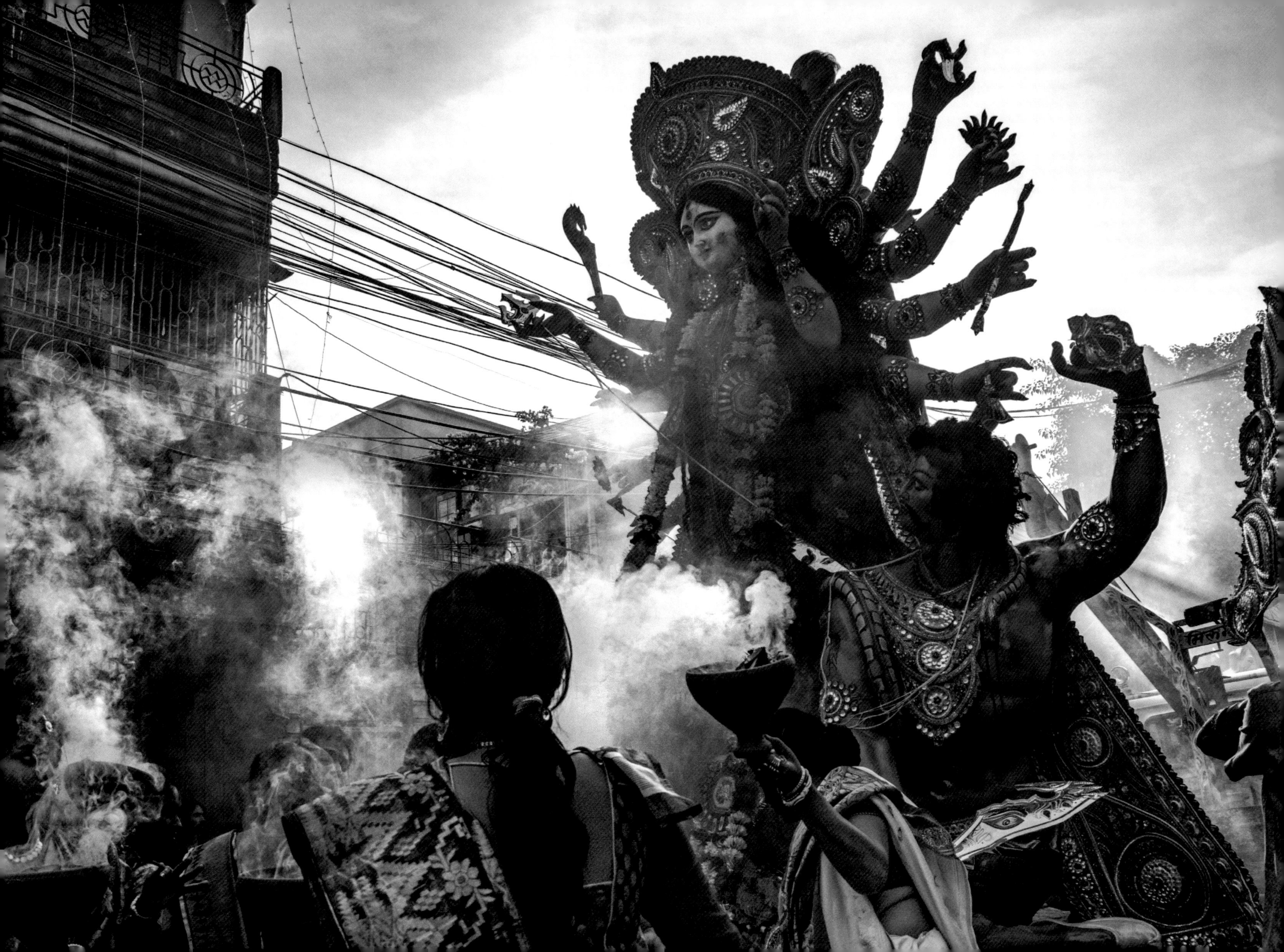

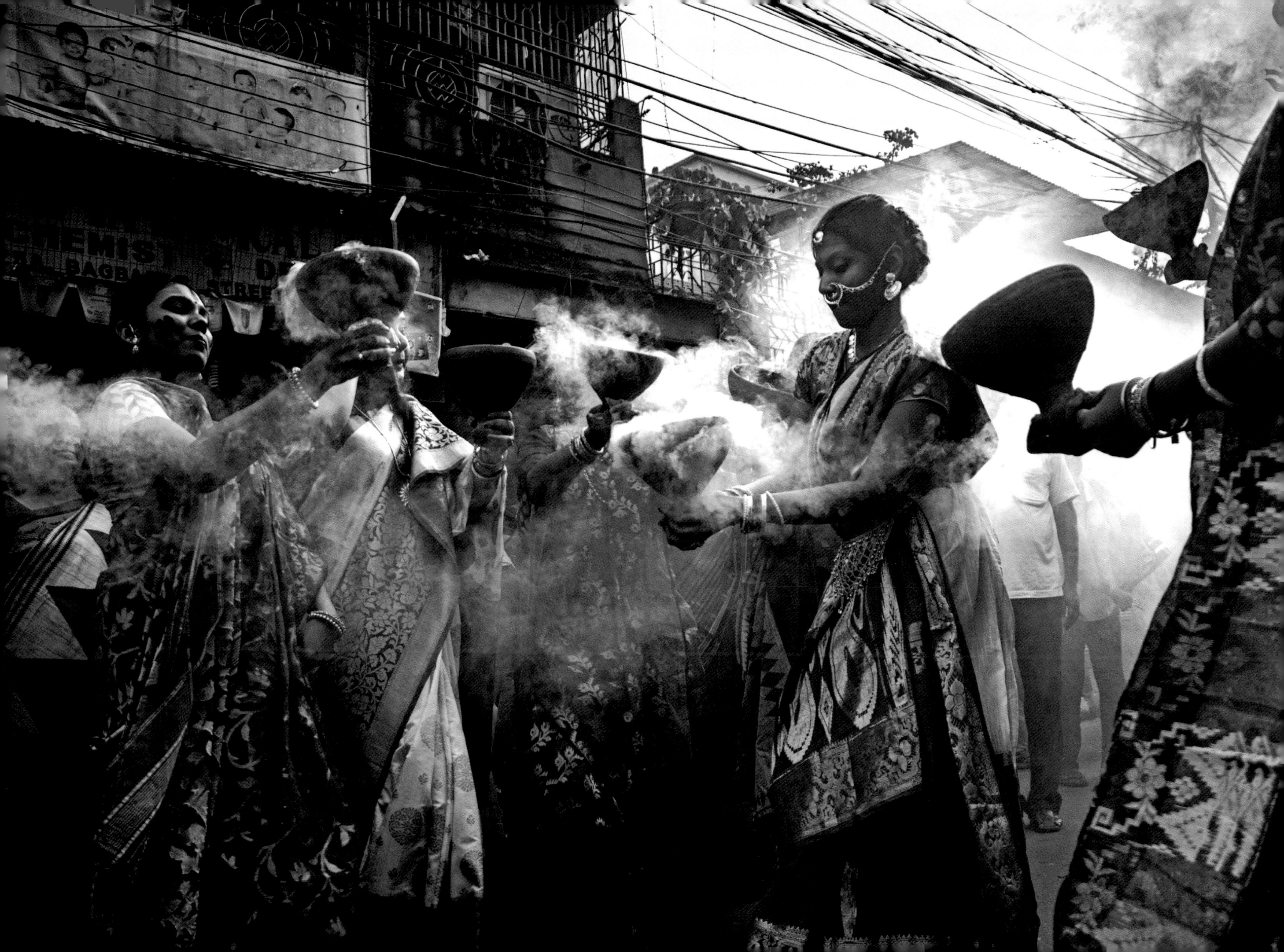

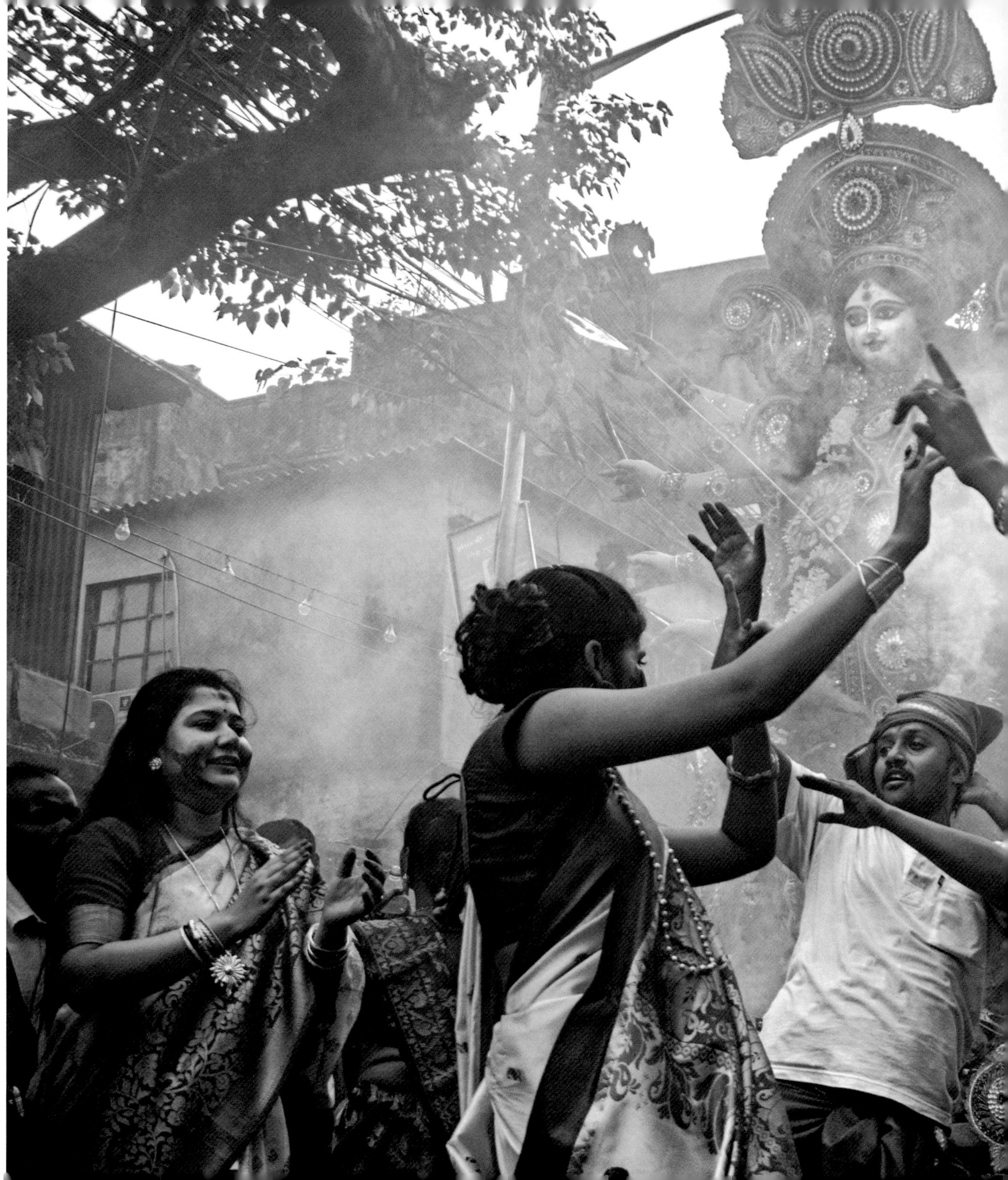

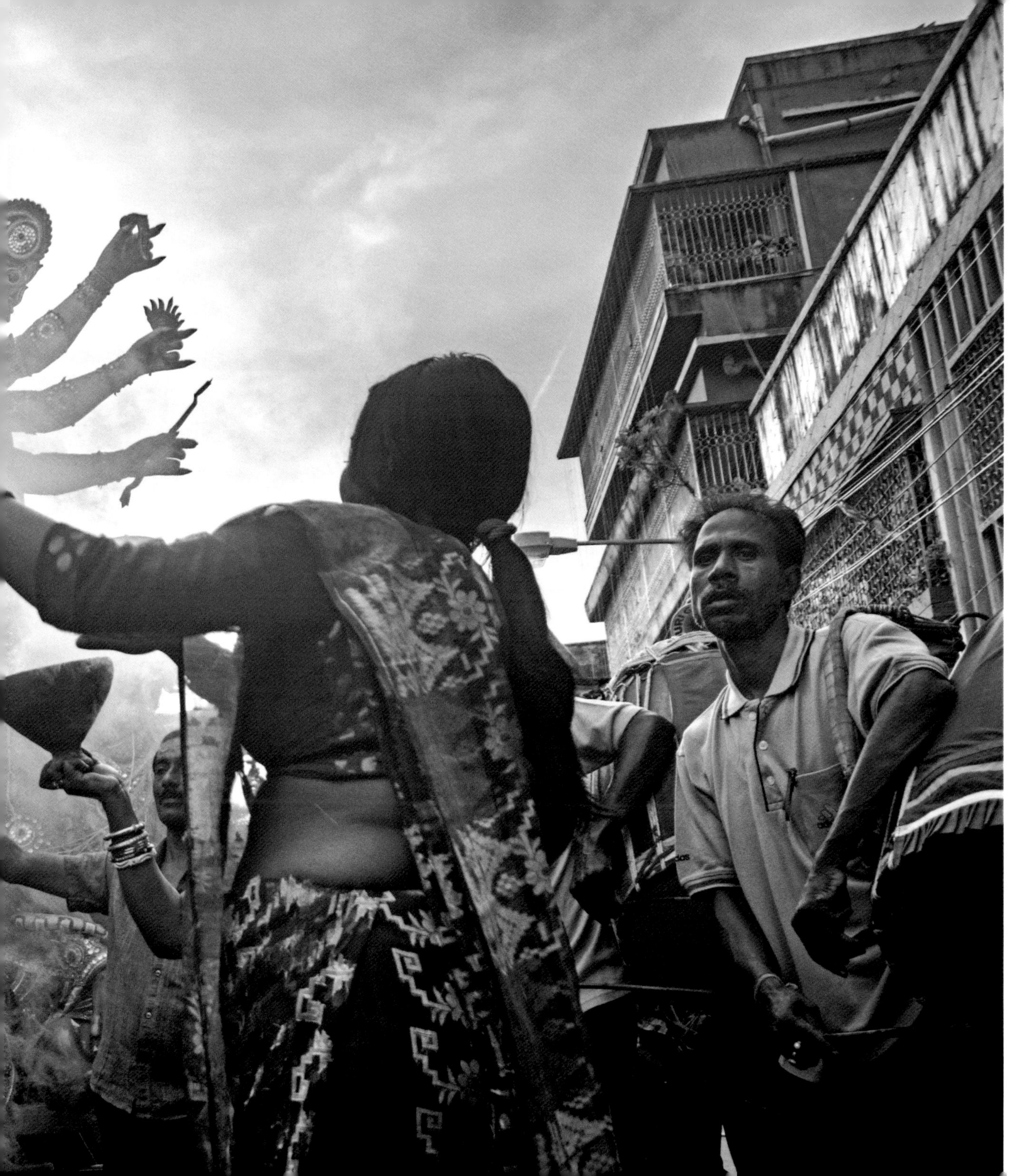

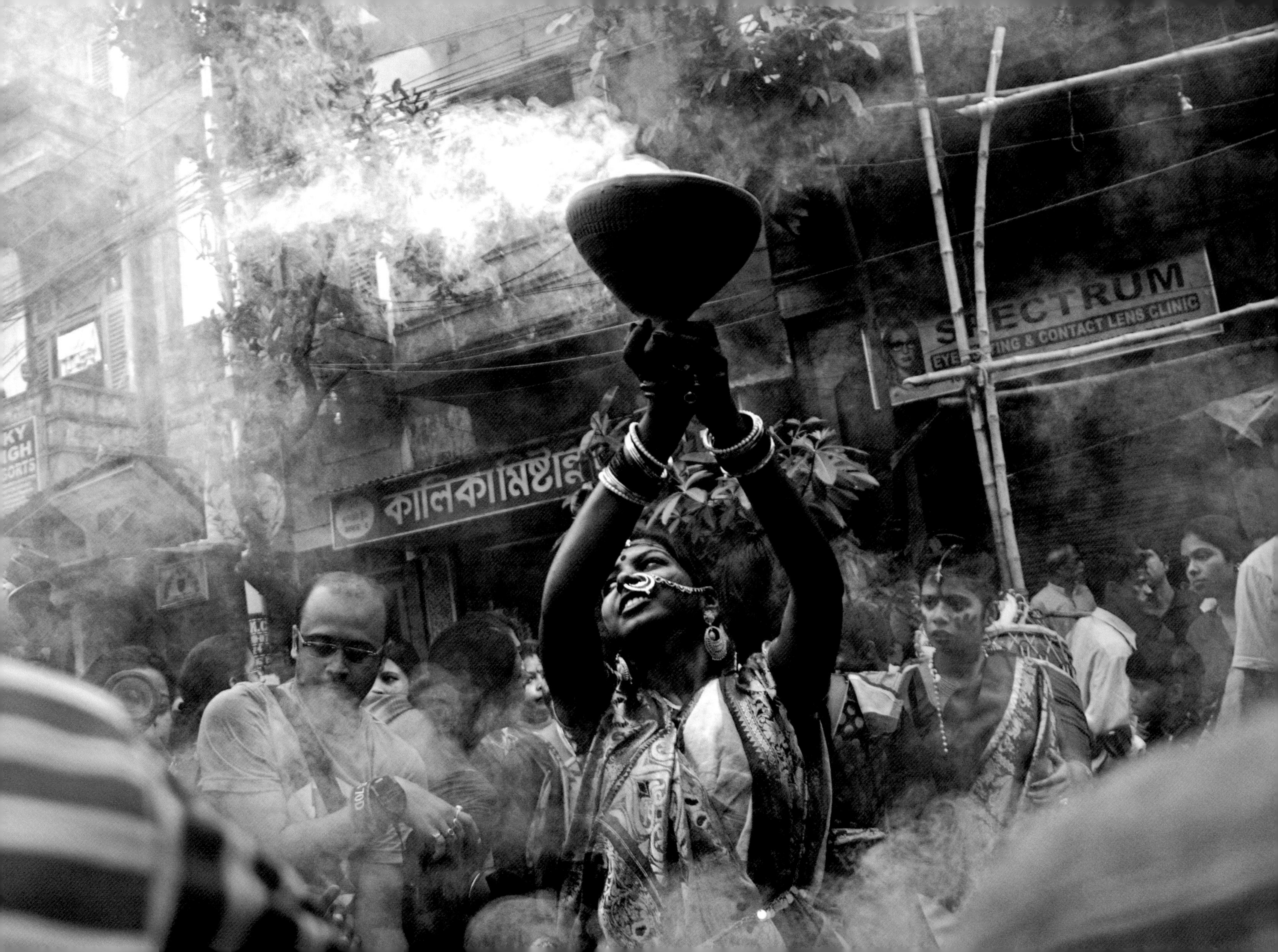
SPECTRUM
CONTACT LENS CLINIC

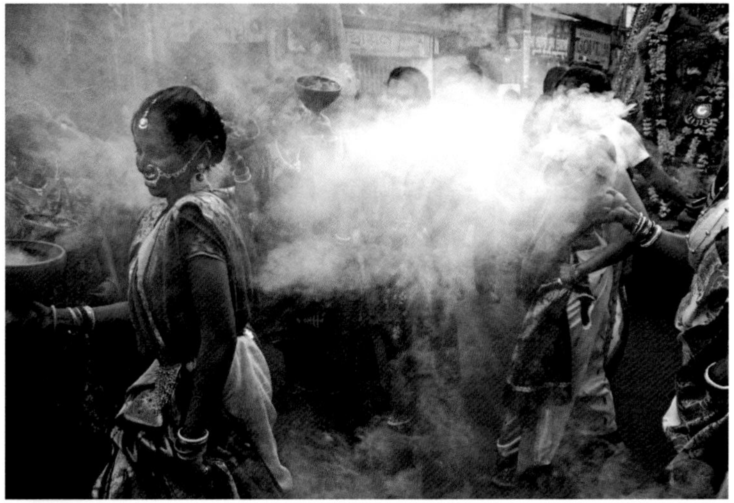
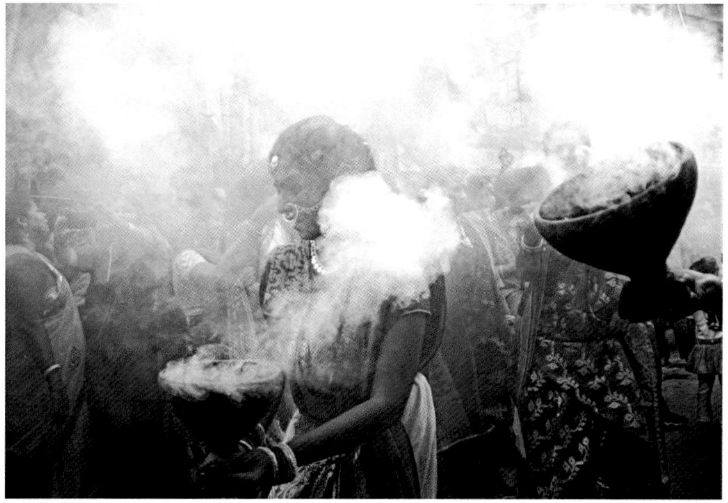
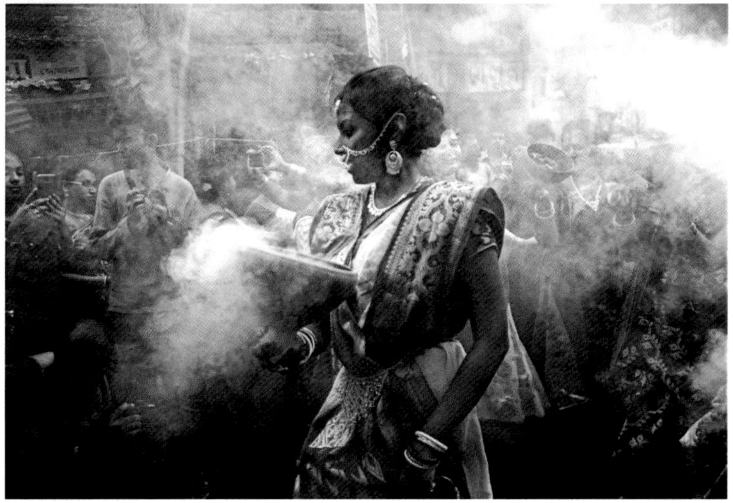
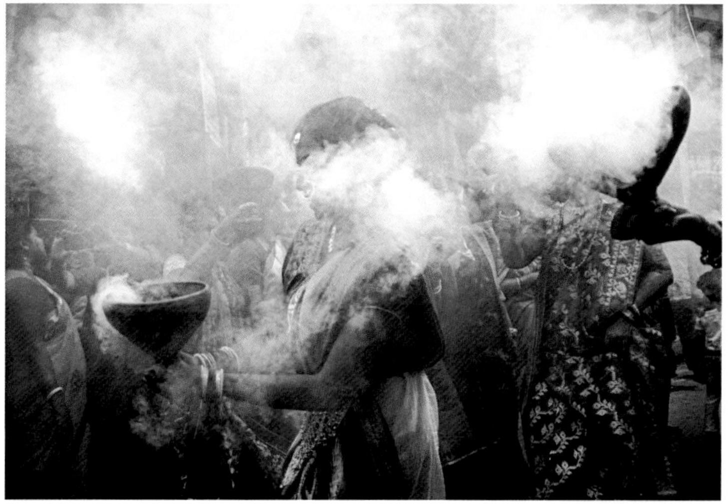
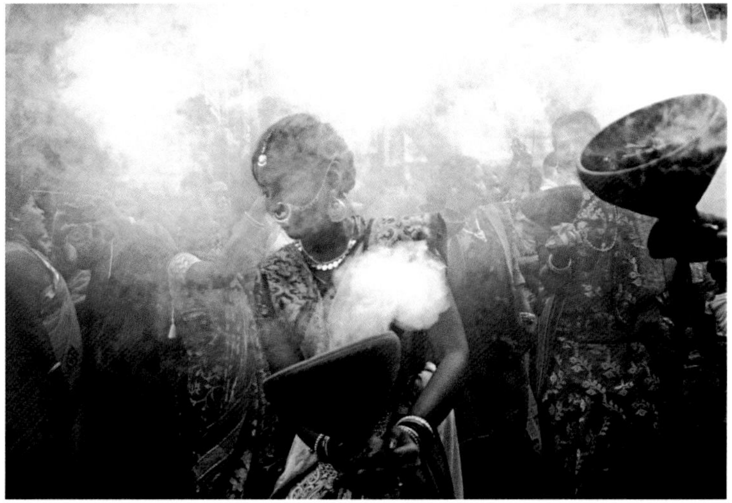
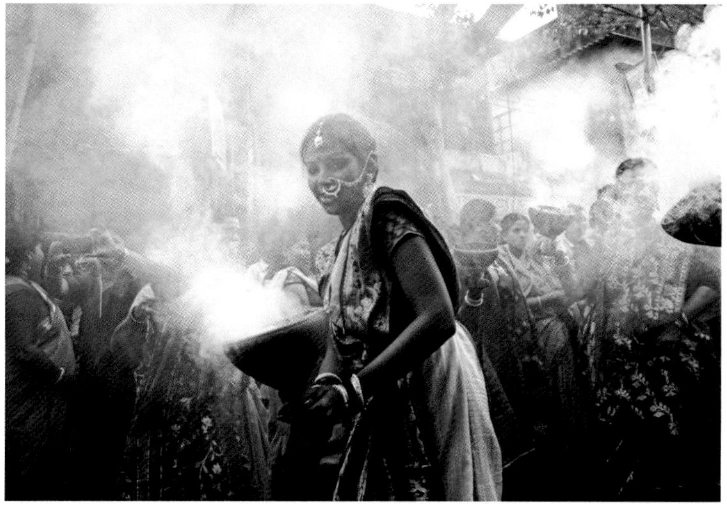

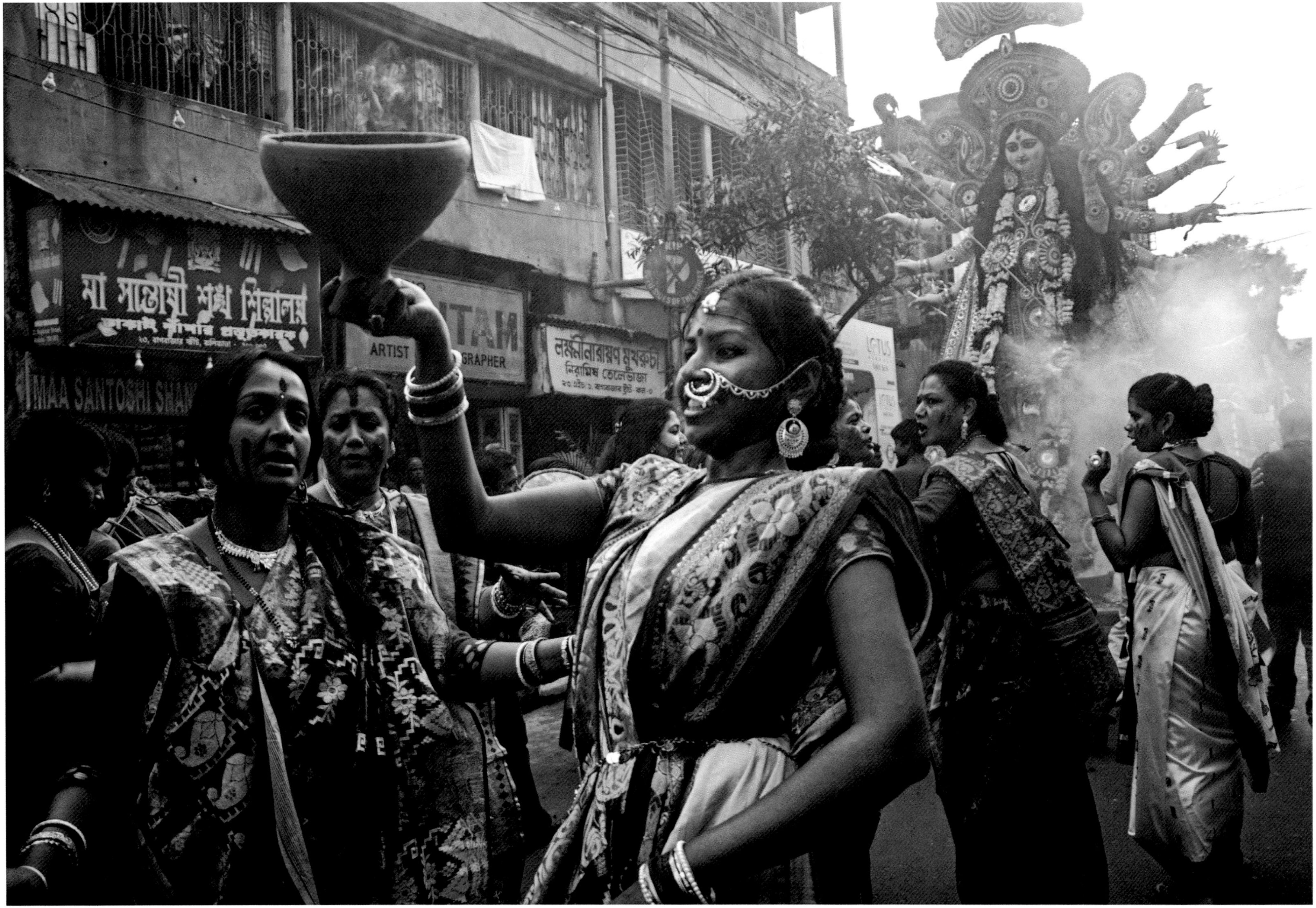
মা সন্তোষী শঙ্খ শিল্পালয়
MAA SANTOSHI SHA
ARTIST
GRAPHER
নিরামিষ তেলেভাজা

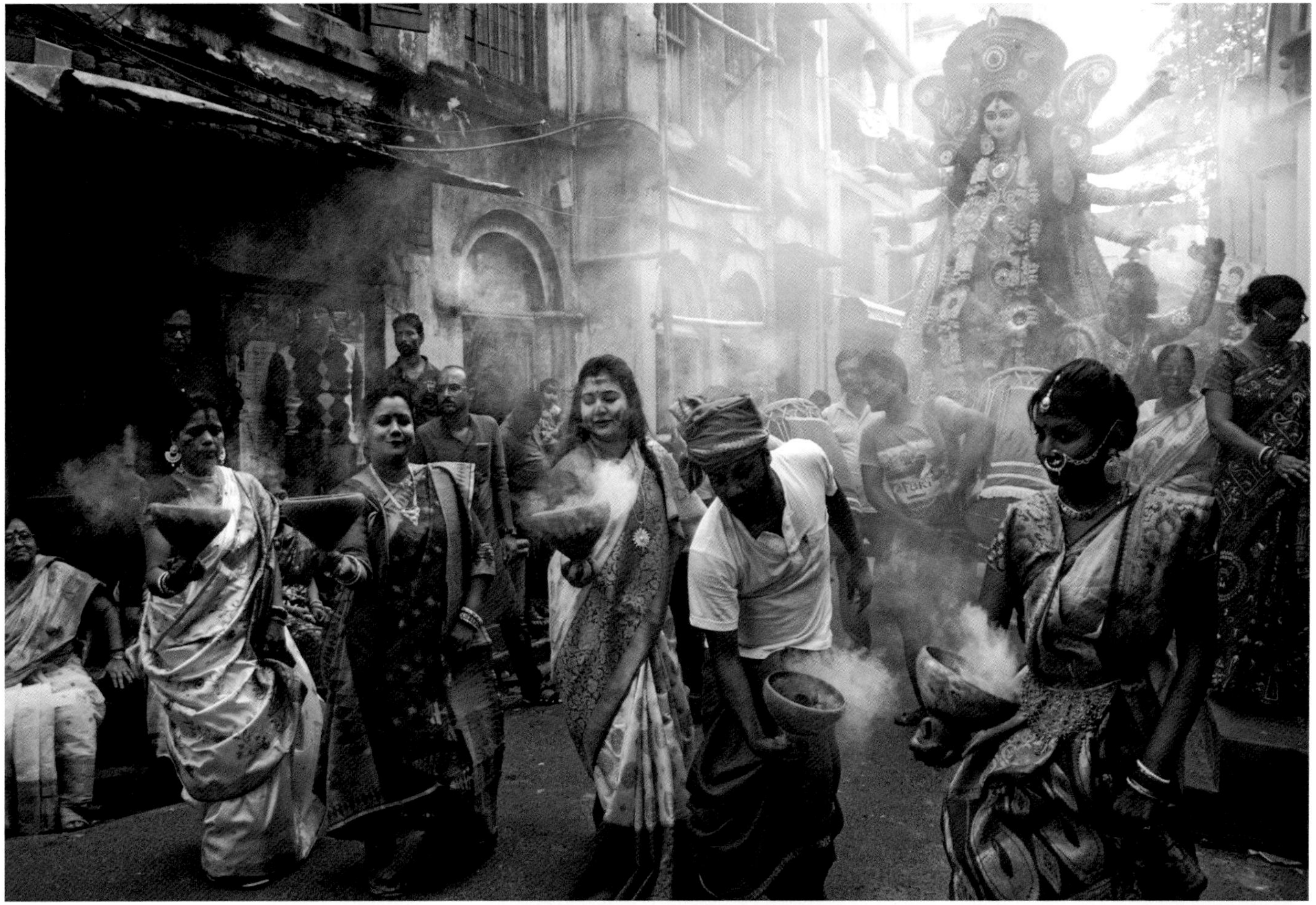

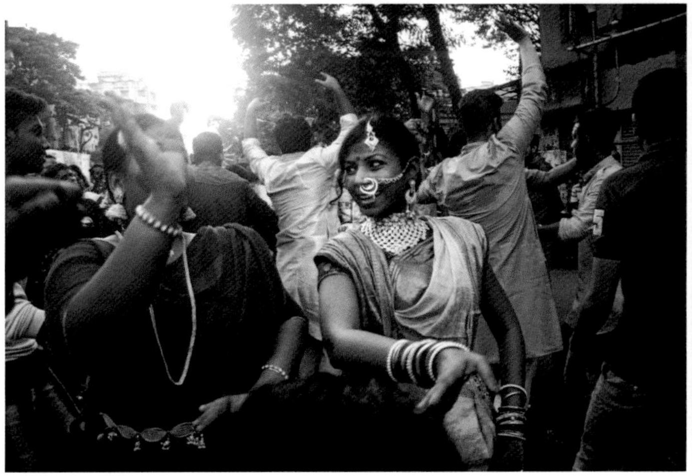

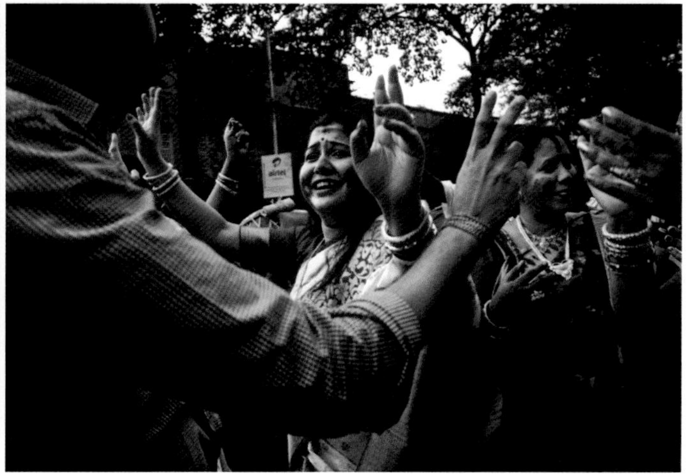

GANGASAGAR MELA

Ganga Sagar Mela is world's one of the largest human congregation at the confluence of holy river Ganga and Bay of Bengal. It is held annually (14th - 15th January), at the southern tip of Sagar island of West Bengal, India. It is the biggest pilgrimage fair of Eastern India. Millions of people from all parts of India gather there to take holy dips. When visited there, I was amazed to see the huge crowd. Thousands of monks and millions of pilgrims stay there in this festival and I tried to capture some moments of their activities.

In very early morning, ignoring the cold wind and the frozen atmosphere, devotees start to take their holy dips in the ice cold water of the river and offer prayers to the rising sun. As the day grows, the bank of the river becomes too much crowded with the pilgrims. This continues till the evening. This place is an attractive tourist spot which attracts both pilgrims and adventure lovers. Thousands of photographers from different parts of the world gather there during this festival.

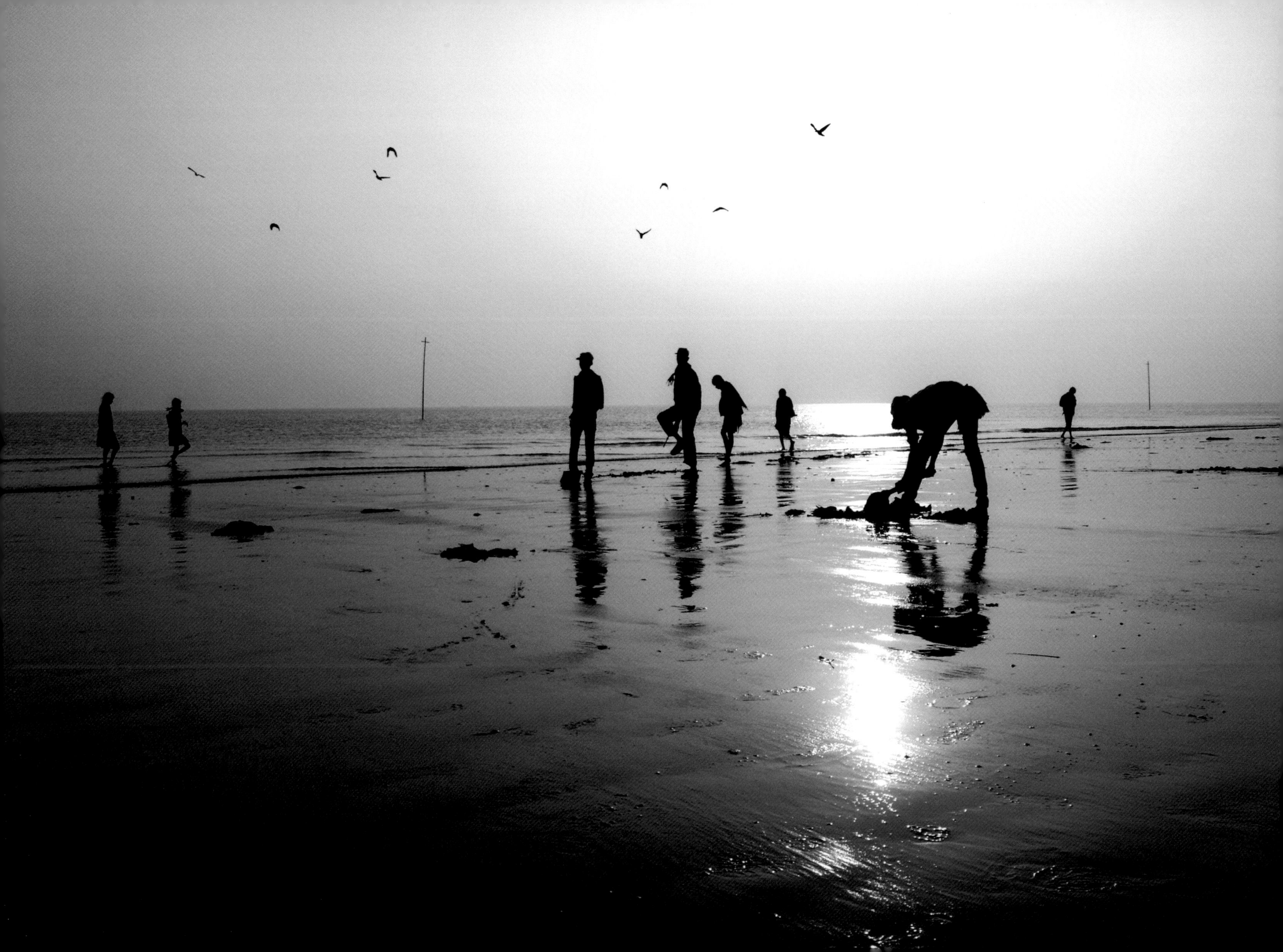

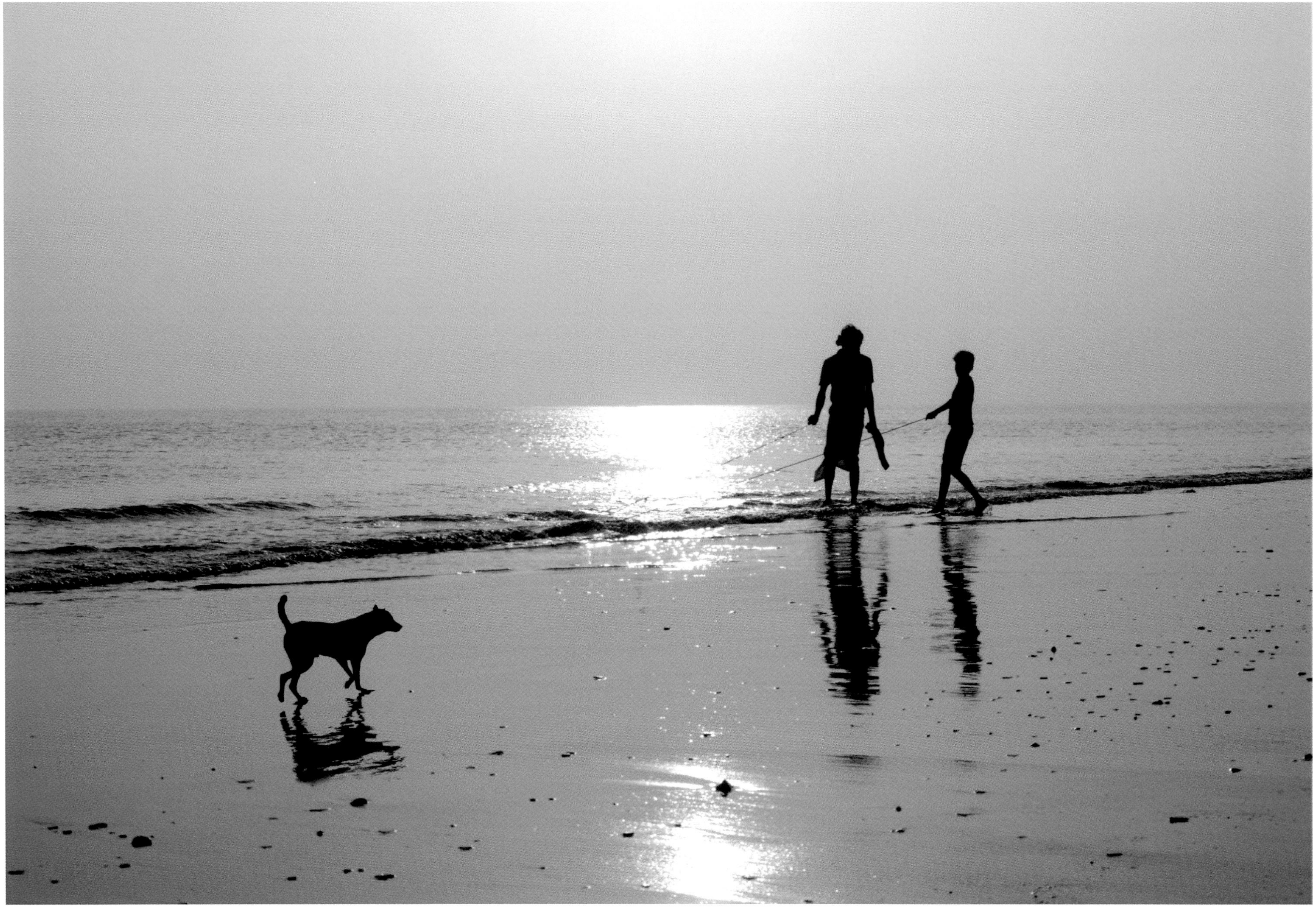

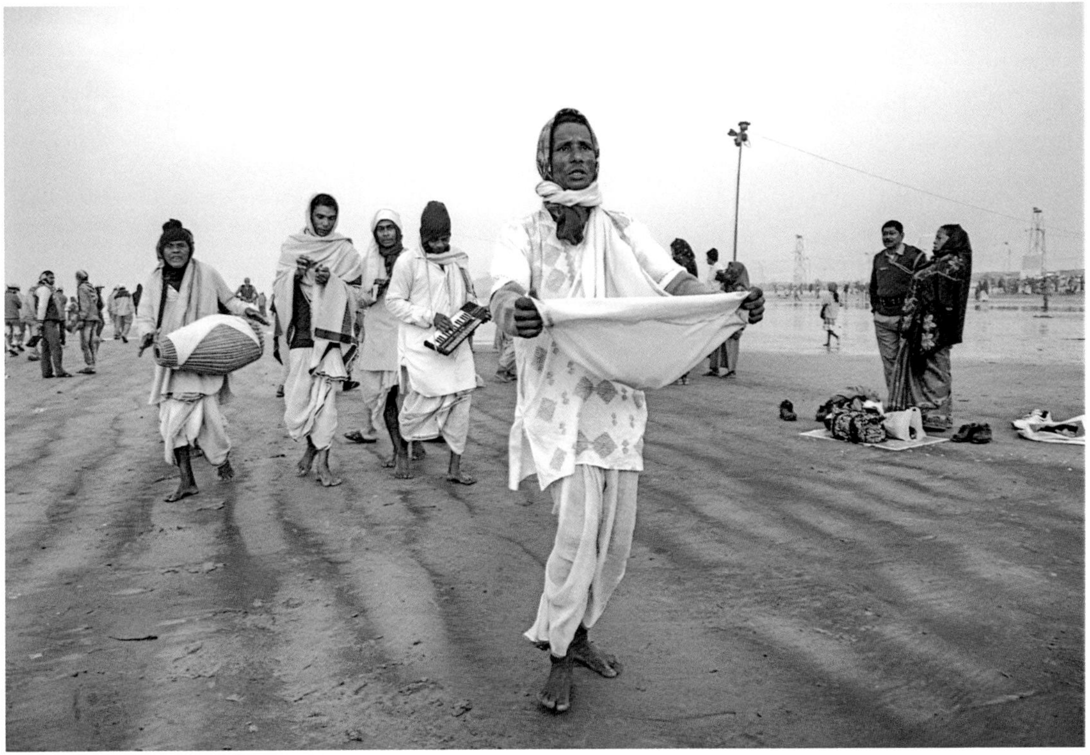

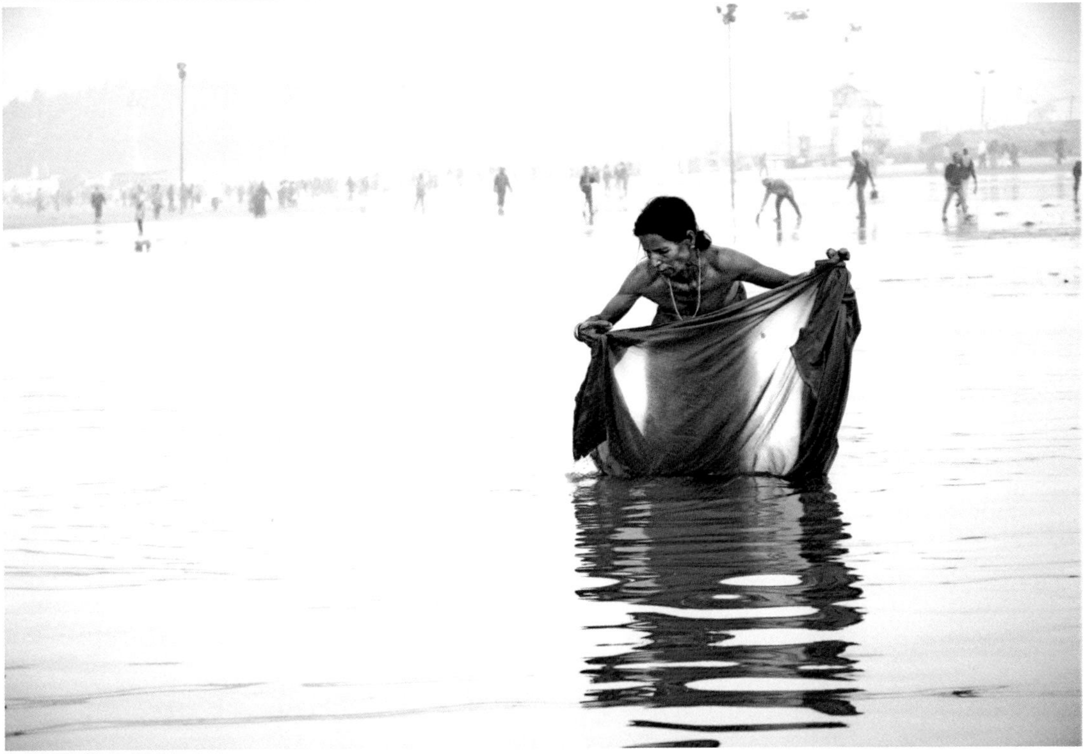

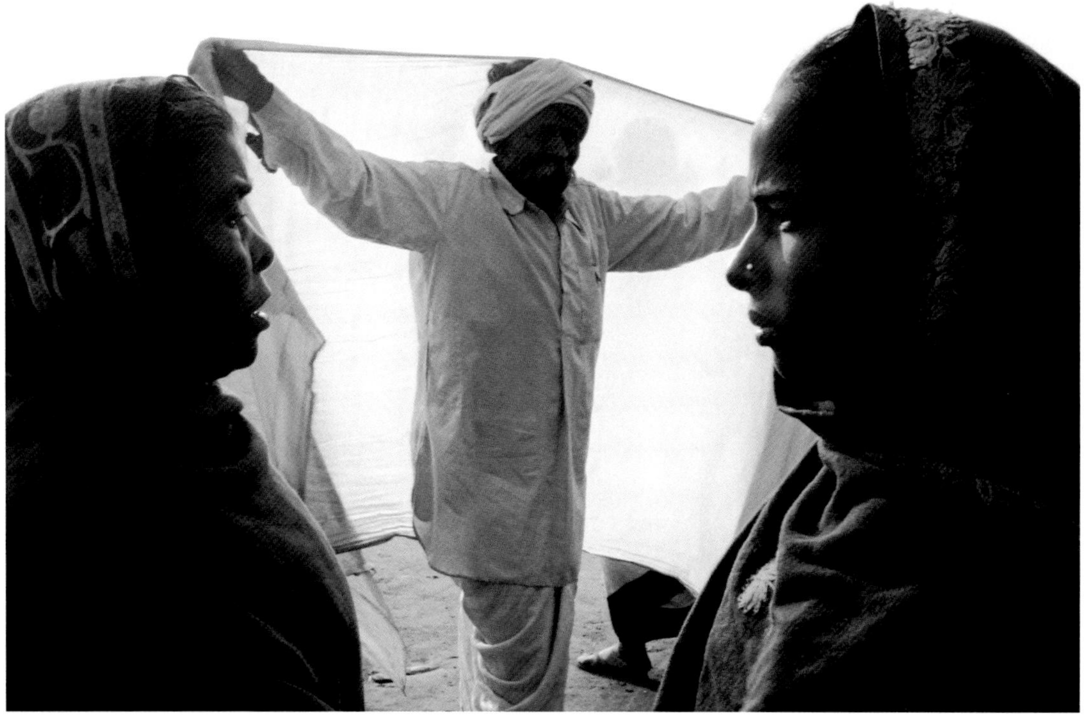

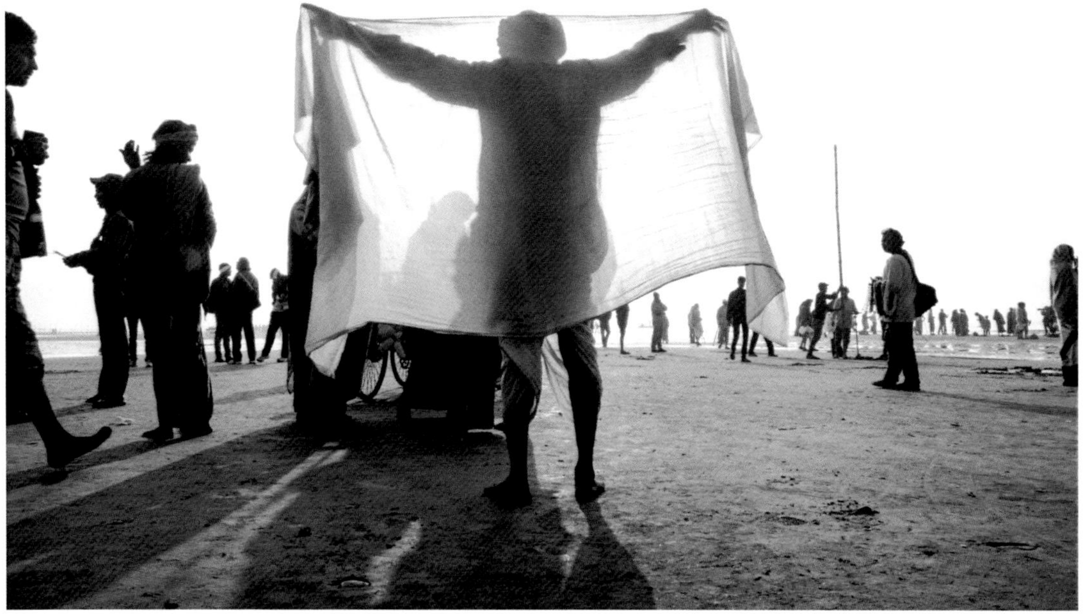

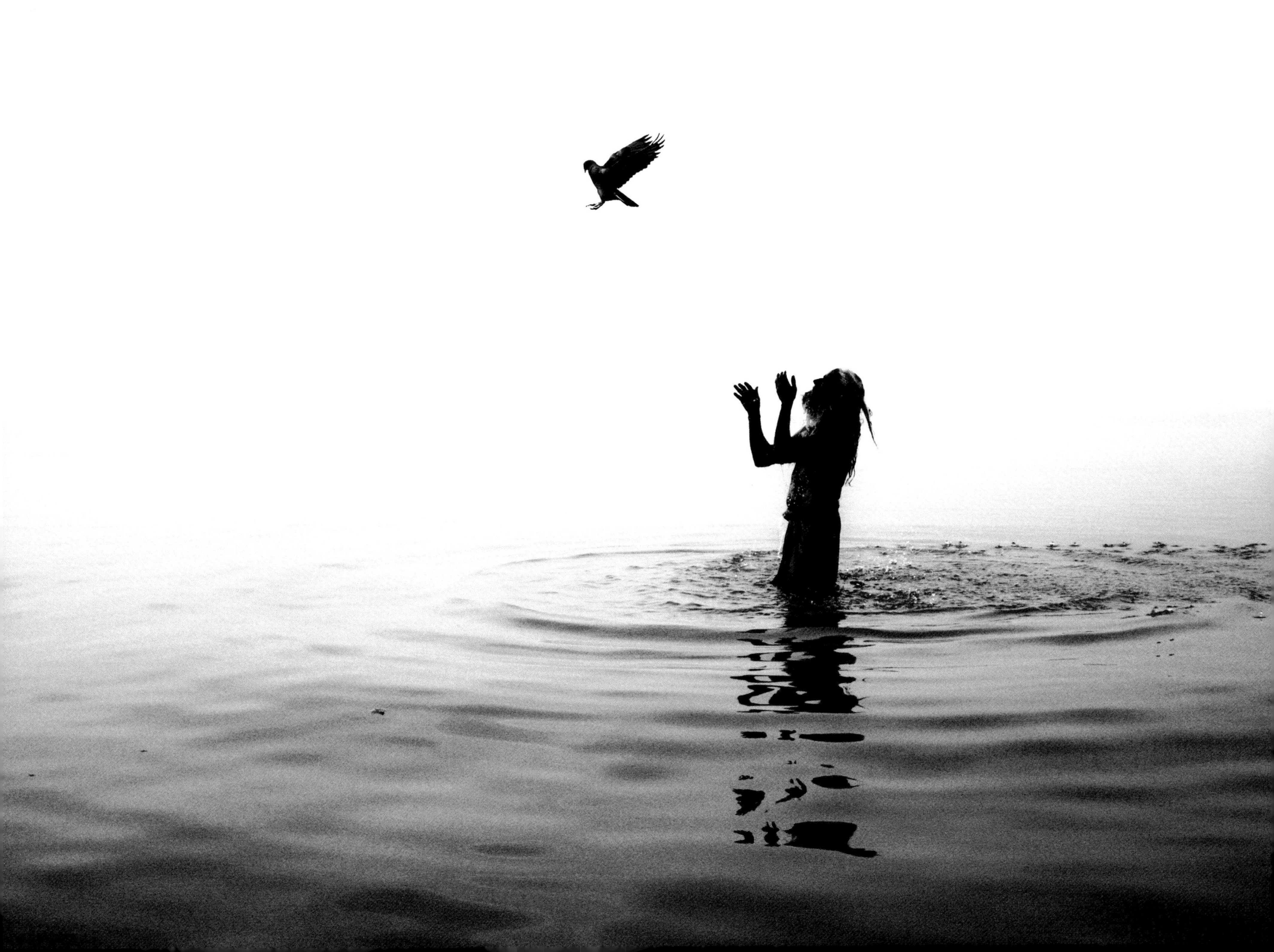

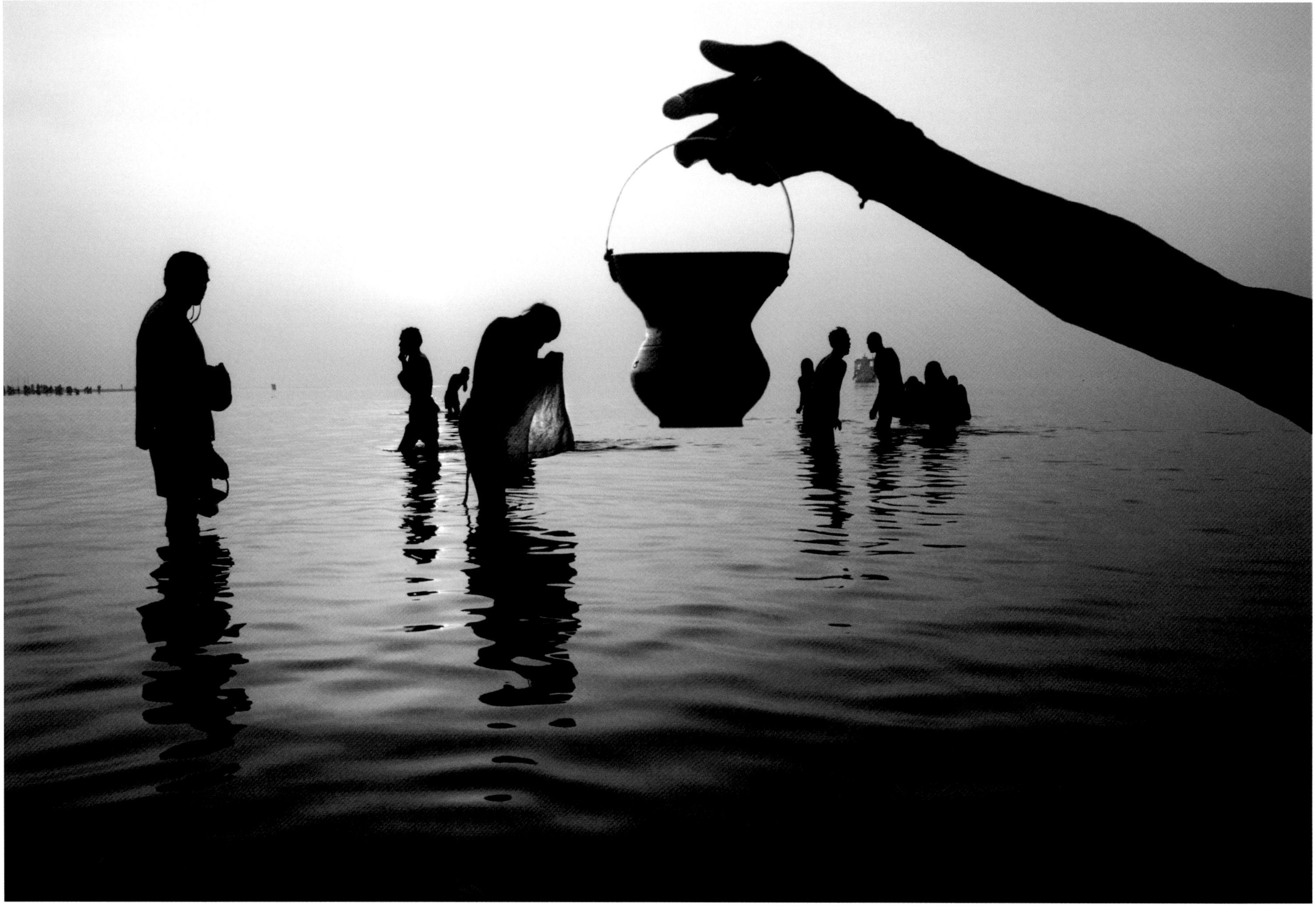

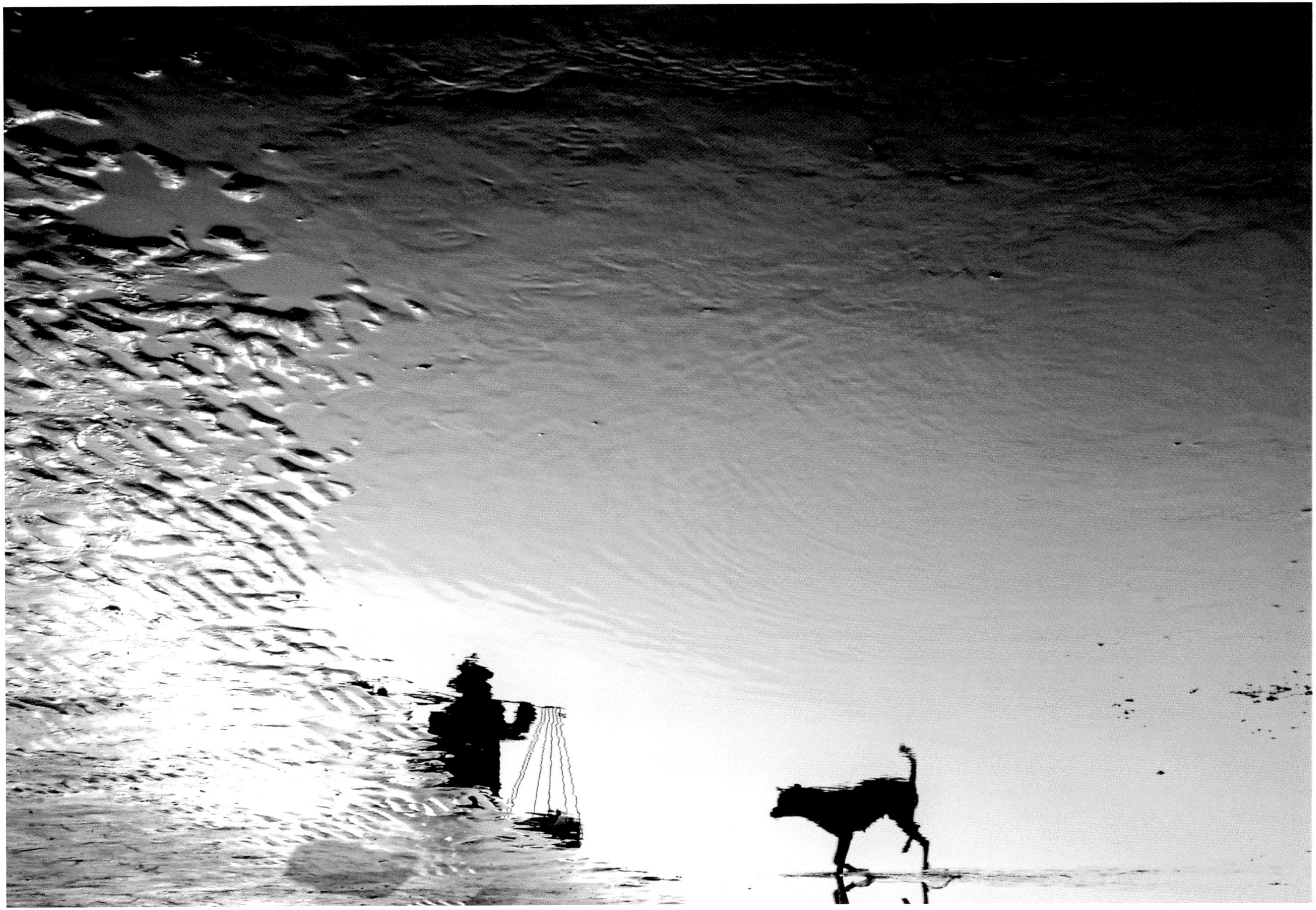

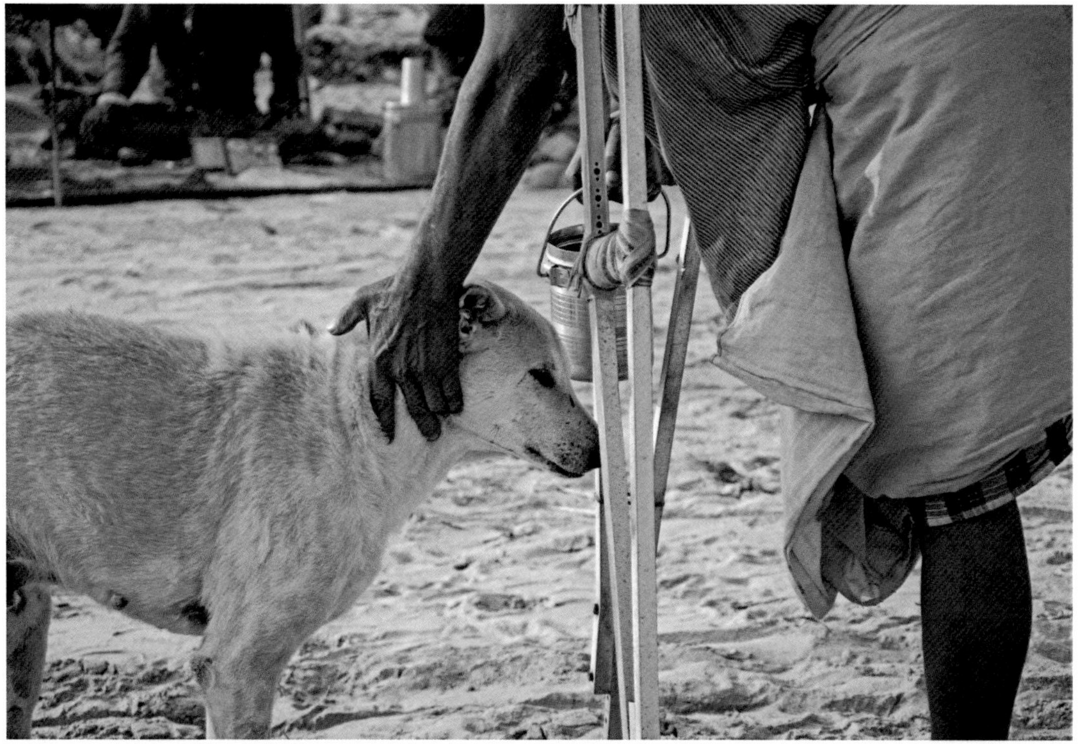

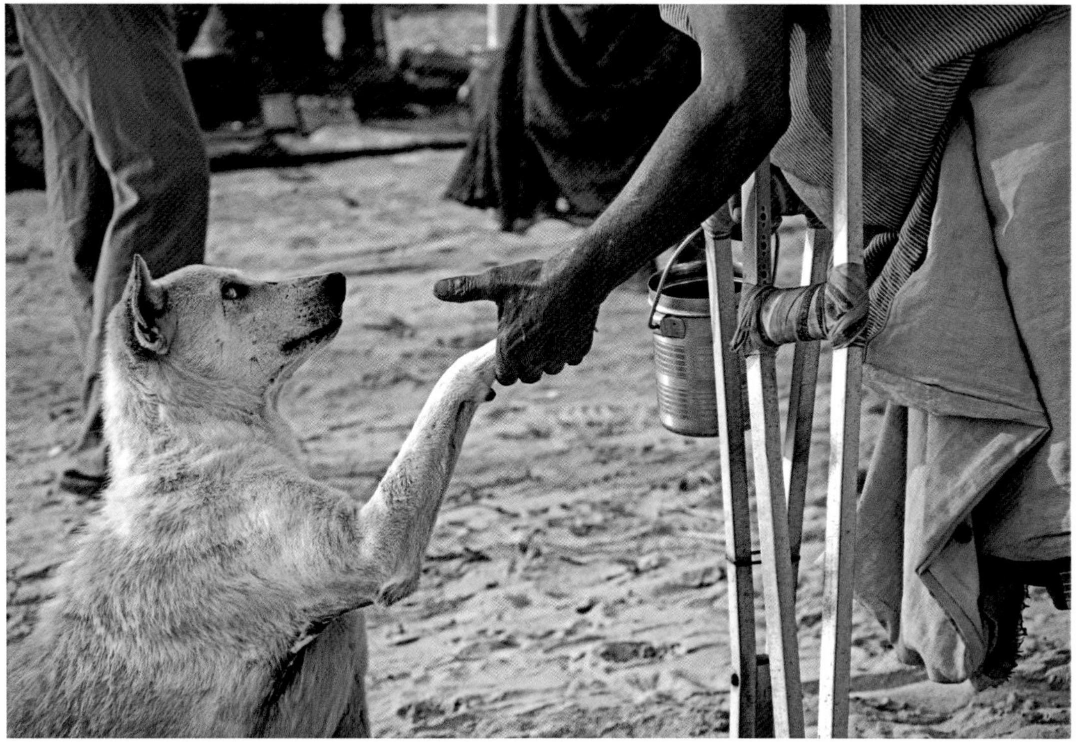

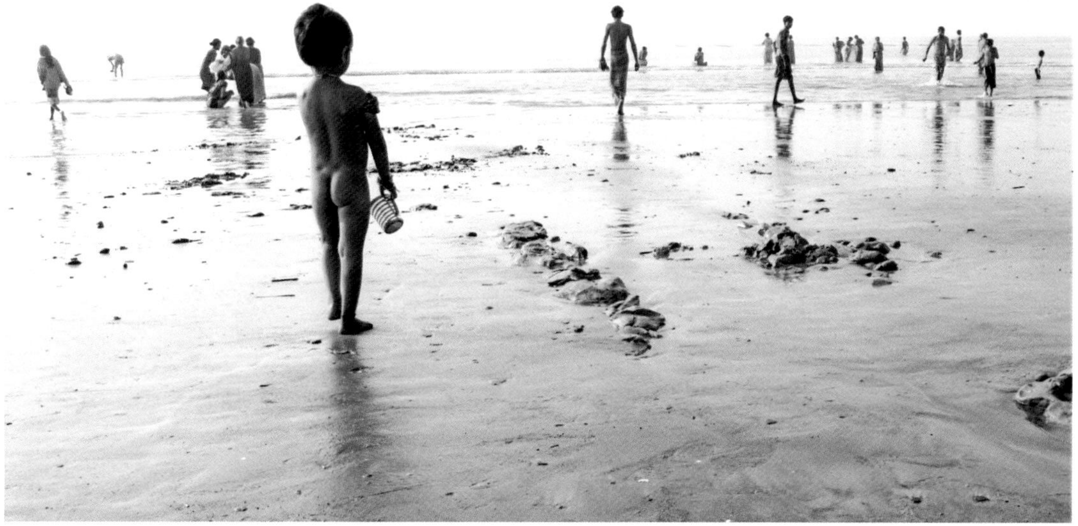

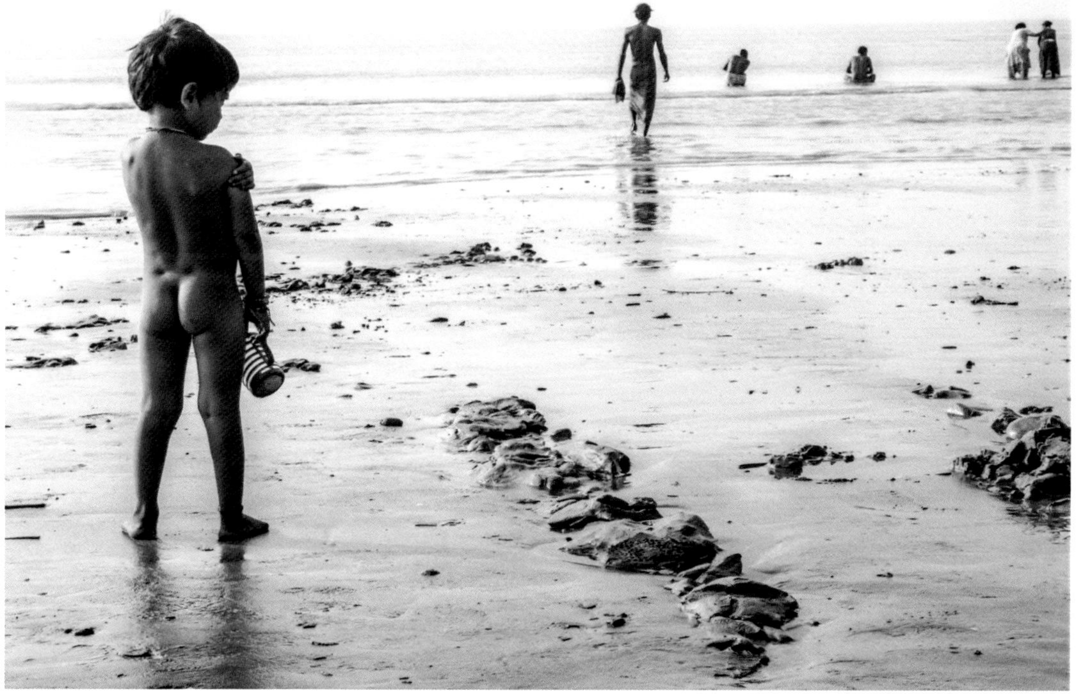

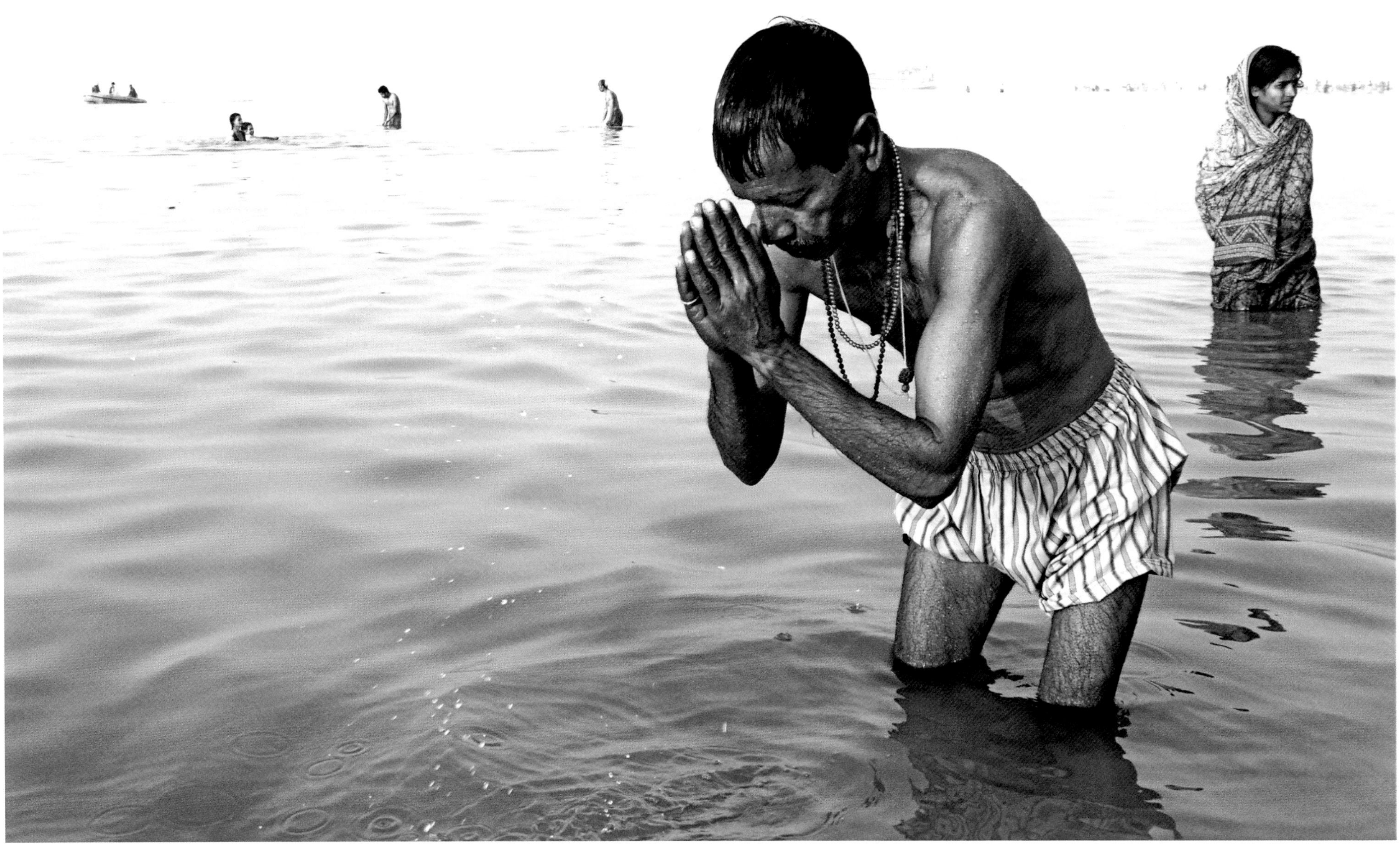

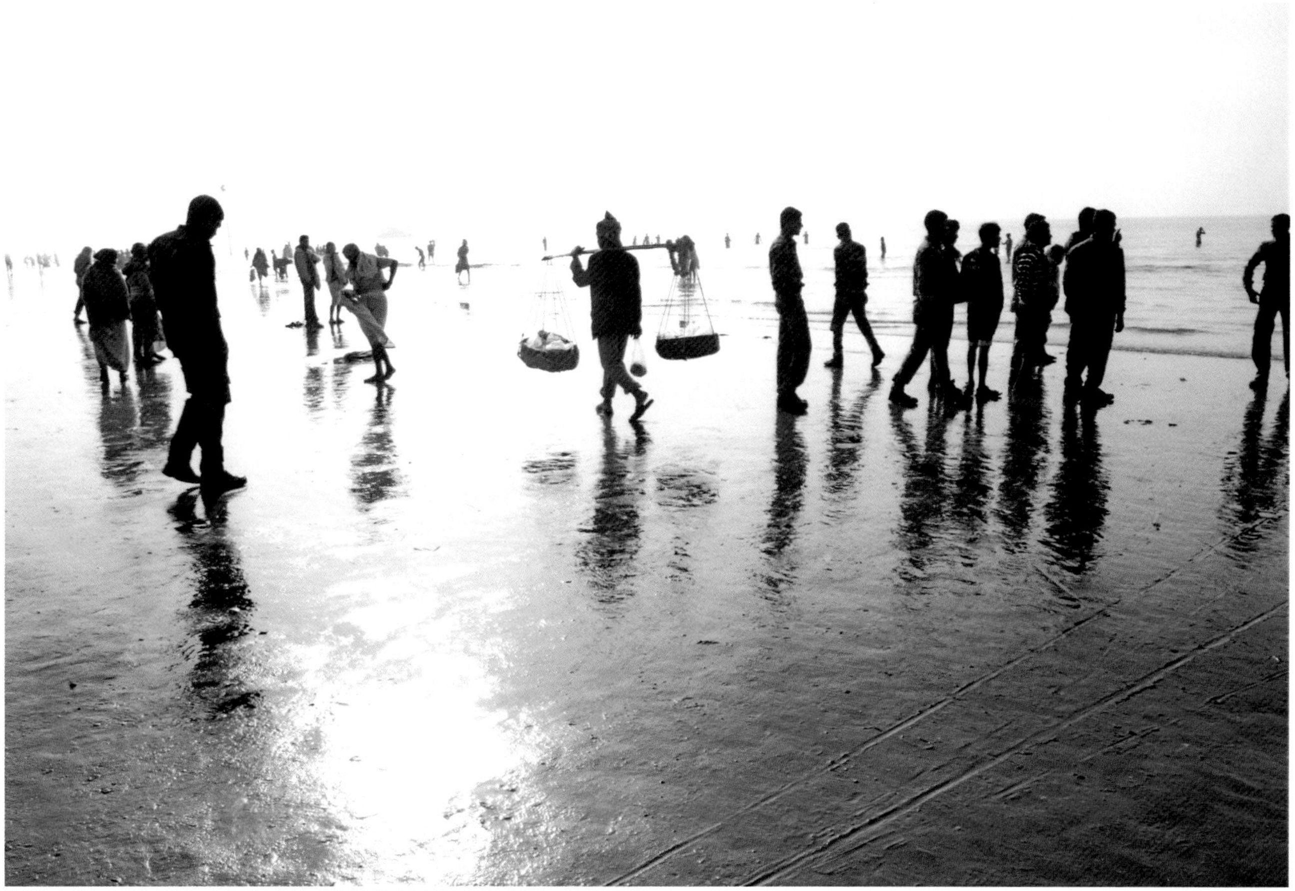

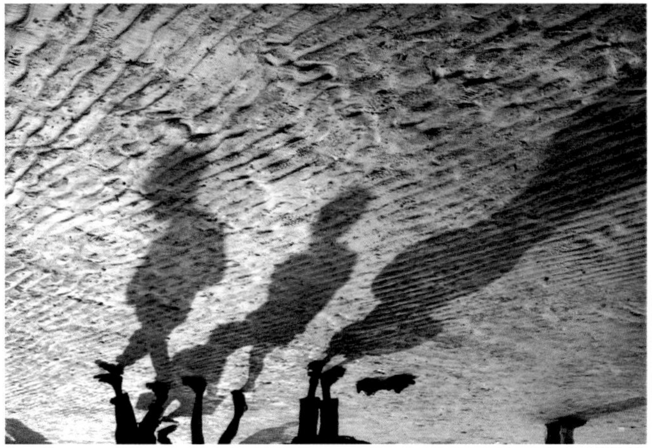

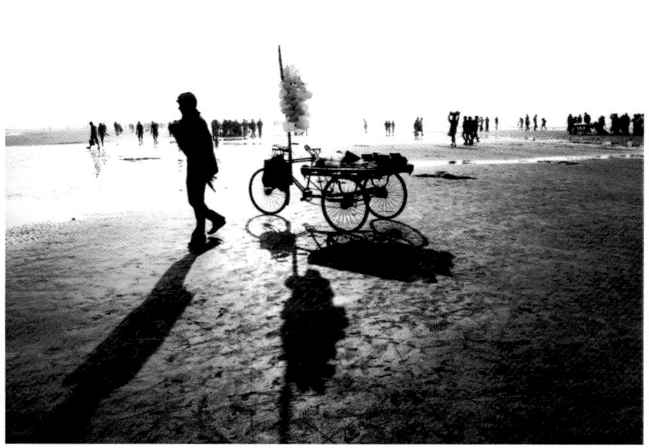

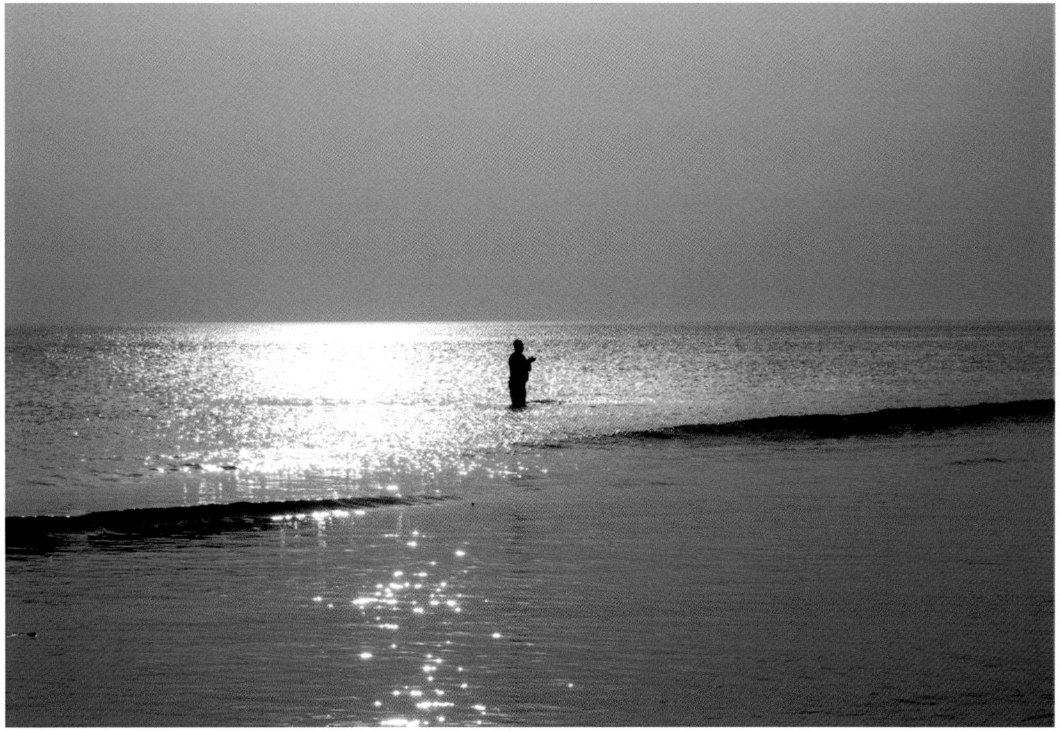

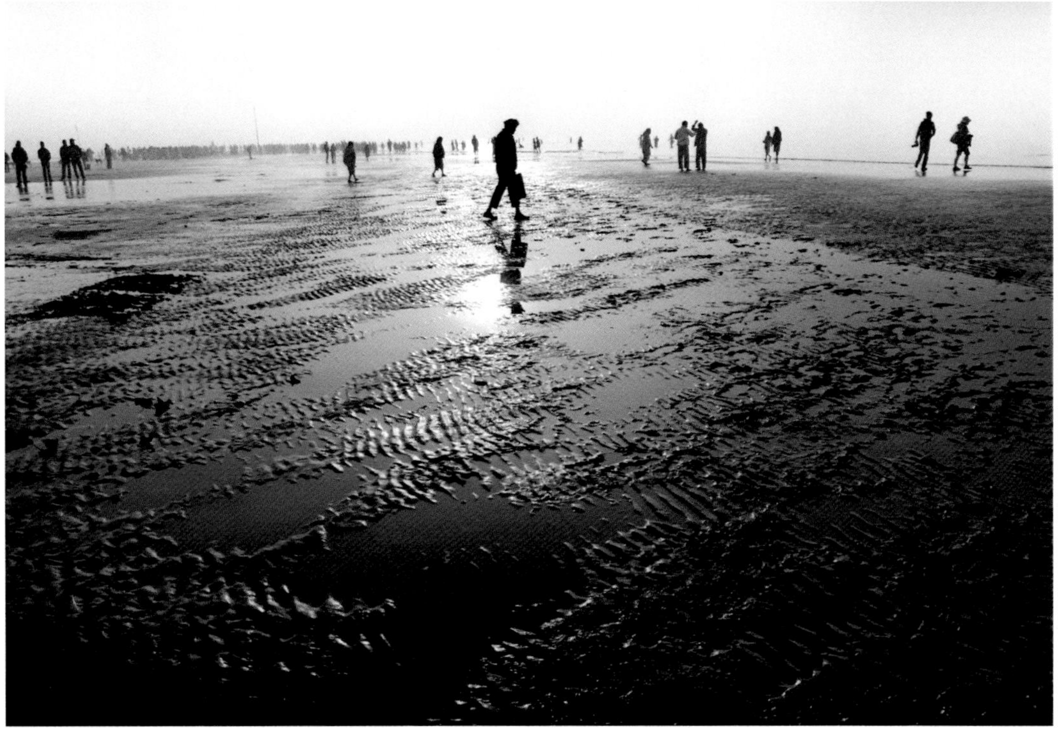

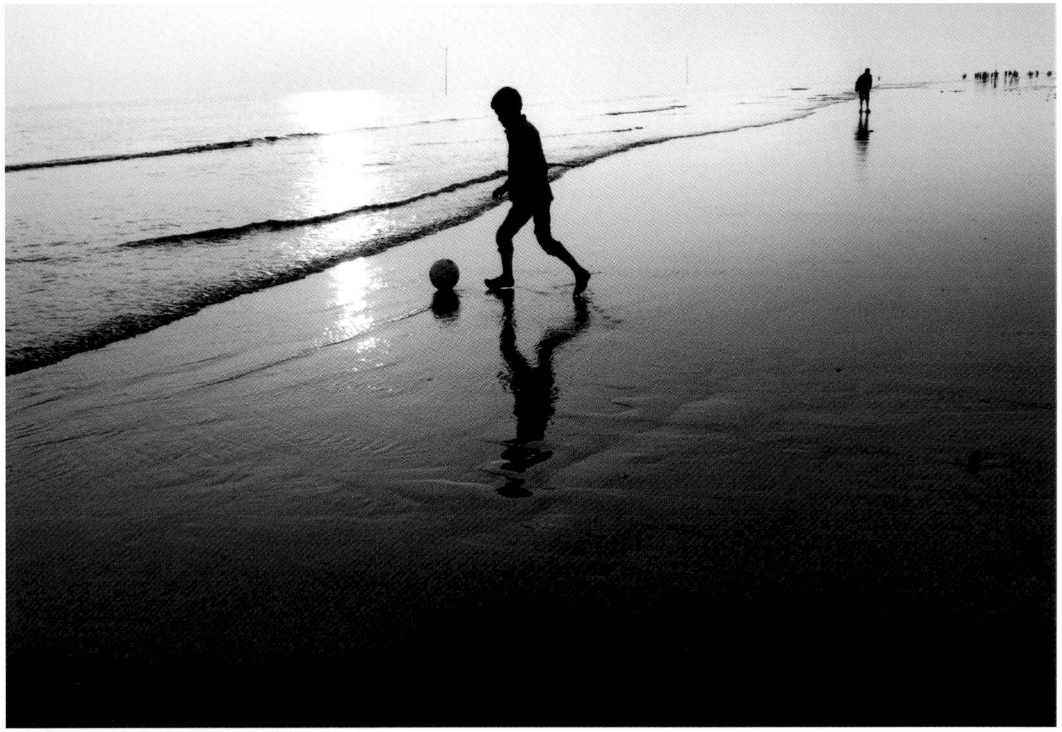

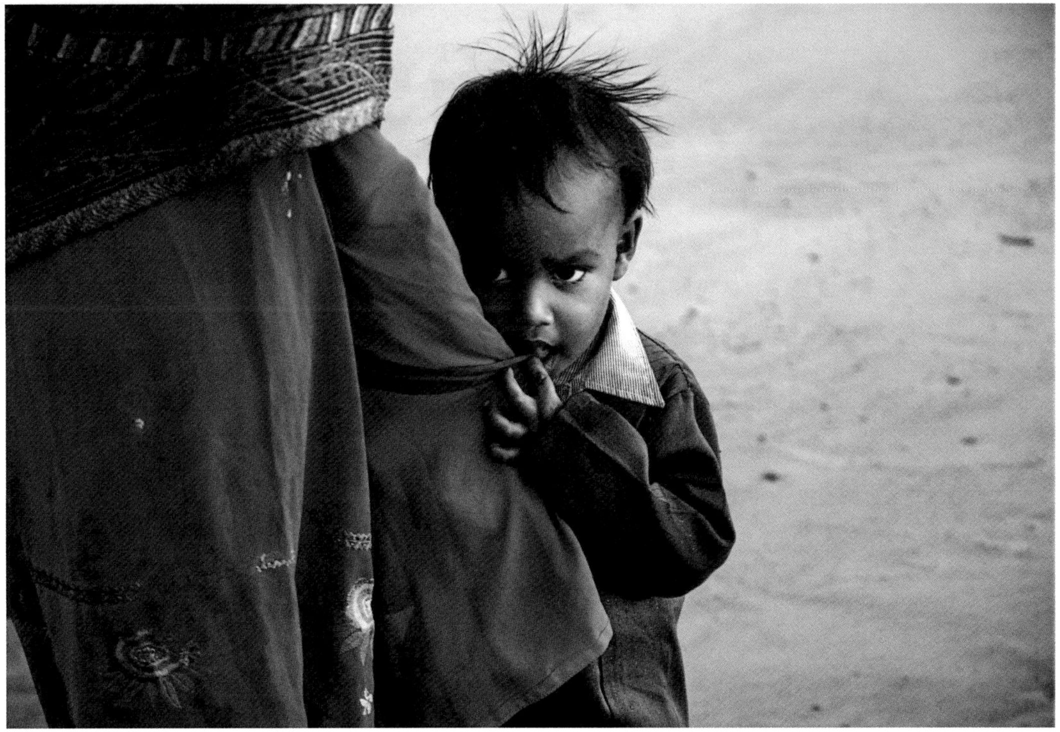

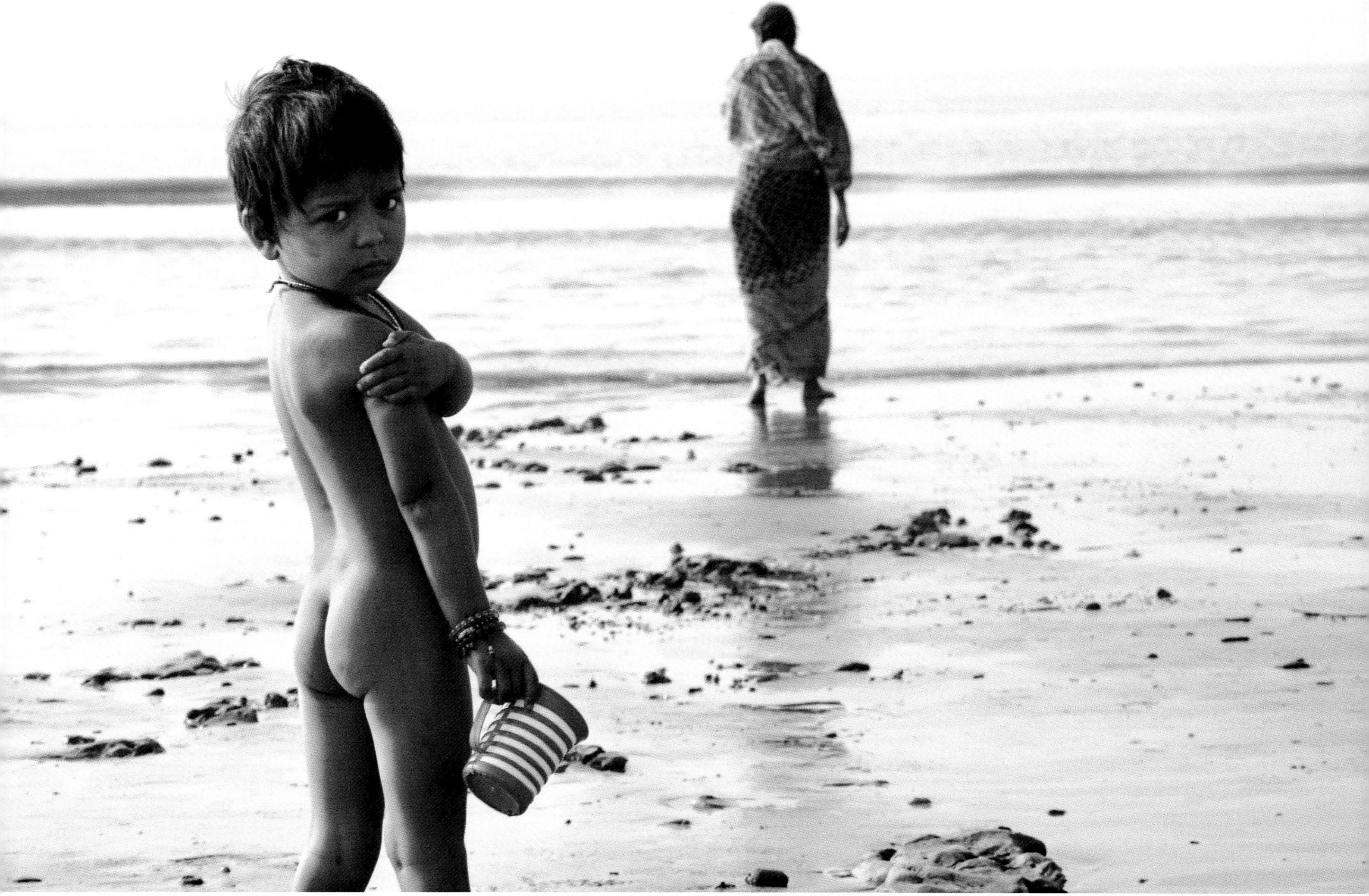

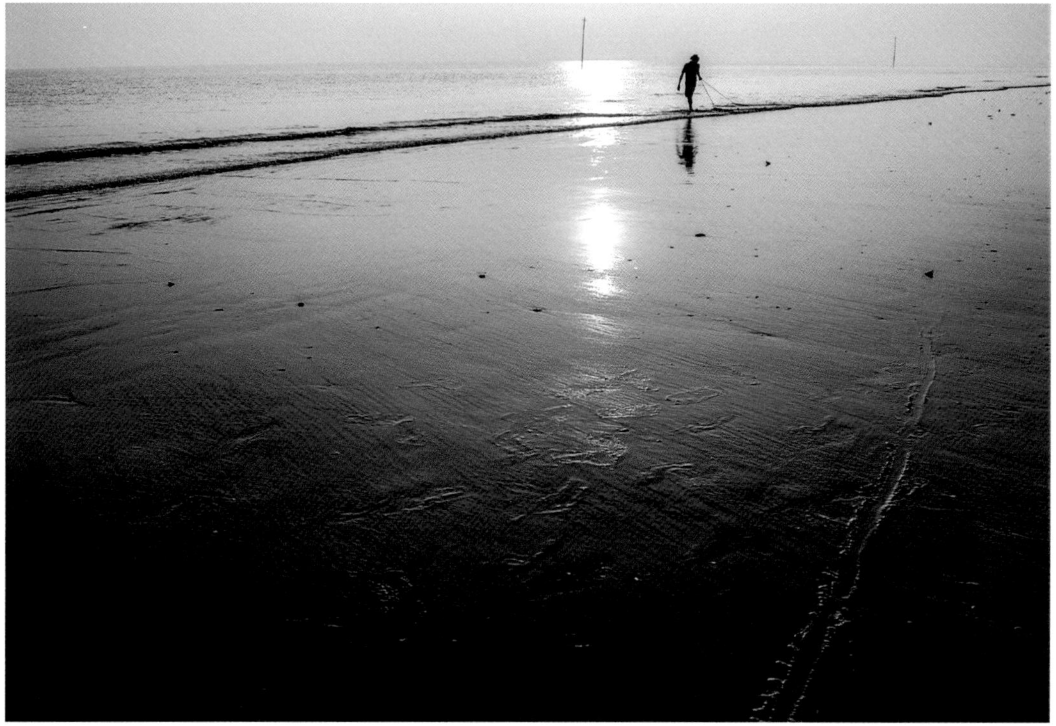

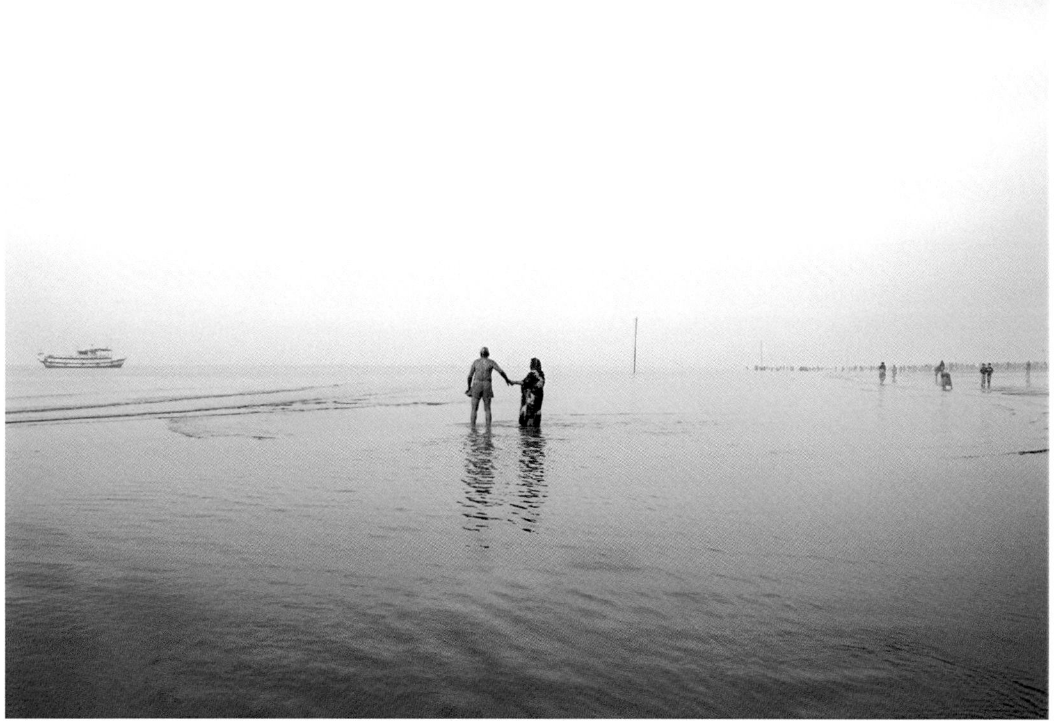

The Maidan, also known as the Brigade Parade Ground, is a large public park located at the centre of Kolkata, India. The ground is owned by the Indian Army and thus horse mounted Army men are often seen there. It is considered as the lungs of the city. Its vastness with lots of old trees and lush greenery is its beauty. It is used by the Kolkata's residents for yoga, morning walk, jogging, spirited football and cricket matches, family outing and general idling.

Though the Maidan has the most refreshing appearance throughout the year, it acquires its best form in the early mornings of winter seasons. In winter, the ground is mysteriously blanketed with dense fog in early mornings. People do their regular exercises, yoga, running, playing amongst the thick layers of fog. Beautiful sunrise through extremely foggy weather and activities of people and horses, create the place extra ordinarily attractive. One can witness how a night changes into day with a series of changes of colors and thinning the blanket of fog.

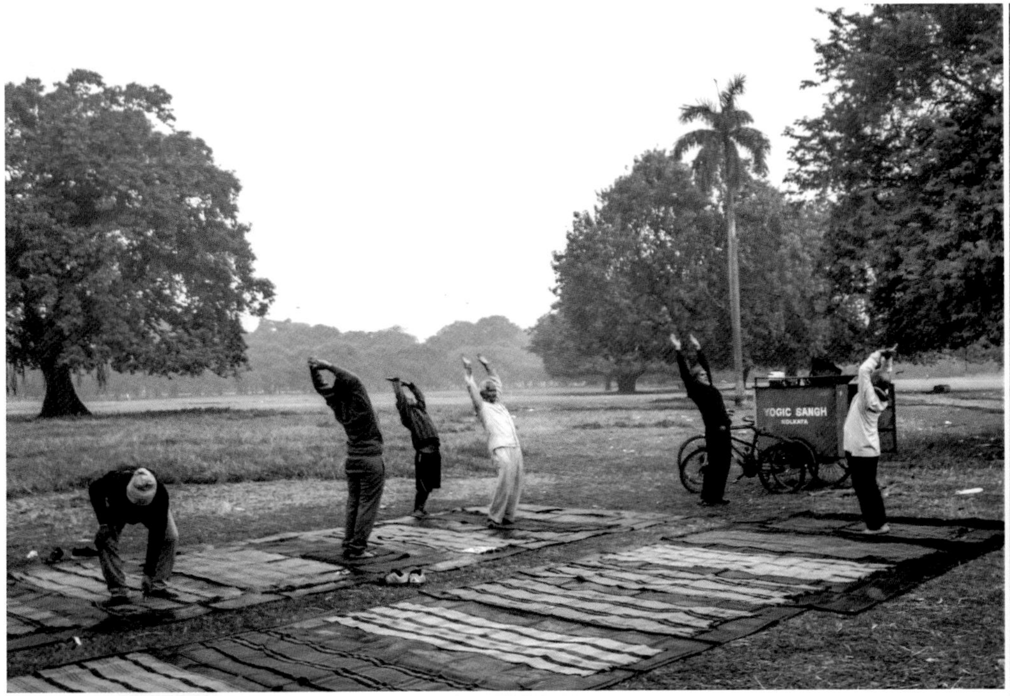
YOGIC SANGH
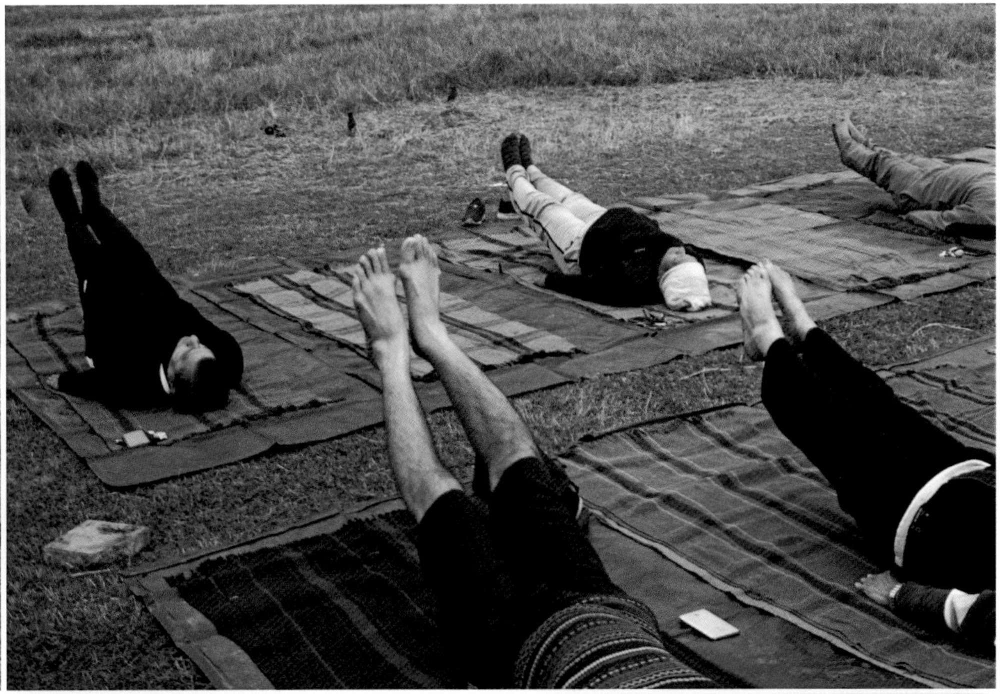
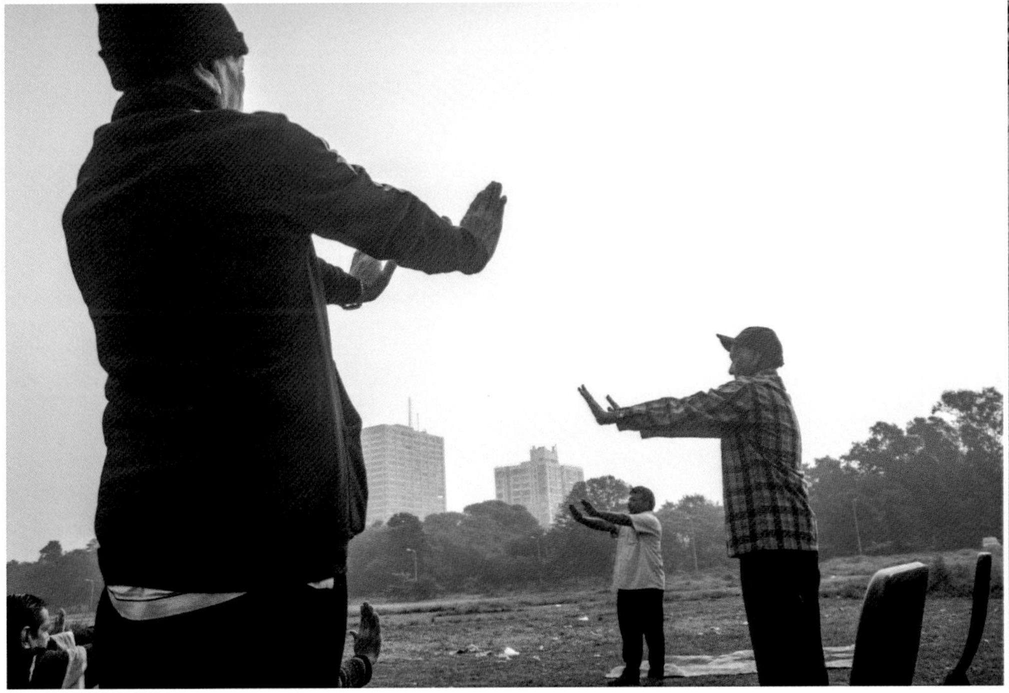
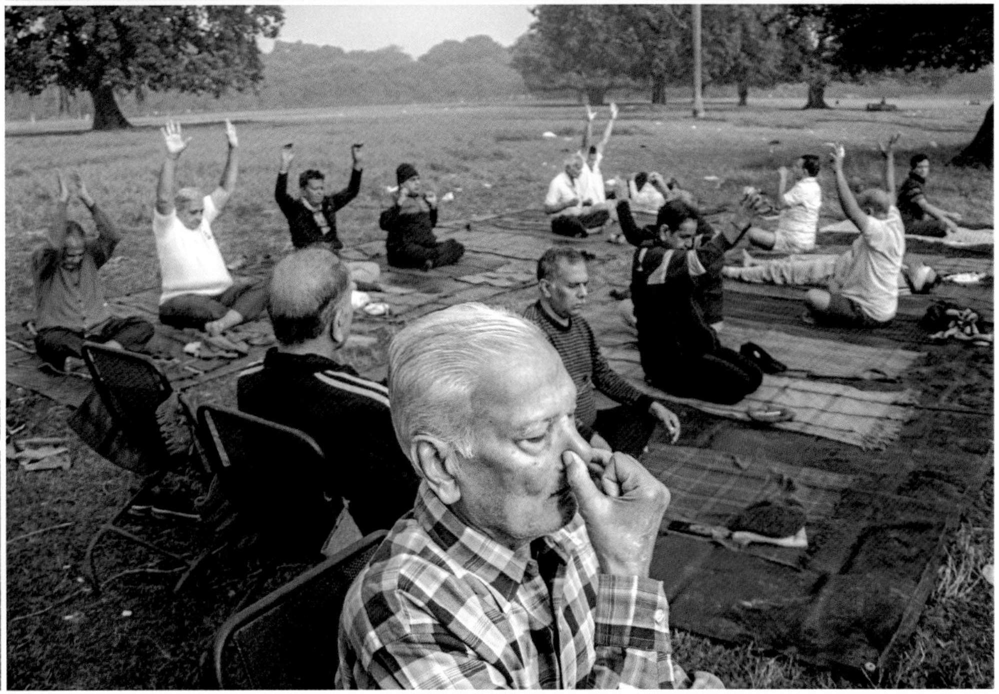

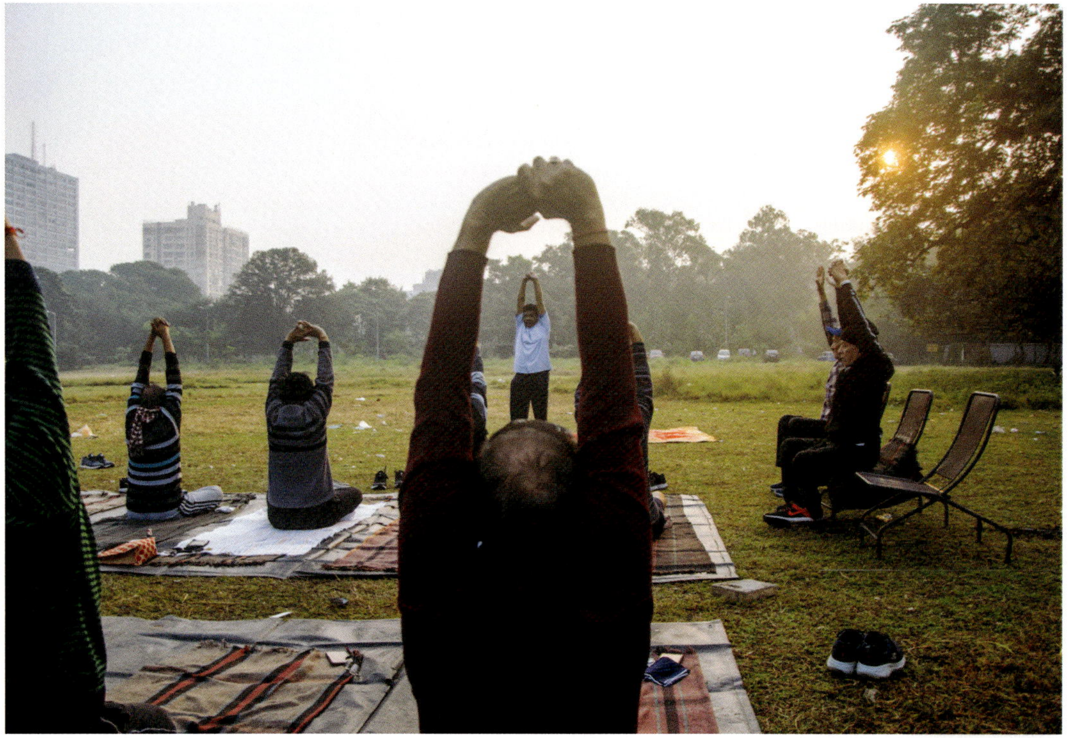

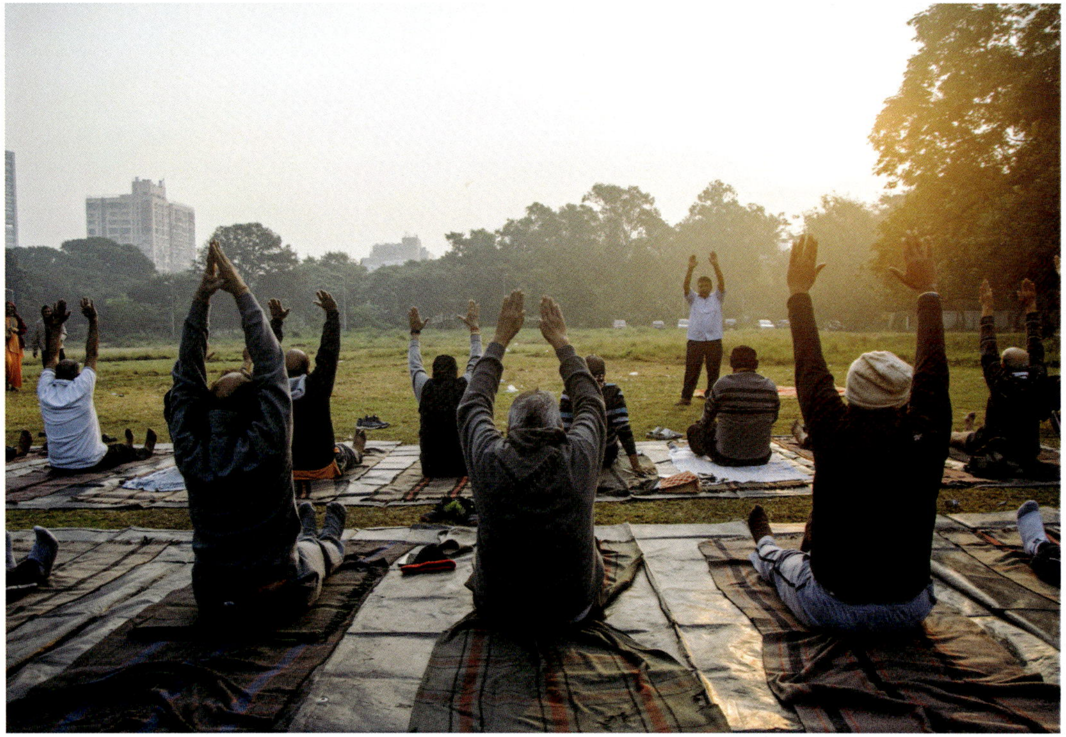

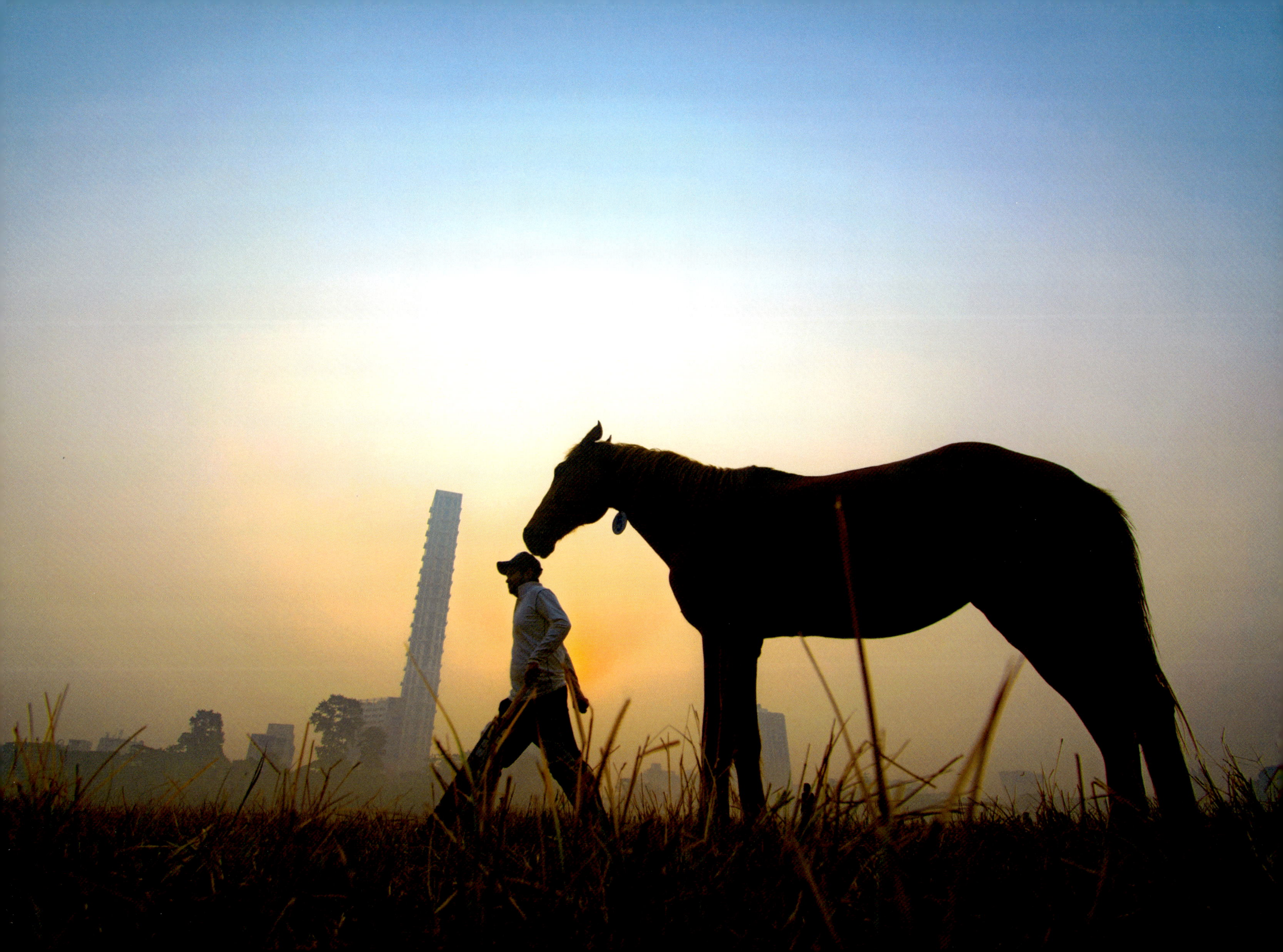

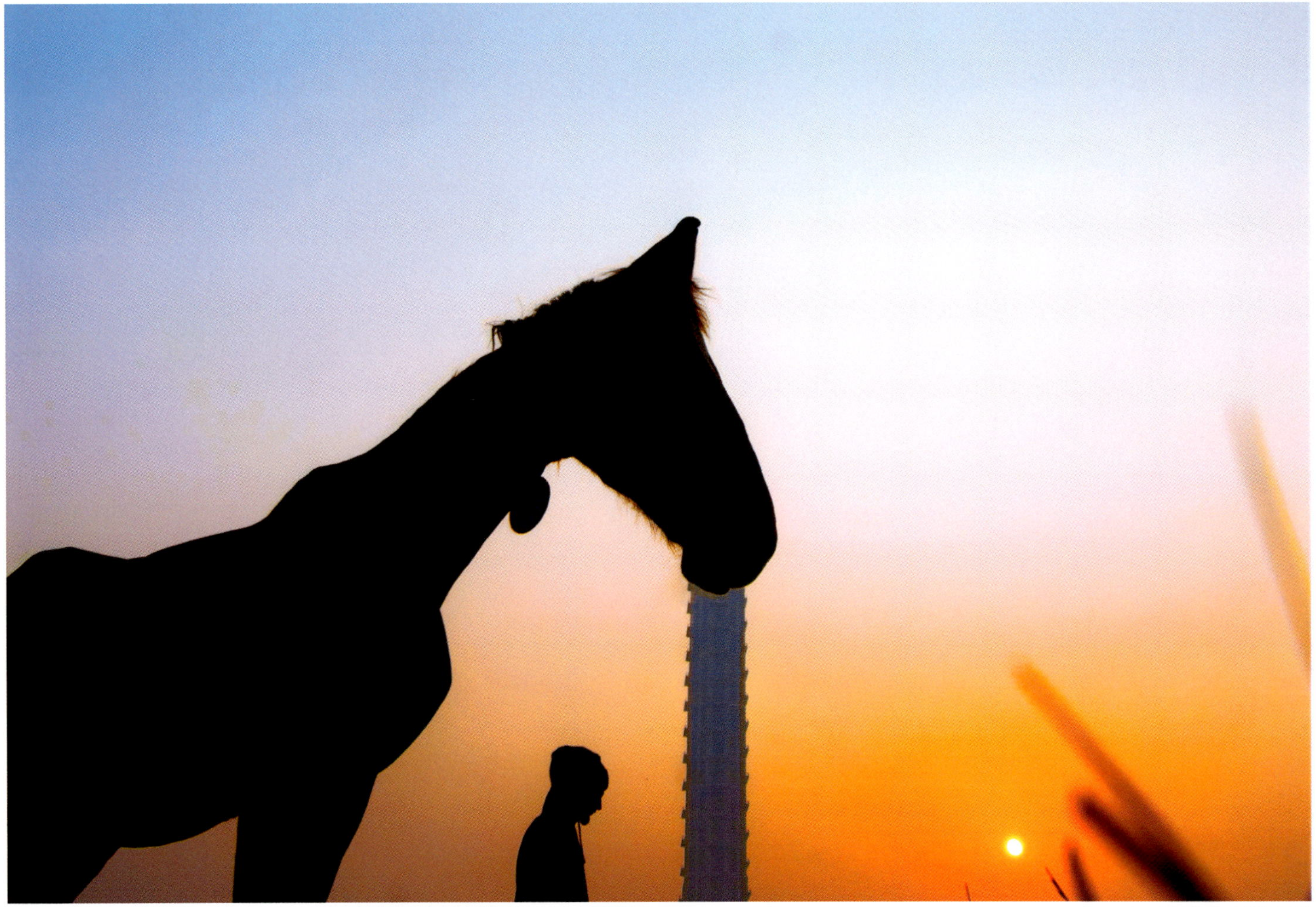

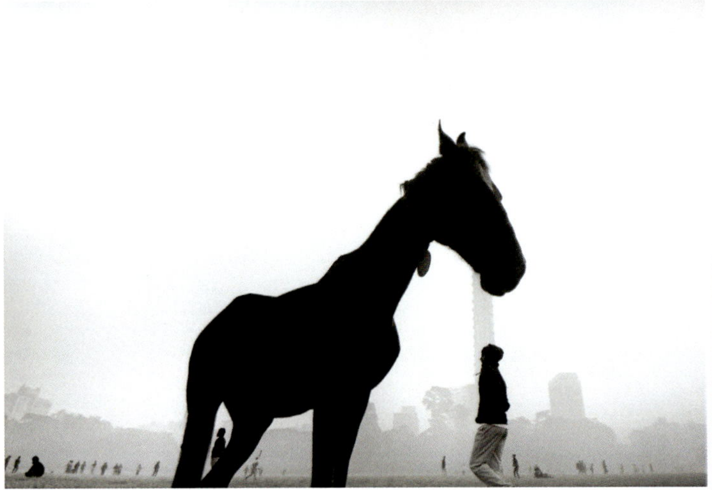

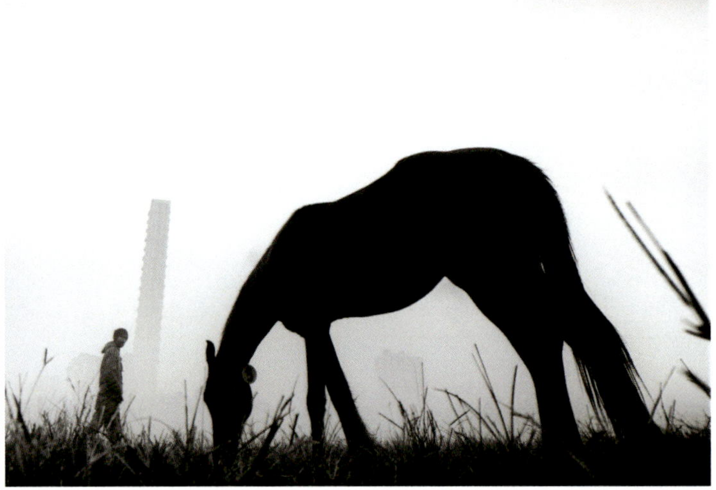

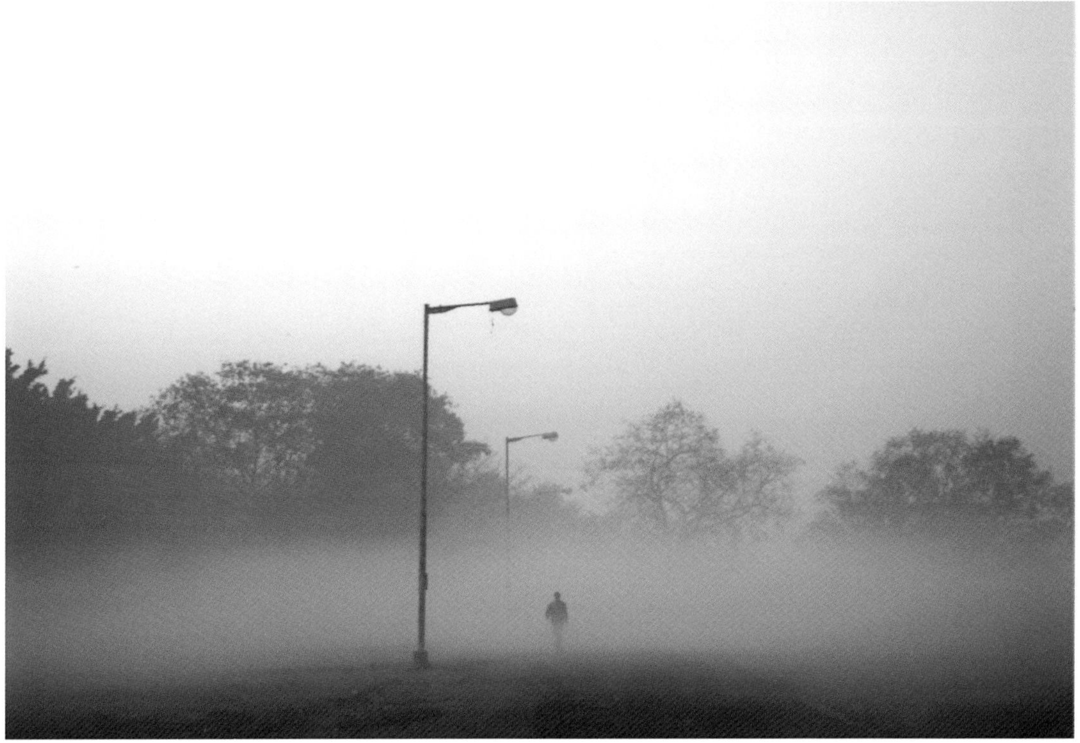

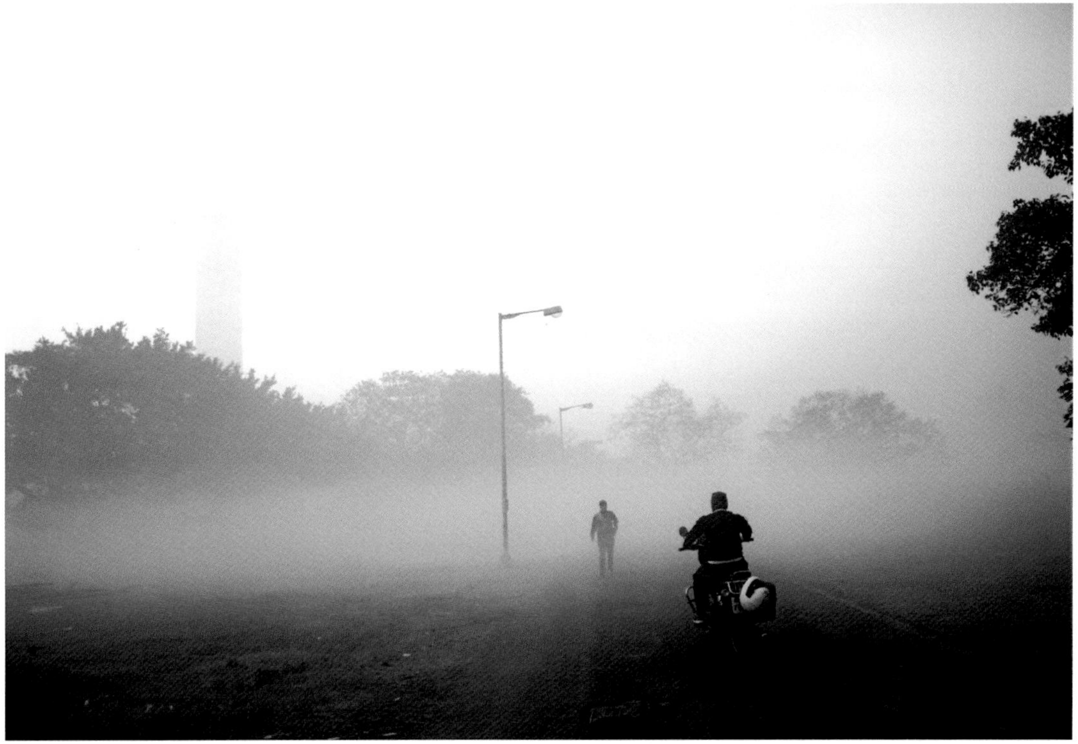

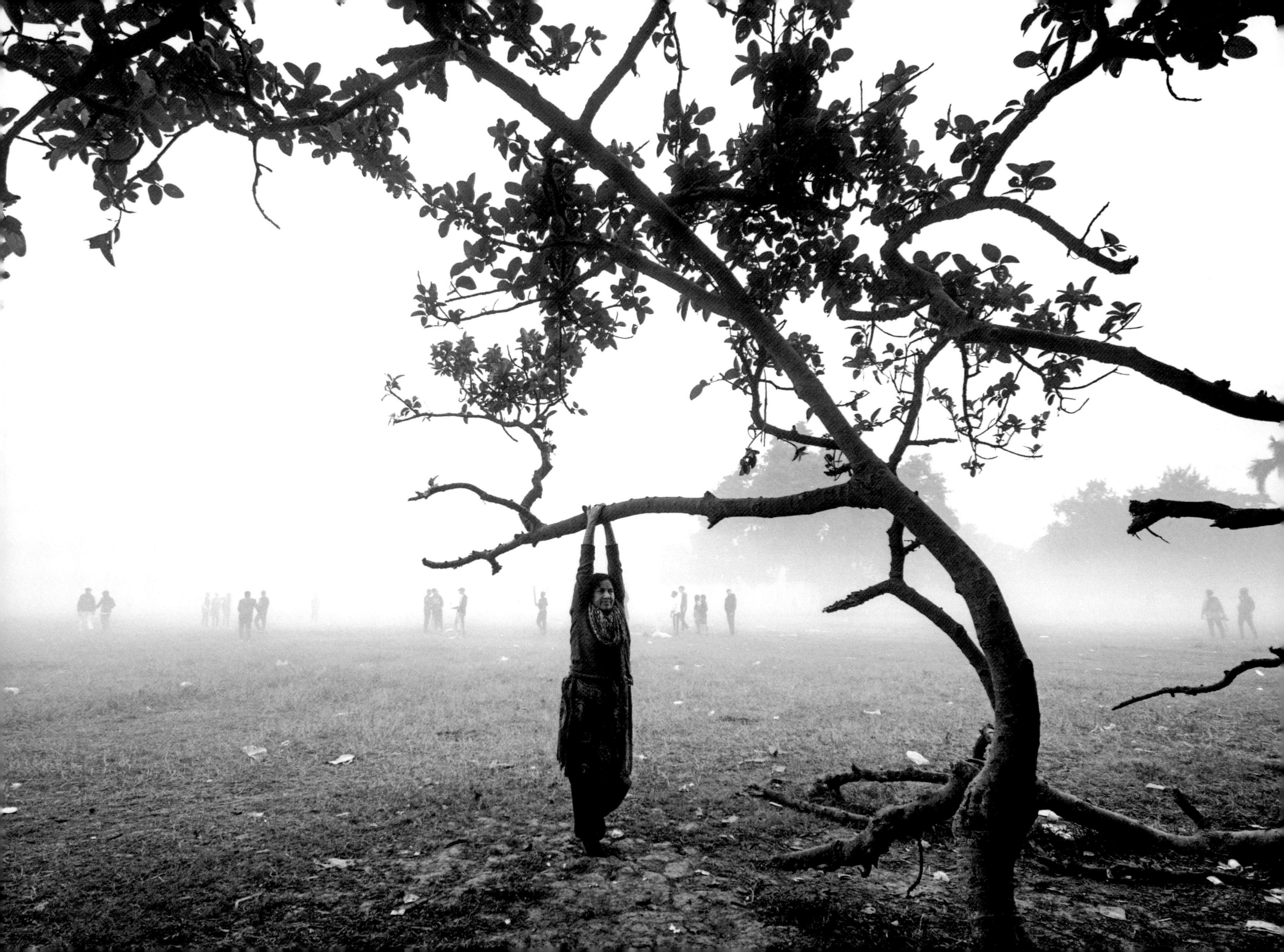

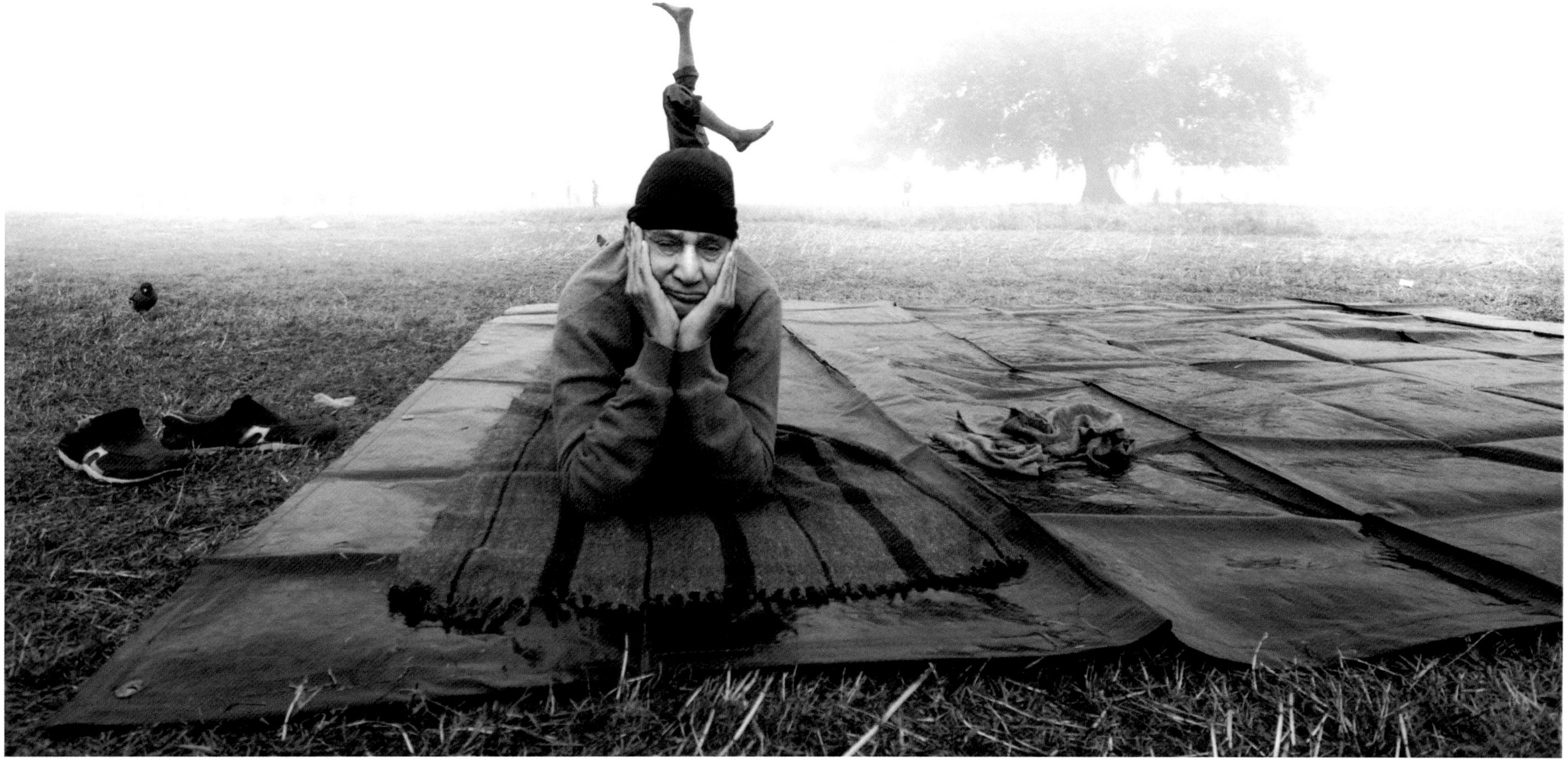

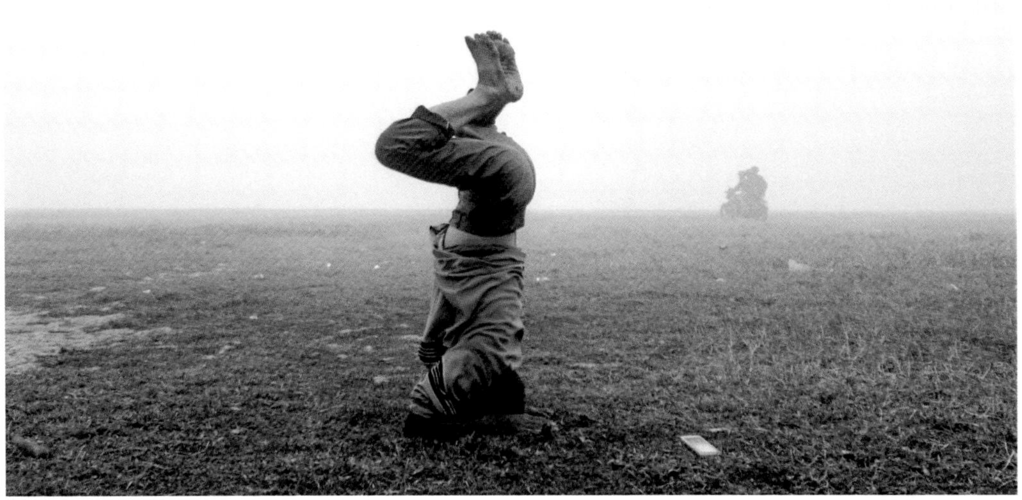
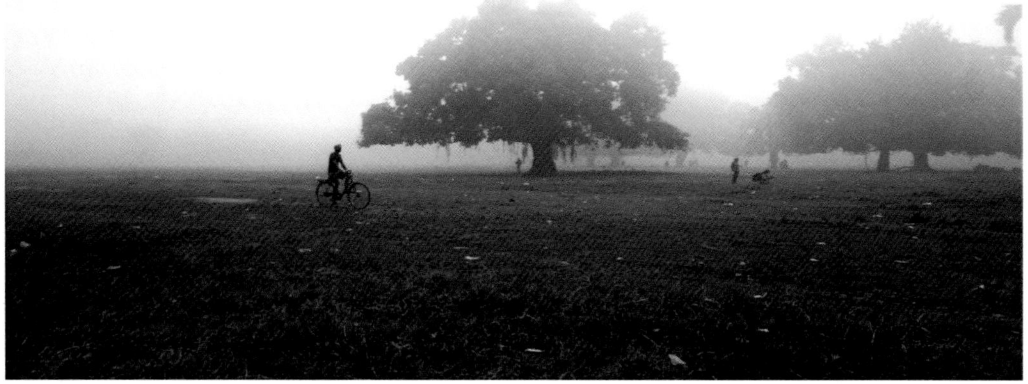
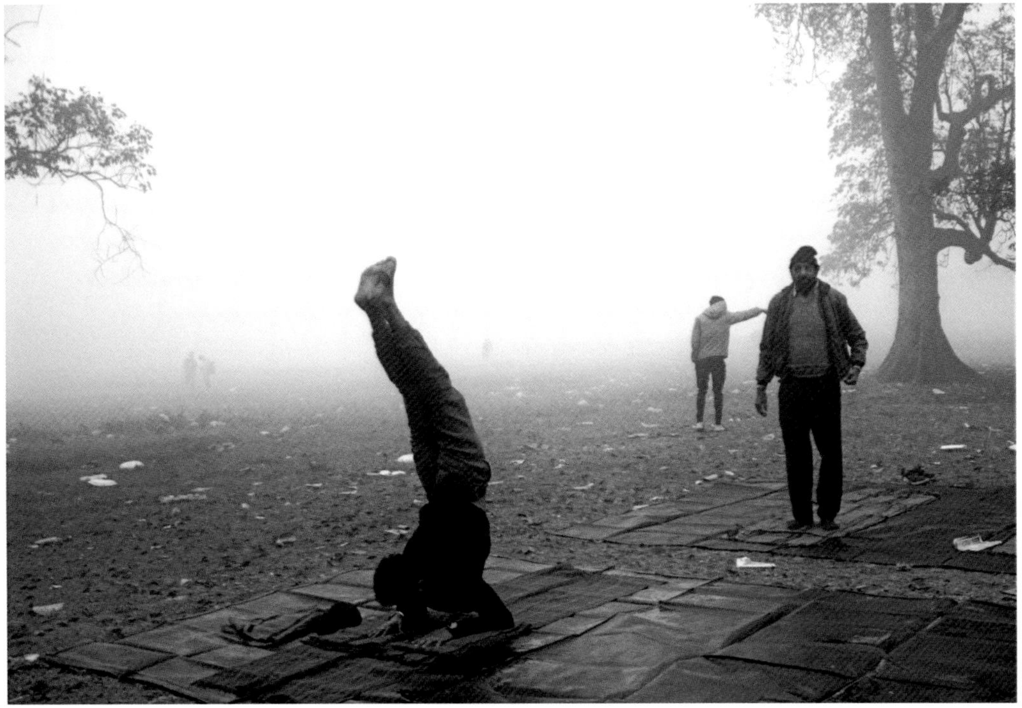
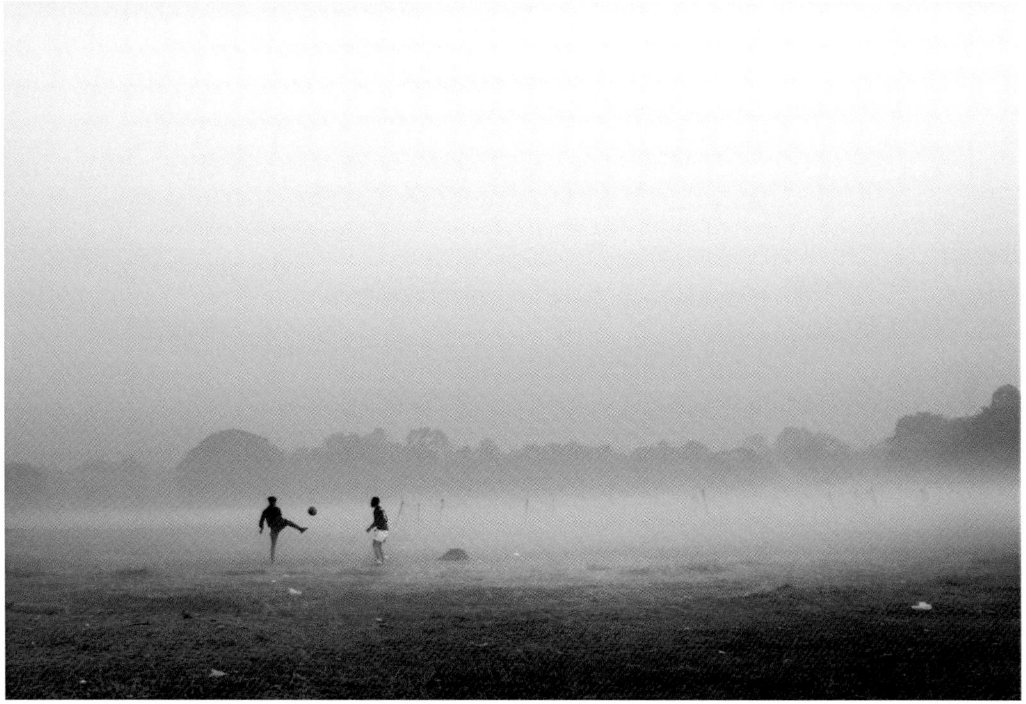

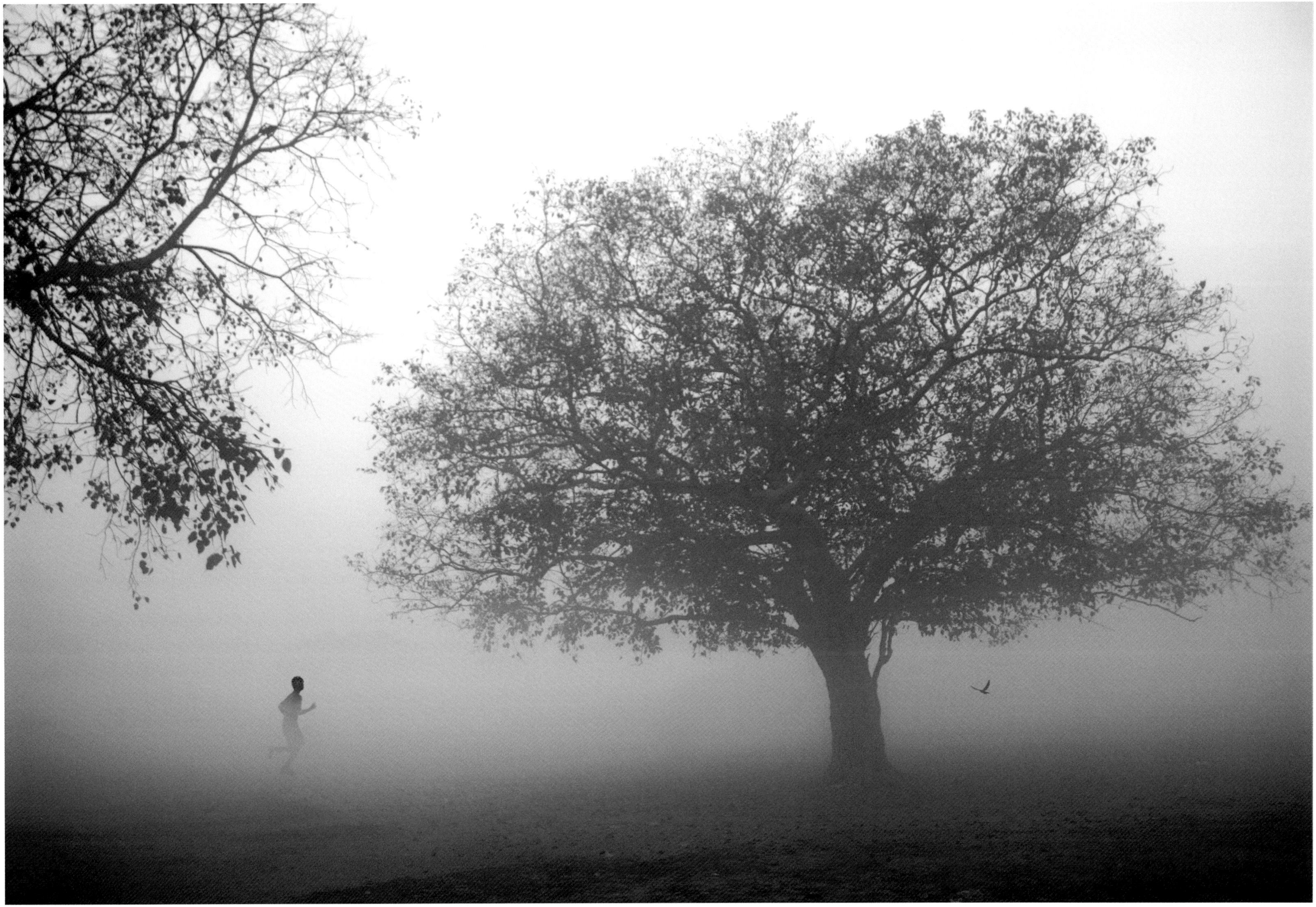

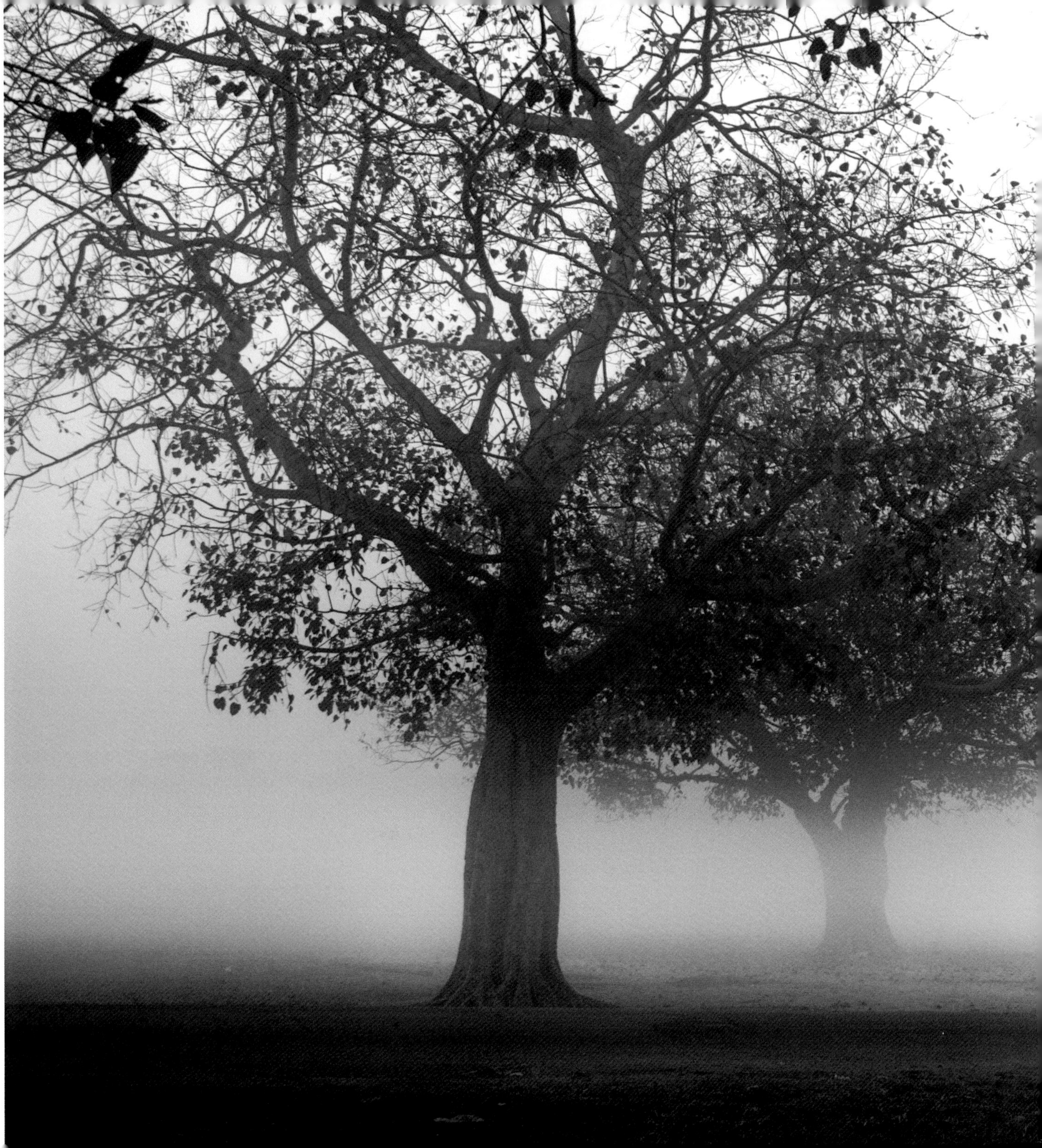

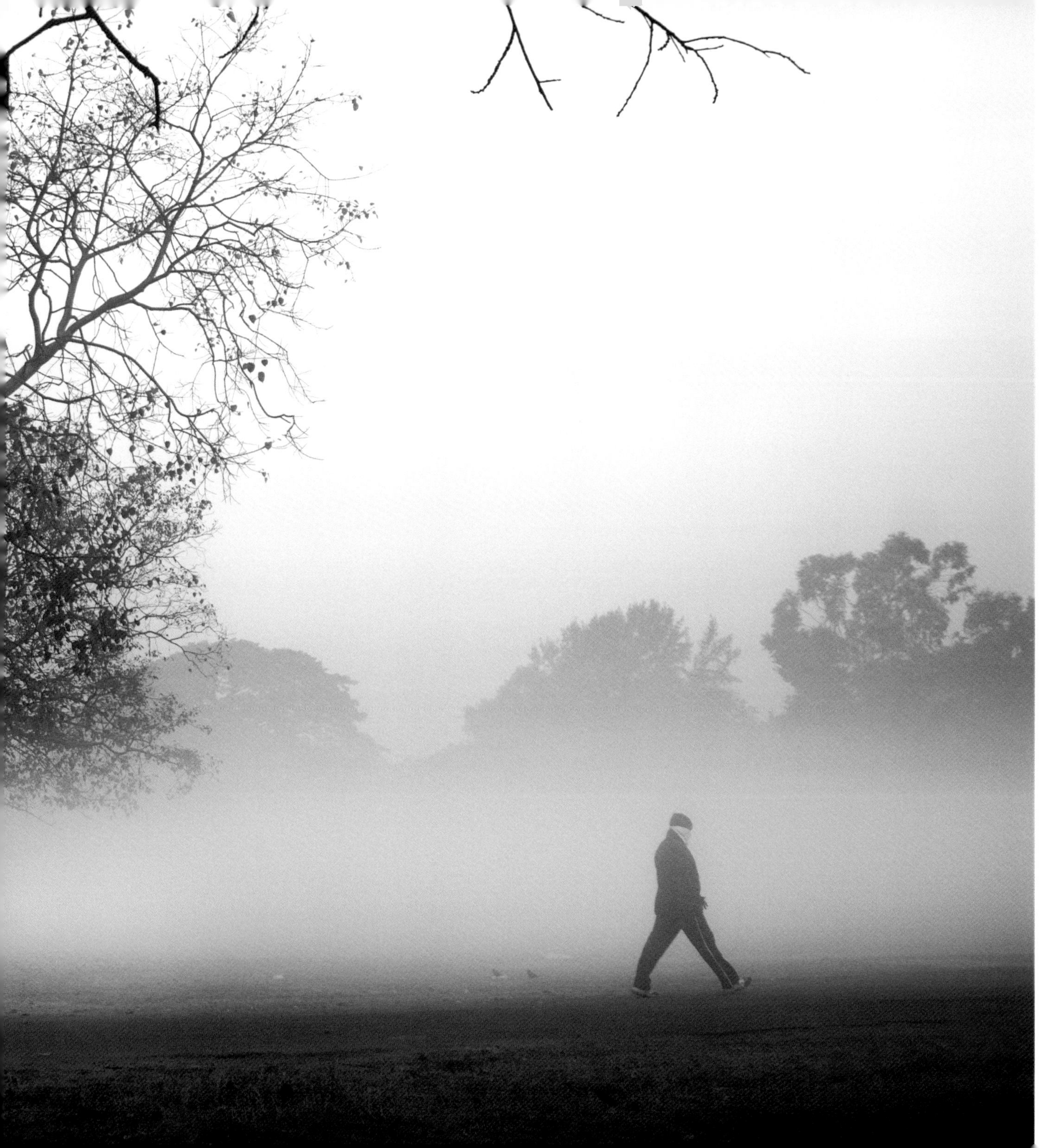

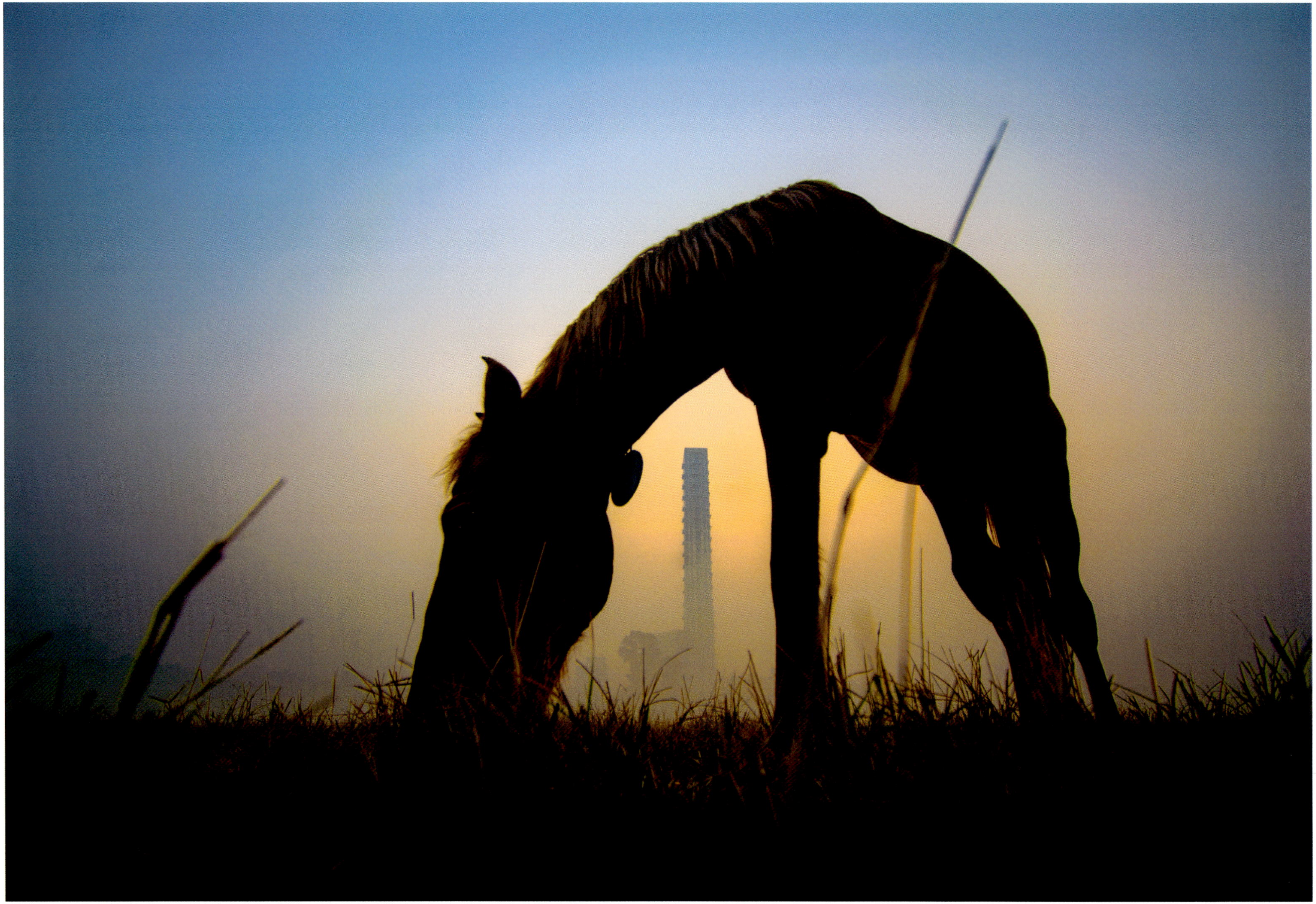

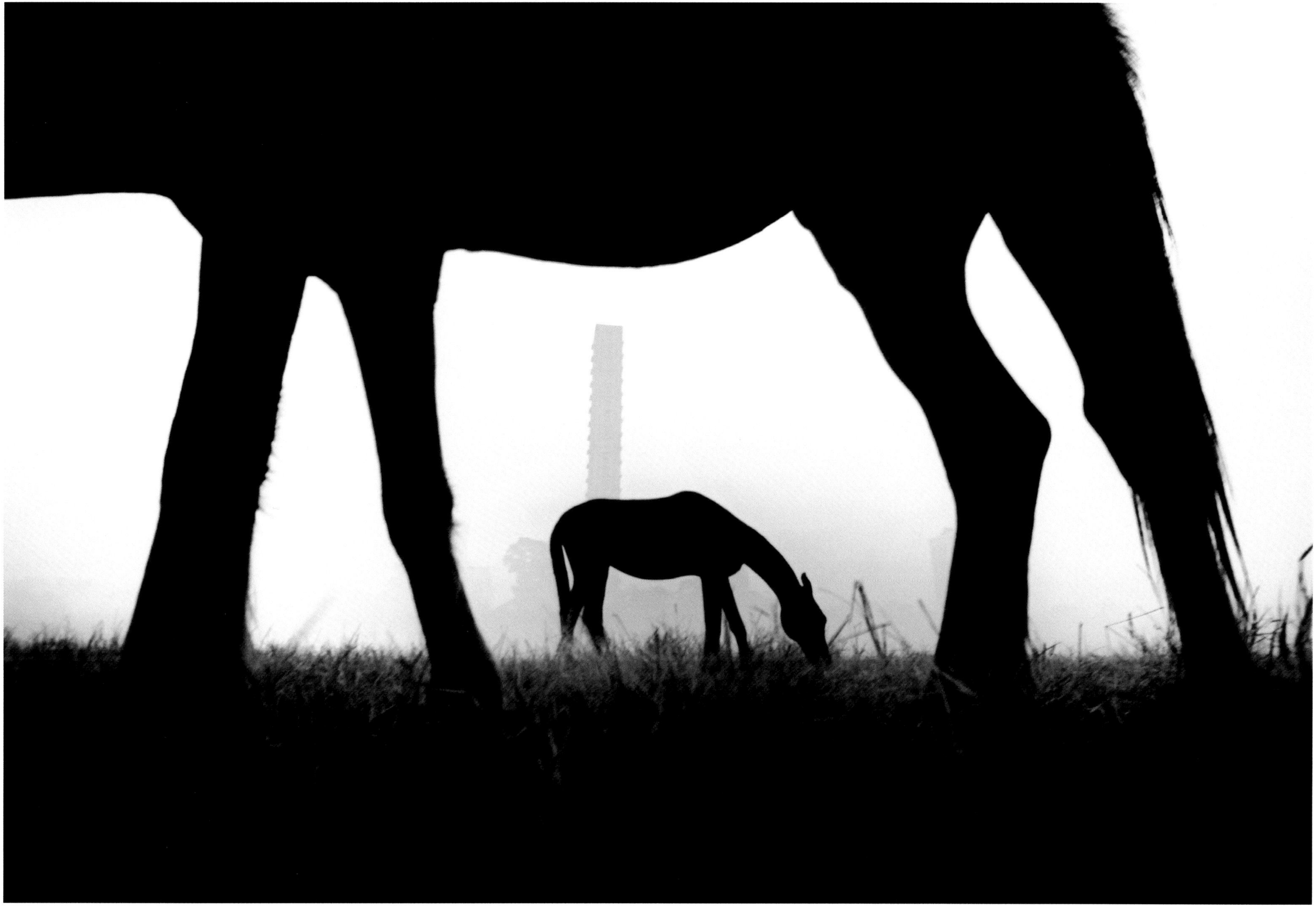

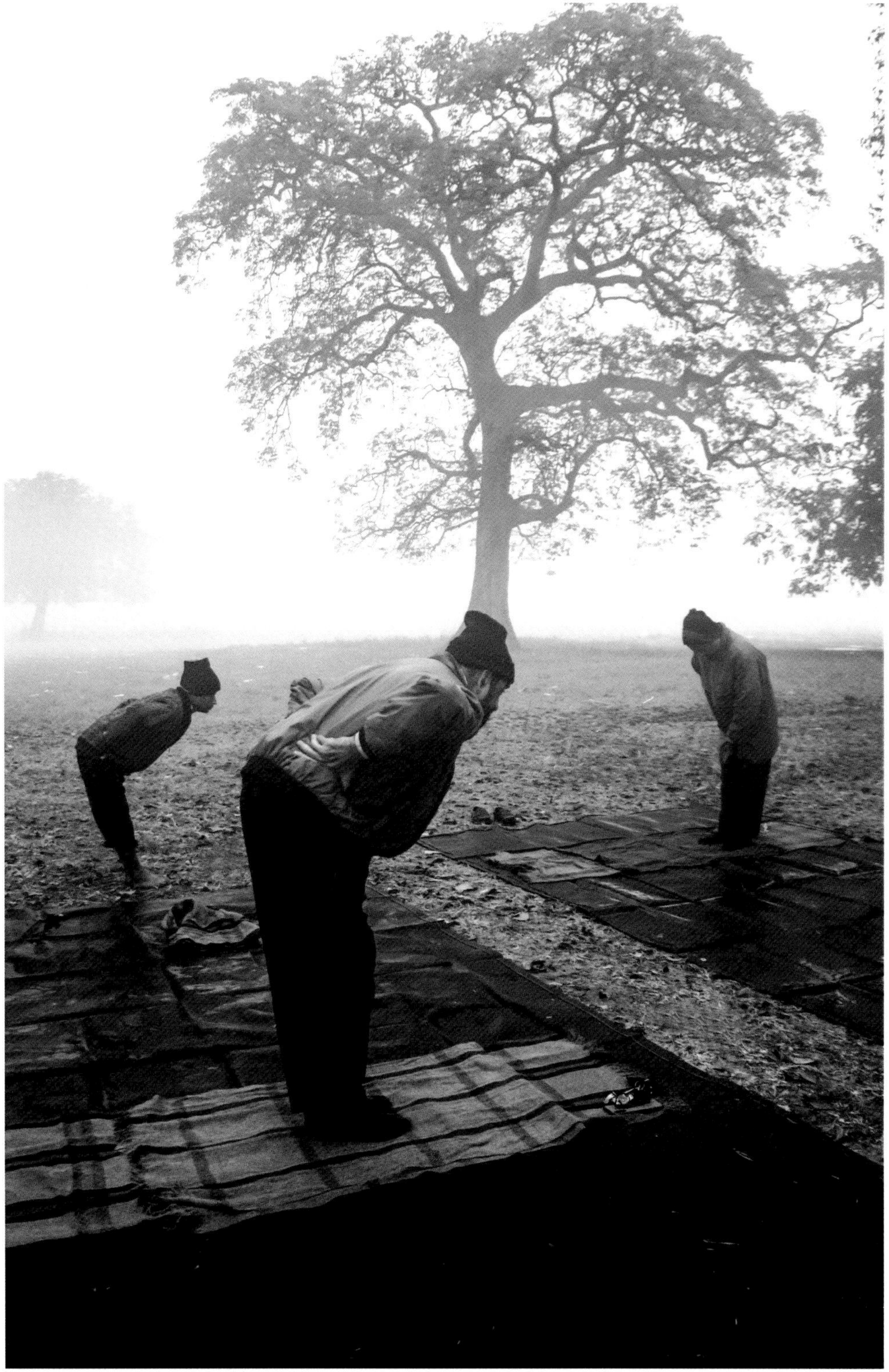

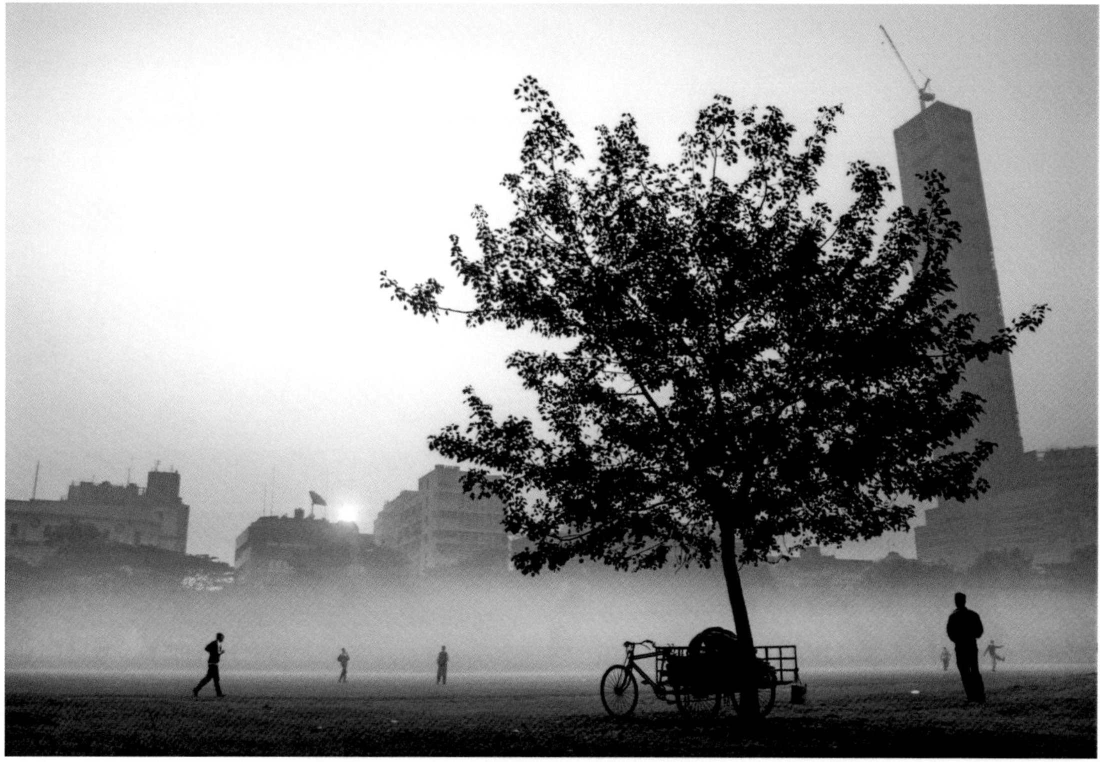

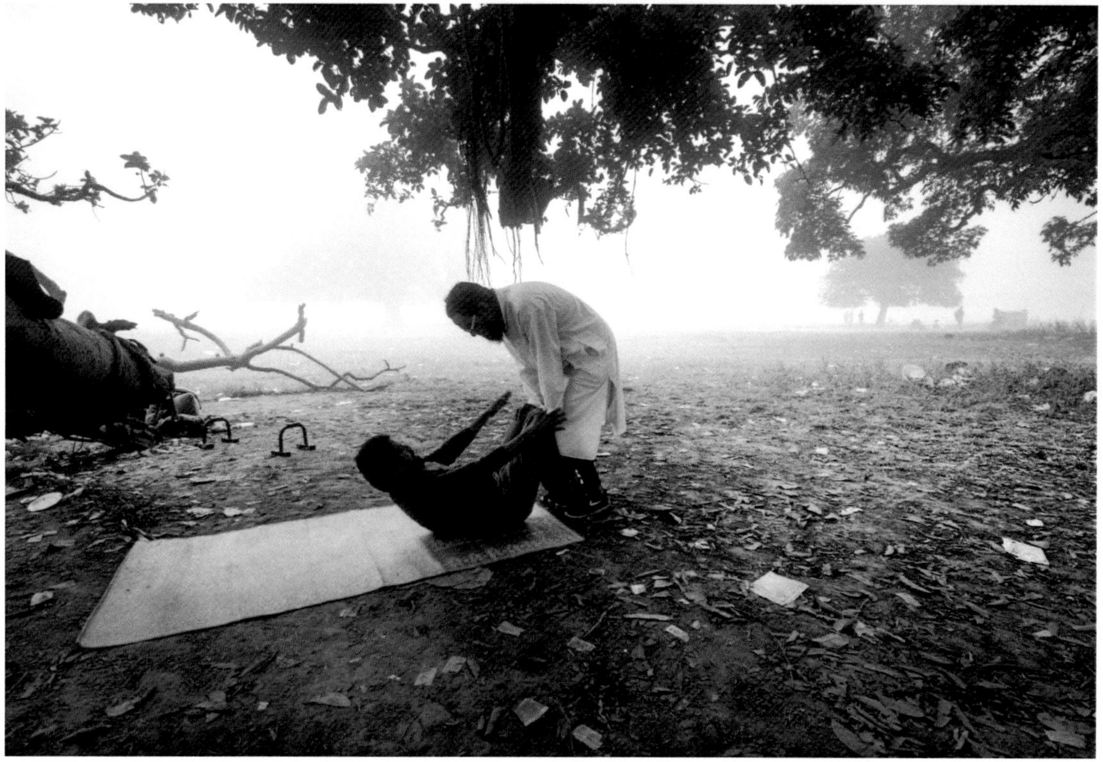

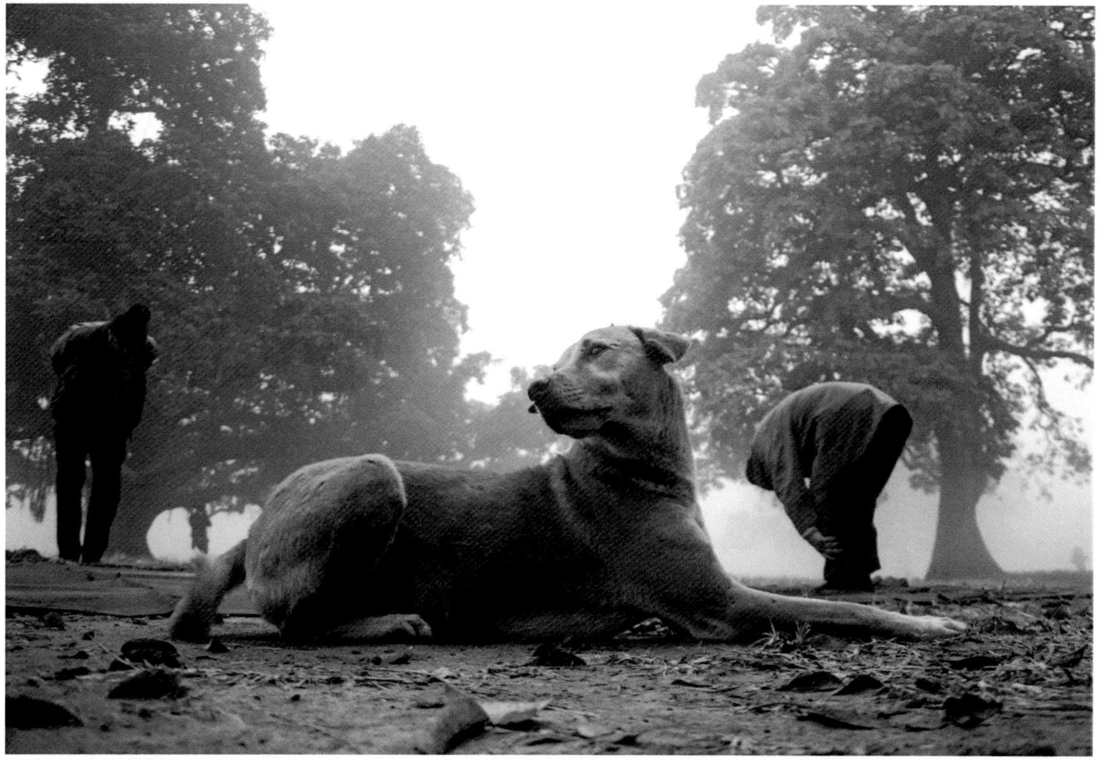

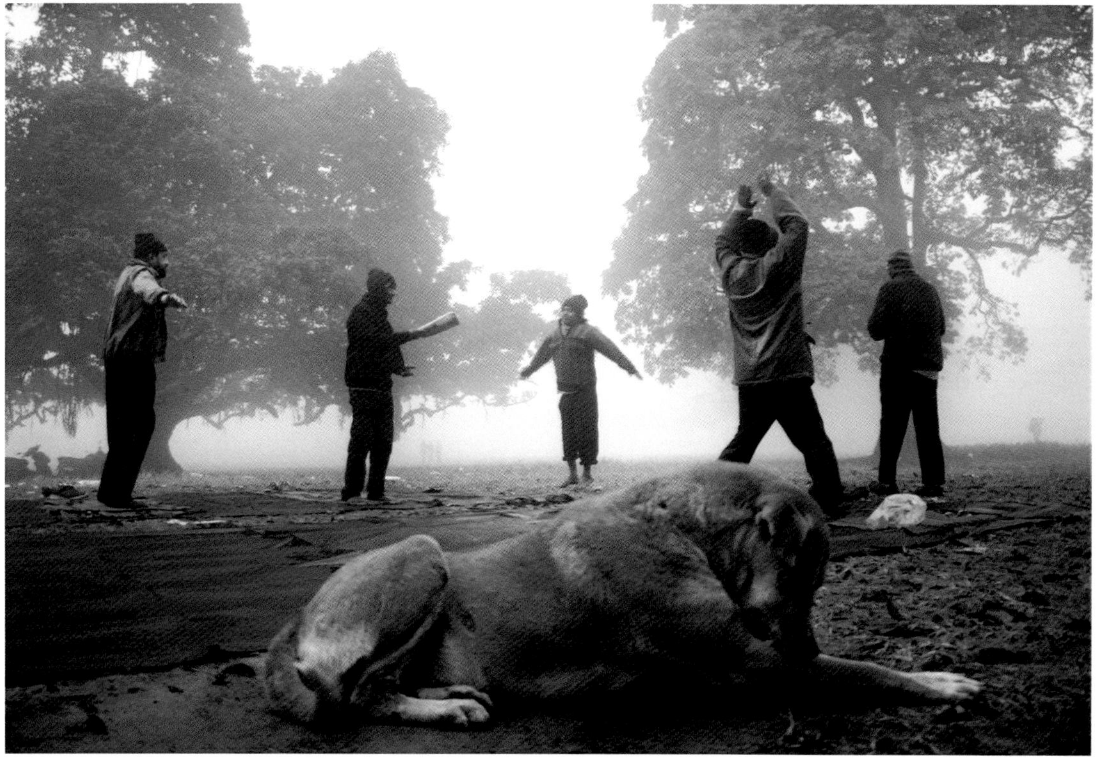

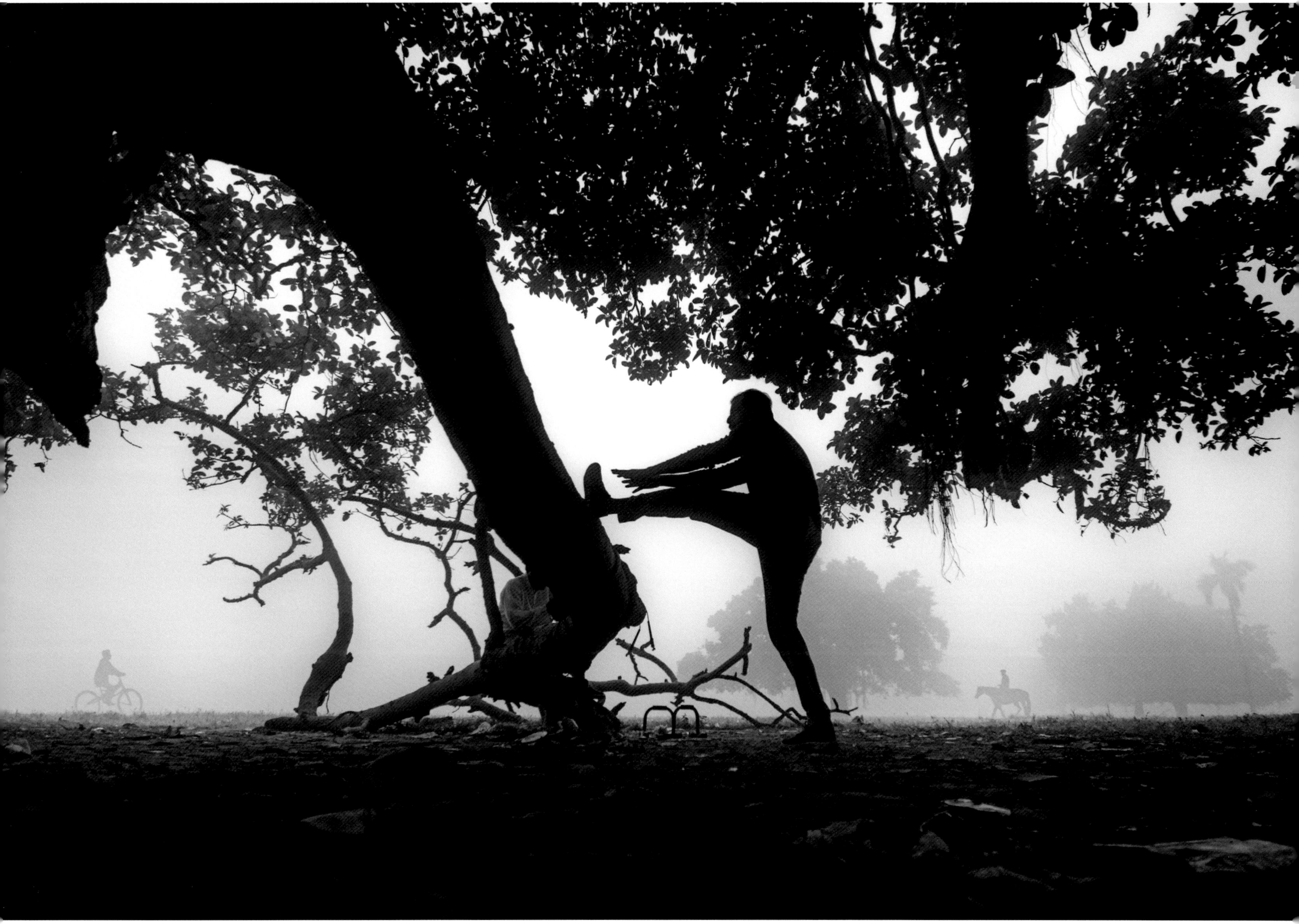

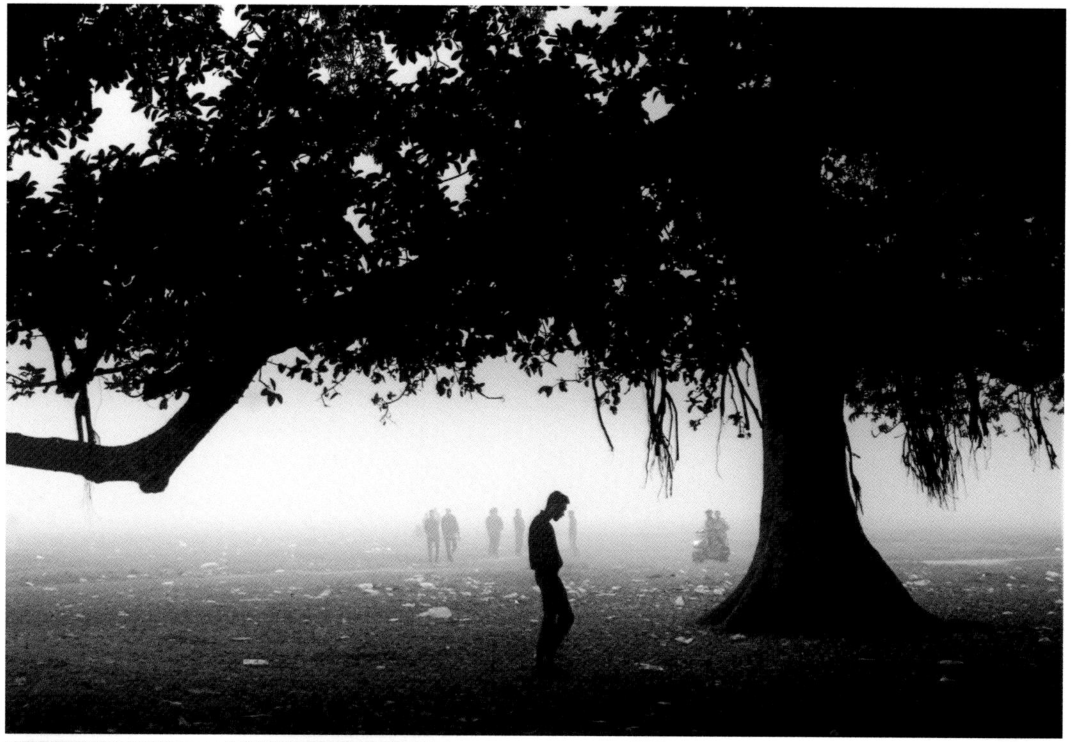

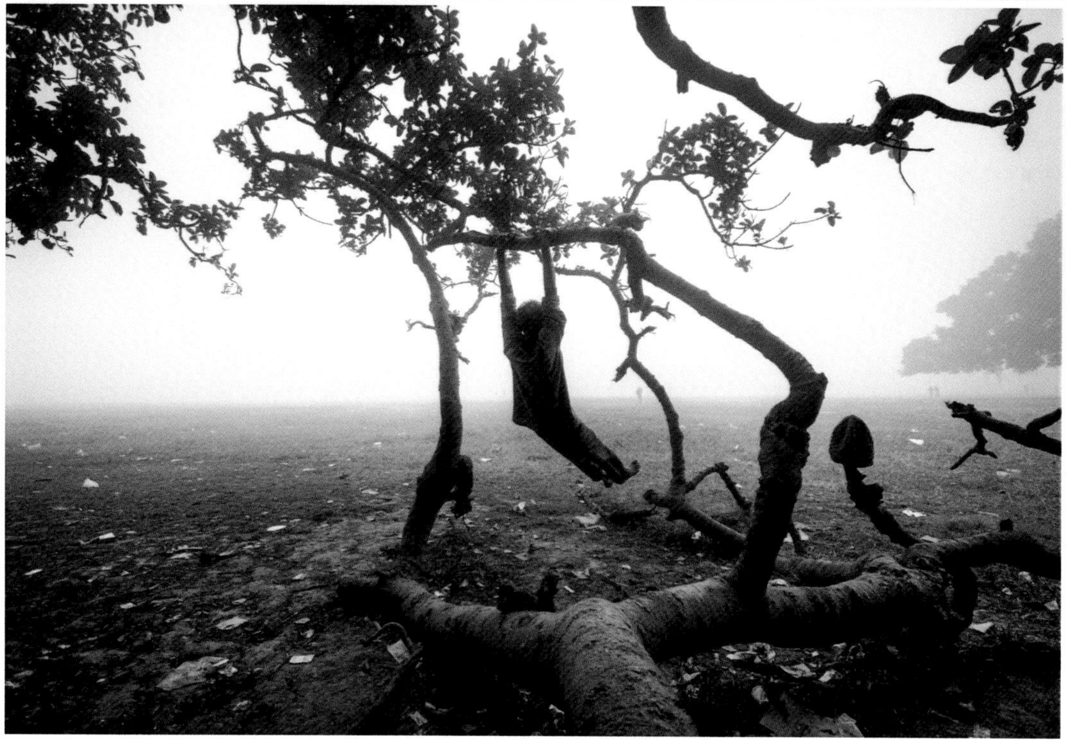

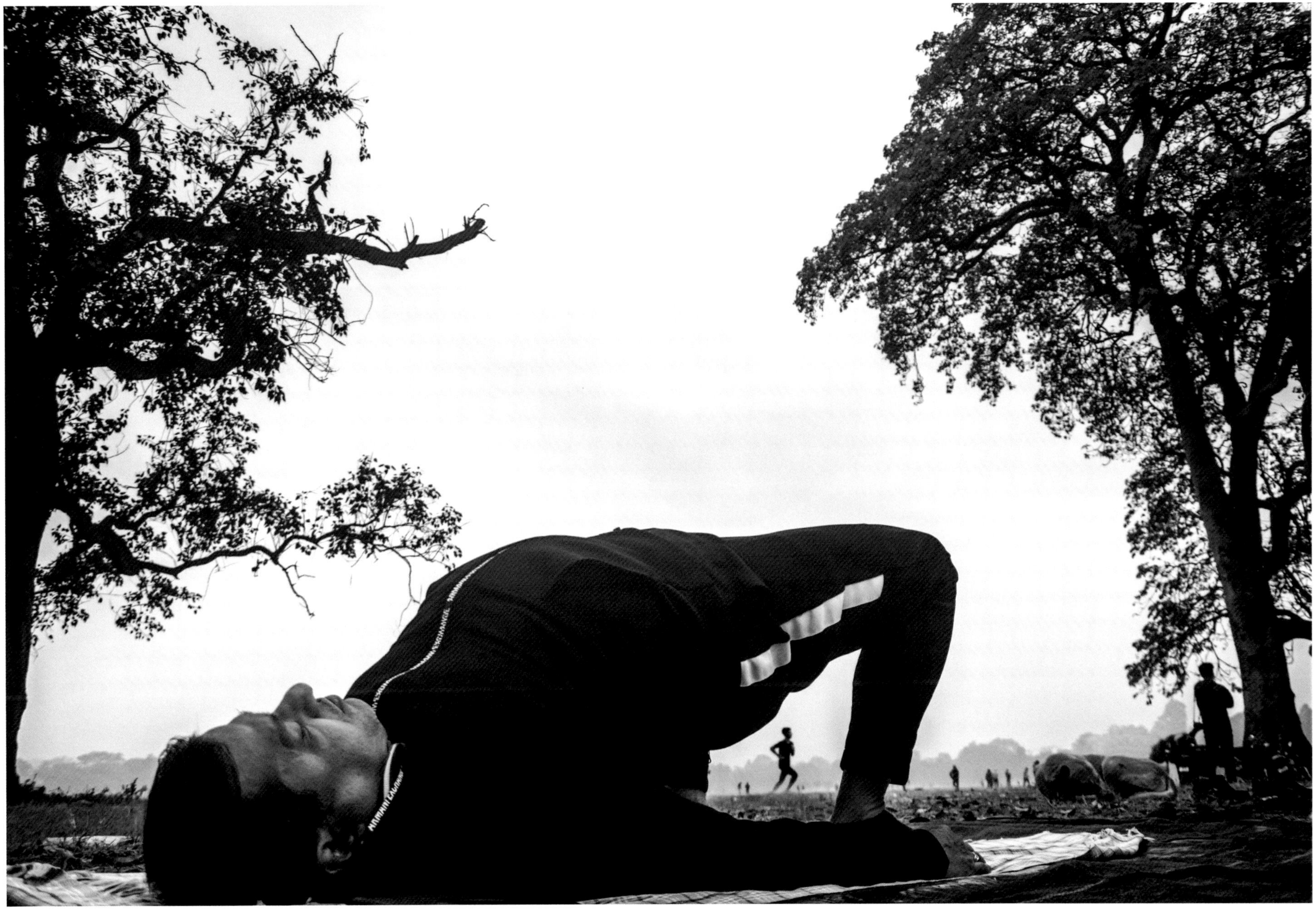

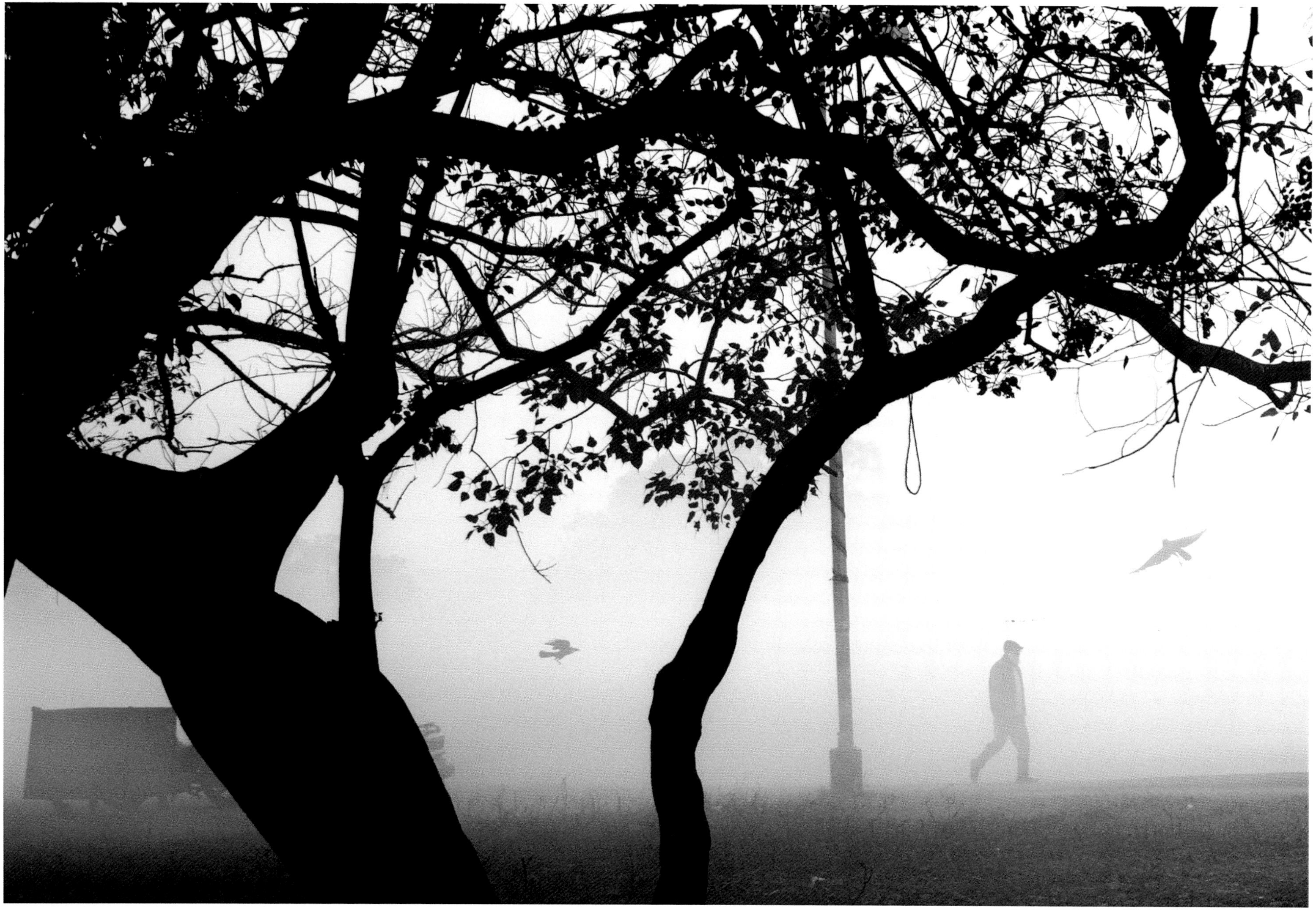

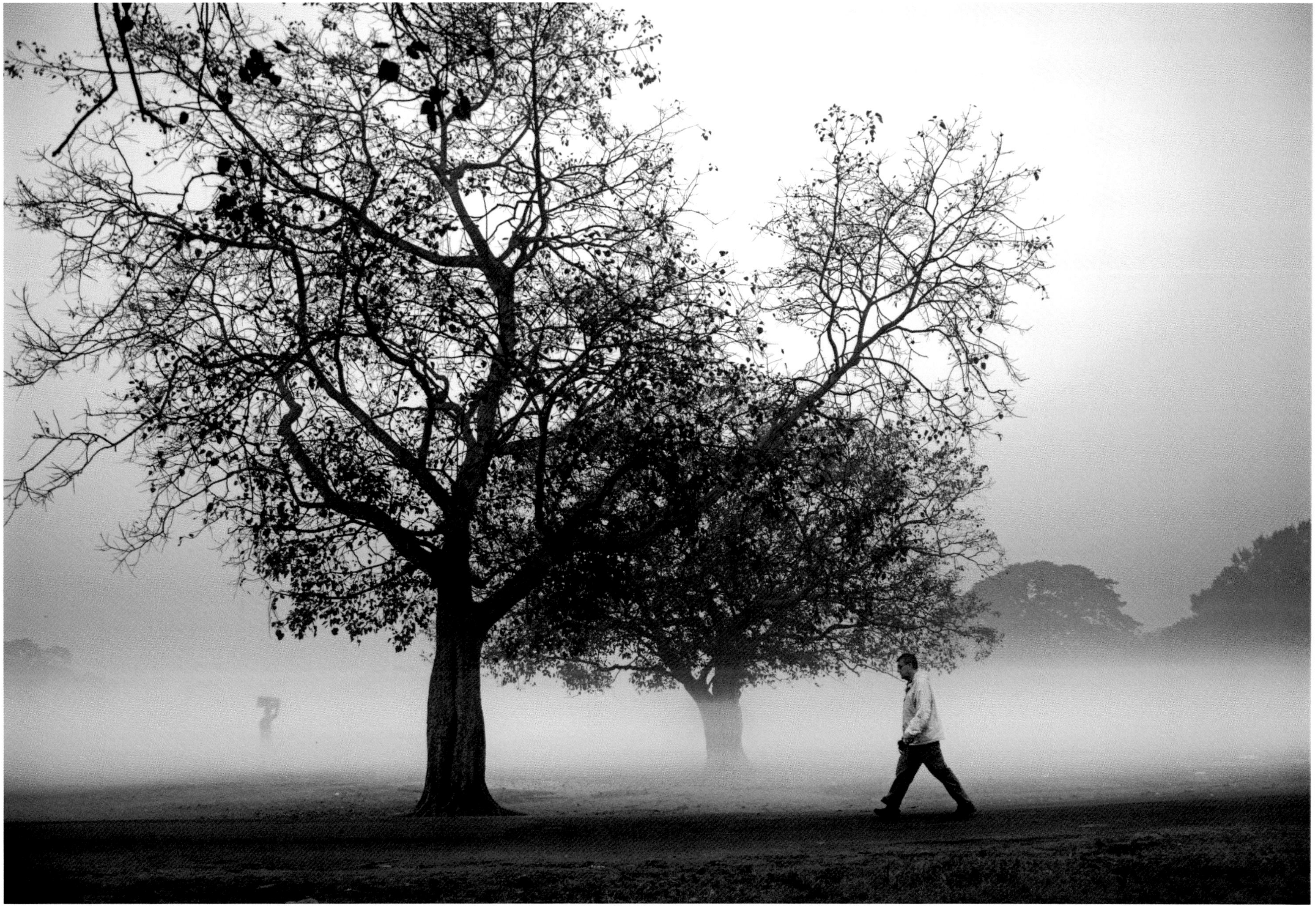

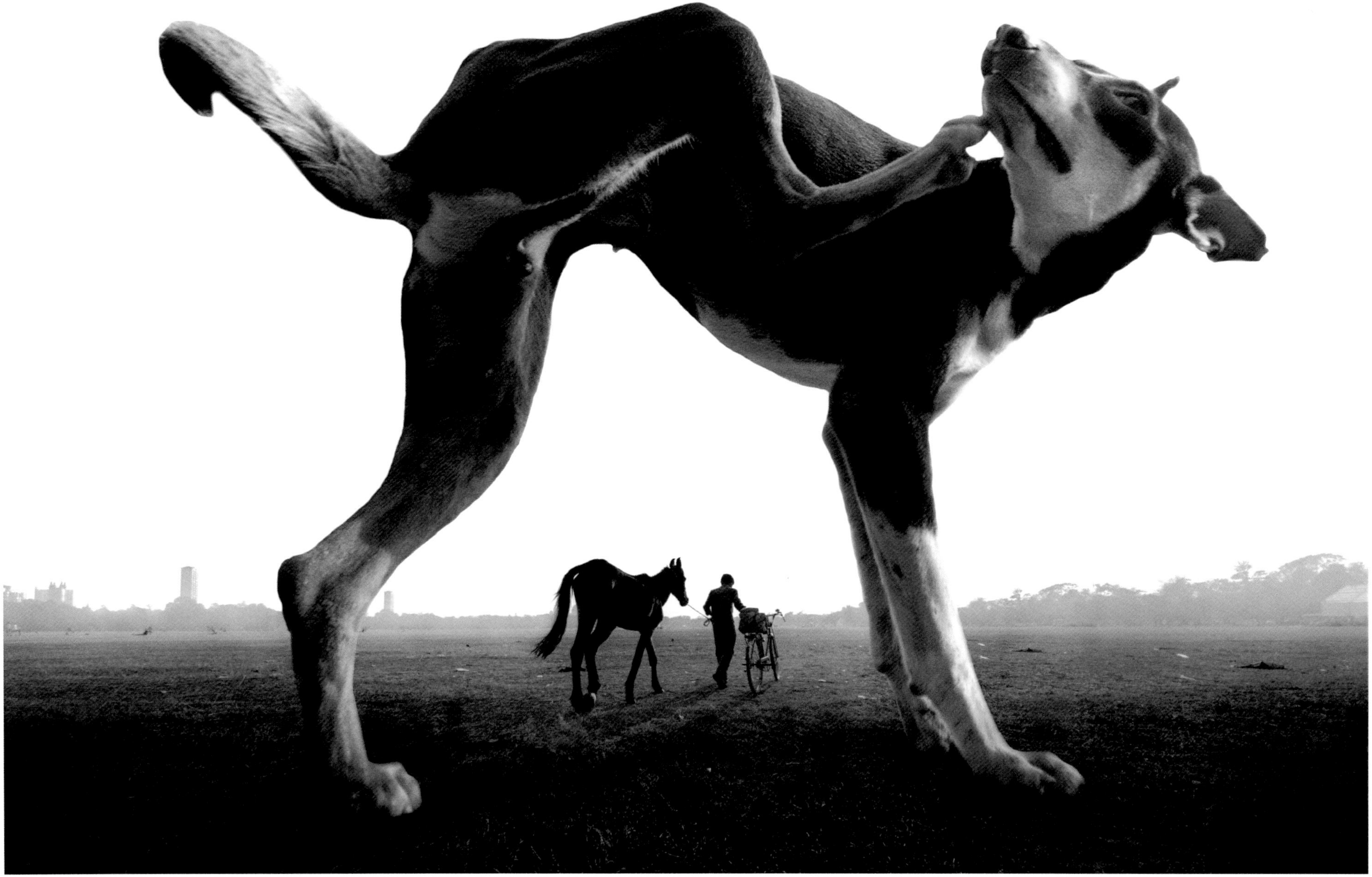

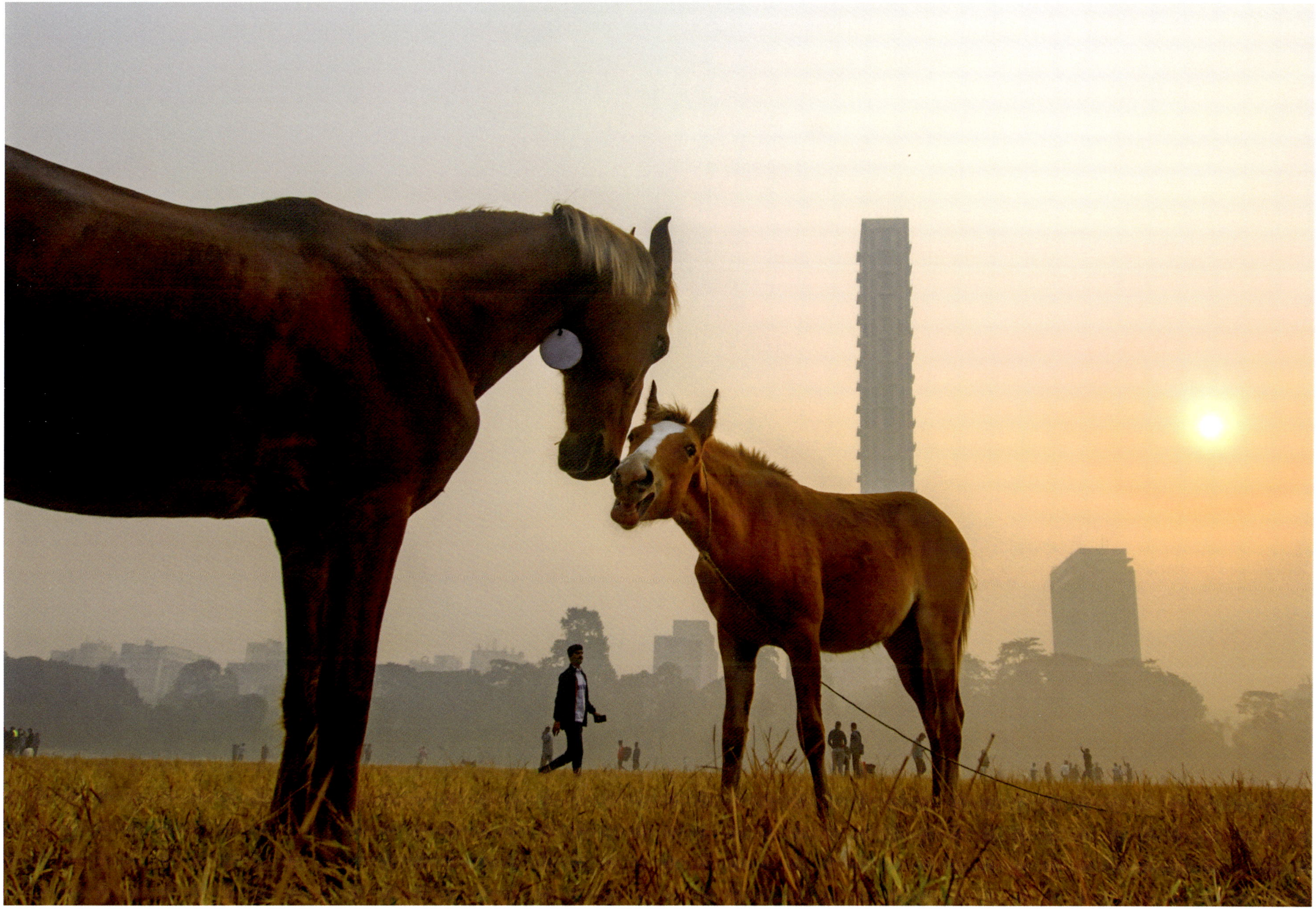

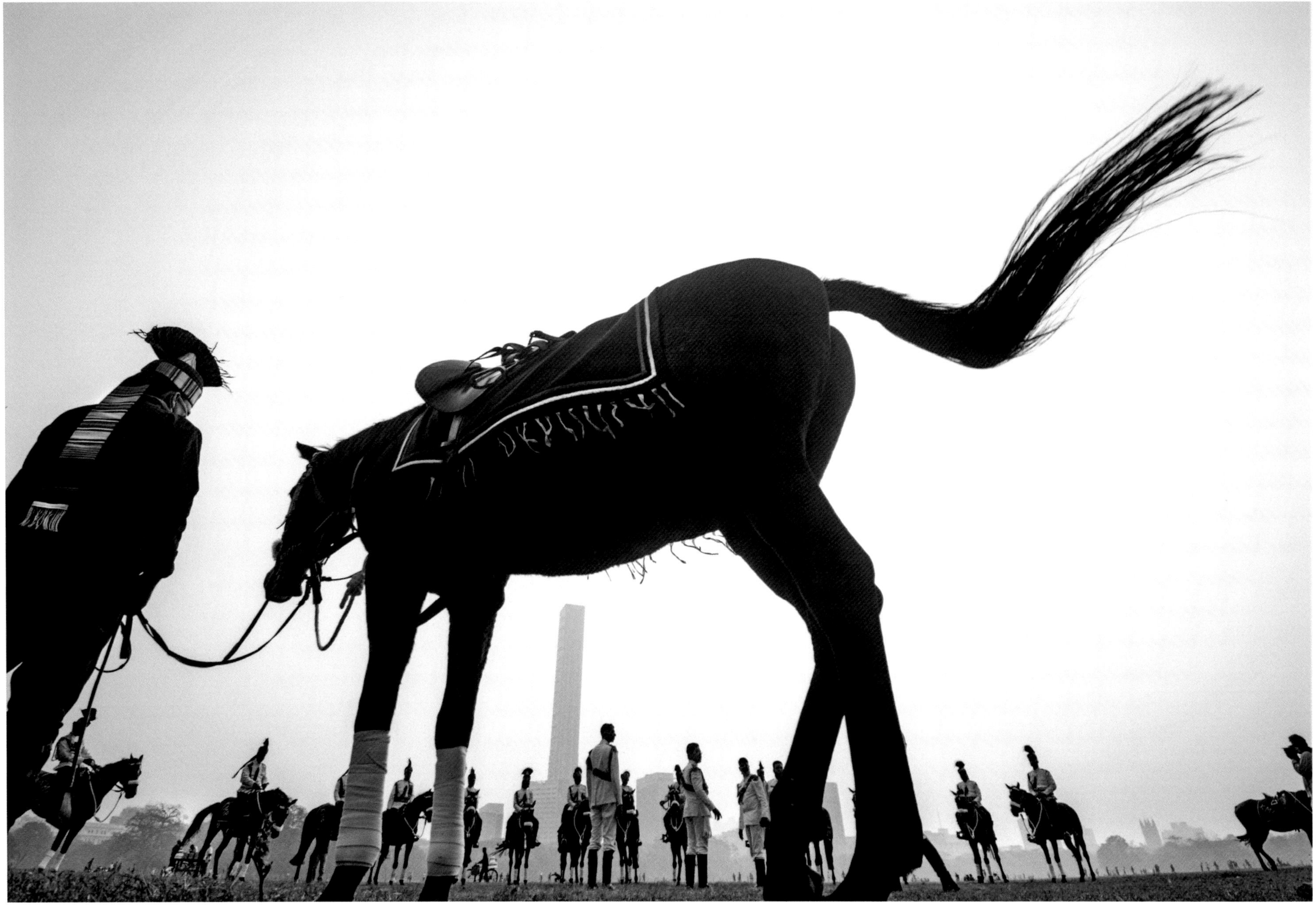

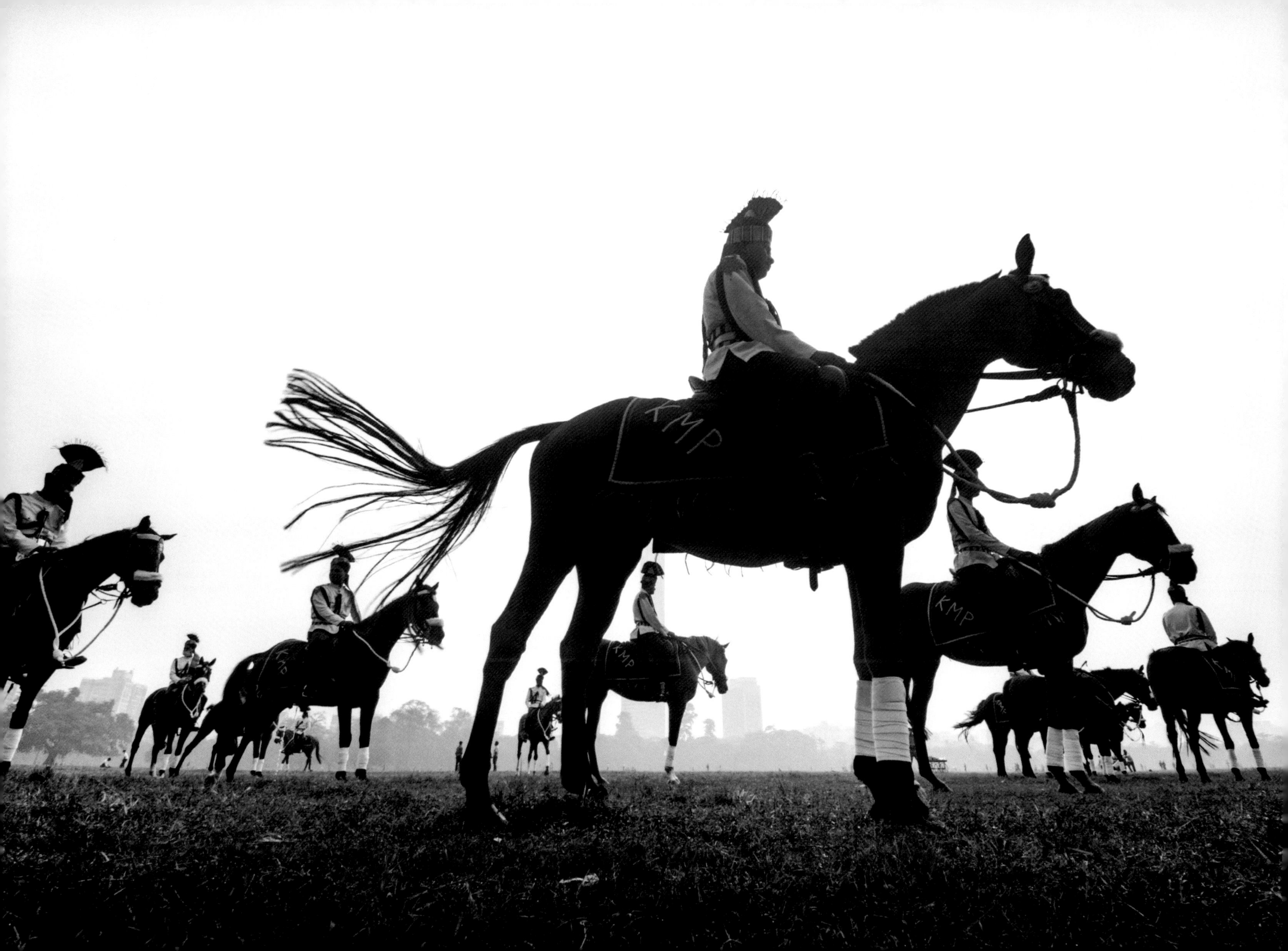
KMP
KMP

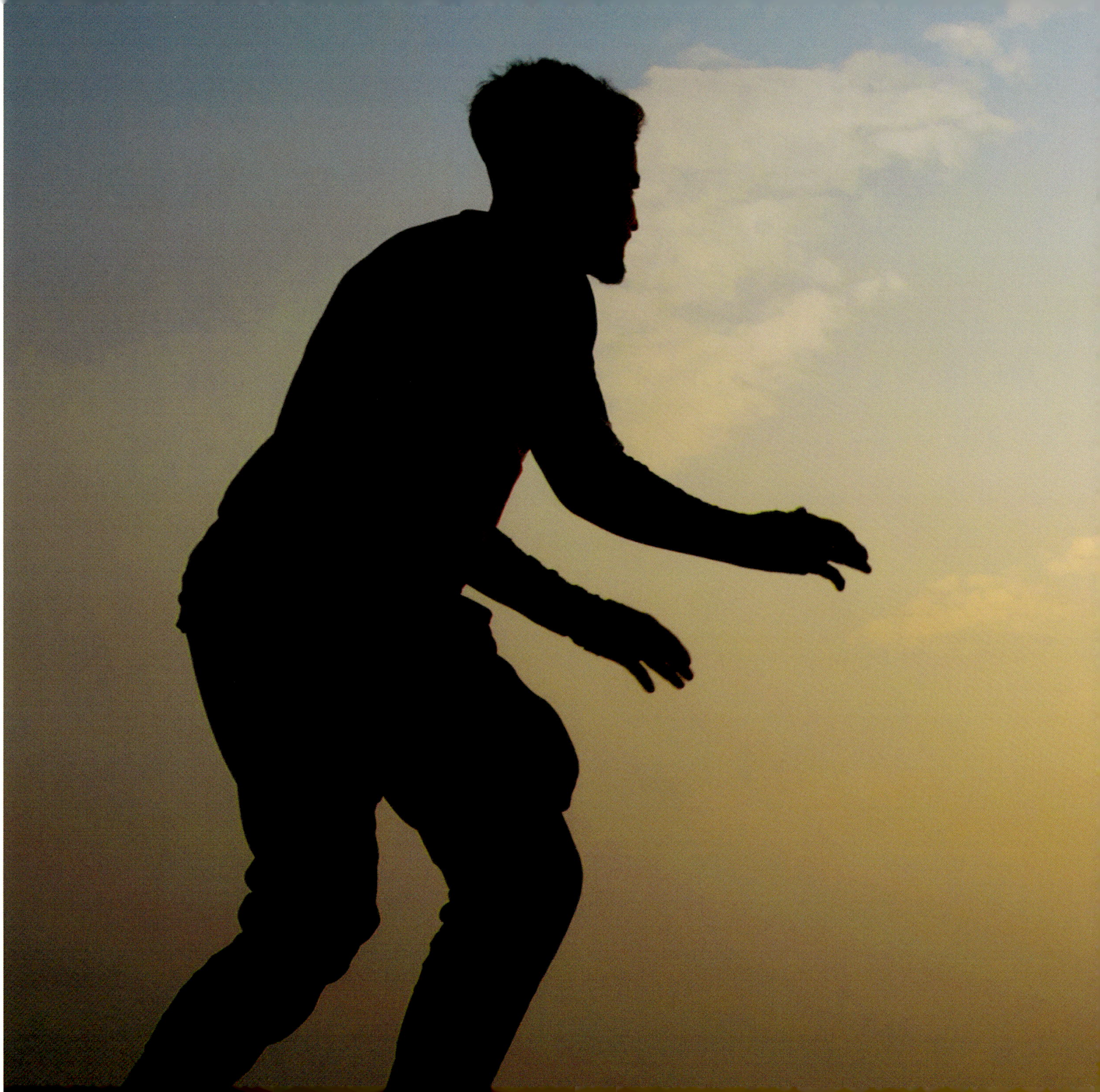

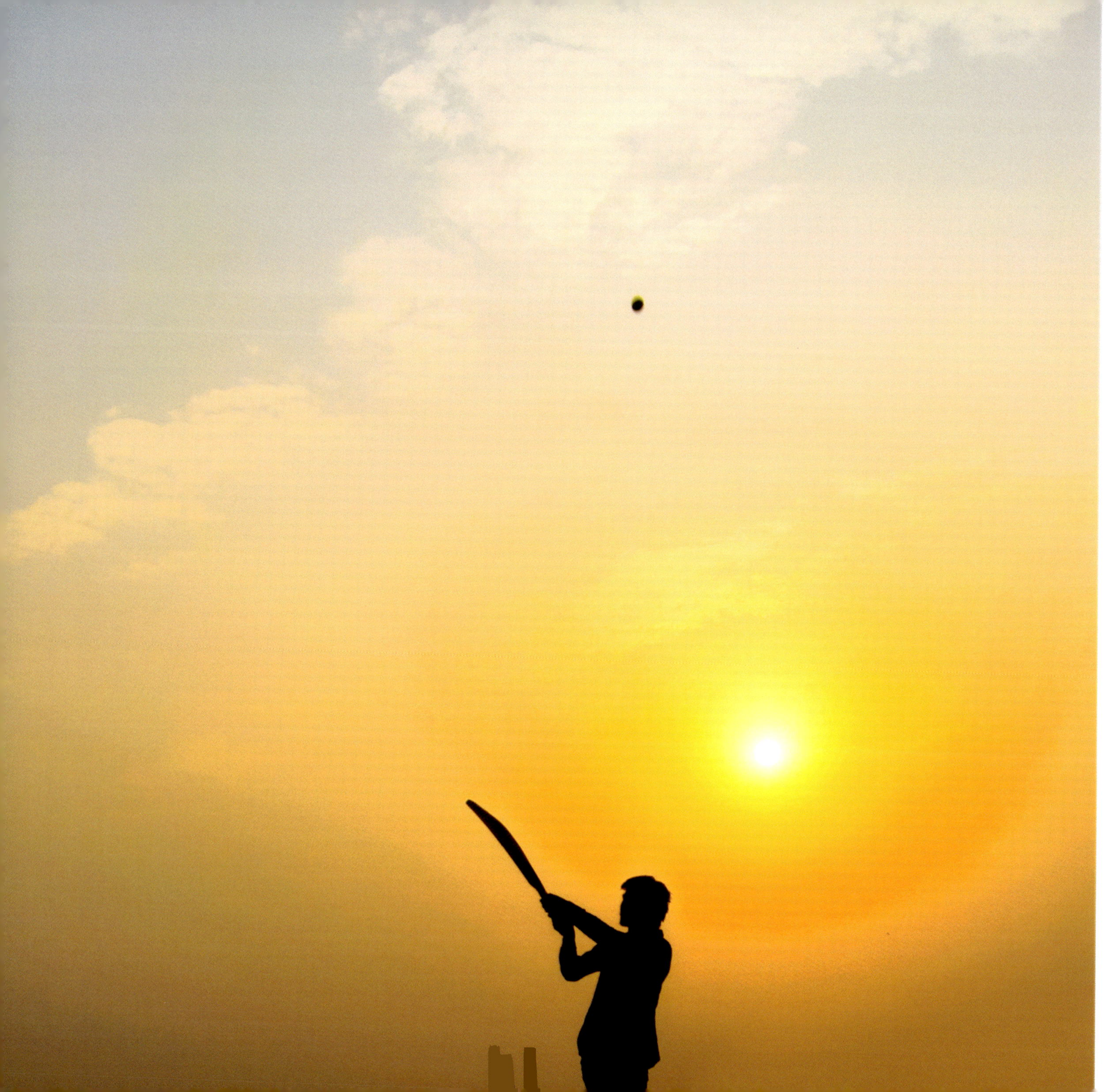

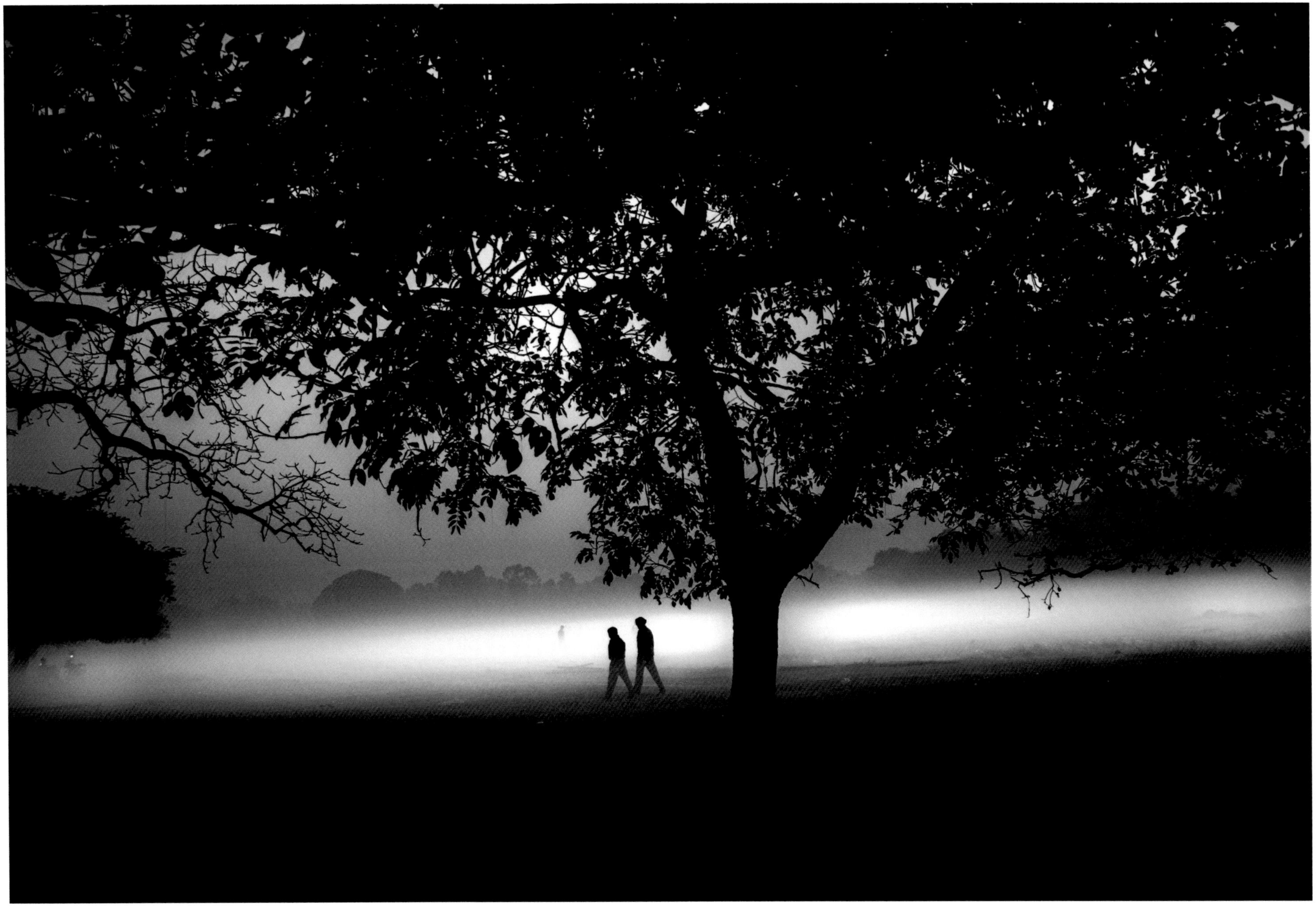

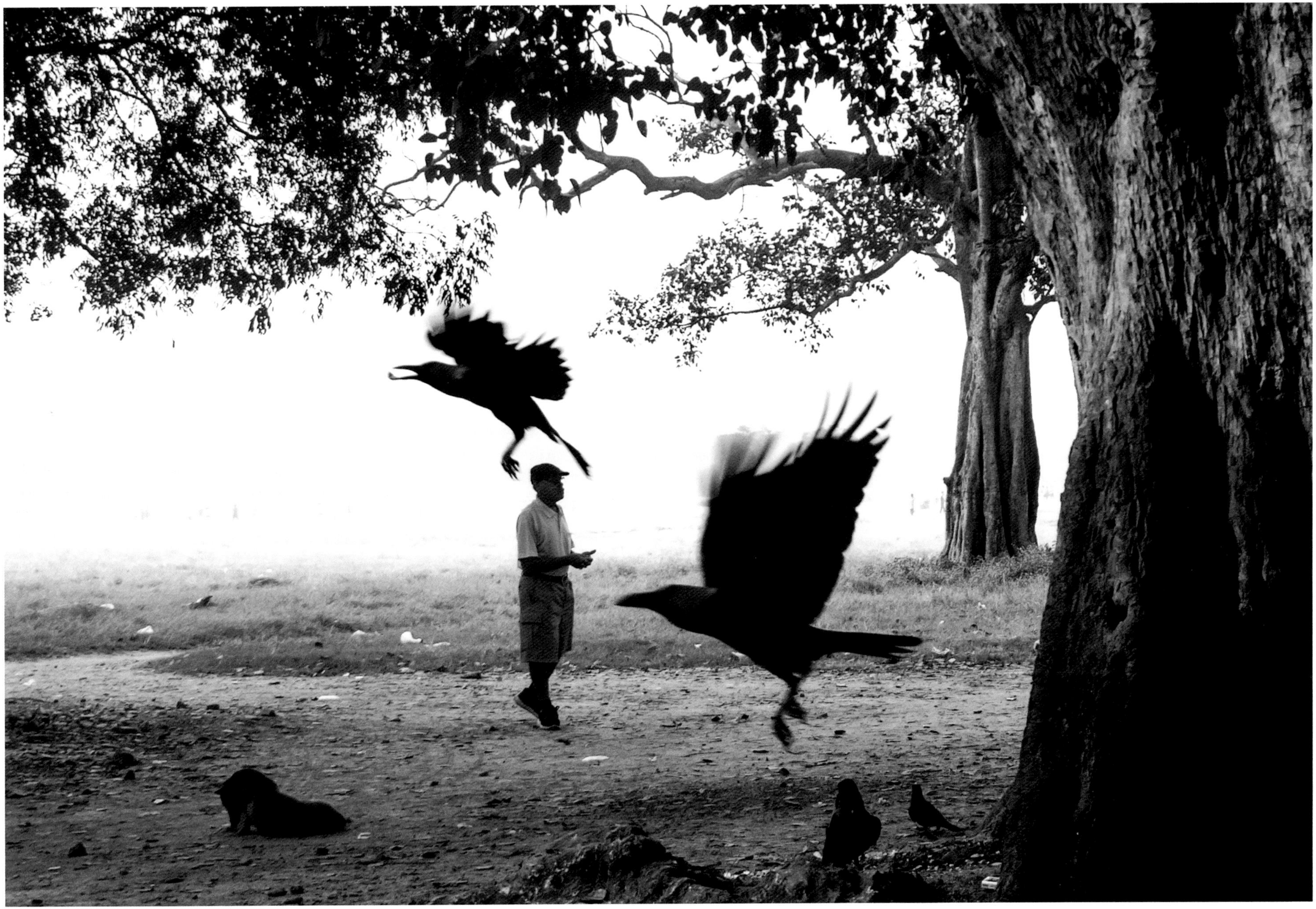

In Kolkata, there are a number of Ghats along the banks of the river Hooghly (Ganga). Amongst them, Mallick Ghat is an age old Ghat which is located in Howrah, West Bengal. It took part in the history when it was used first for purifying river water before distributed for public use.

From the ancient time, the water of Ganga is considered as holy to Hindu religion and used for religious and auspicious occasions. It is believed that this water can destroy sins and gives salvation. People gather at this Ghat to collect the holy water. This Ghat is famous for Hindu Religious ceremonies, like, Tarpon, Kola Bou Snan (bathing of sapling of banana tree) during Durga puja and the Chhat etc.

Mallick Ghat is a popular site for tourists and photographers. This Ghat is also used for bathing by the local people. They come here to take their bath and dry their clothes and take water for their different purposes. The light and shadow creates a dramatic environment in the sunny ambience. From this Ghat, the nearby magnificent Howrah Bridge is seen with its full glory.

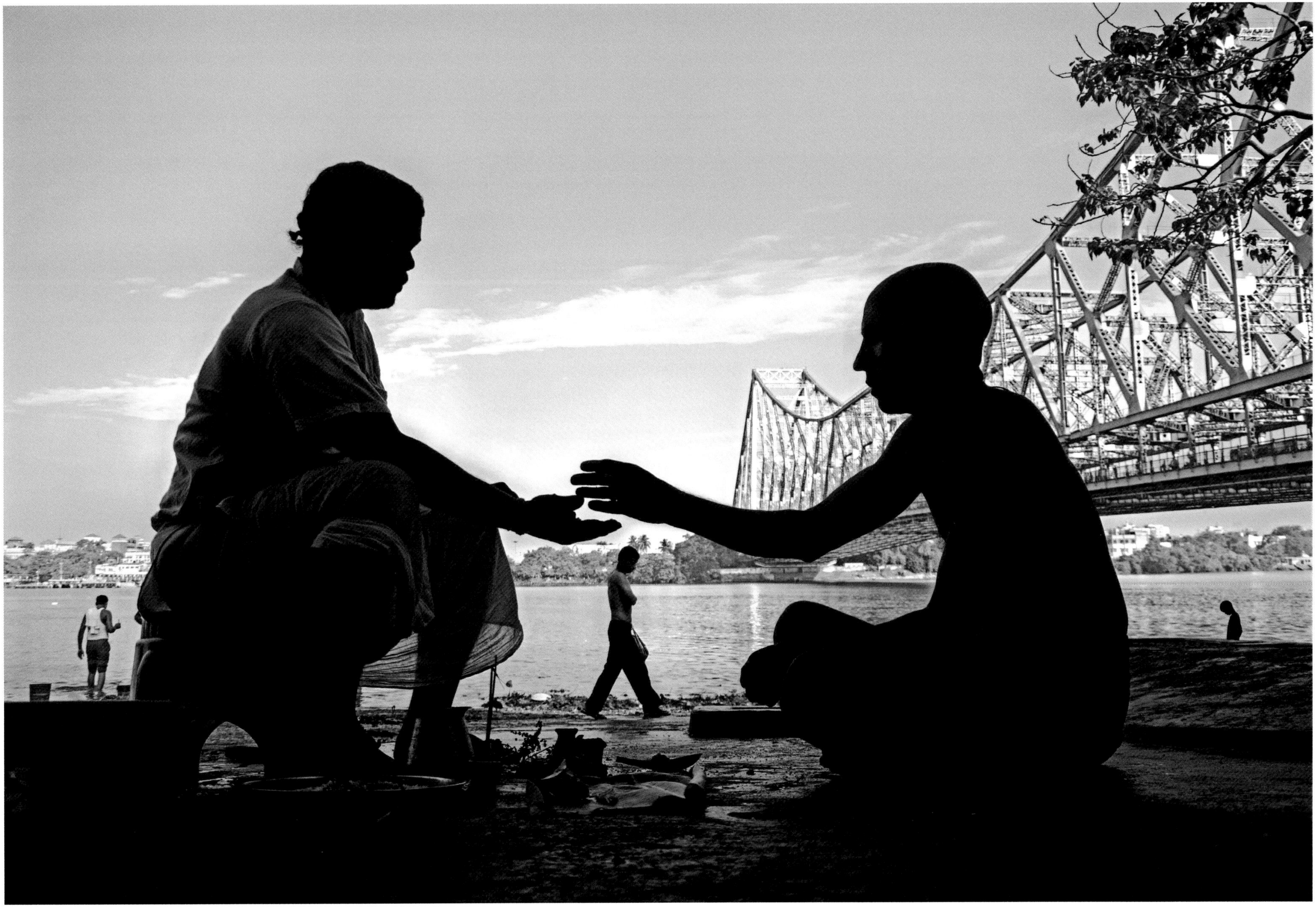

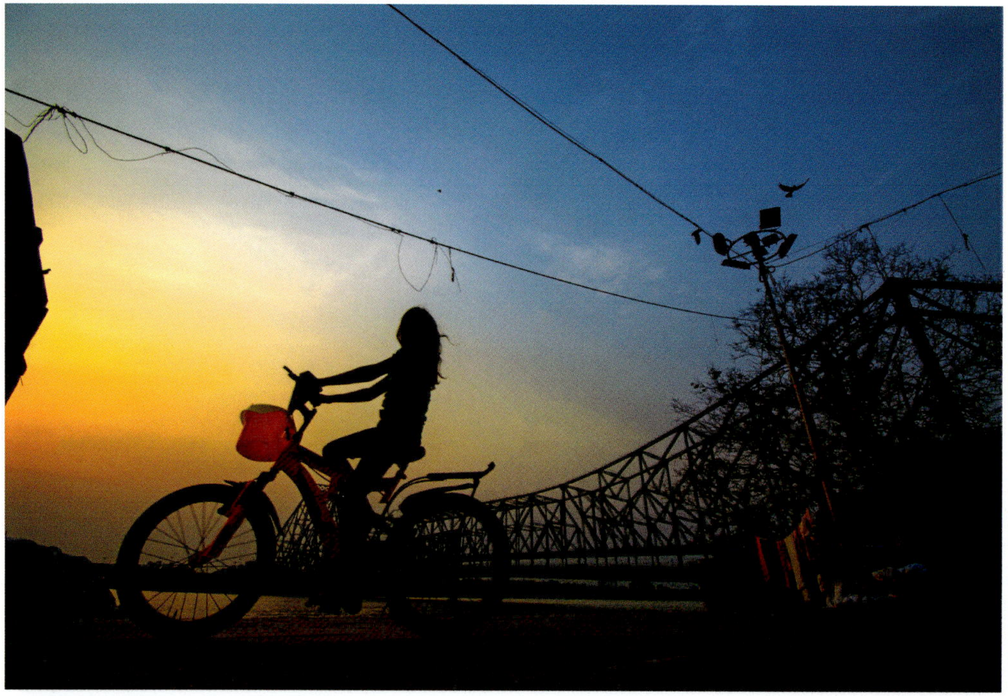
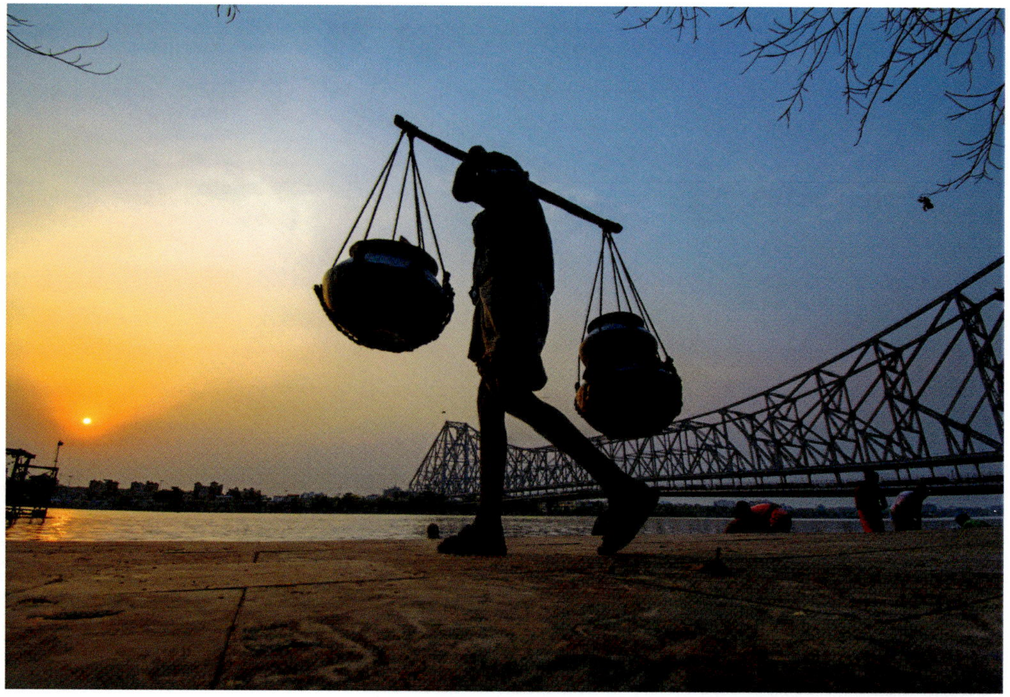
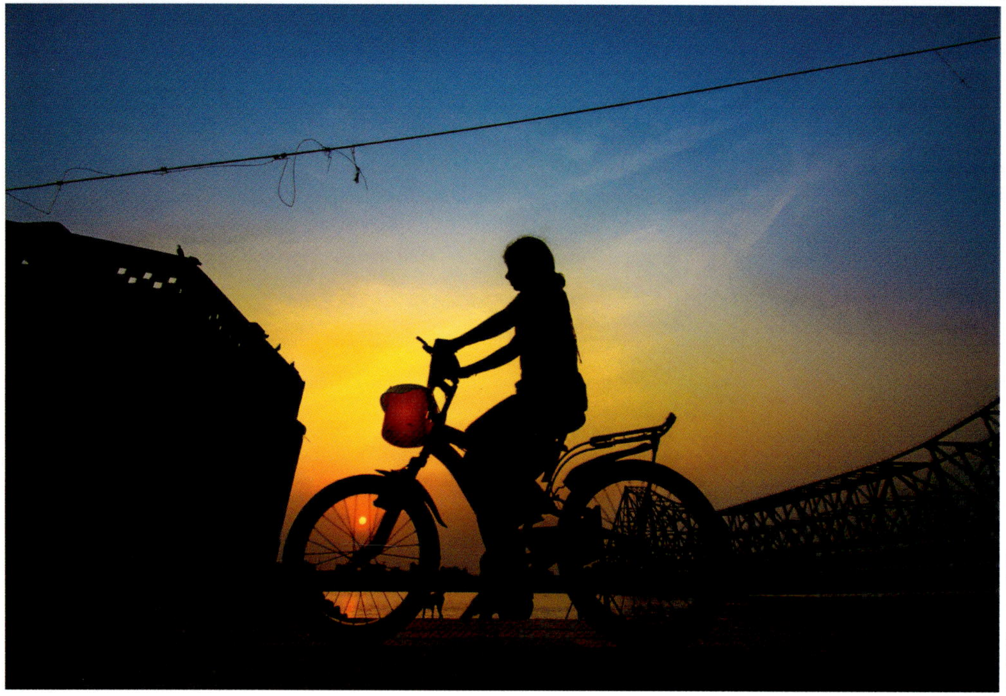
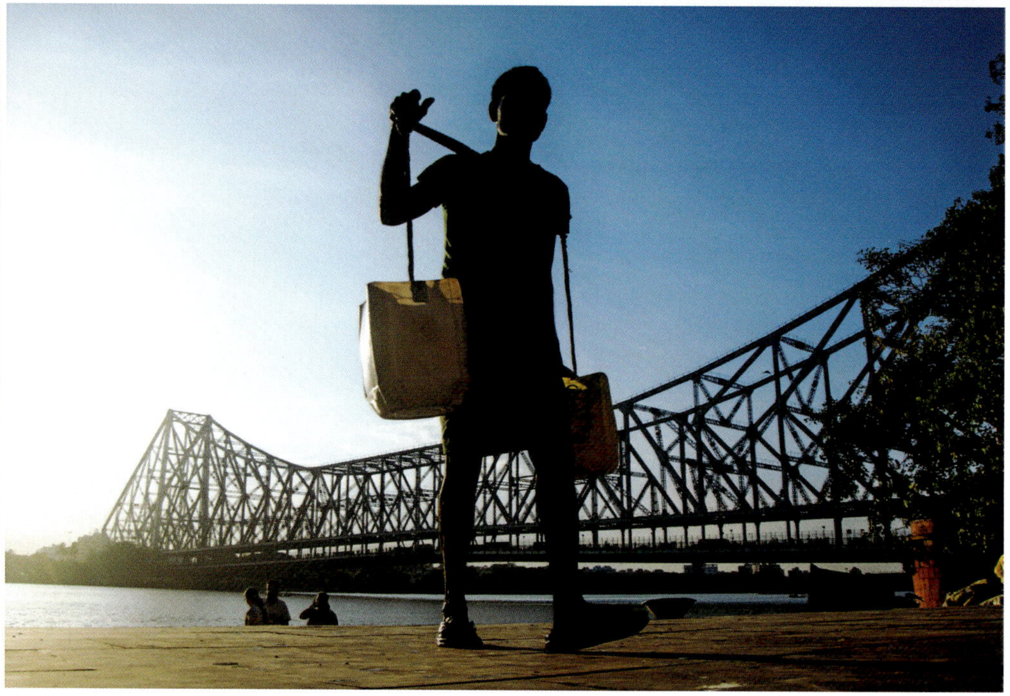

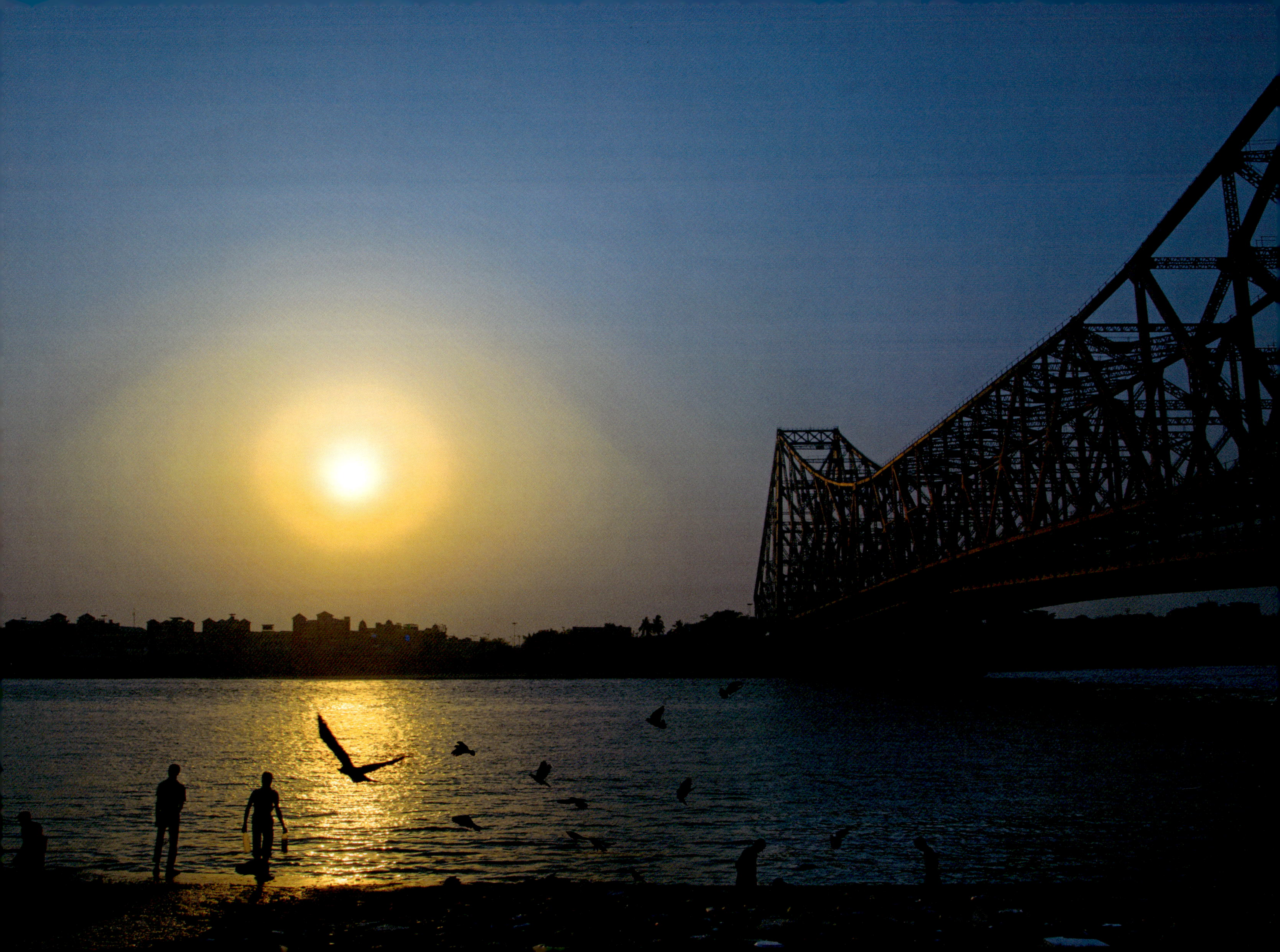

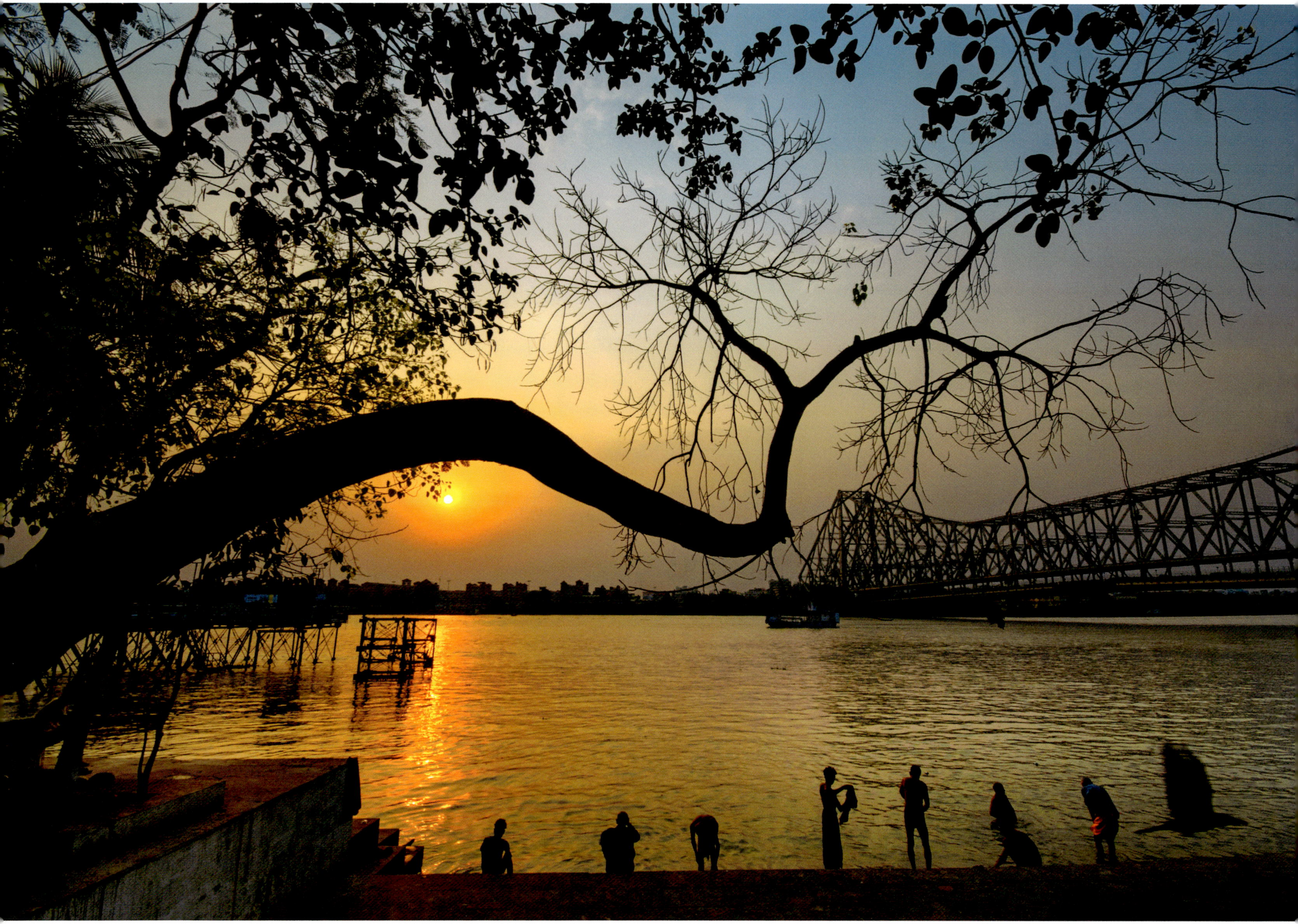

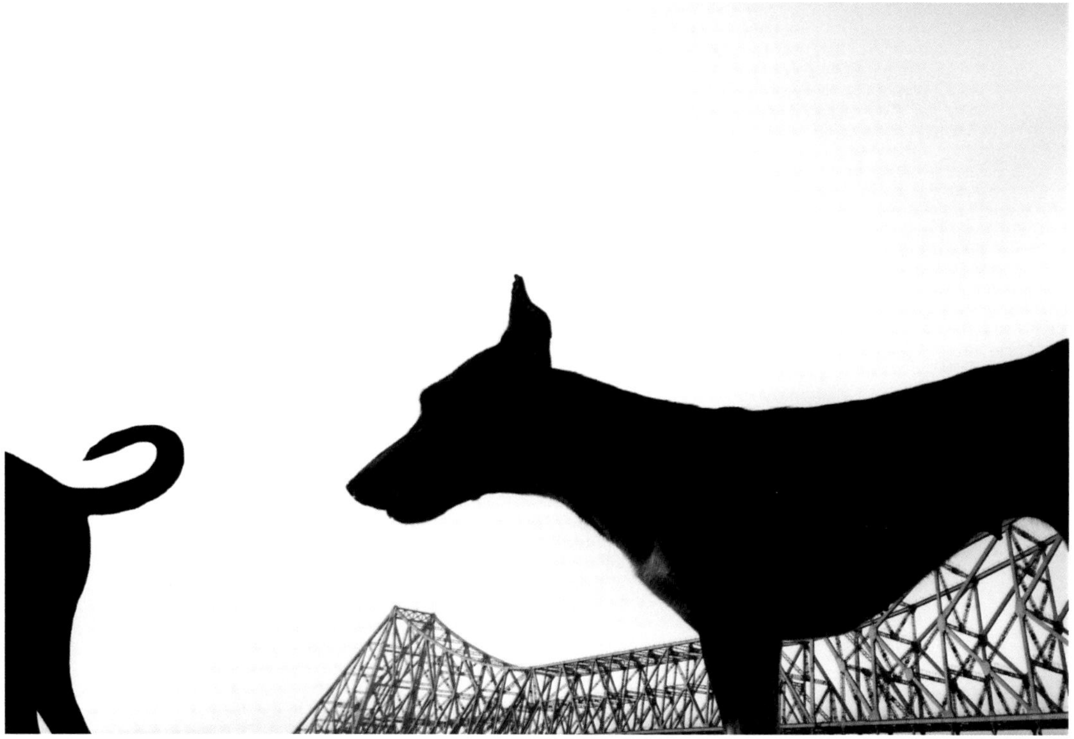

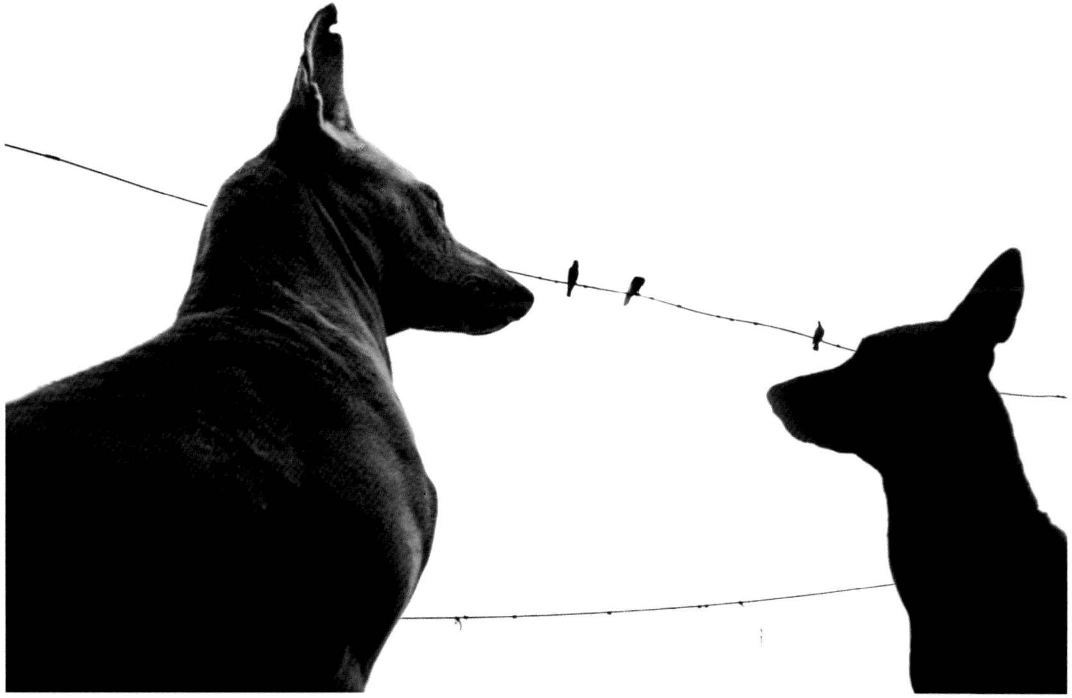

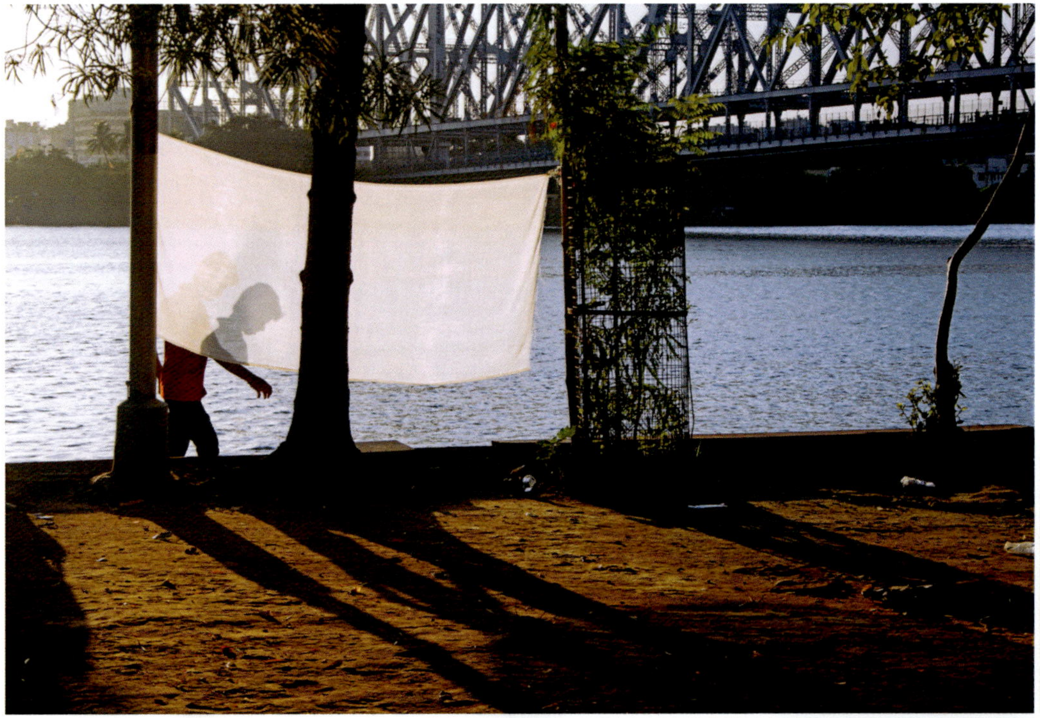
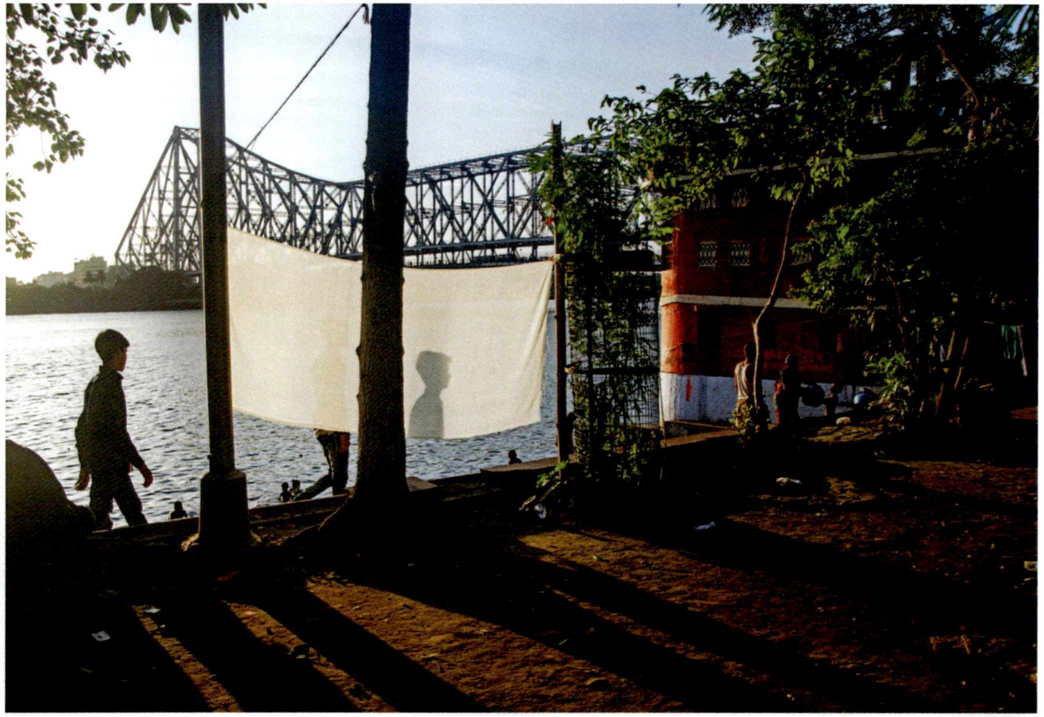
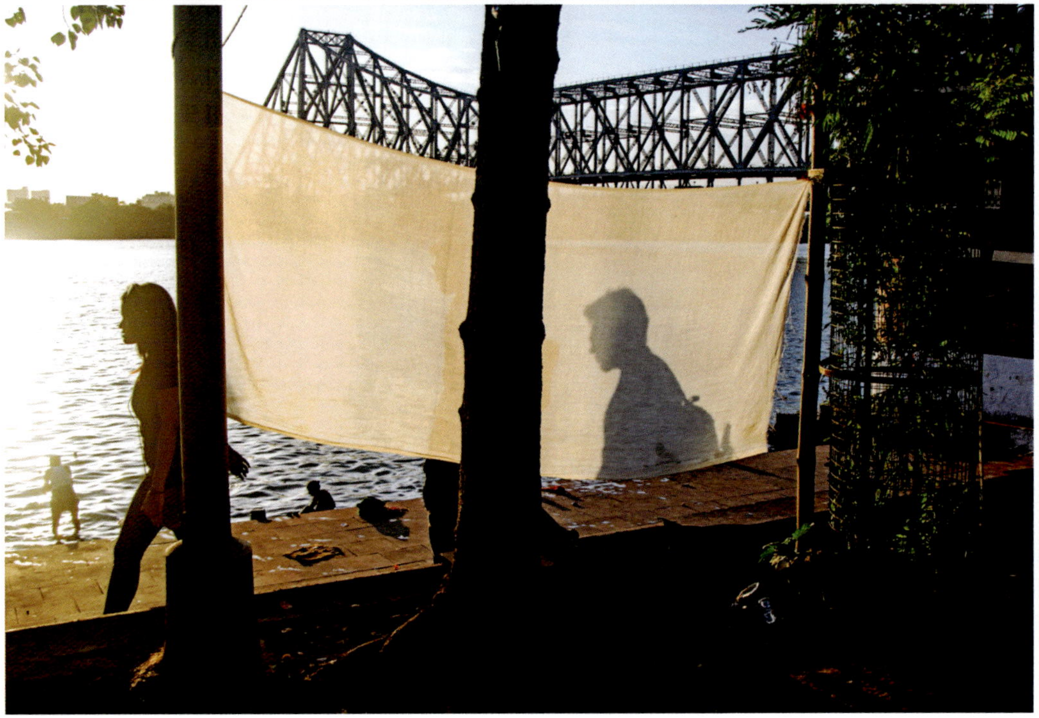
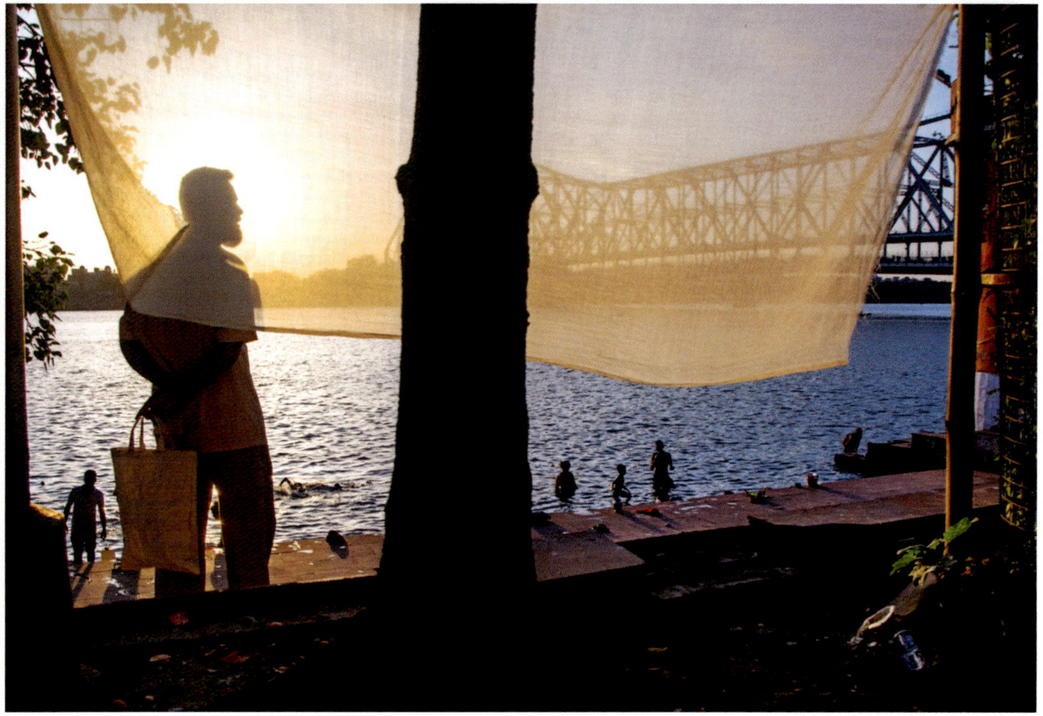

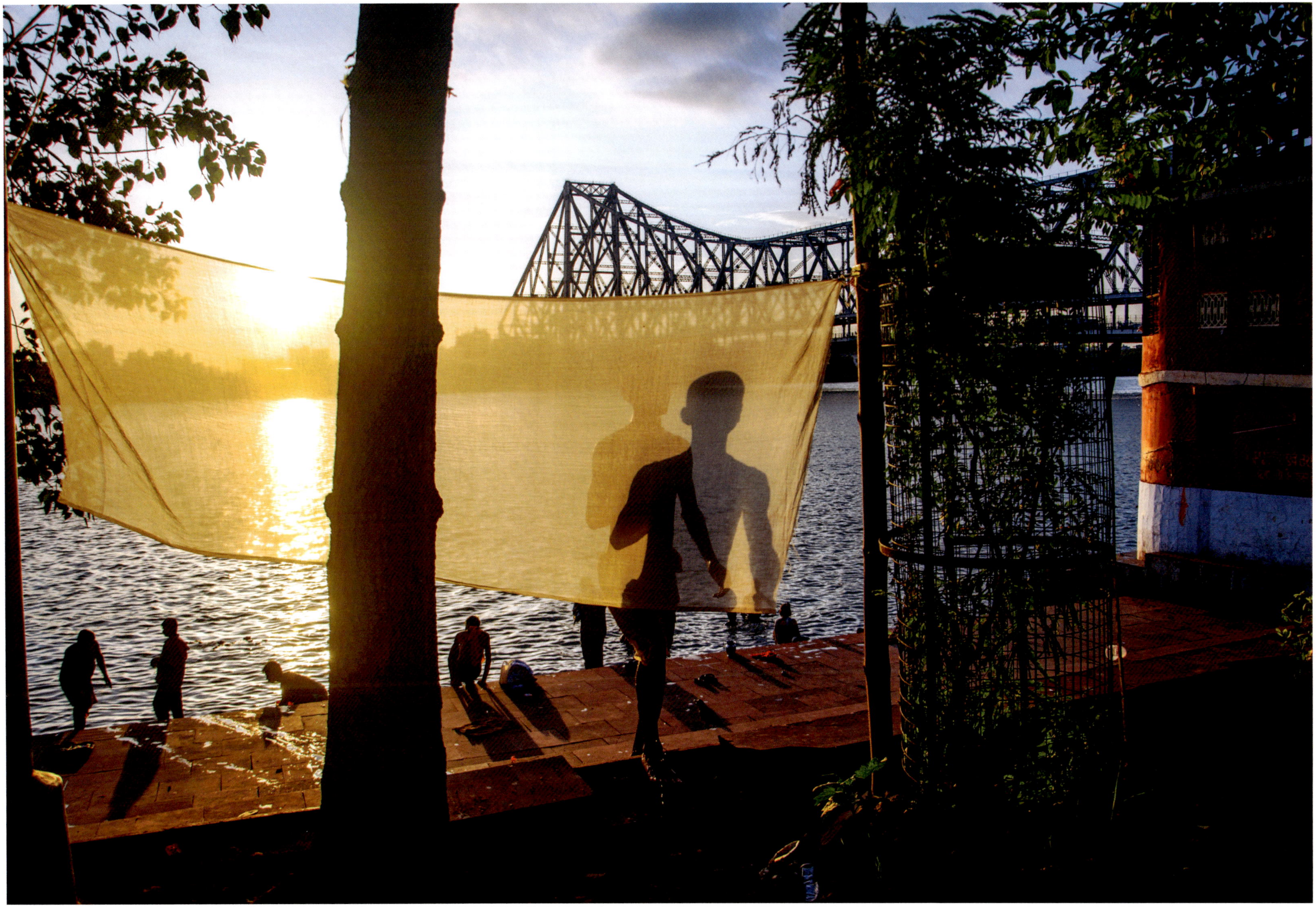

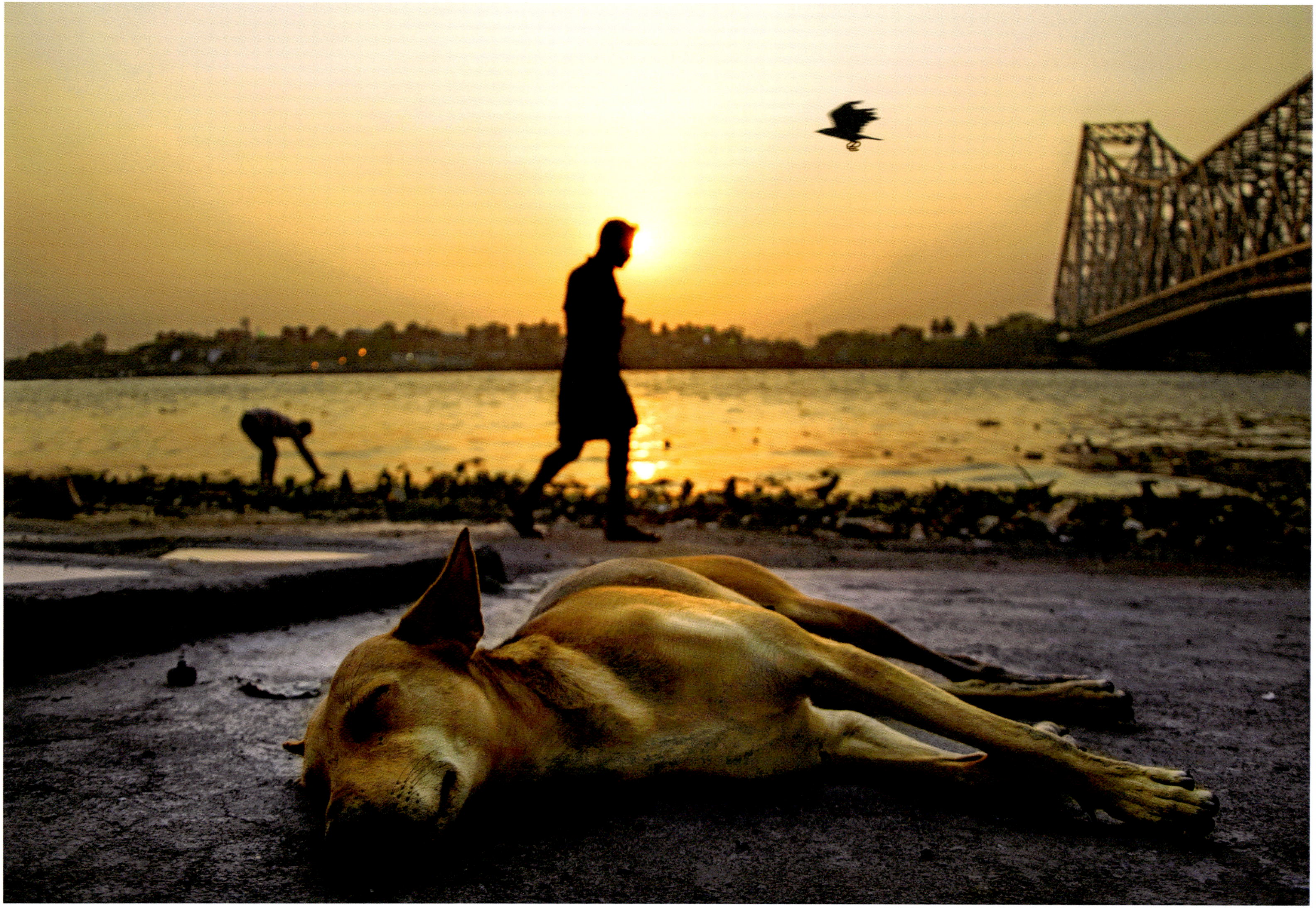

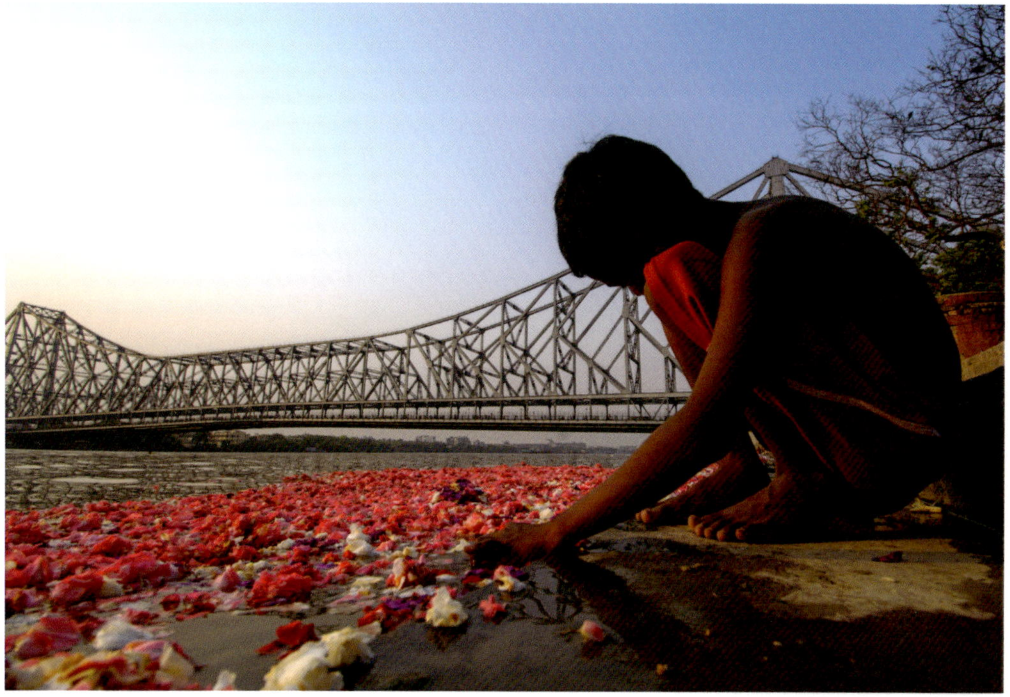

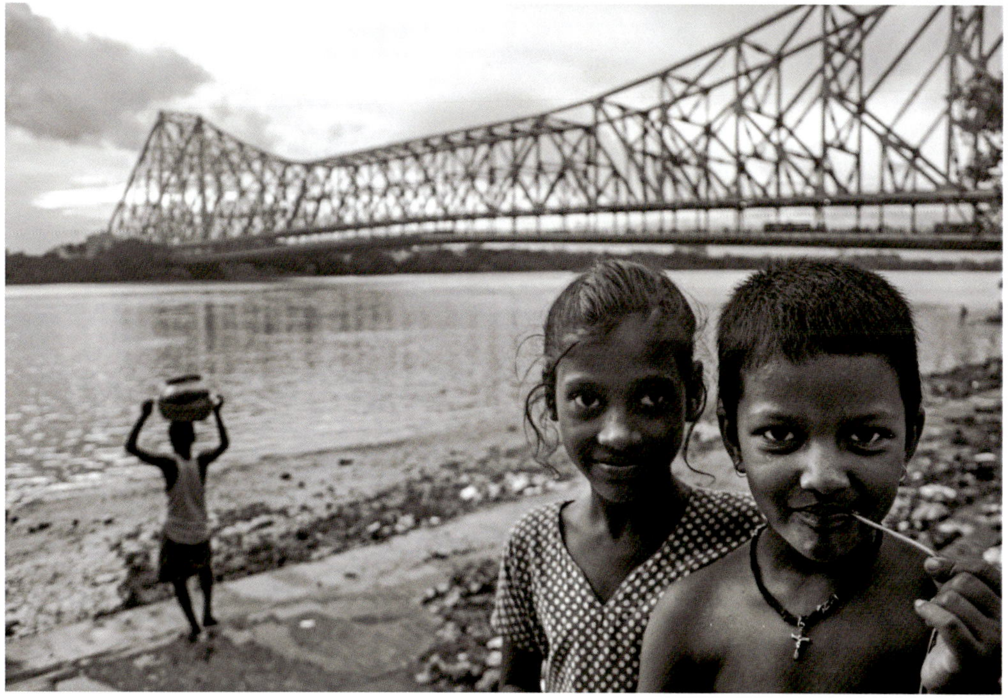

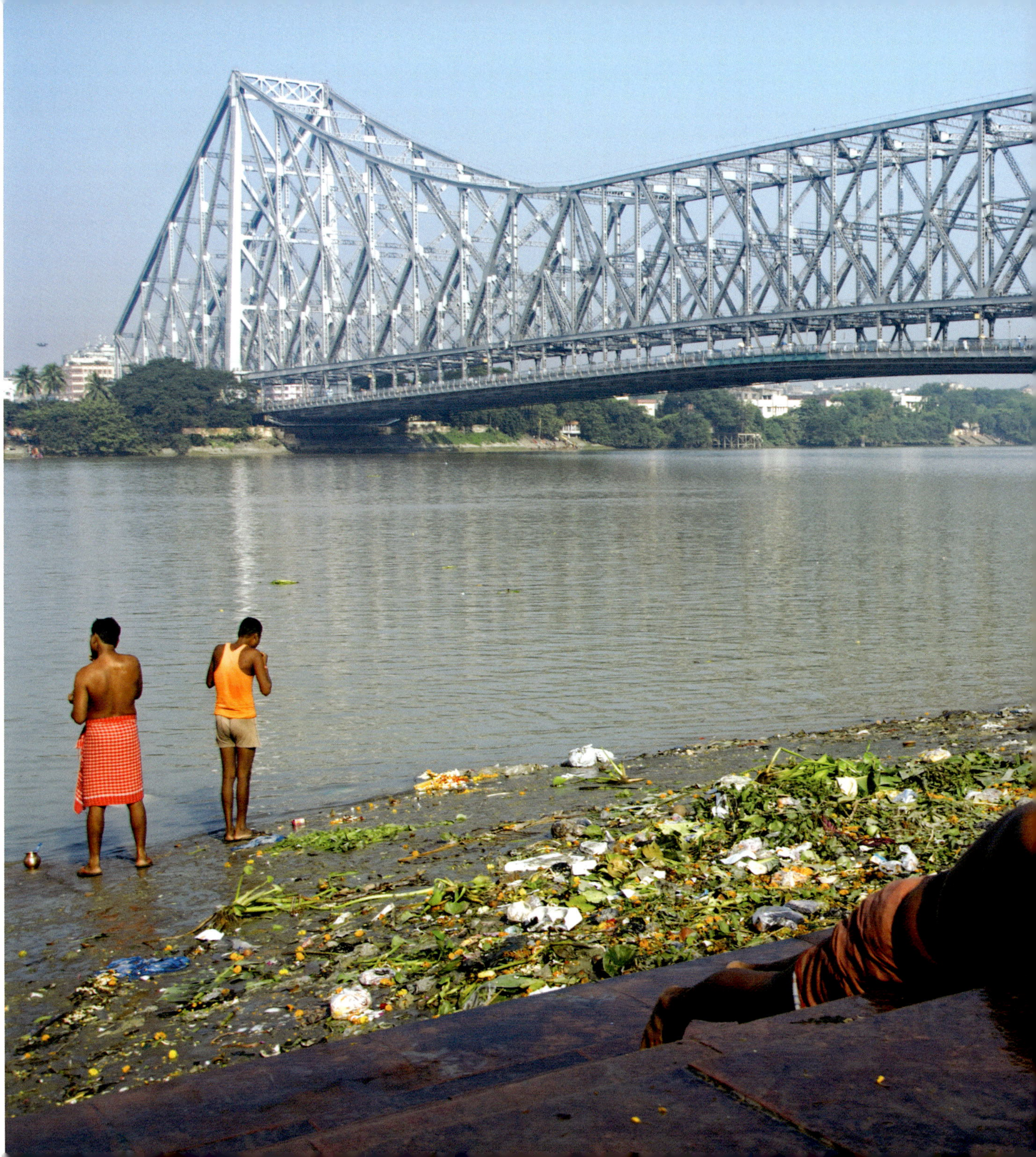

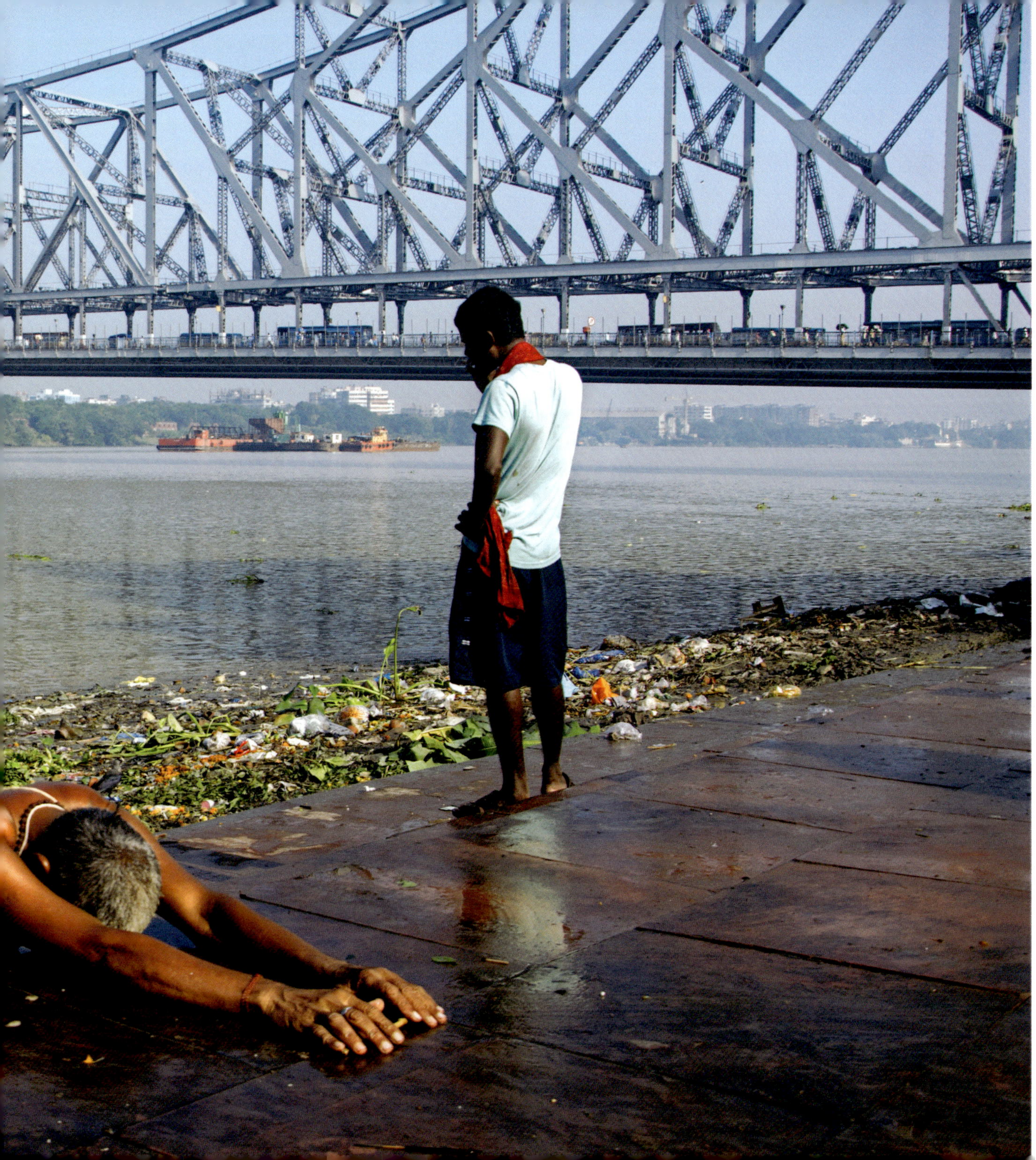

MANNEQUIN REPAIRING HOUSE

One of the inevitable parts of fashion technology is the use of mannequins. Nowadays the whole retail industry stands on the immense help provided by the mannequins. Visual advertising has an important role in enhancing sales in any retail store. The presentation and display of merchandize on mannequins attracts customers into the stores and encourage them to buy the product. Other than in-store displays and window decorations, mannequins are also used by many online sellers to show their products photos. They are also used in health sectors for teaching the first aid applications.

As I belong to Kolkata, I got the opportunity to take some pictures of the place where they are repaired and reshaped for using again. This place is the narrow alleys of north Kolkata, near Kumortuli. They are brought there in the form of different body parts and made ready to reuse. Then they are presented to us wrapped in gorgeous dresses. They are the main attraction of the great lucrative looks of shopping centres of Kolkata. But they start their journey from very filthy, unhygienic places. Their destiny awaits there too.

I took these pictures to show how the mannequins are reformed, by joining different body parts to regain their beauty. Some people are engaged there in this work. Once I got a glimpse of an old peeping lady, who lost her young age beauty and possessing a wrecking structure. She symbolized the ultimate destiny of this mannequin's beauty. When we see them usually wrapped in gorgeous dresses, we like to look ourselves just the way they look like. We never try to think how they are going to end up.

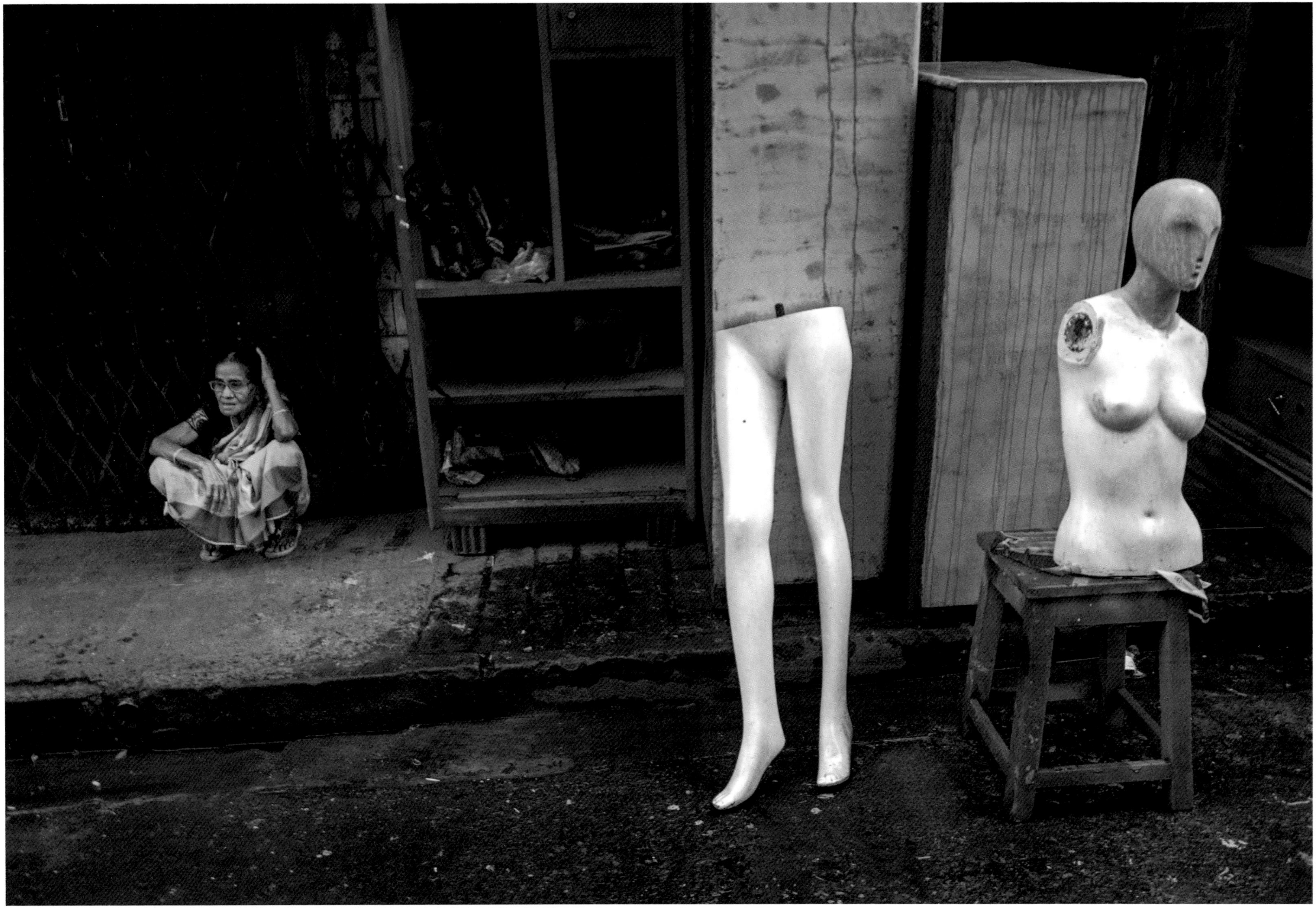

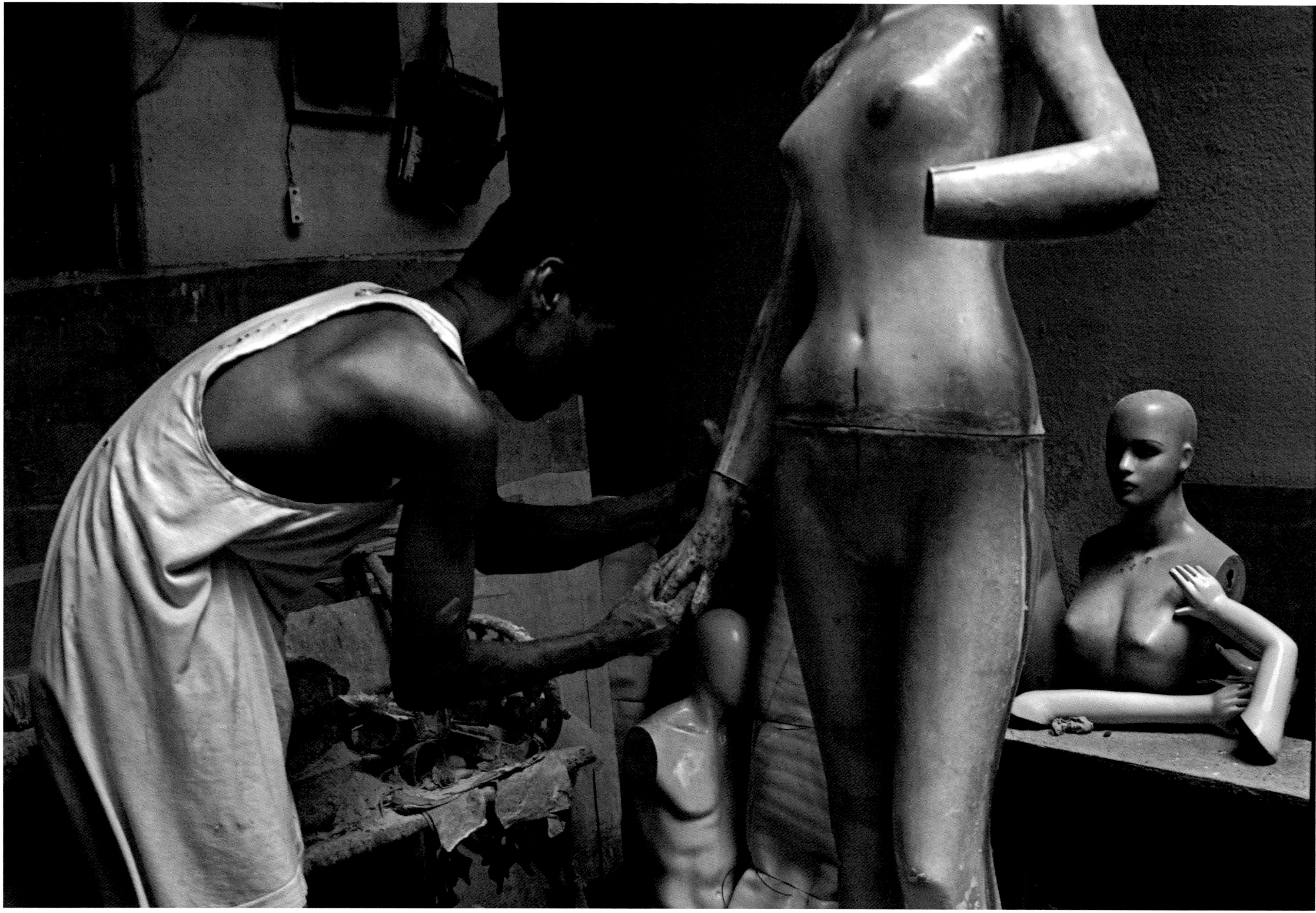

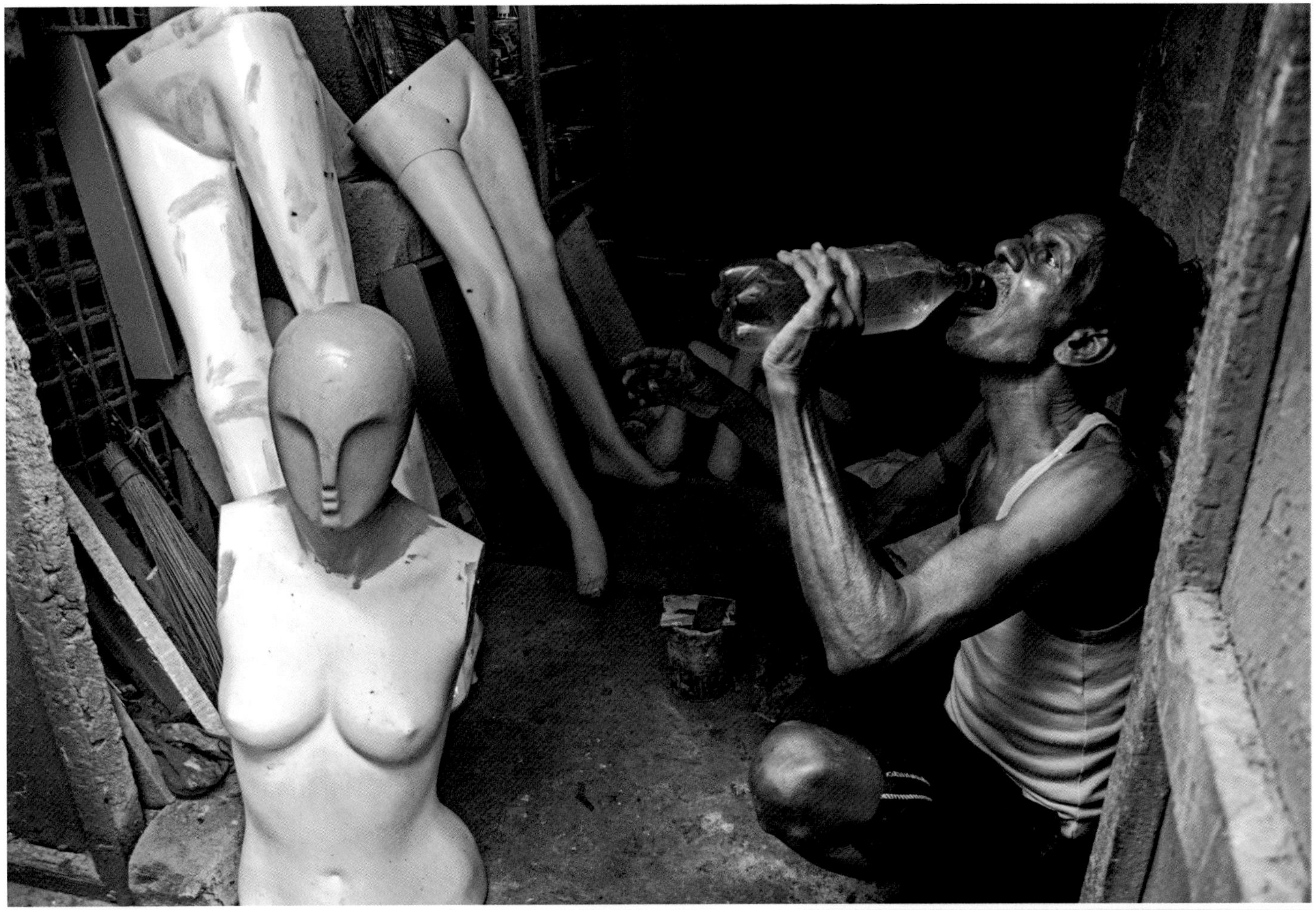

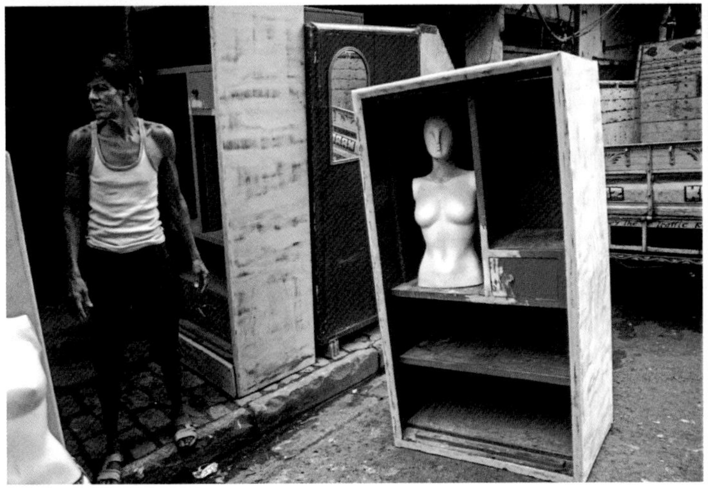

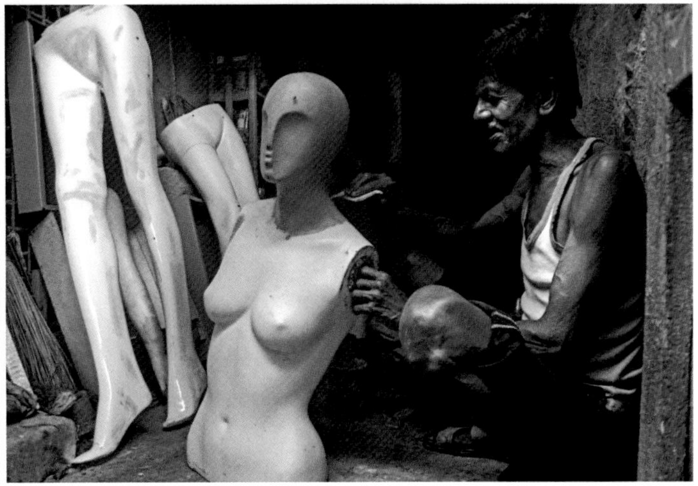

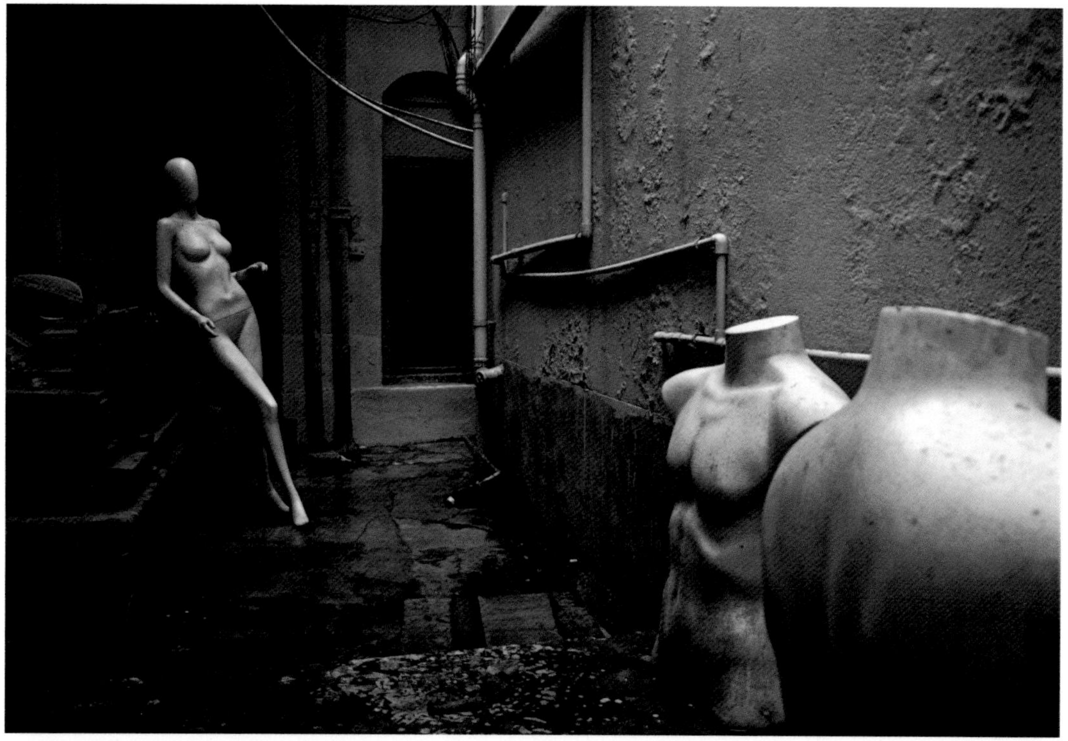

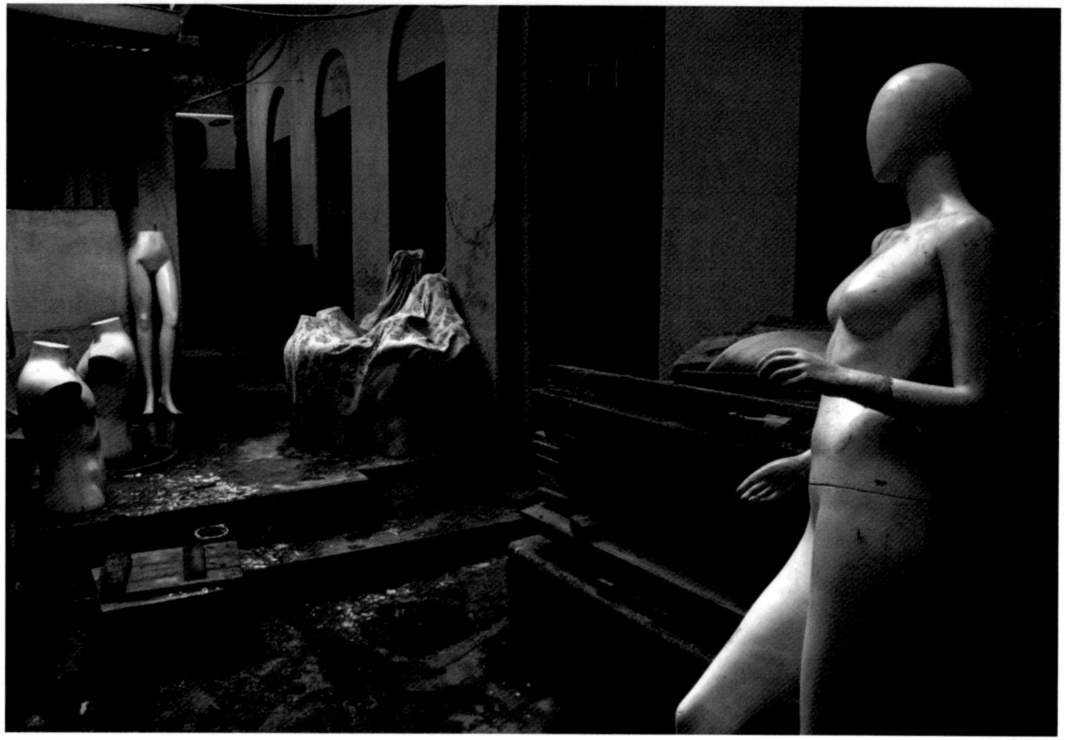

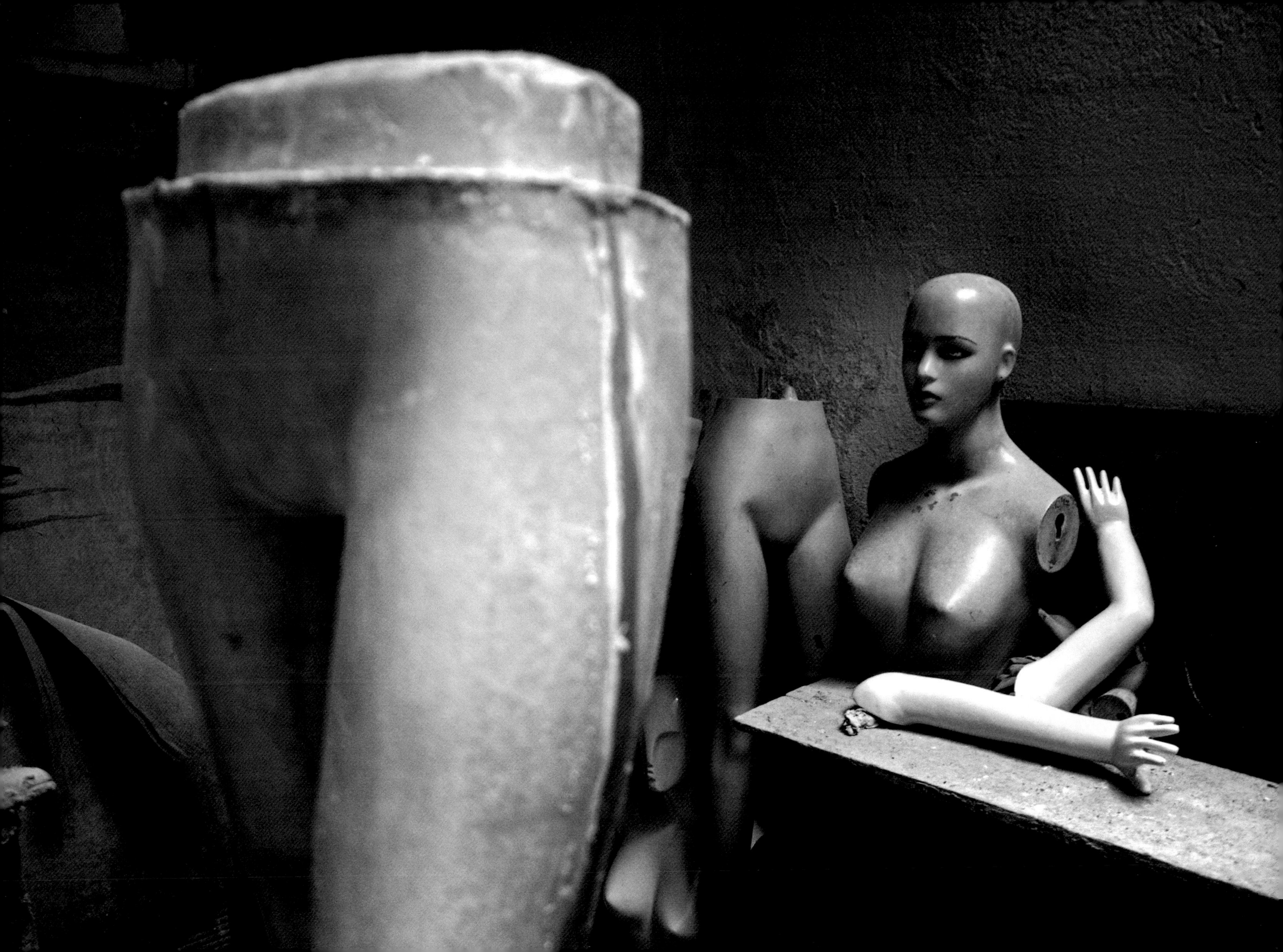

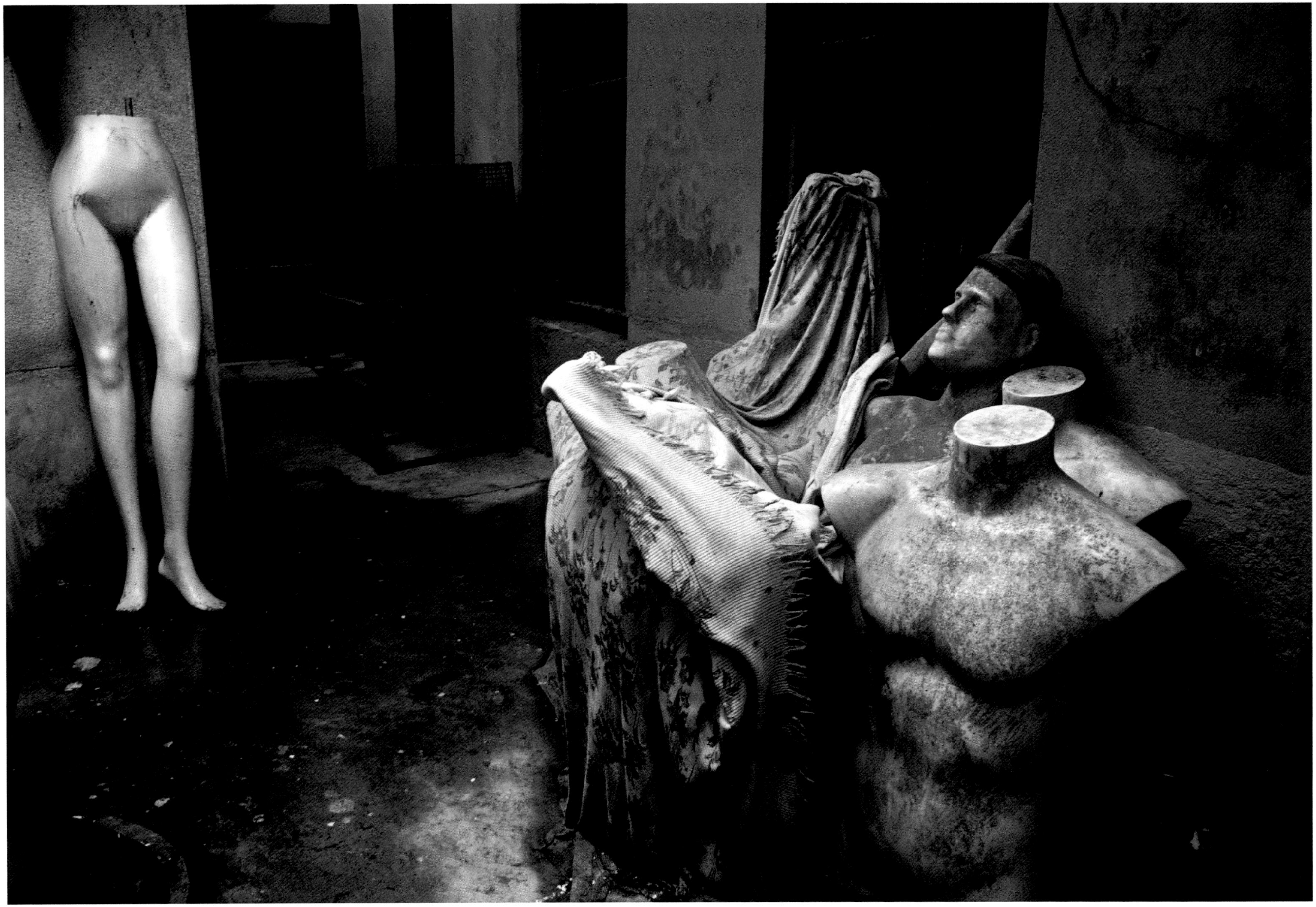

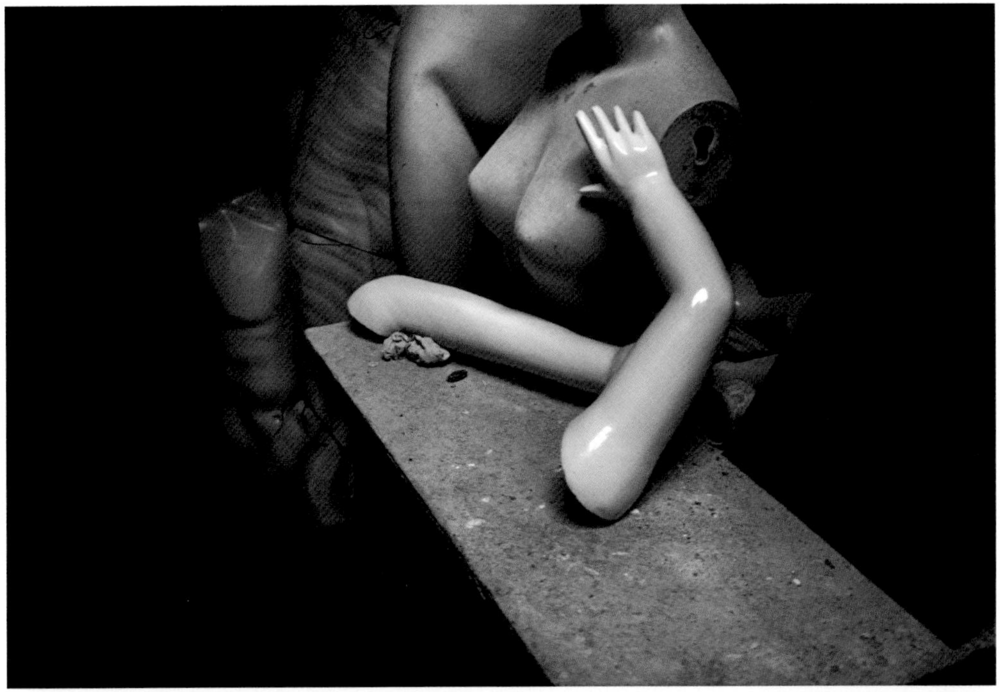

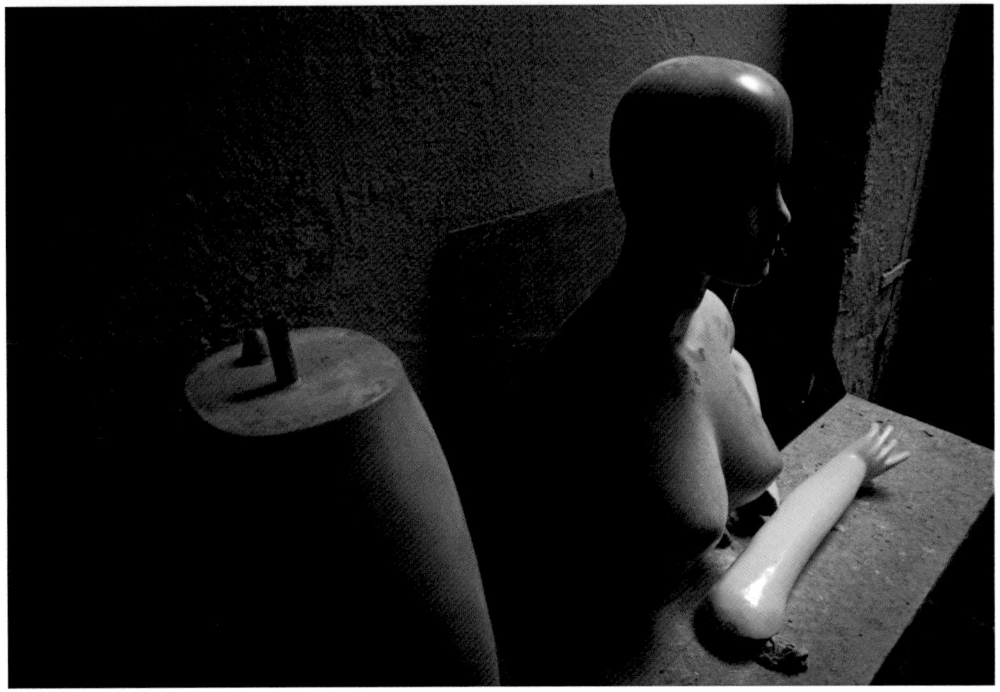

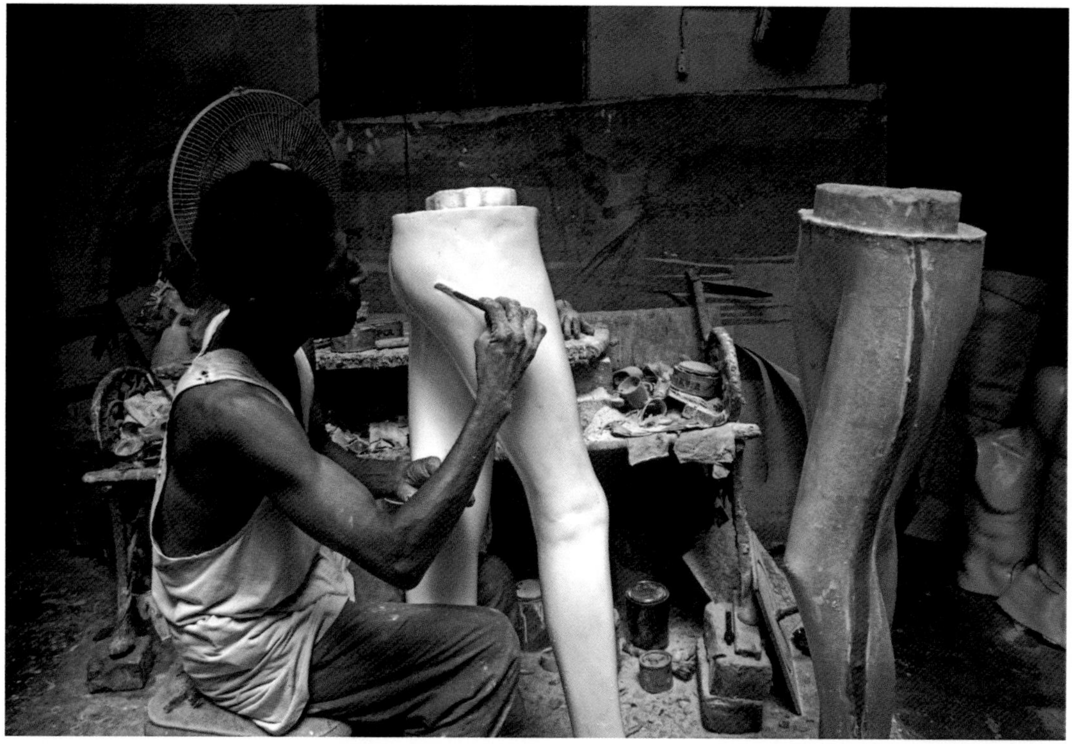

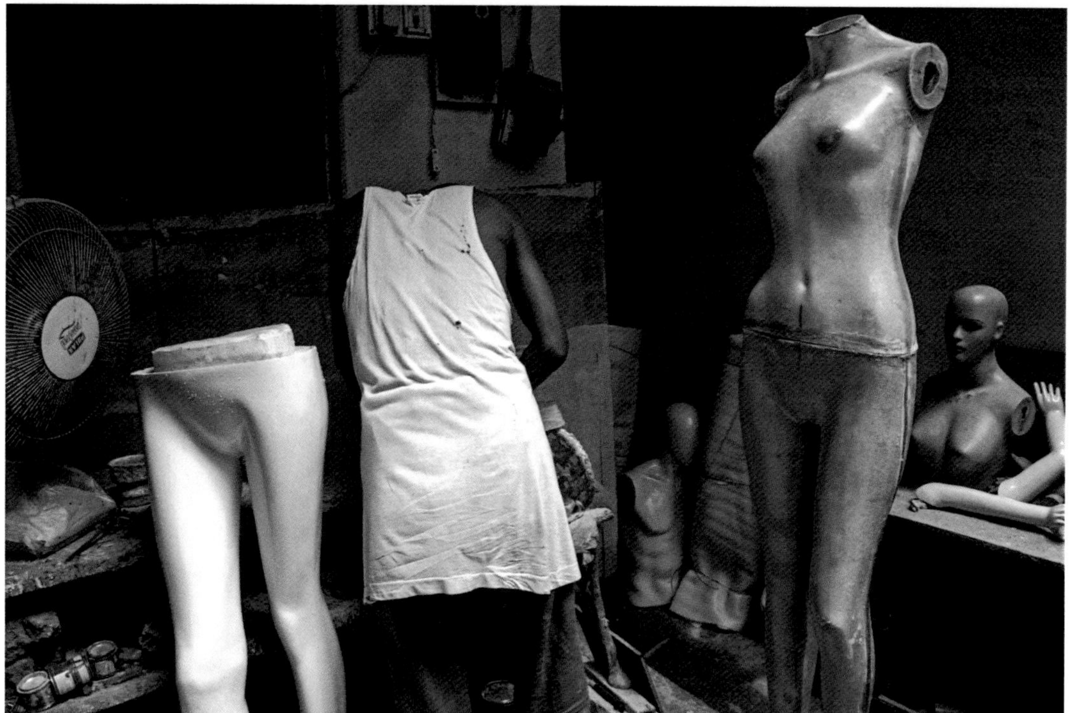

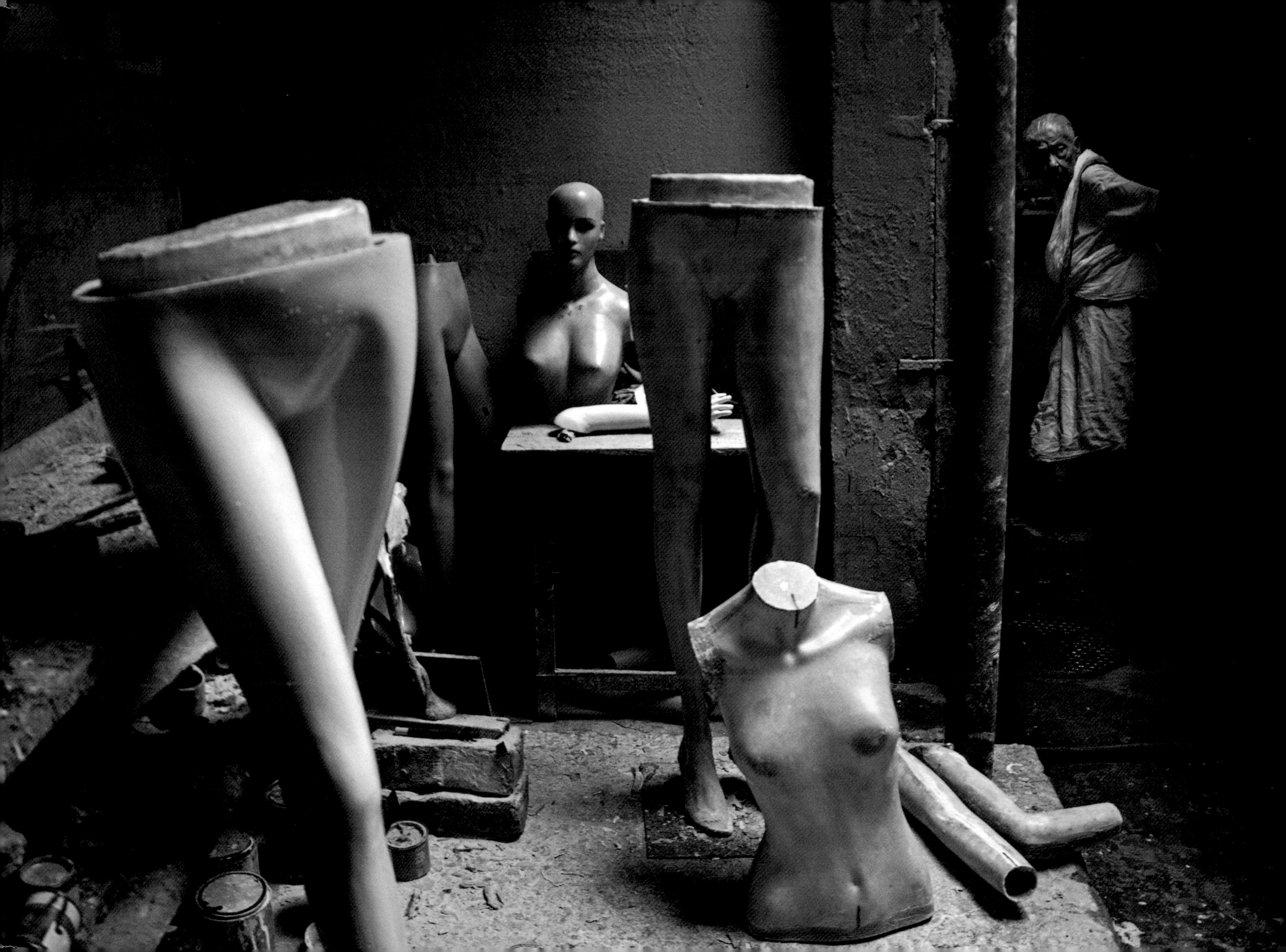

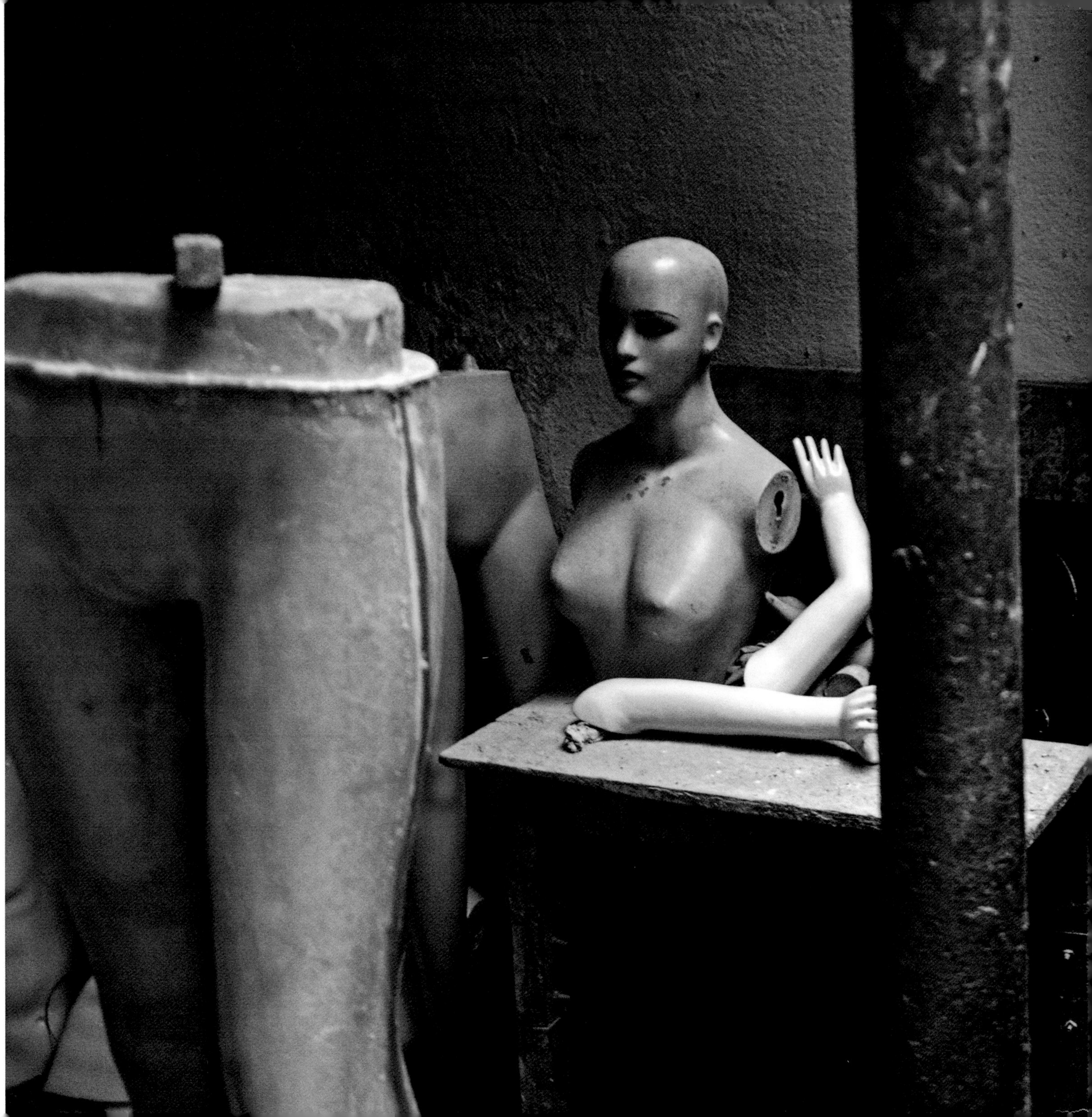

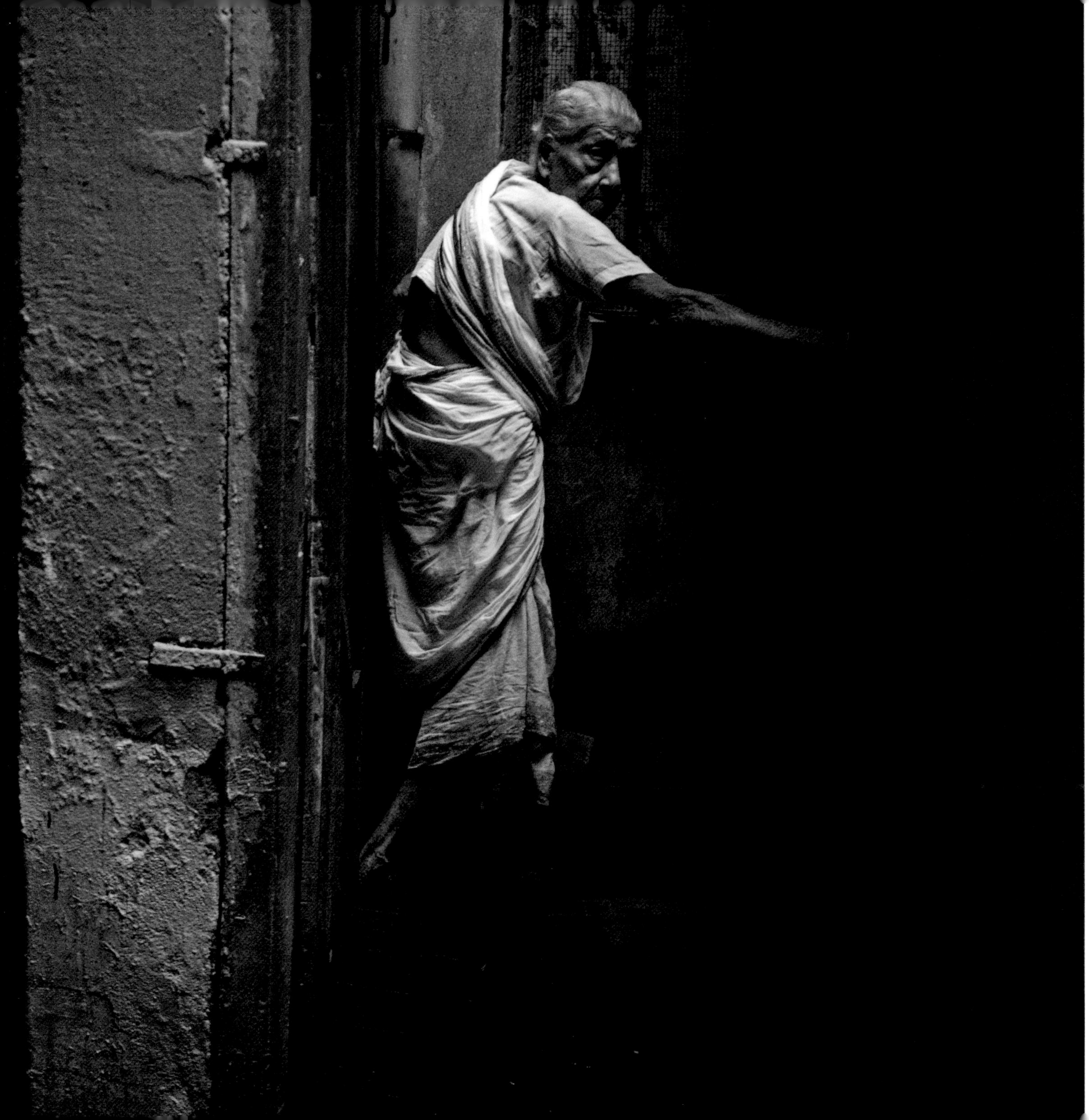

The Nakhoda mosque is the largest and the principal mosque of Kolkata, located in Chitpur area, in central Kolkata. It is an iconic landmark in the City of Joy. The architecture of this grand mosque is based on Indo-Saracenic architecture. The true combination of Hindu, Islam and western elements of architecture are found. The mosque has three domes and two minarets, each 151 feet high. There are additional 25 smaller minarets ranging from 100 to 117 feet height. The entrance of the mosque has a noticeable similarity with the Buland Darwaza at Fatepur Sikri. This magnificent mosque can accommodate around 10,000 devotees at a time, for their prayer meetings or 'Namaaz'. The interior of the mosque stakes its claim for excellent creativity. The walls are painted in bright red terracotta colour and the minarets are in metallic gold and silver. This combination gives this mosque a true majestic look. There is a small artificial pond with colored fishes and there is a fountain in it too. Before going to offer prayers, people use to wash their hands and feet with the water from this pond. A huge number of men and women gather there for their holy prayer. Different bright colorful dresses make this place beautiful. During the time of Eid prayer, the interior of Nakhoda fills to its capacity and the crowd spills out to the adjoining Zakaria Street. Though located at the loud and chaotic point of Kolkata, the ambiance of this mosque is calm and quiet. This place is wonderful to visit anytime of the day. One can offer namaz, read a book or just relax. Especially in the evening, one can fee the calmness of the place, watch people talking and offering prayers. This blissful atmosphere gives one the mental peace and the discipline, silence and serenity of the hall acts as a source of comfort, which creates a great environment for prayer. The doors of this mosque are open for all, irrespective of religions, except when it is time for prayers. The cool atmosphere of the interior attracts people to spend some valued time and take rest.

I took these pictures in different times of a year. The activities, the tranquillity, the people offering prayers in the big hall, the reflections of them on the clean, elegant granite floor attracted me a lot and made me mesmerized.

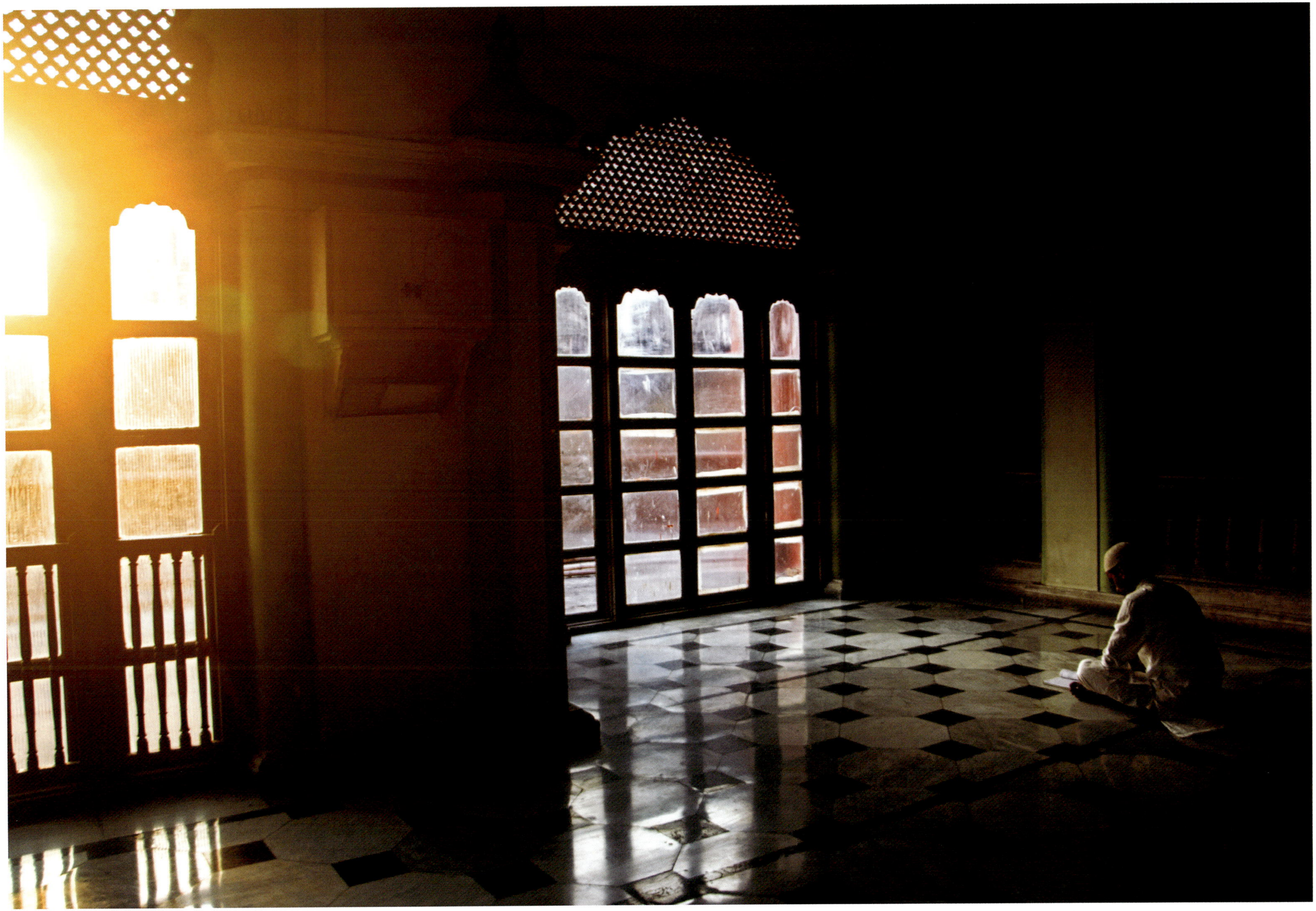

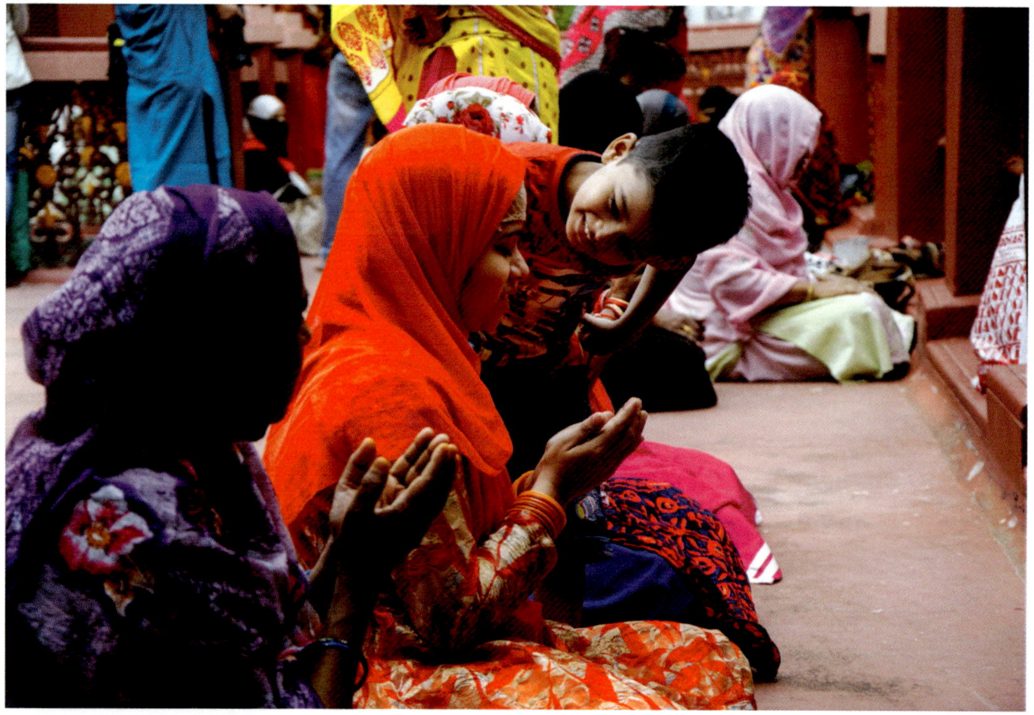

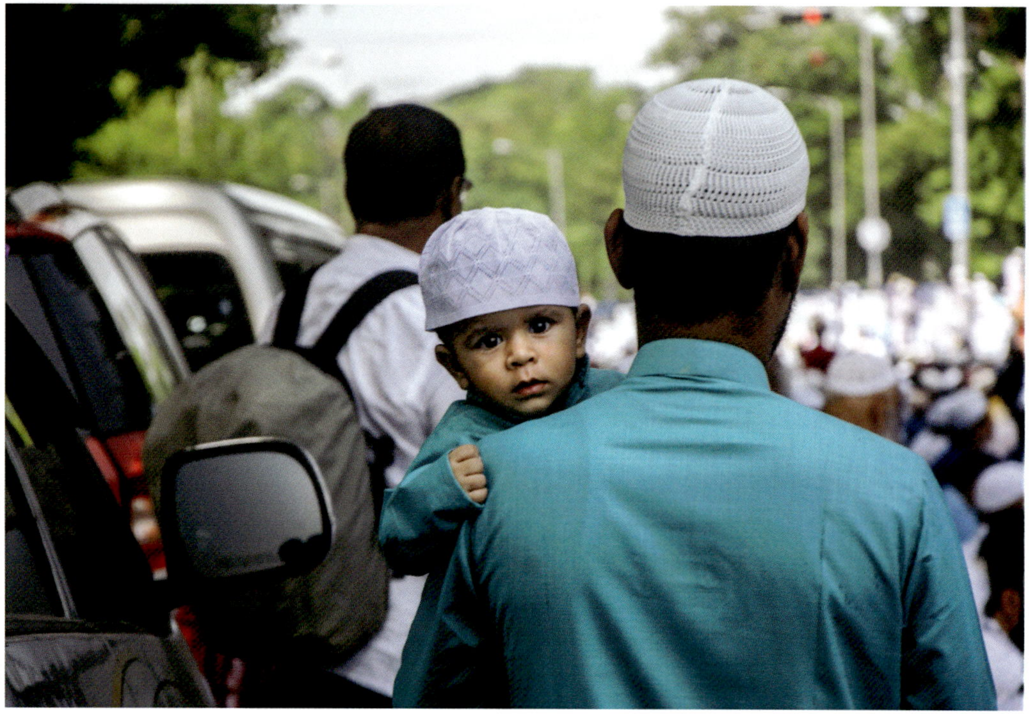

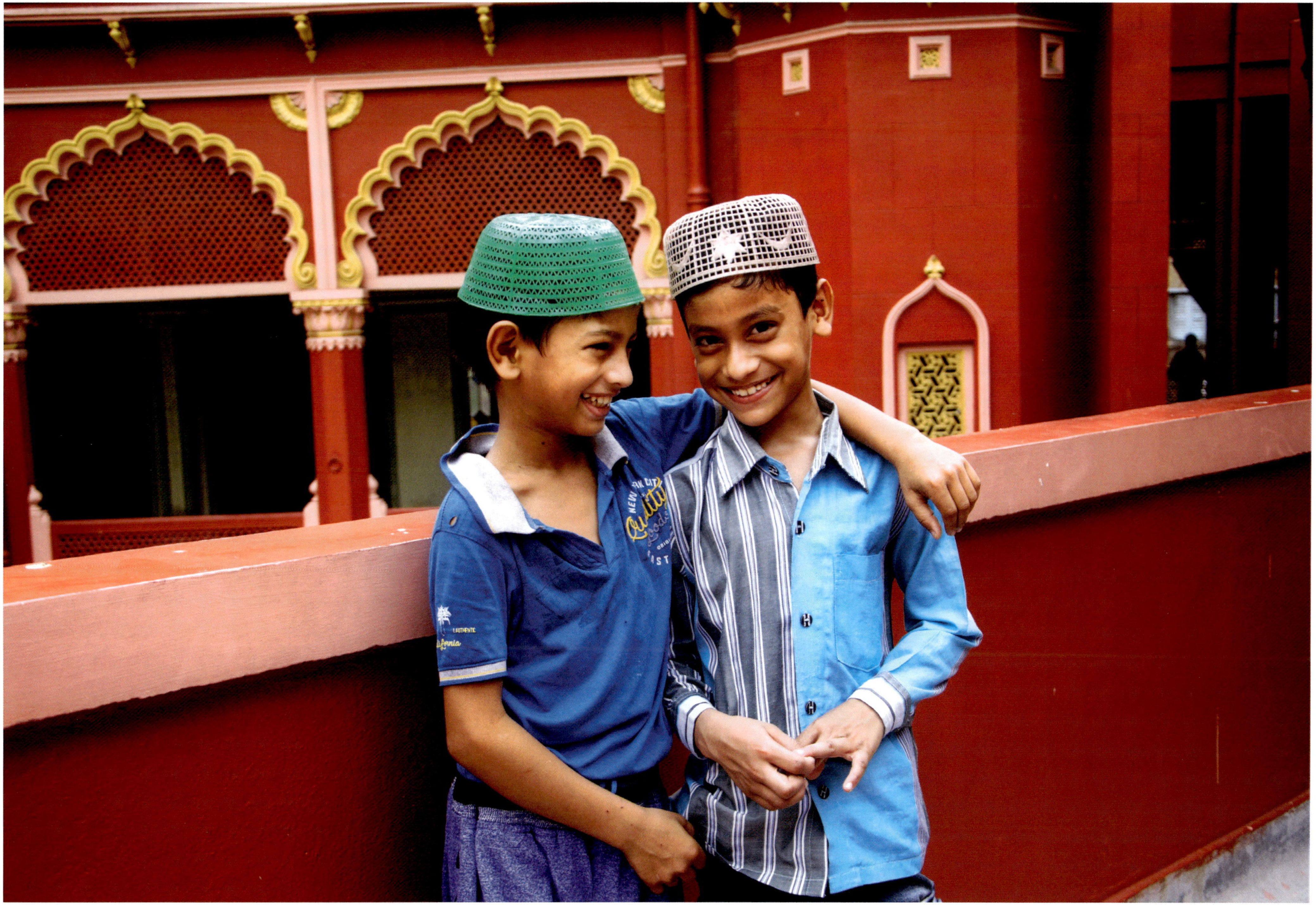

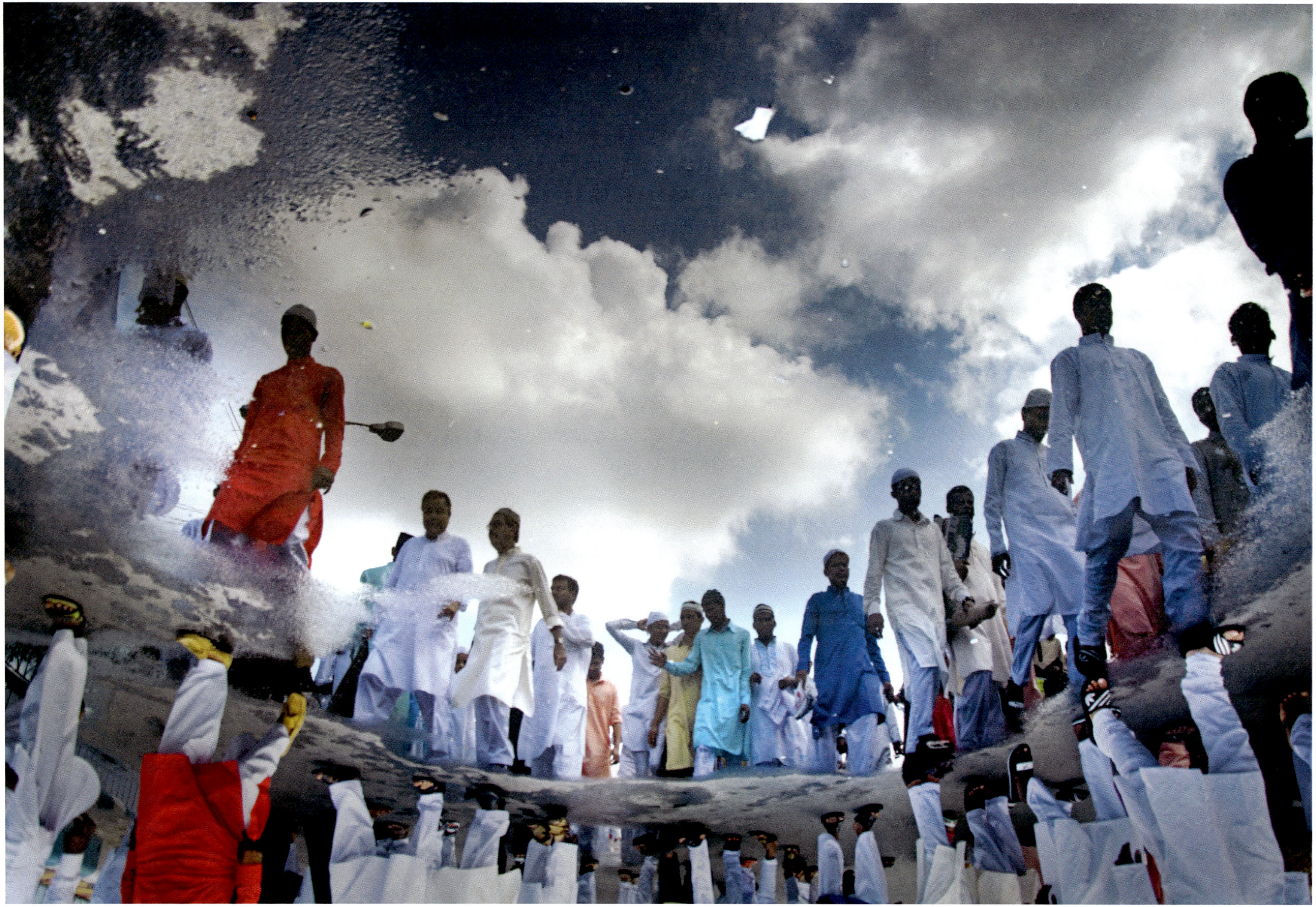

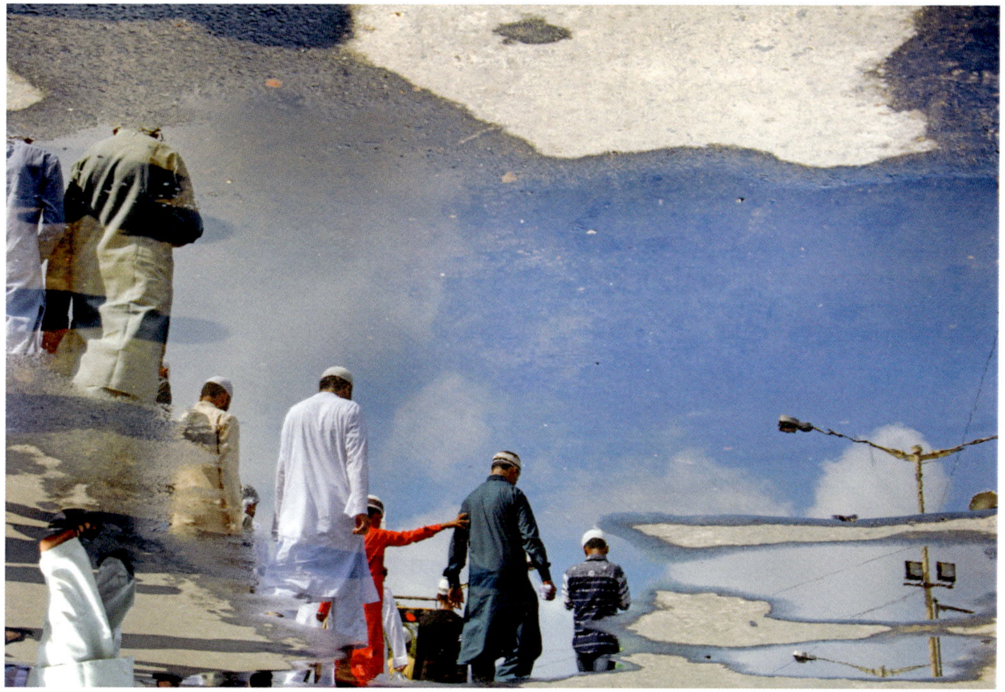

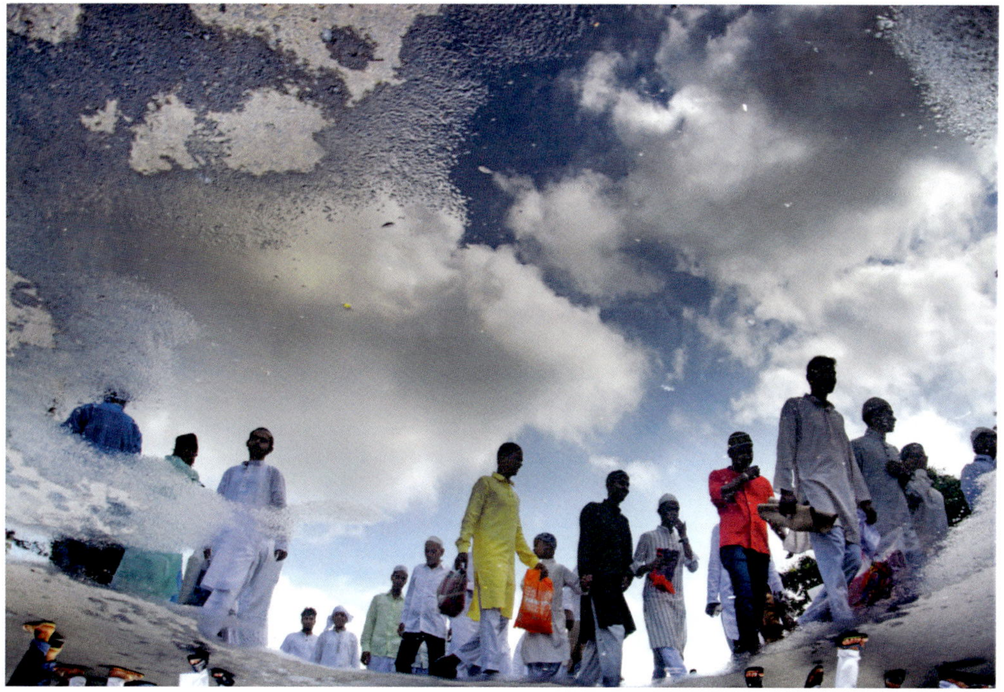

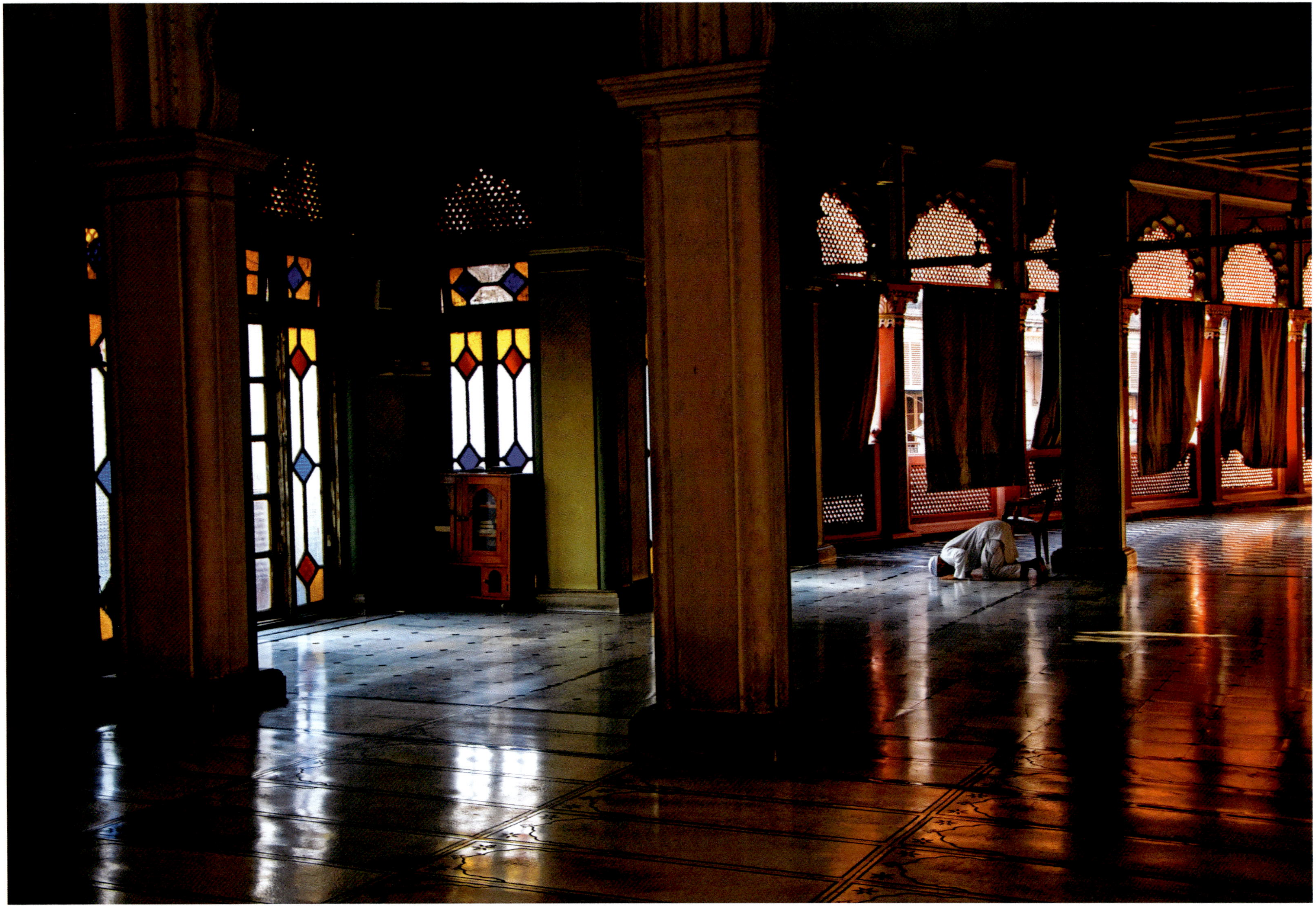

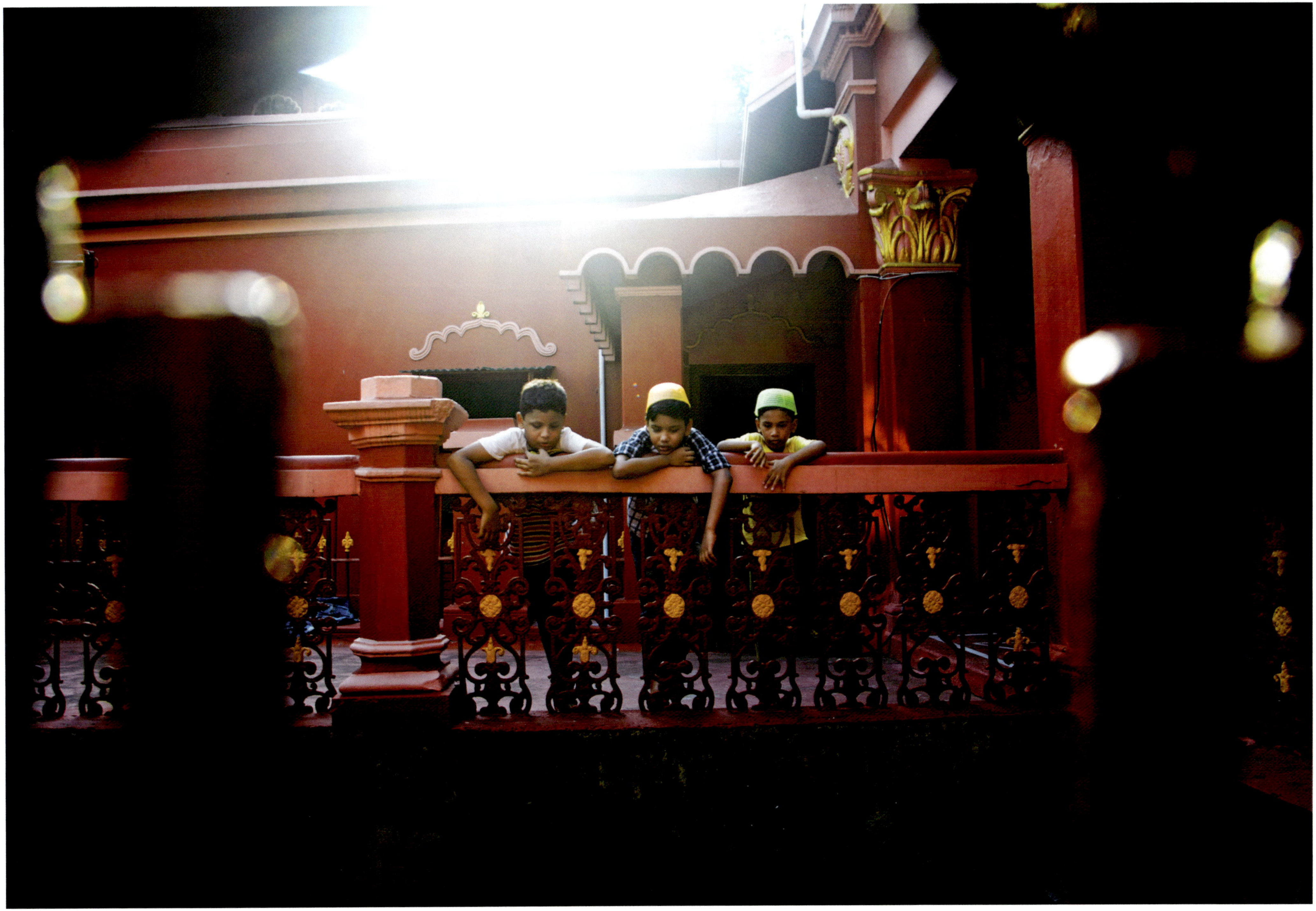

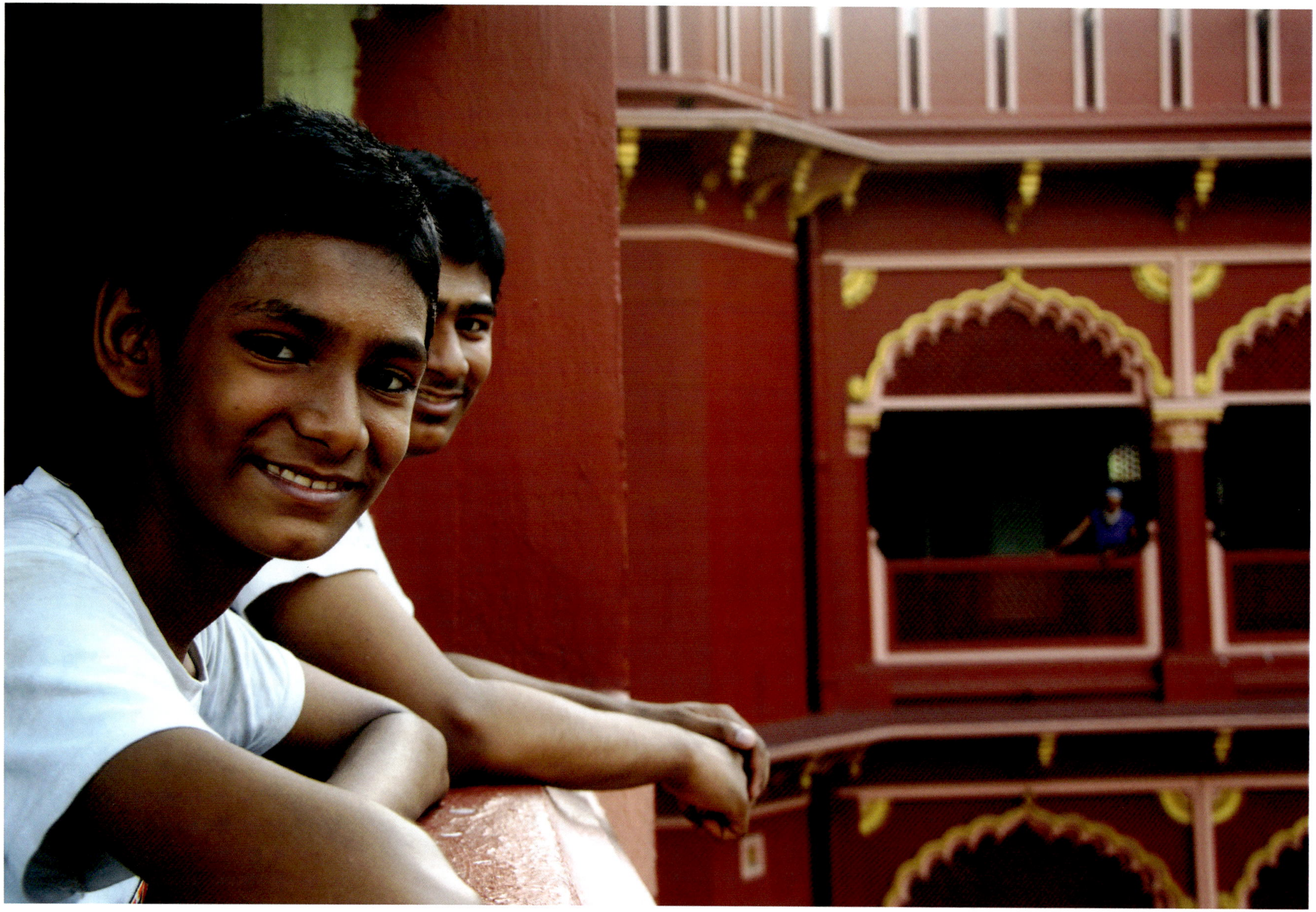

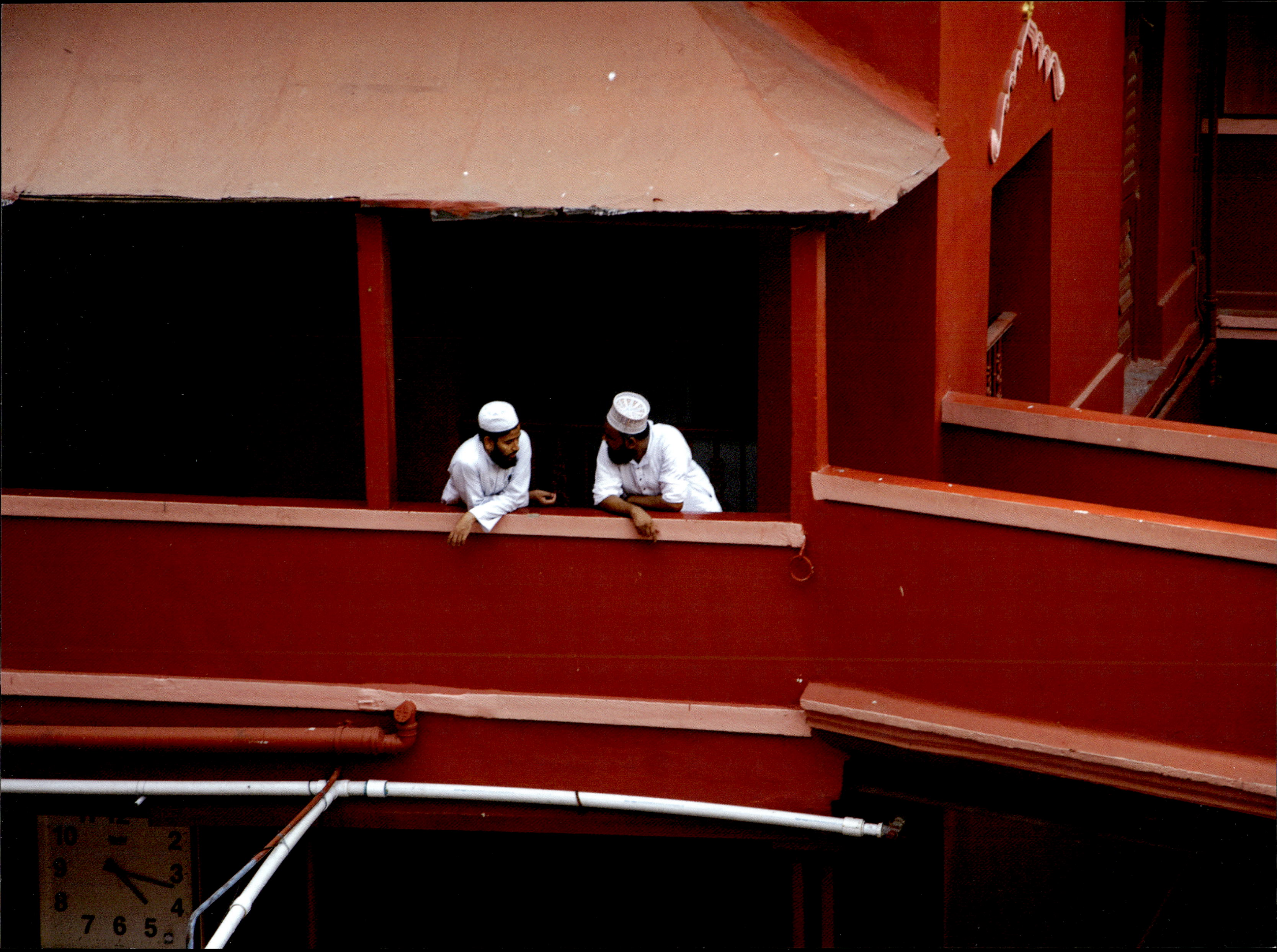

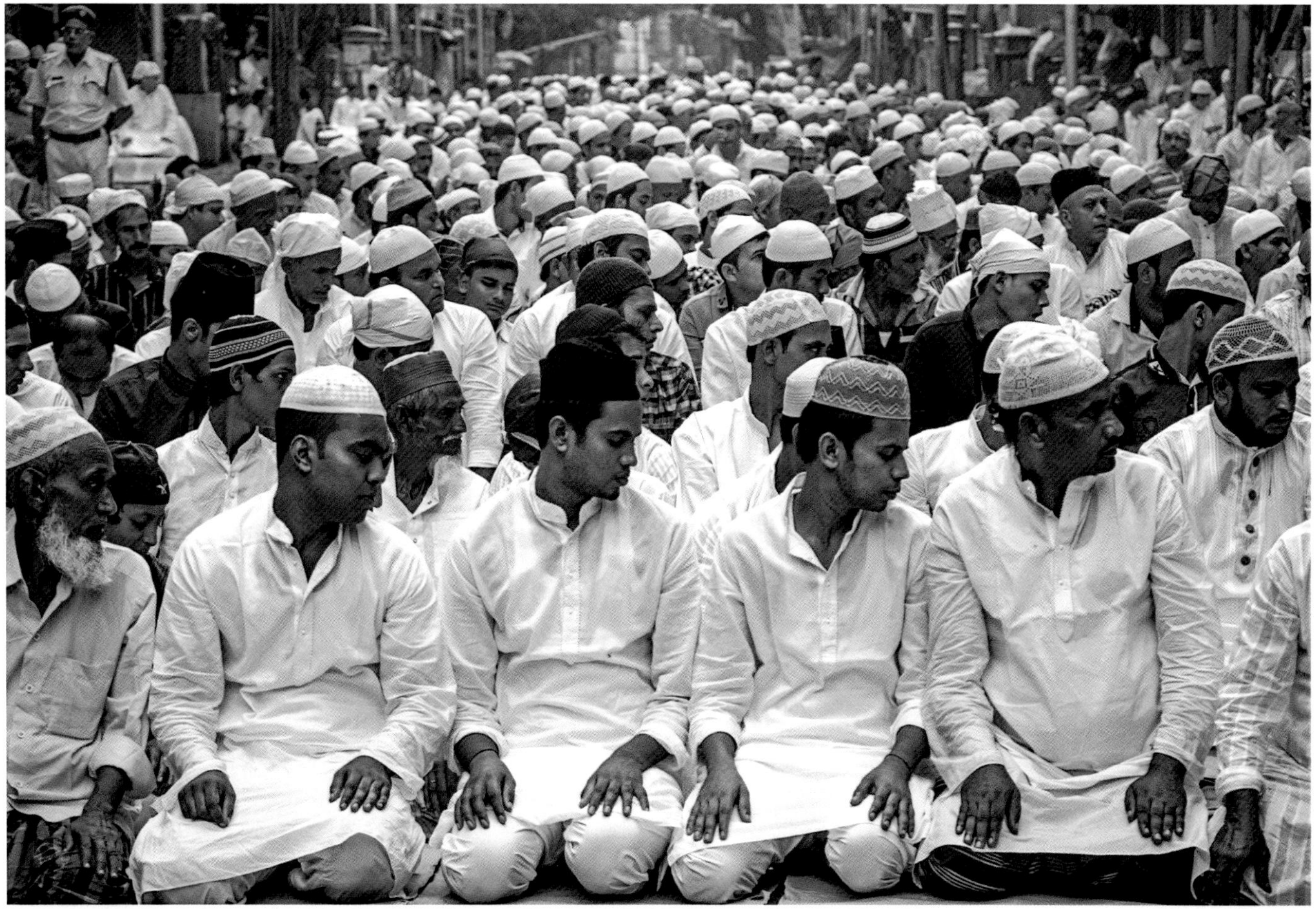

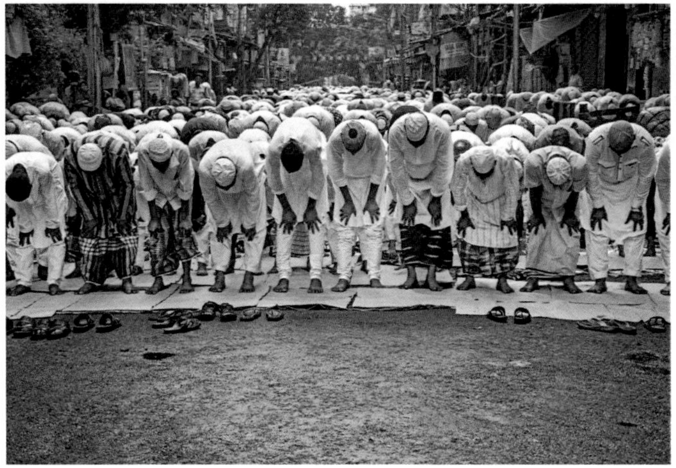

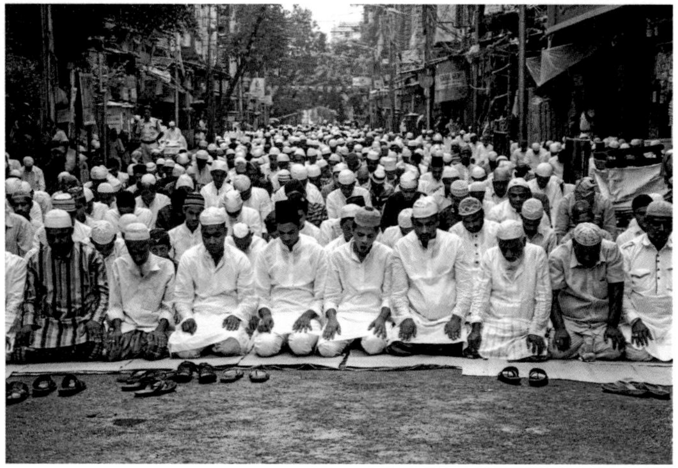

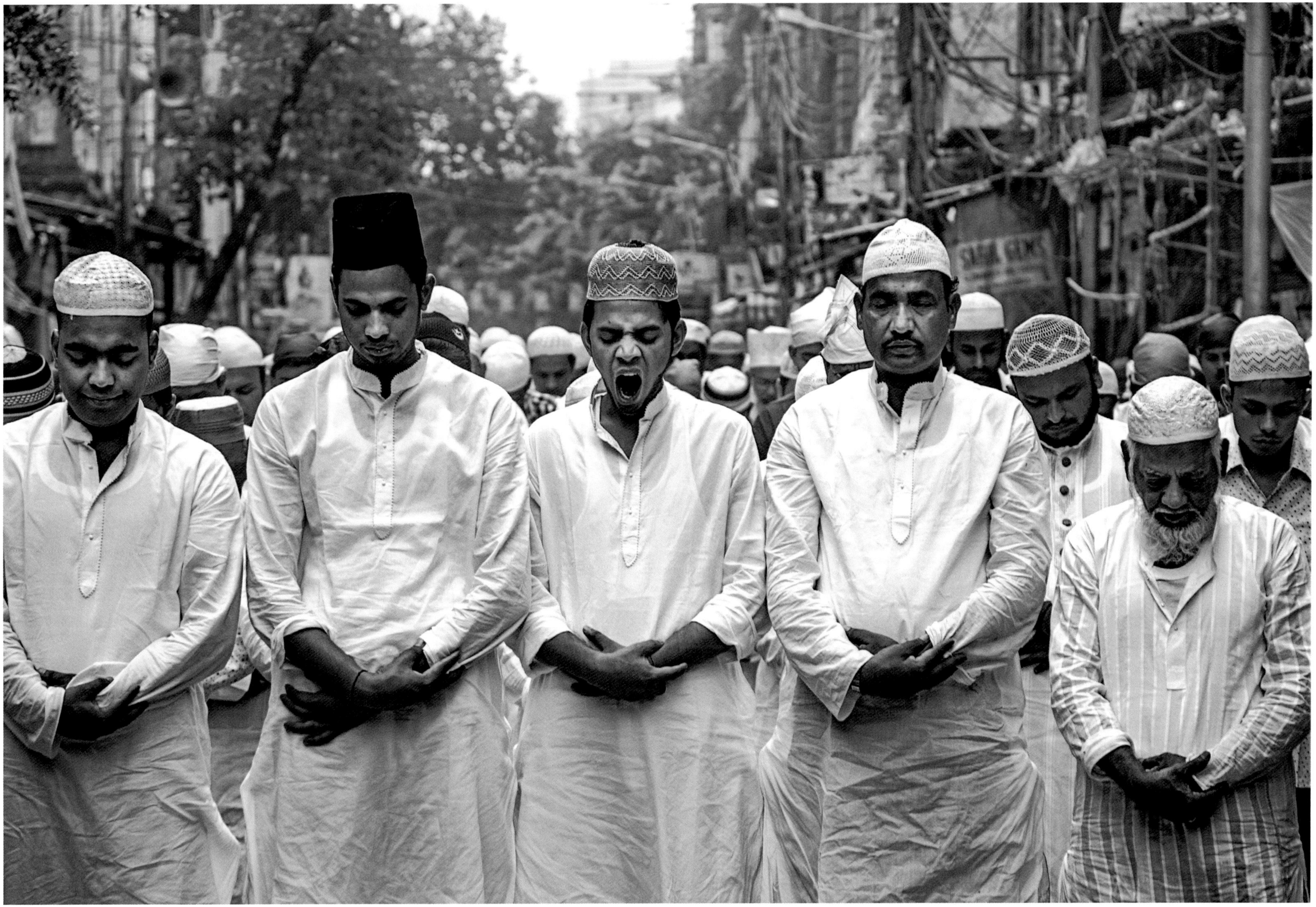

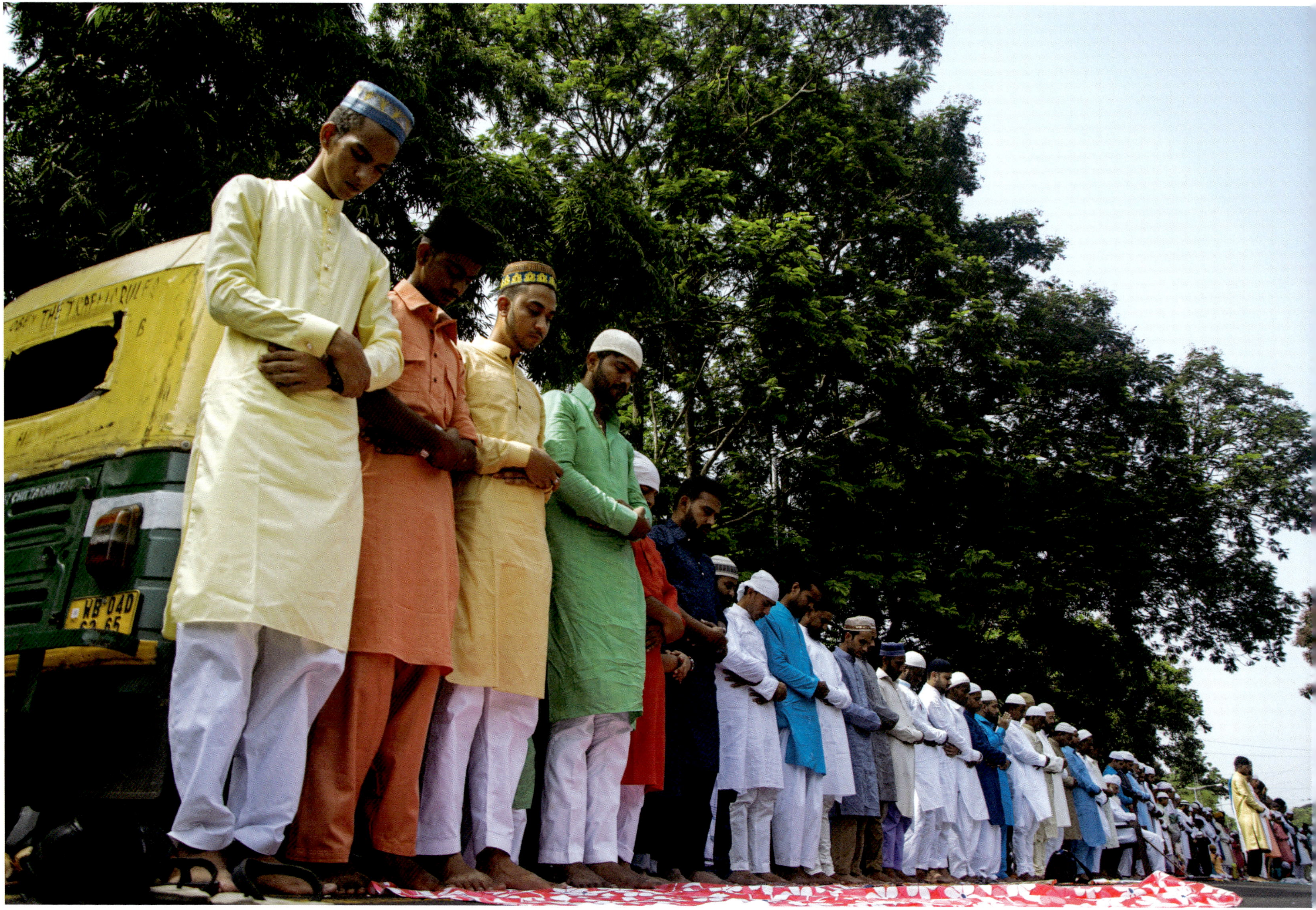

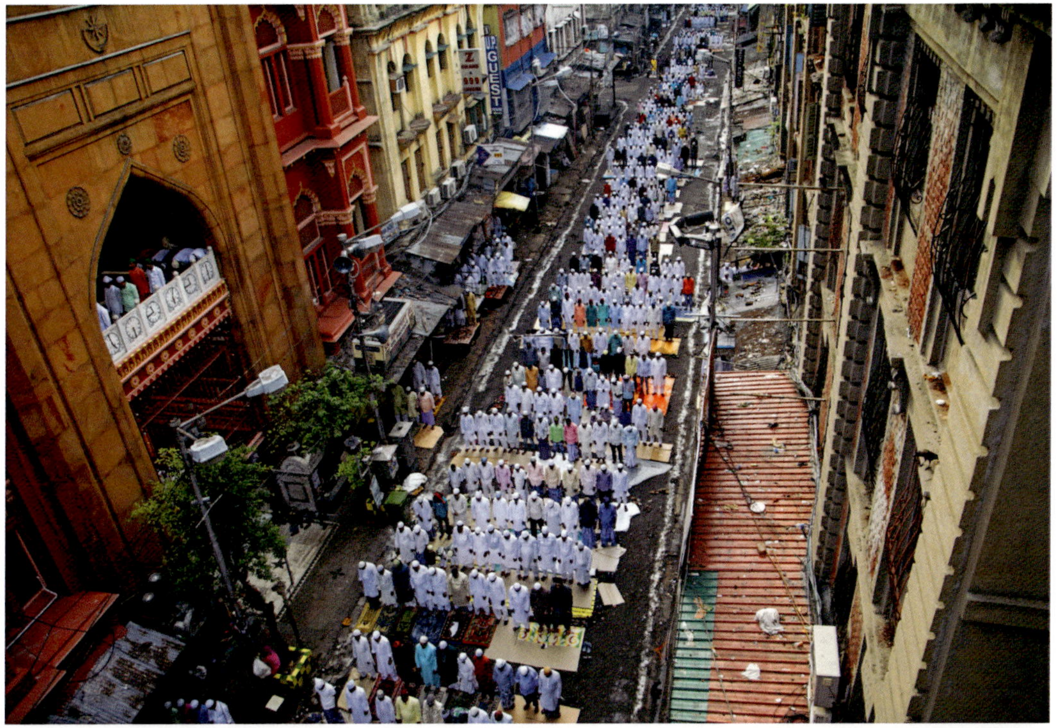

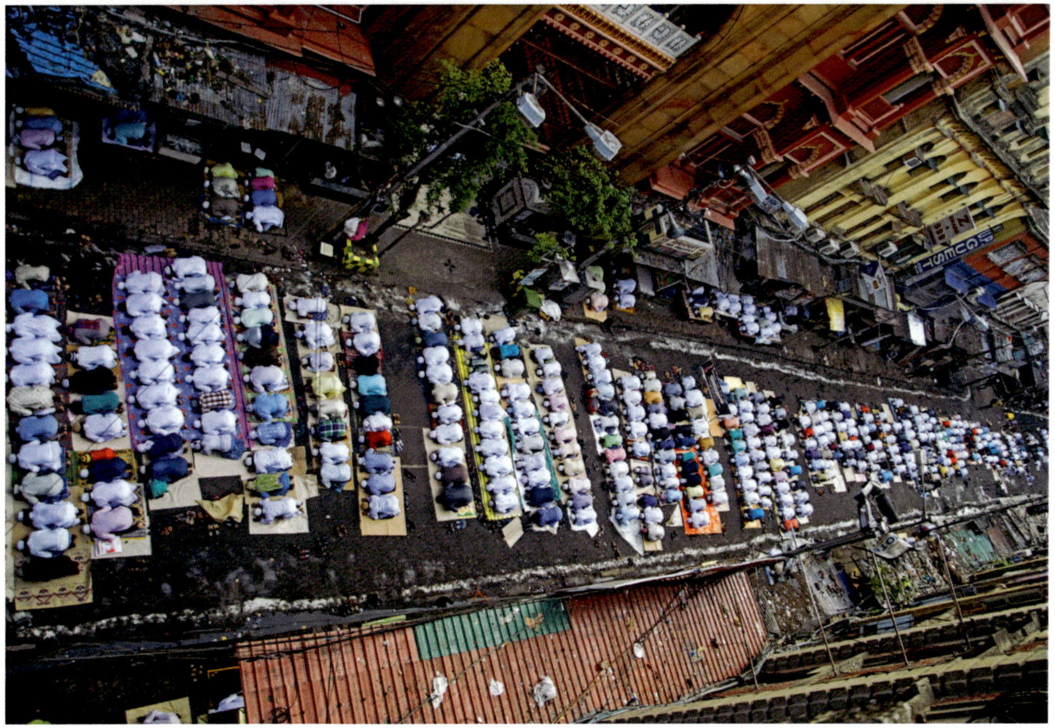

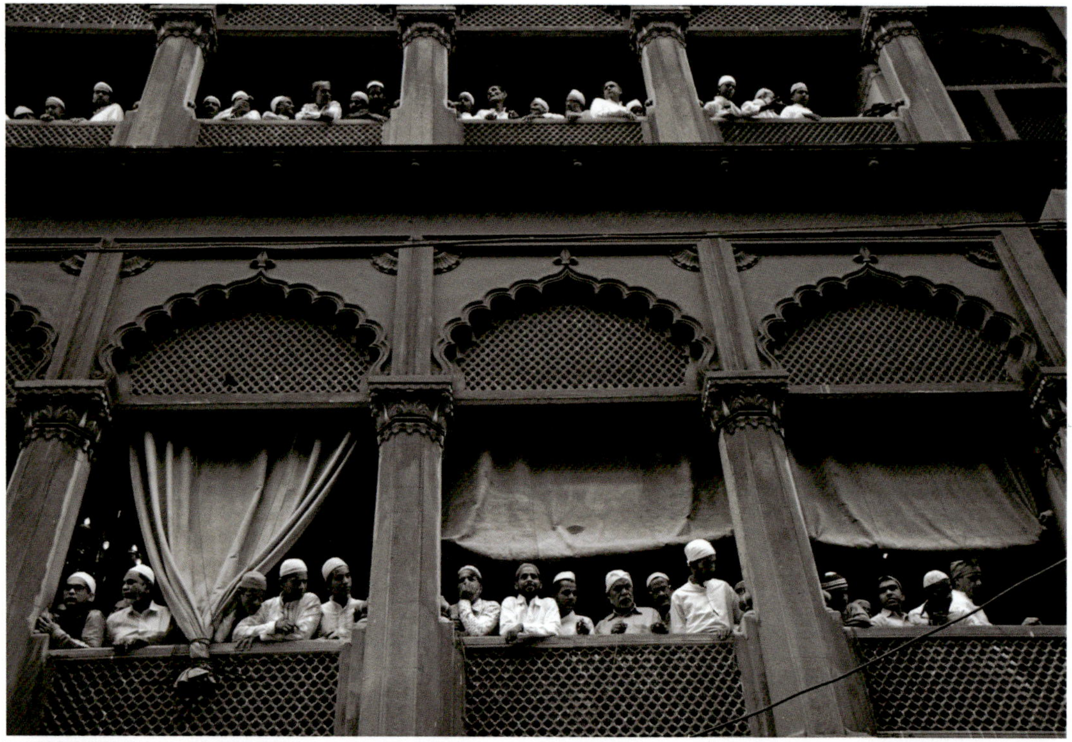
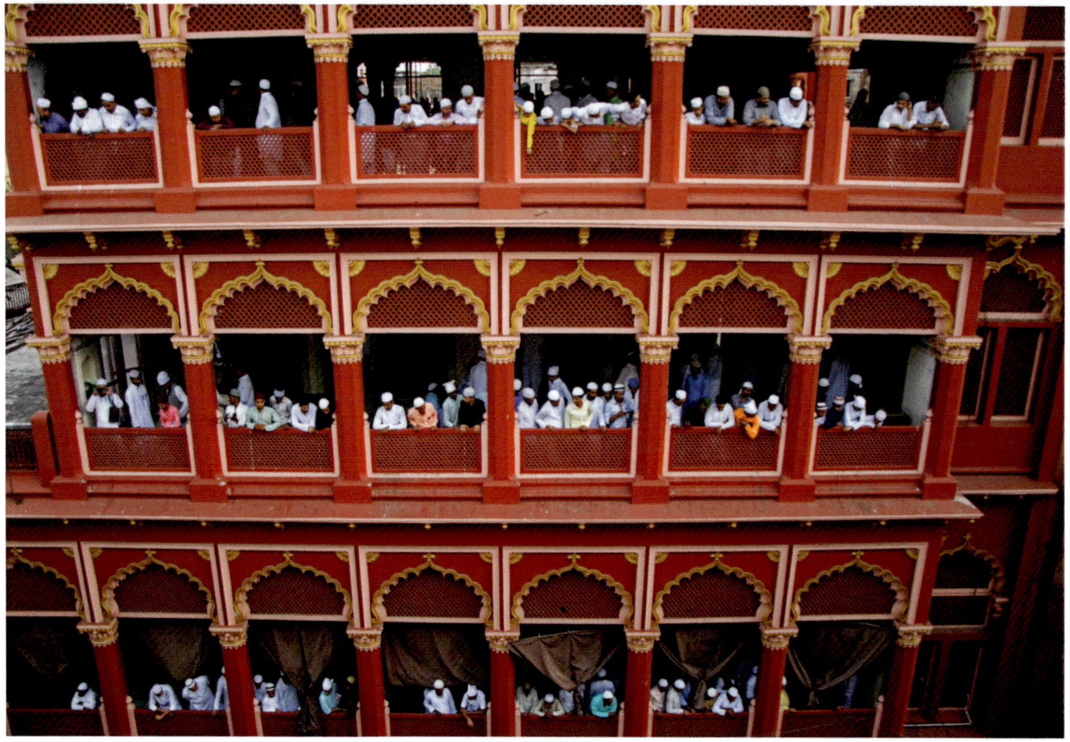

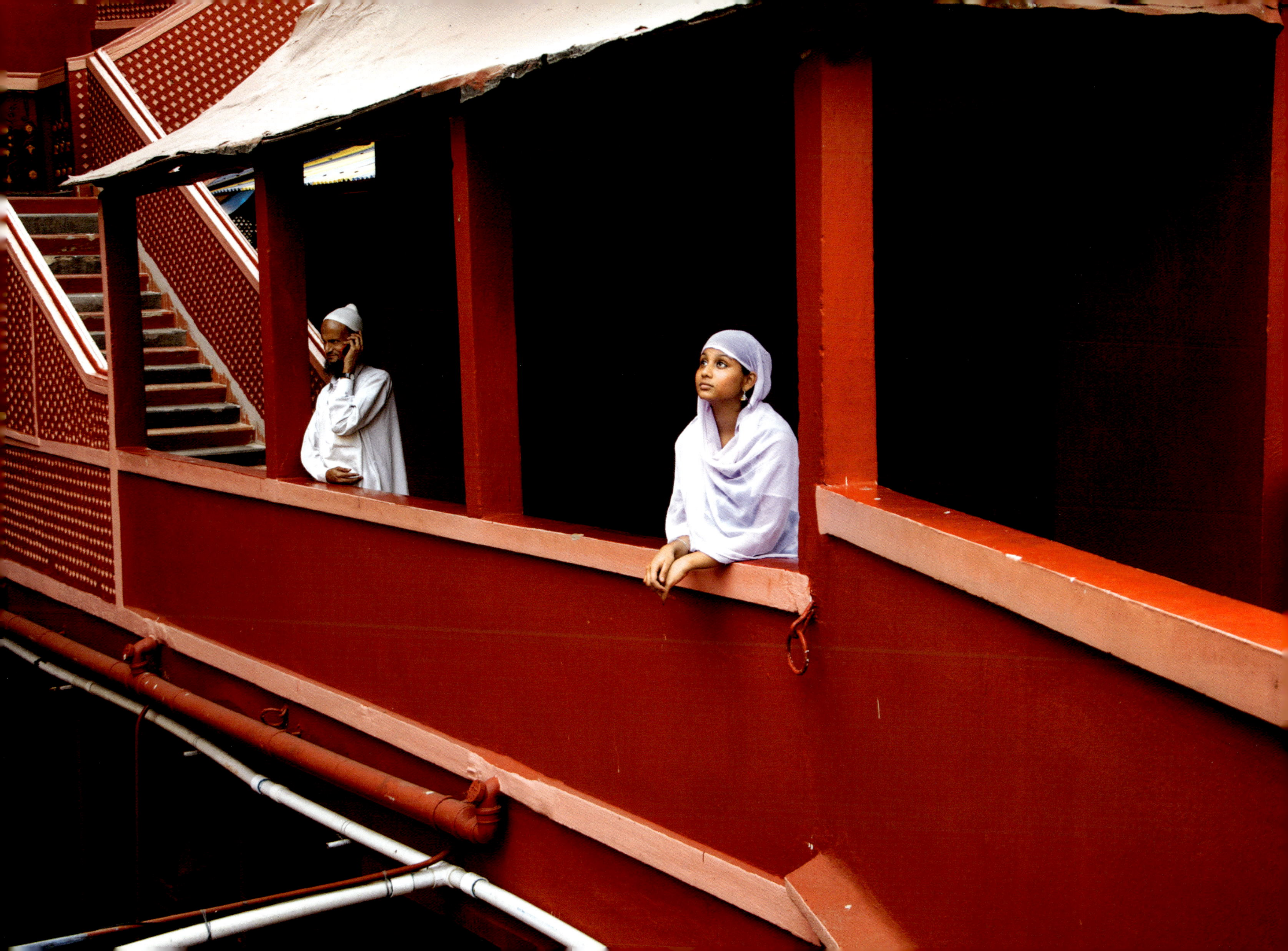

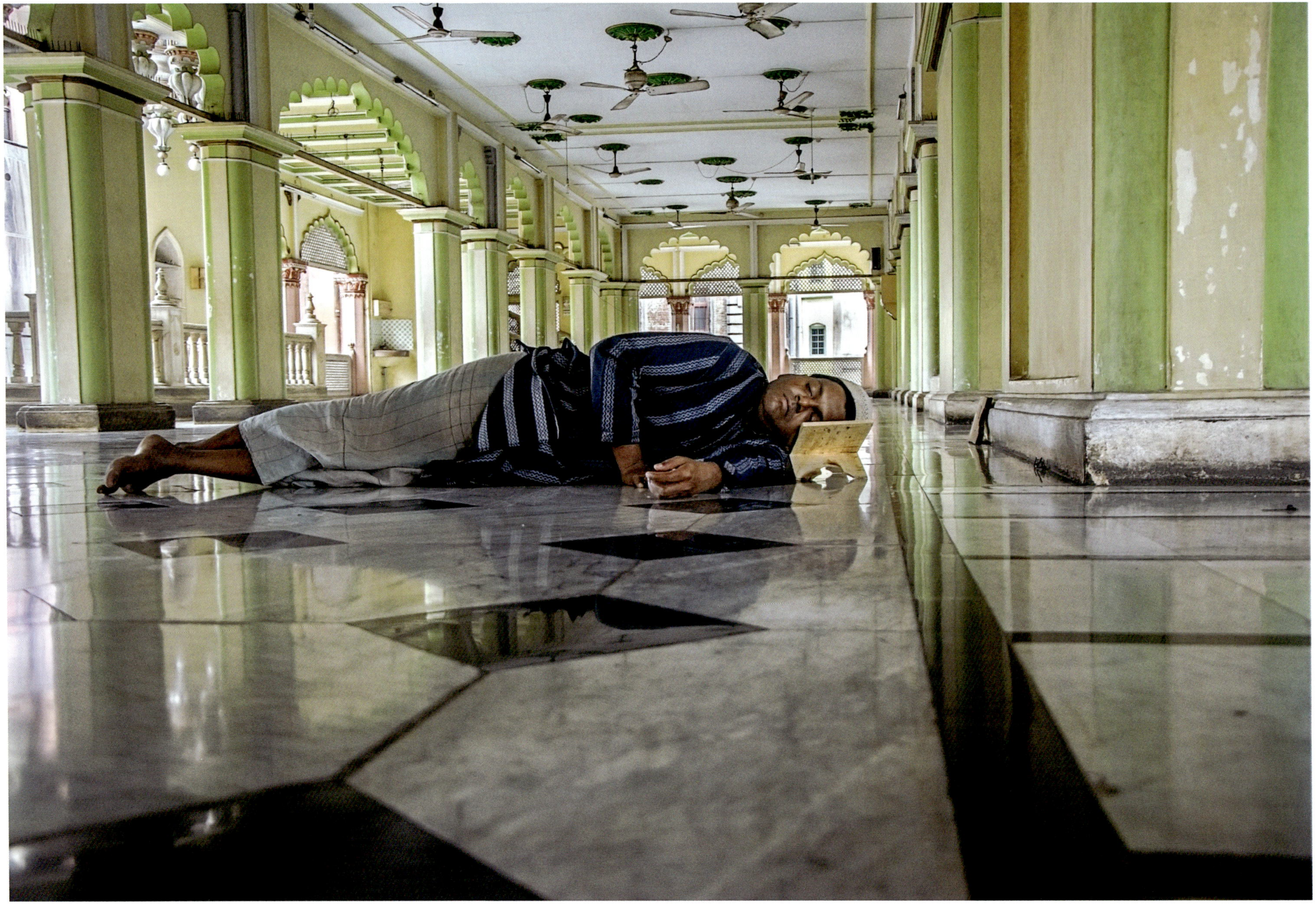

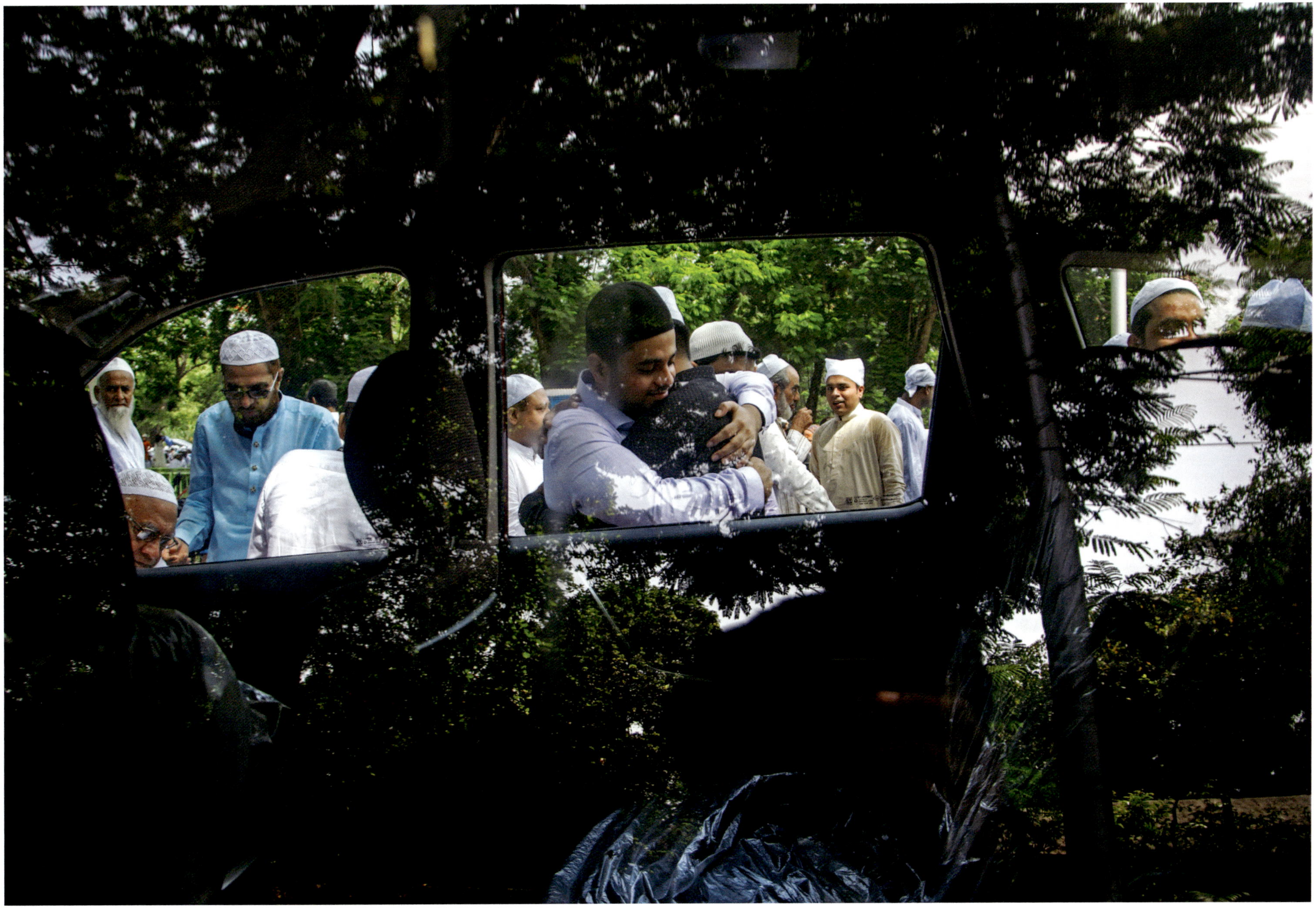

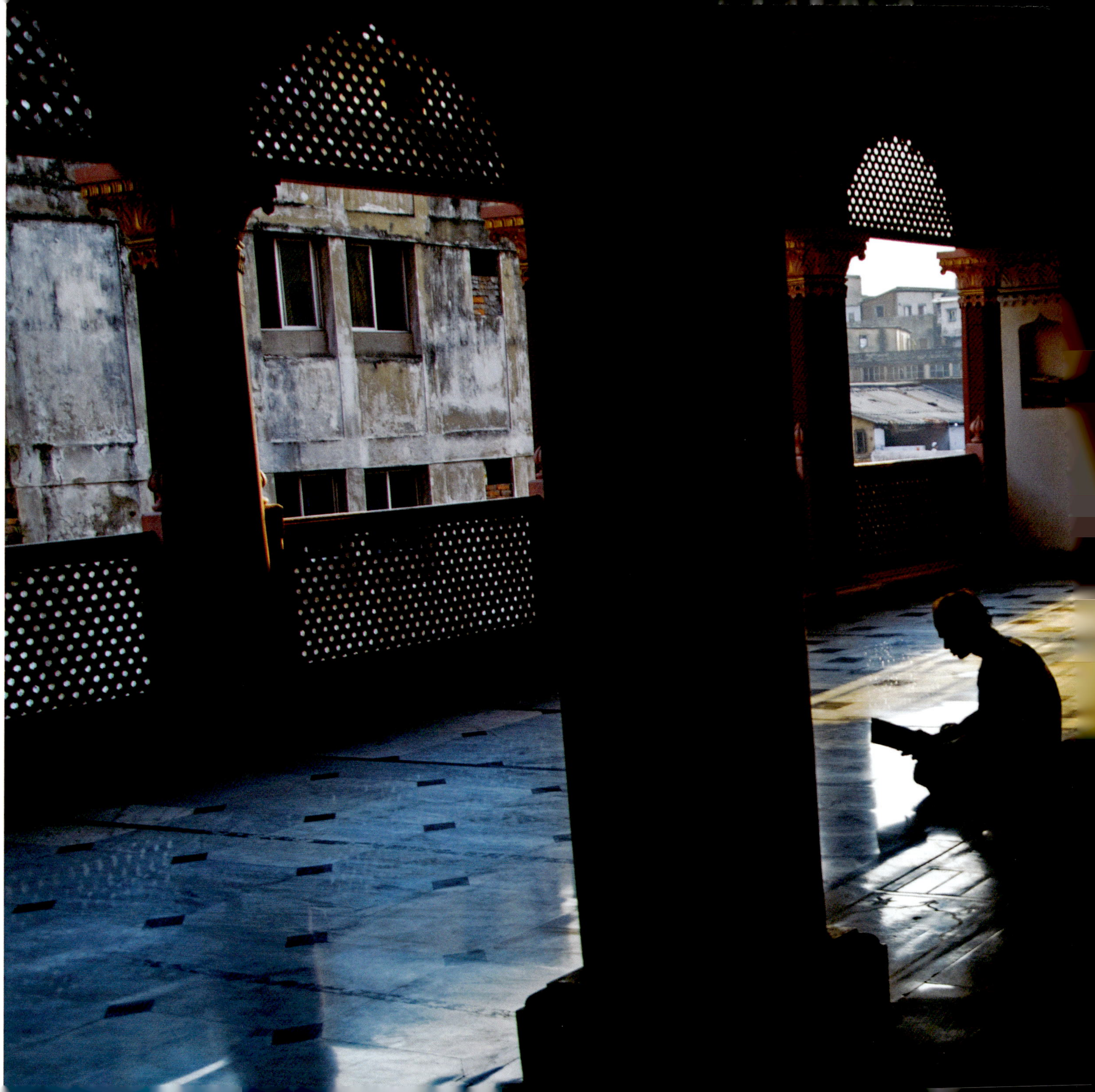

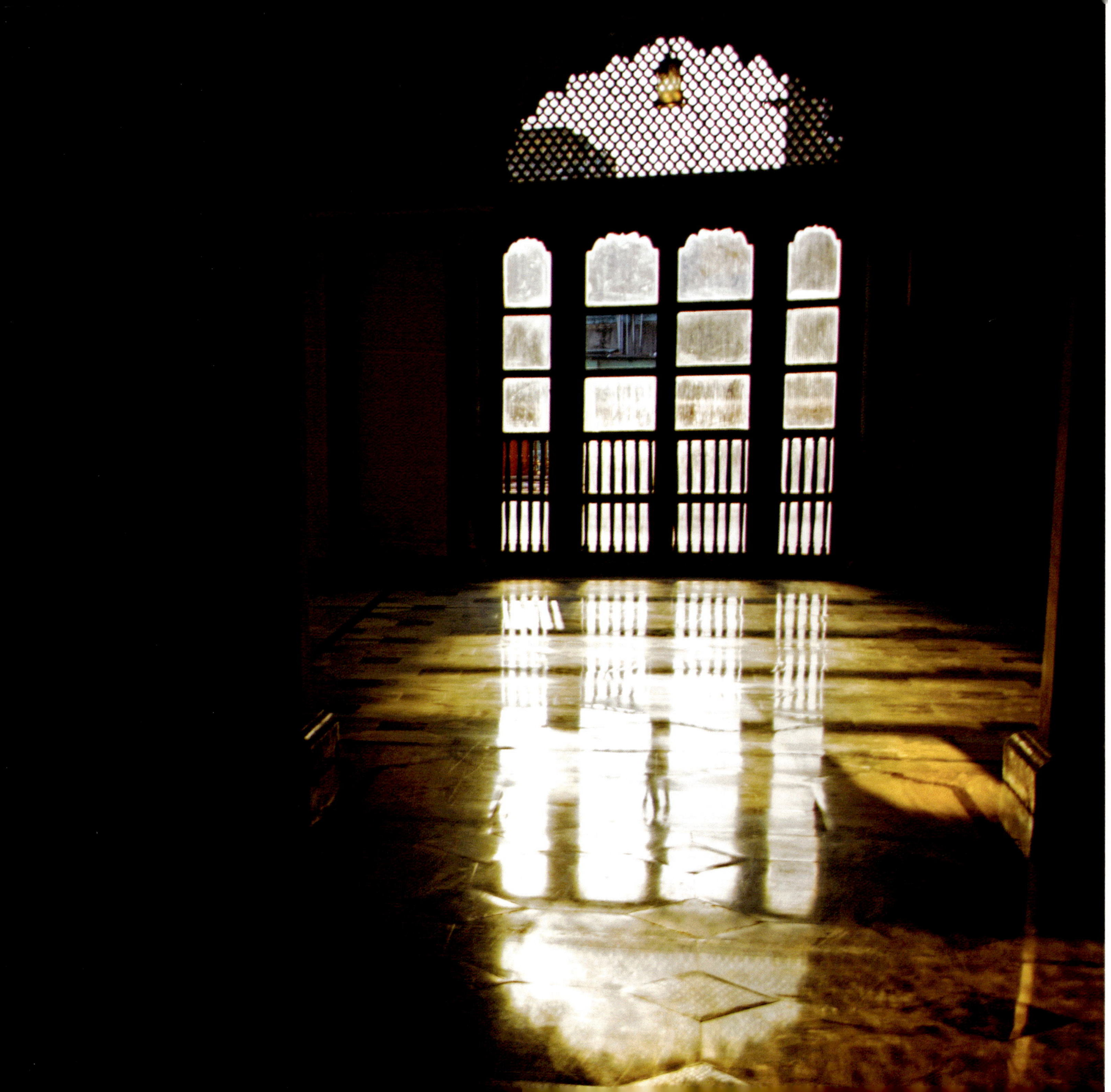

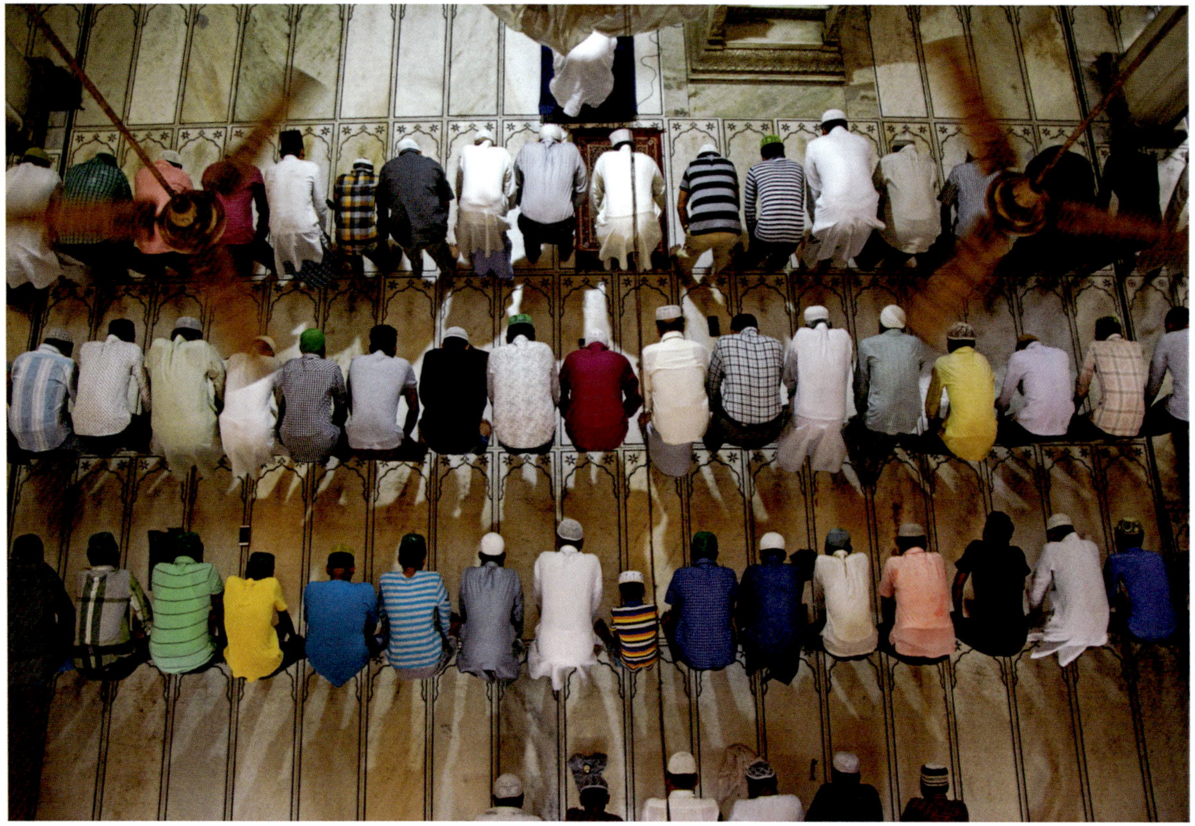

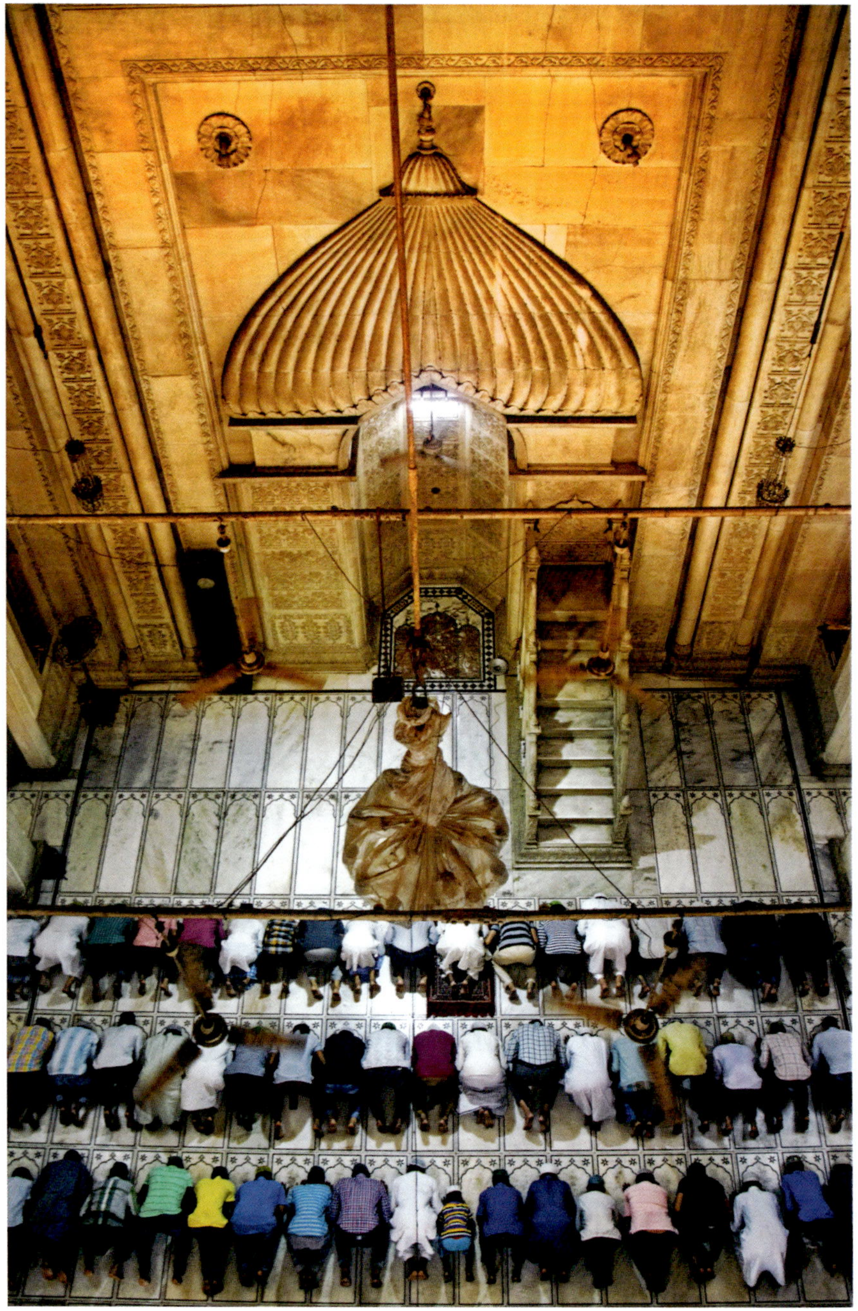

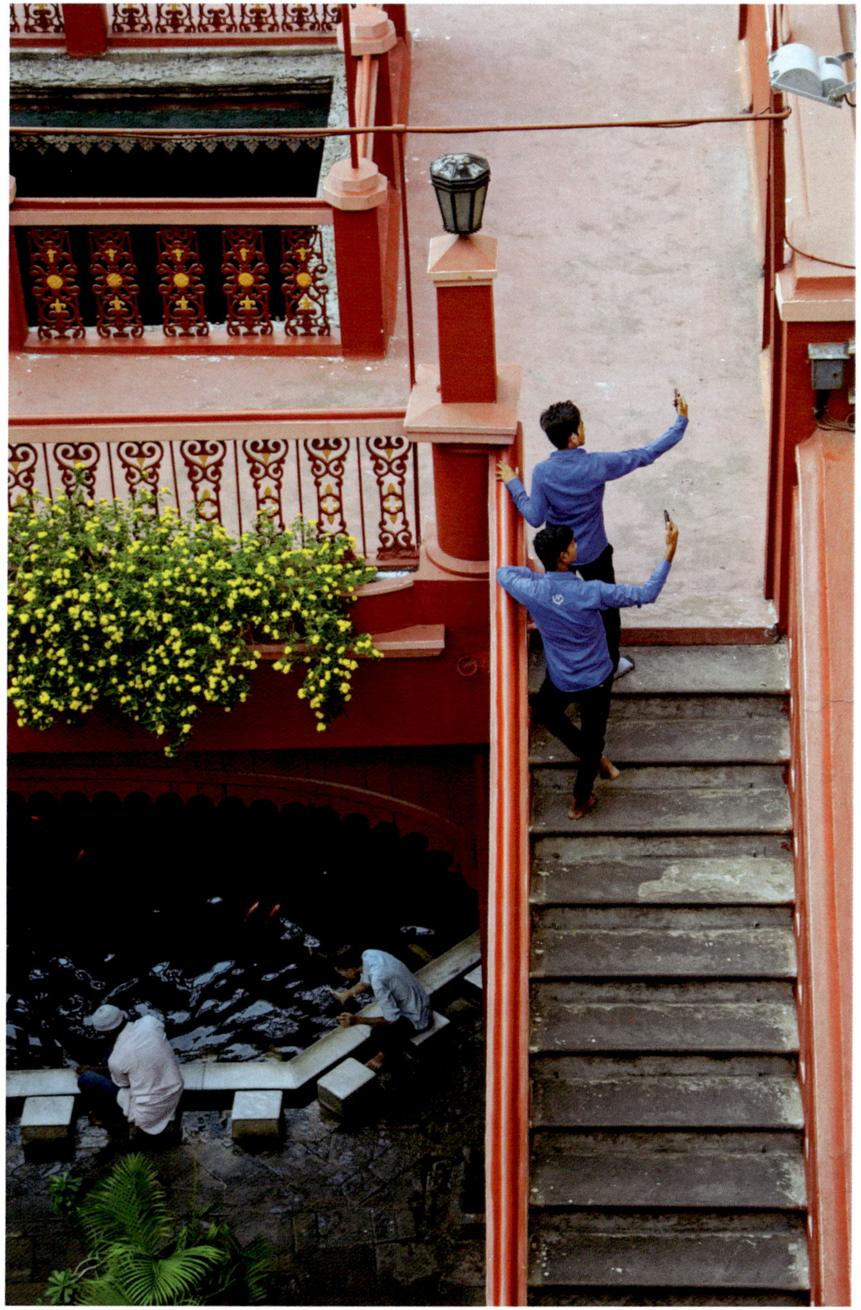

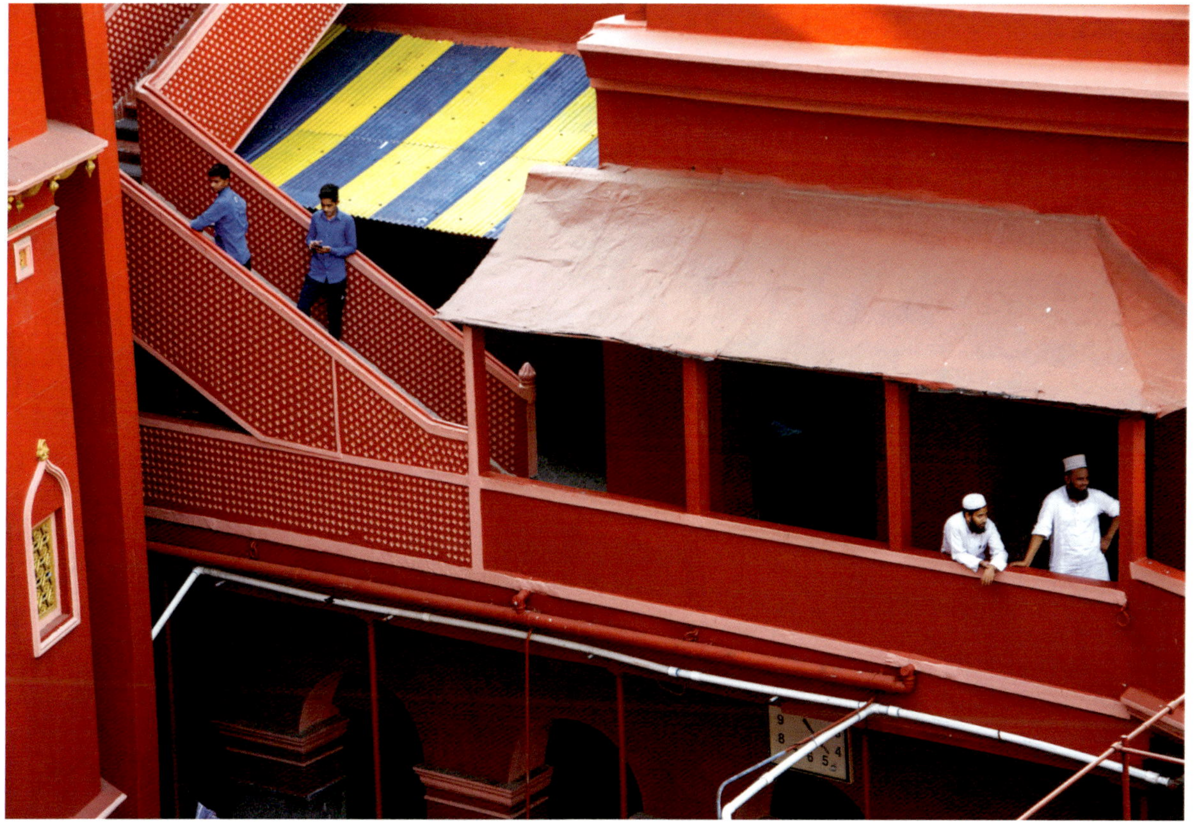

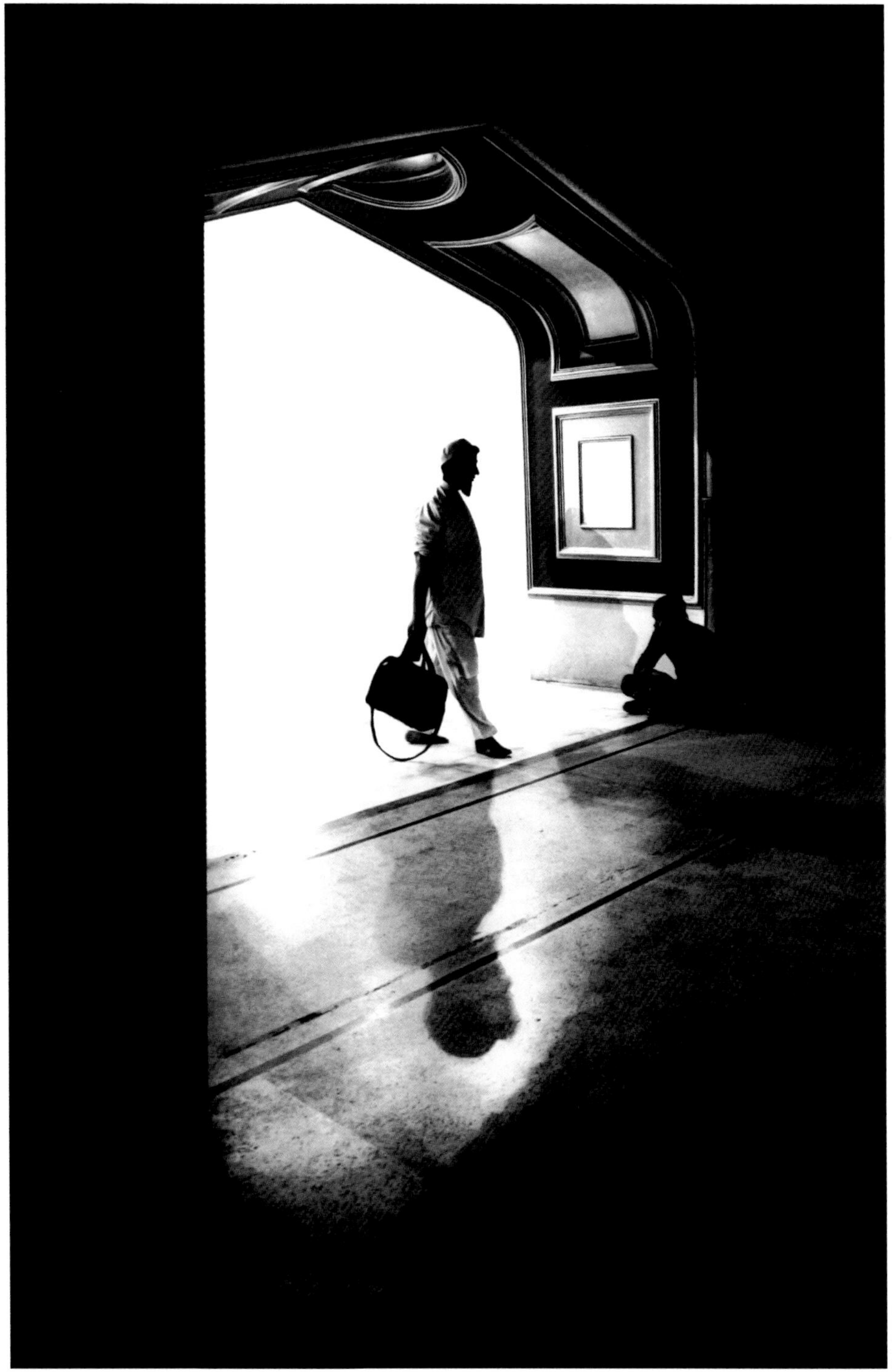

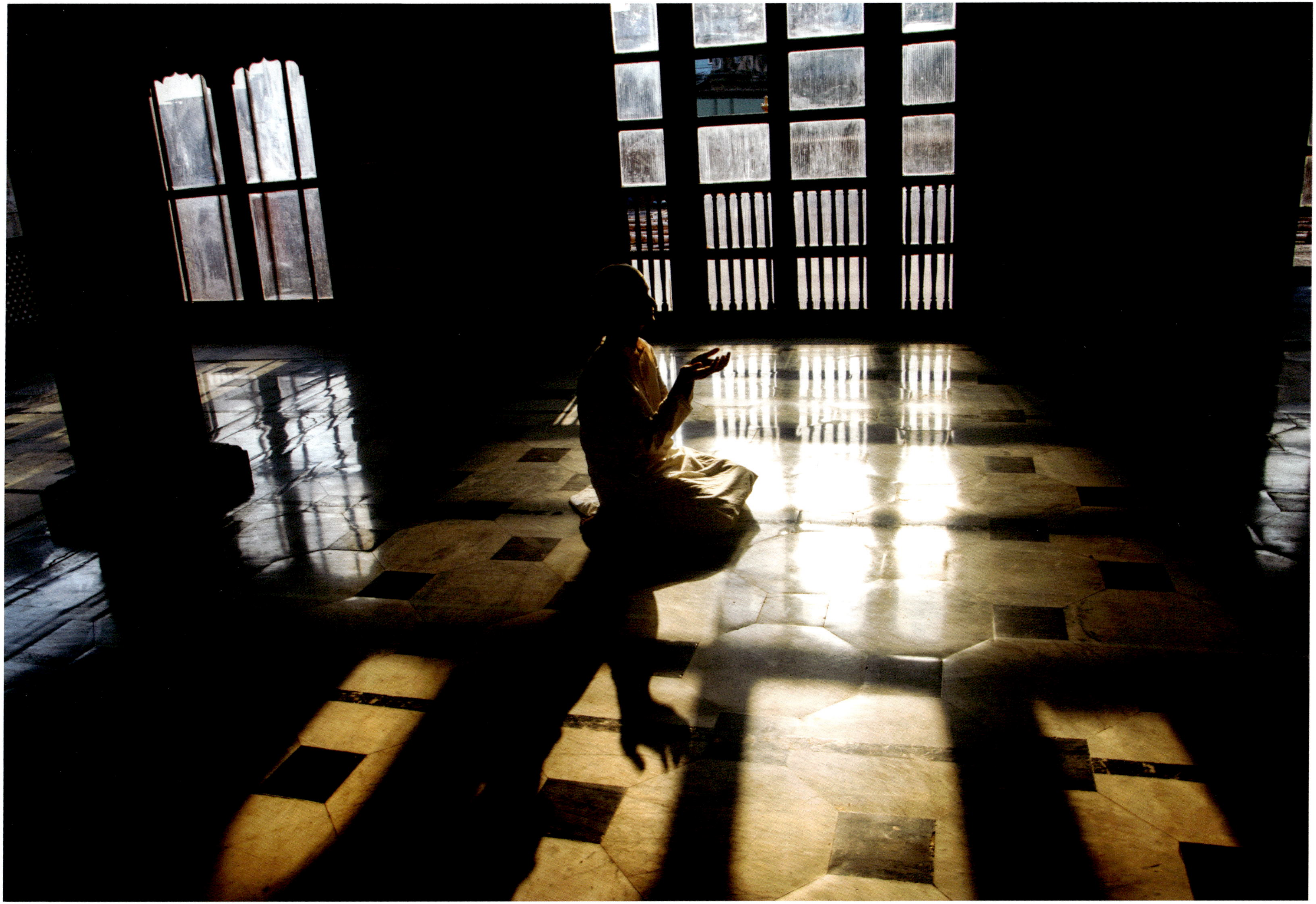

STREET AND PEOPLE

As a photographer, I like to click the streets. Street is my favourite form of photography. The one thing you need for street photography is to keep your eyes open. There is no shortage of stories while you are standing on the street. All we can do is to select the one which moves us the most. Light is the most important factor for all forms of photography. Clever use of light can turn an average picture into an extraordinary one. Another beautiful thing about street photography is that even if we click the same street every day, the stories it tells us will be far from same. Each fleeting moment paints its own unique picture. Almost every click of mine has people in it, so Street and People is an important chapter in my book.

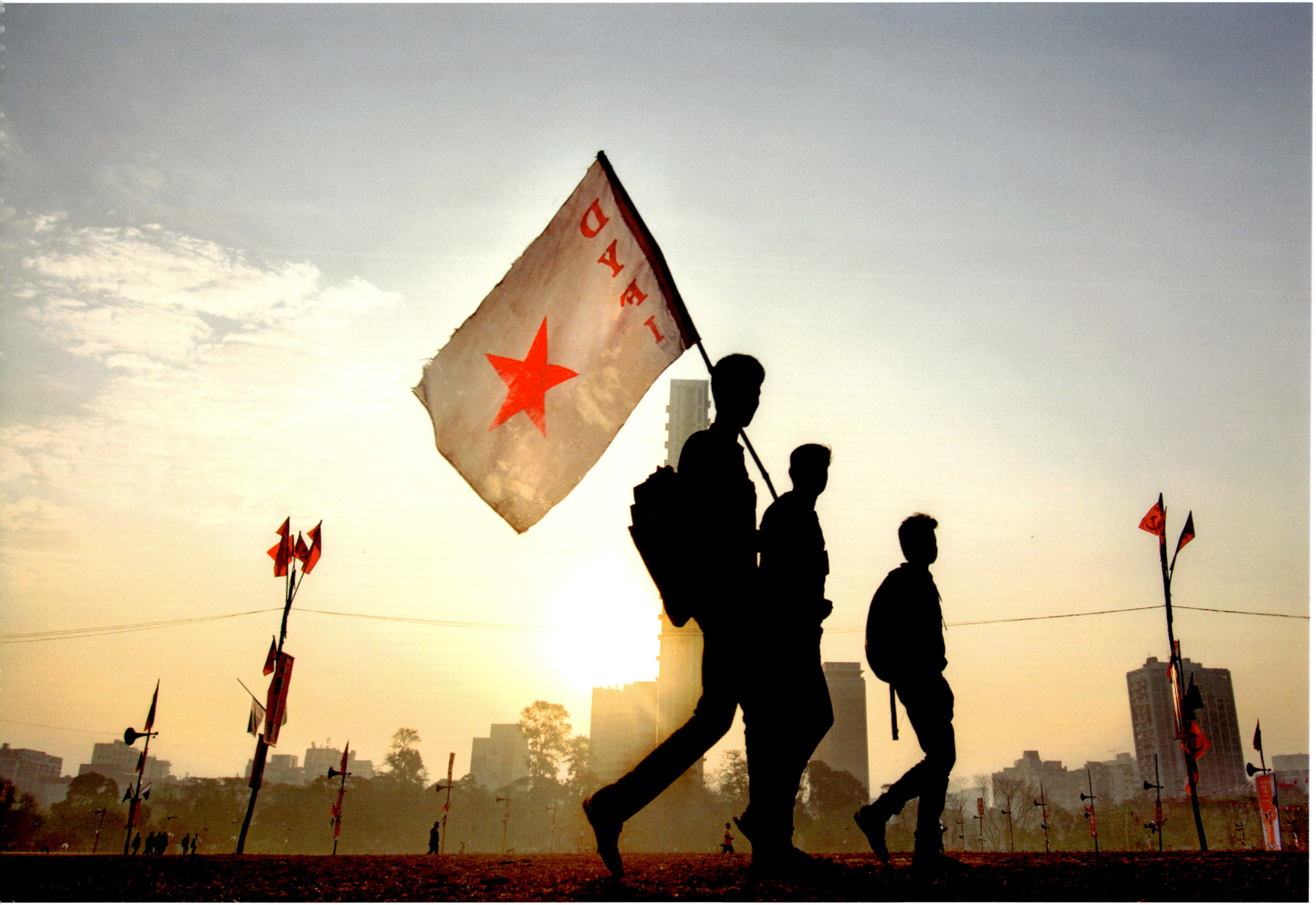

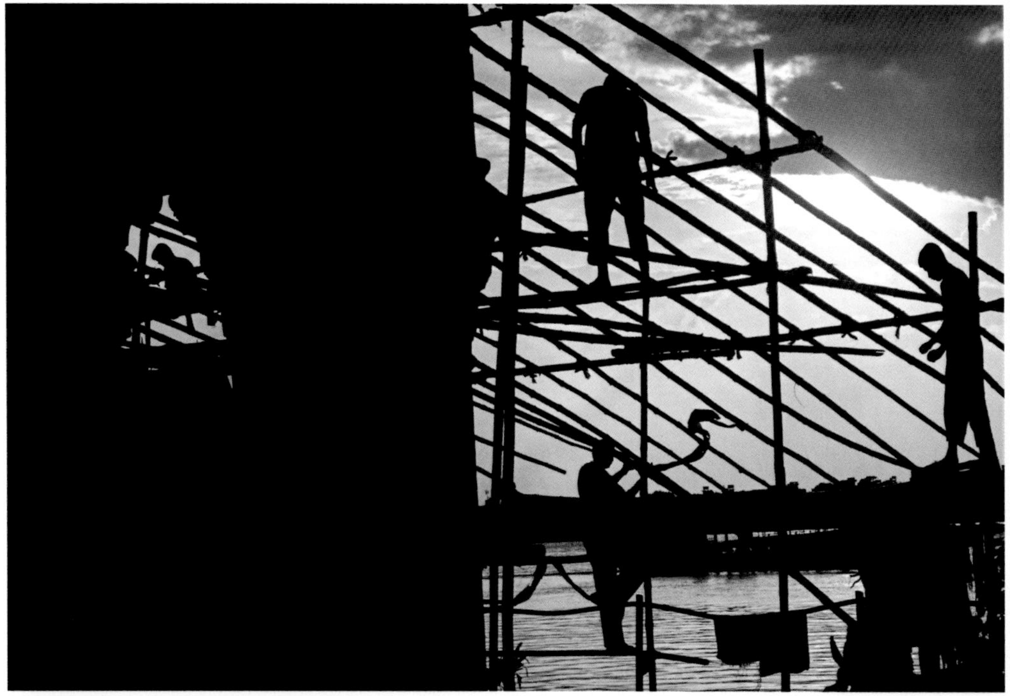
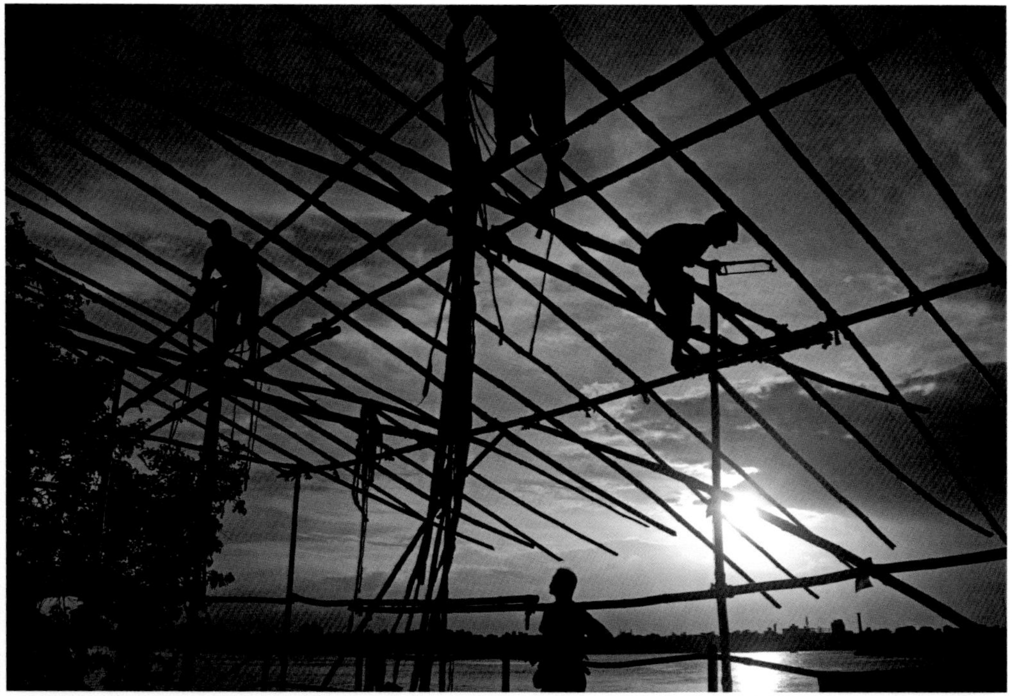
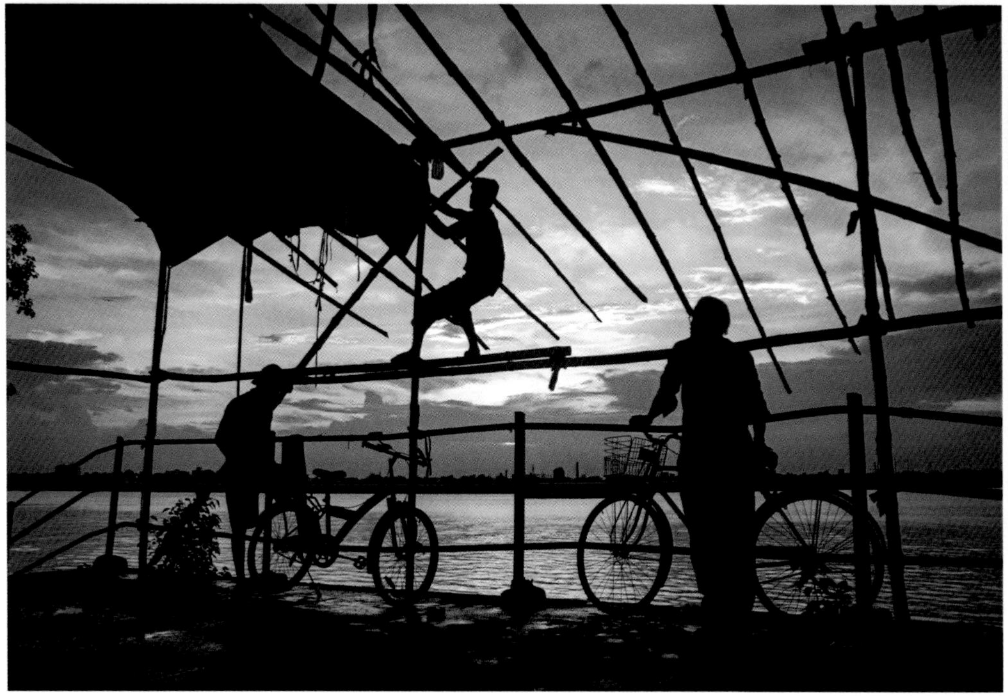
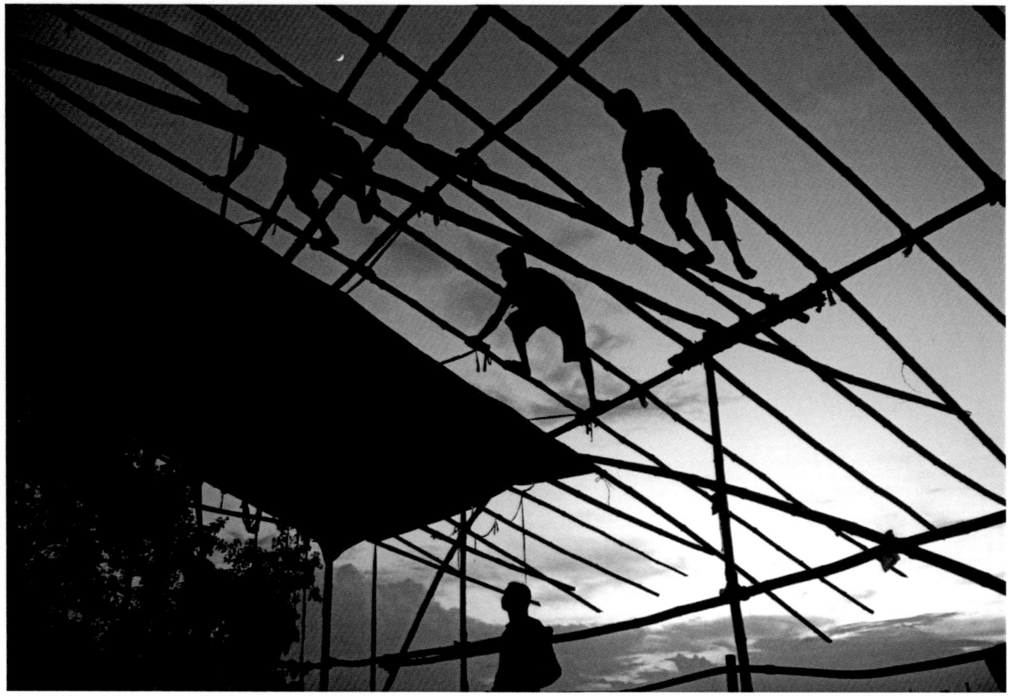

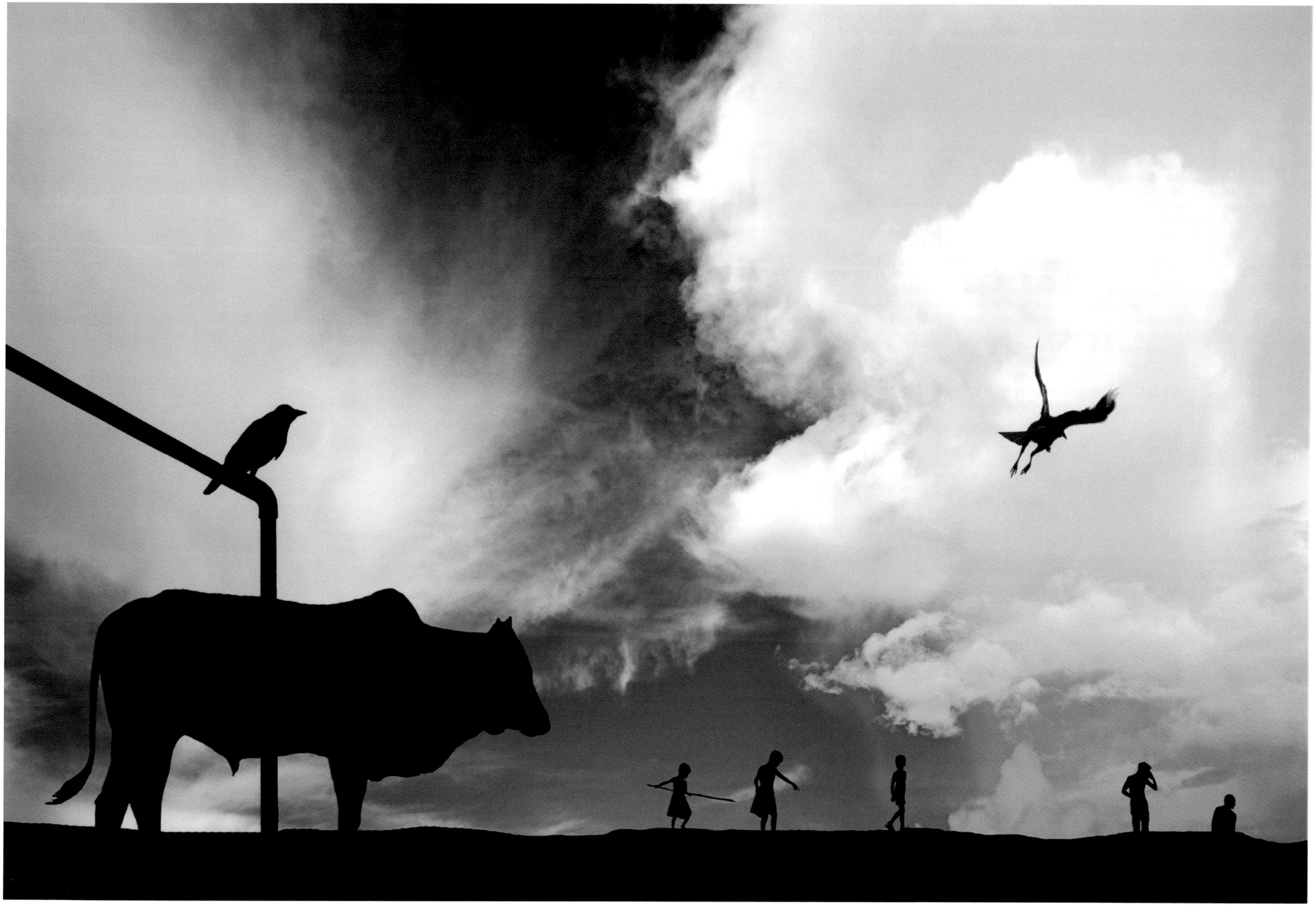

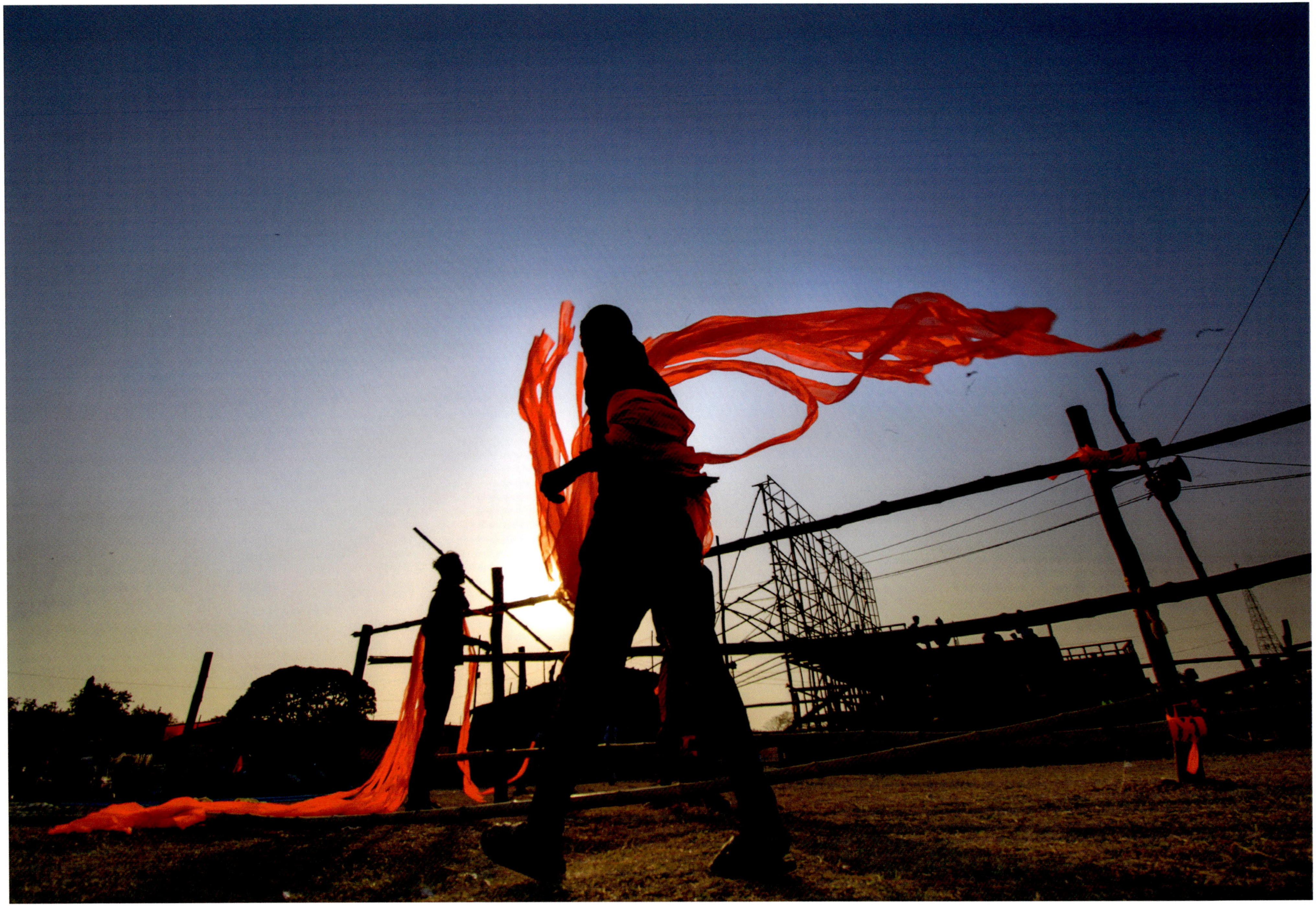

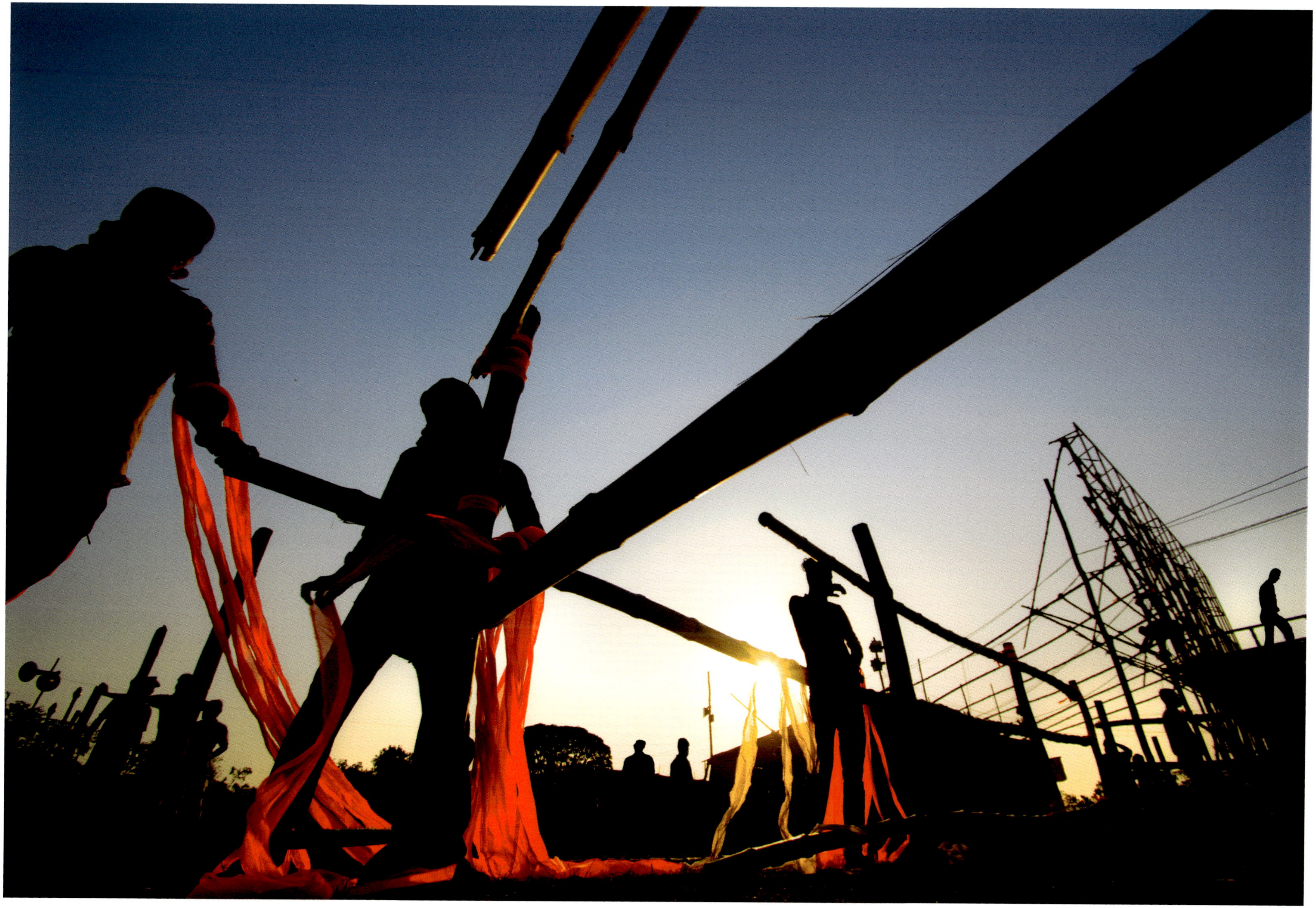

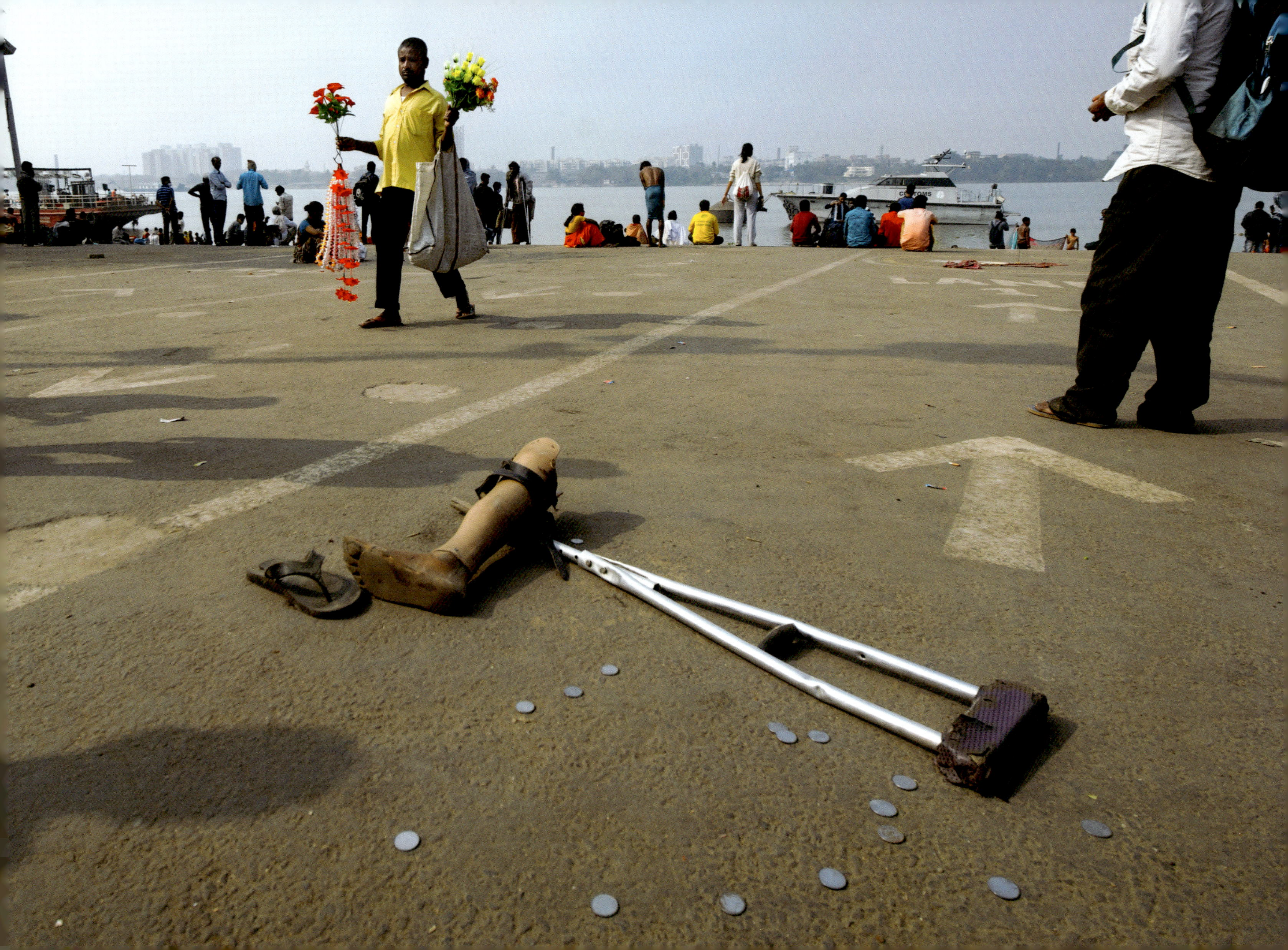

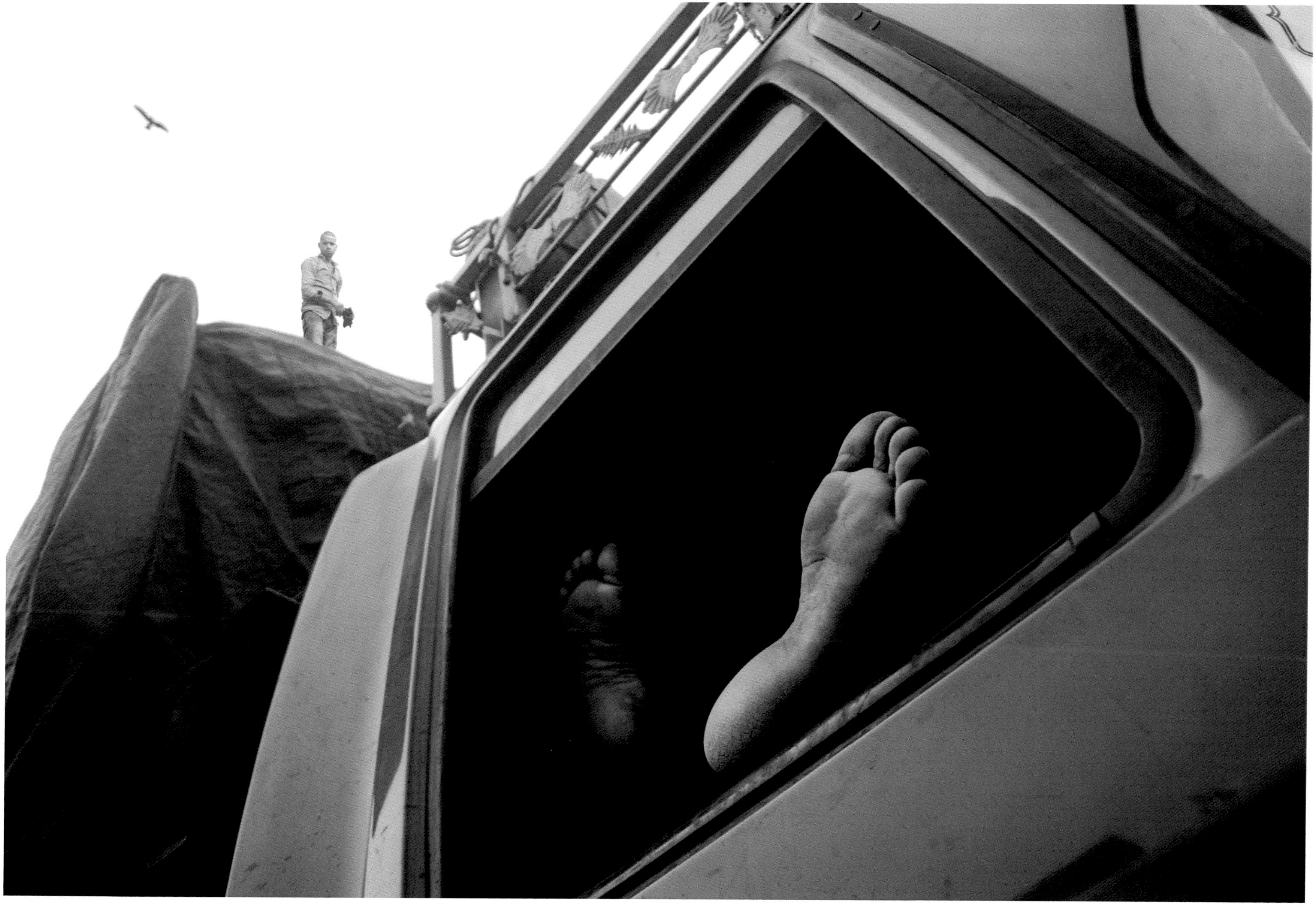

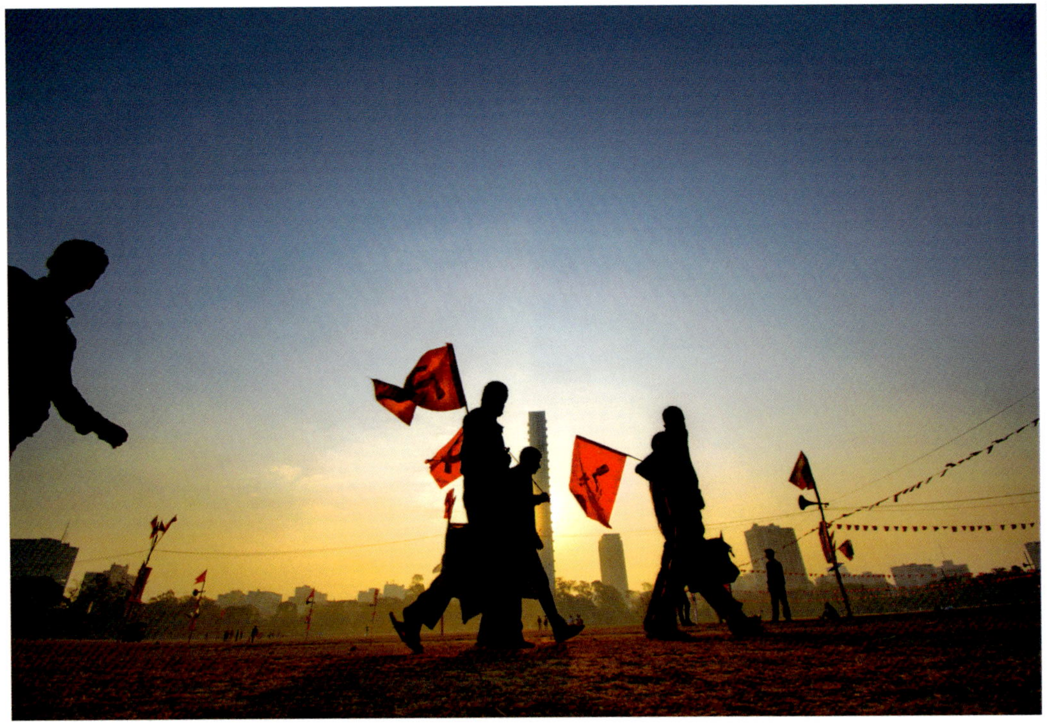
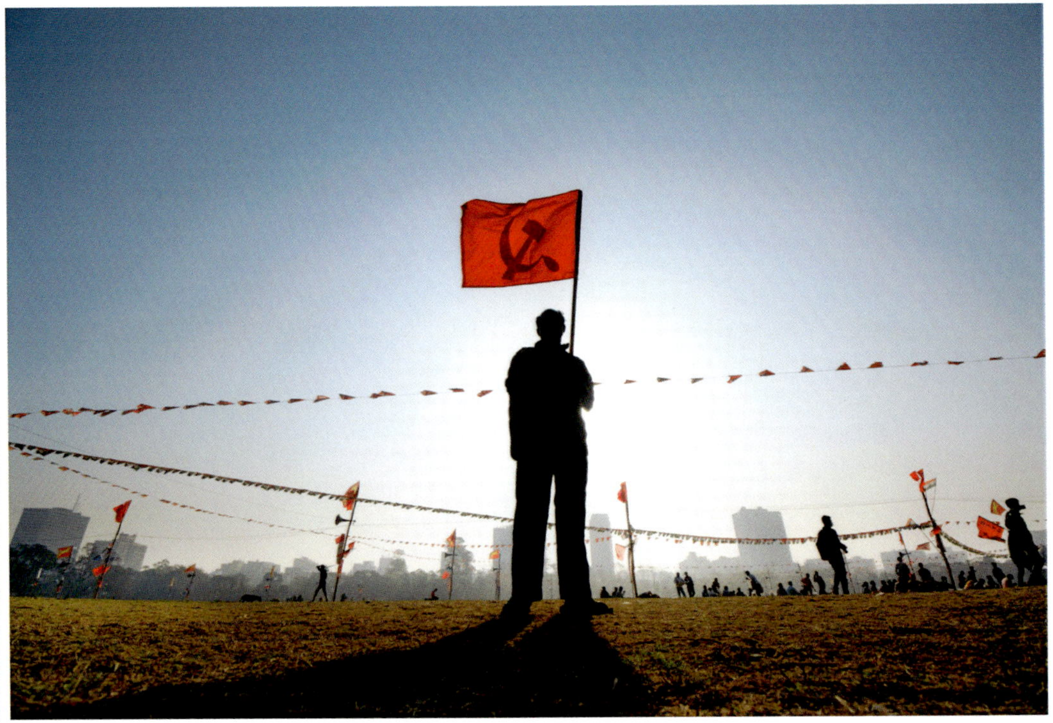

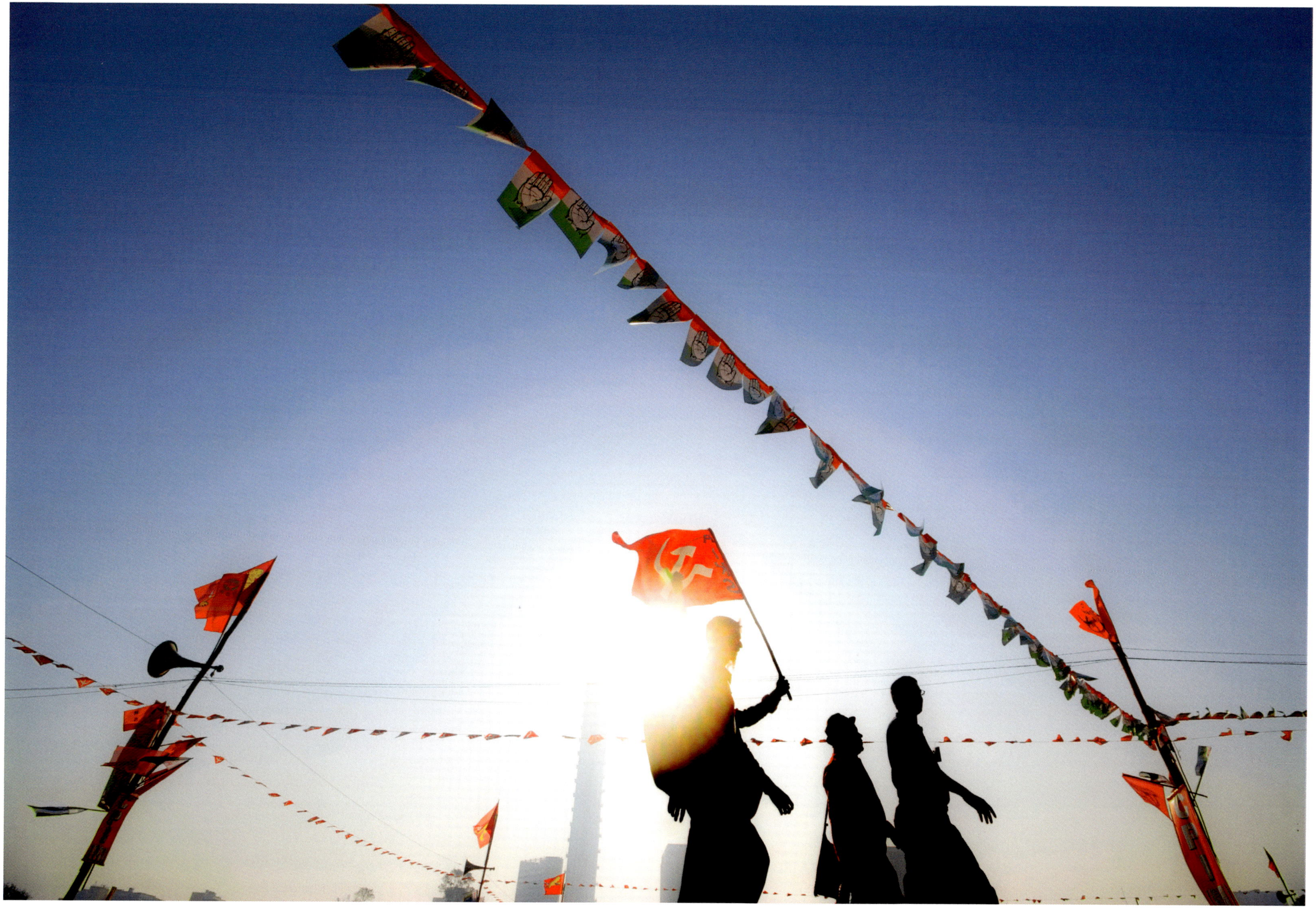

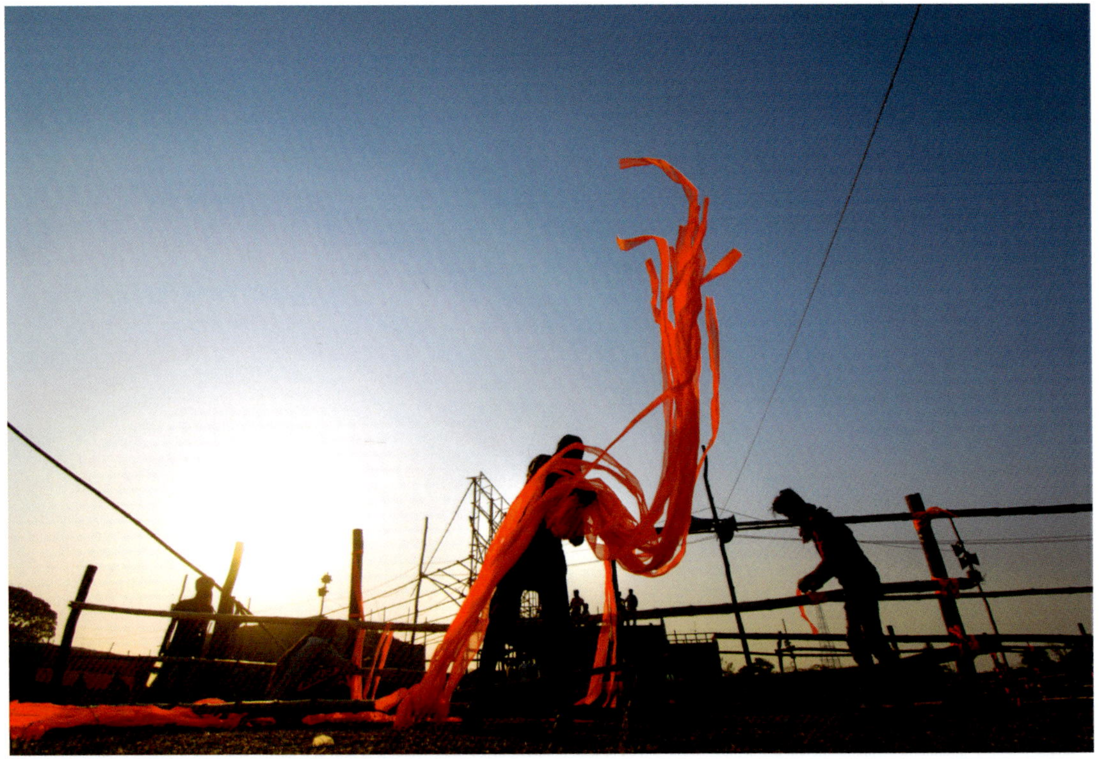

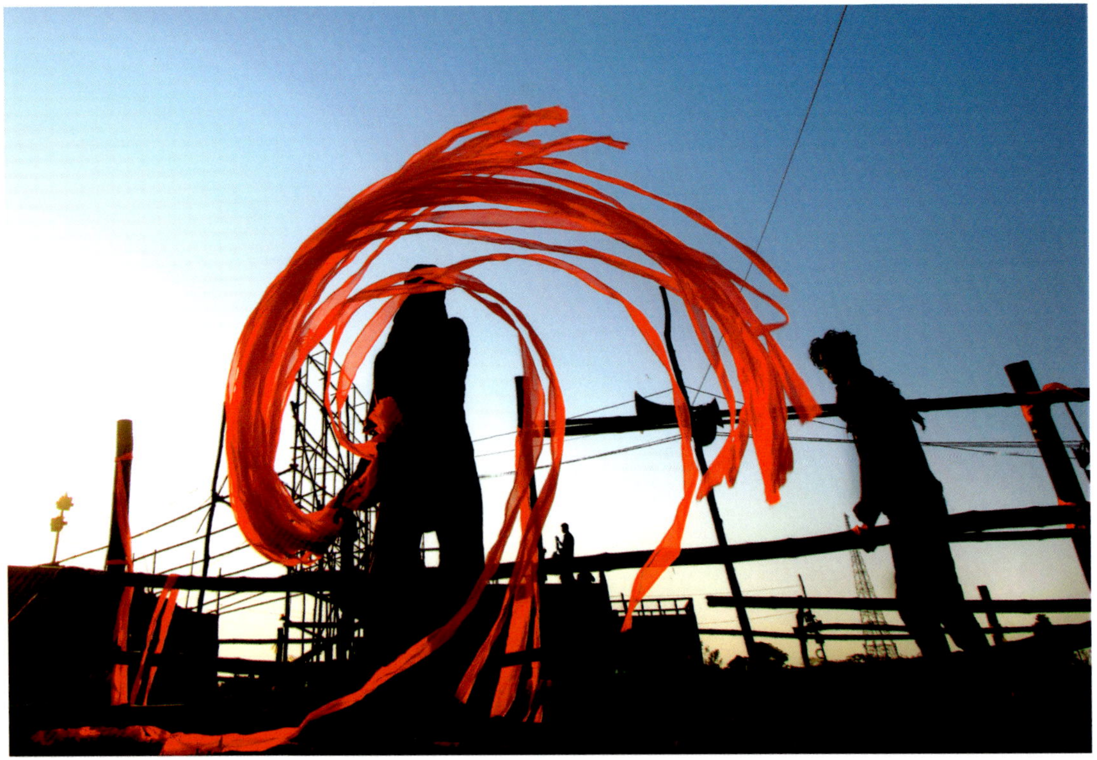

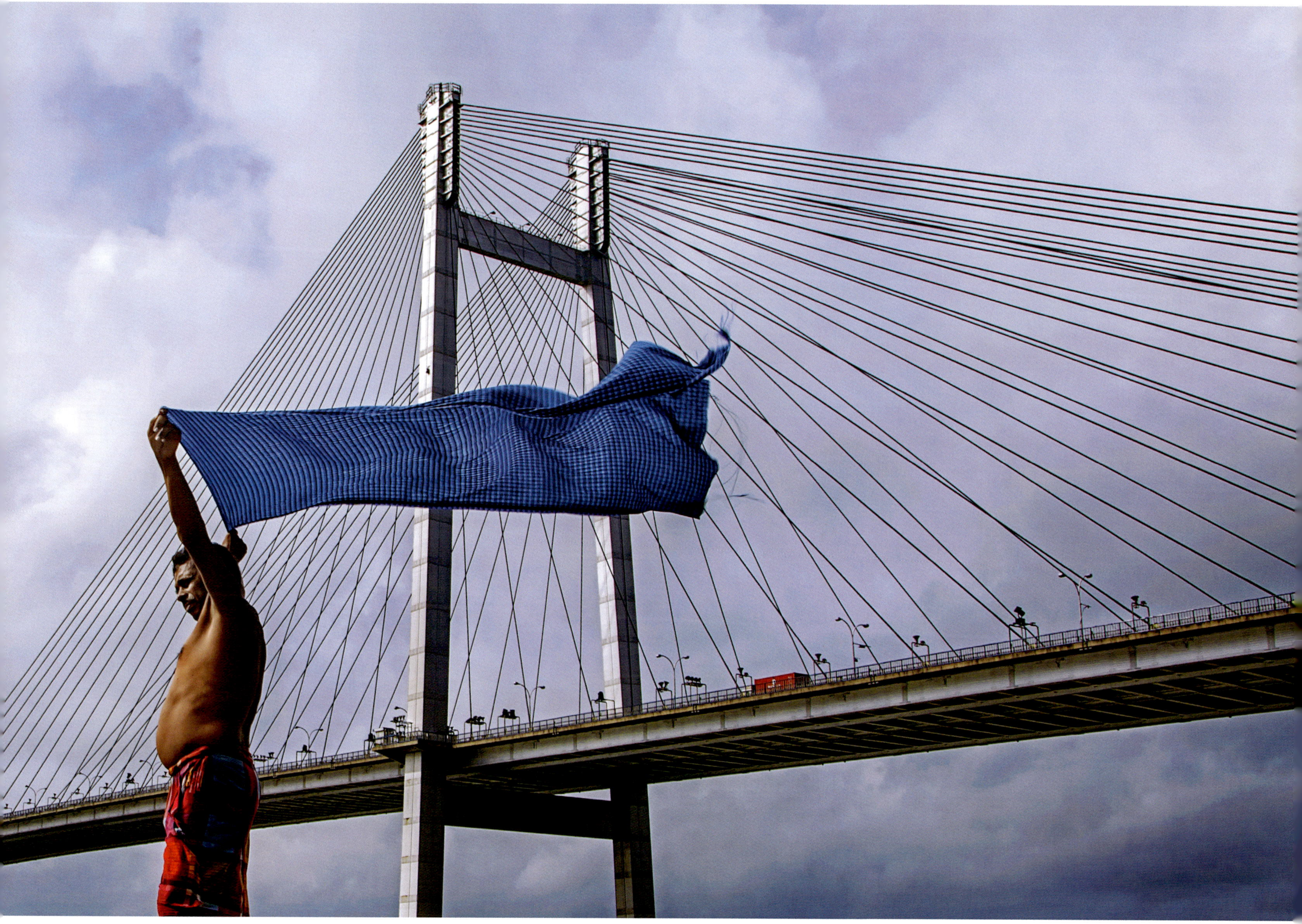

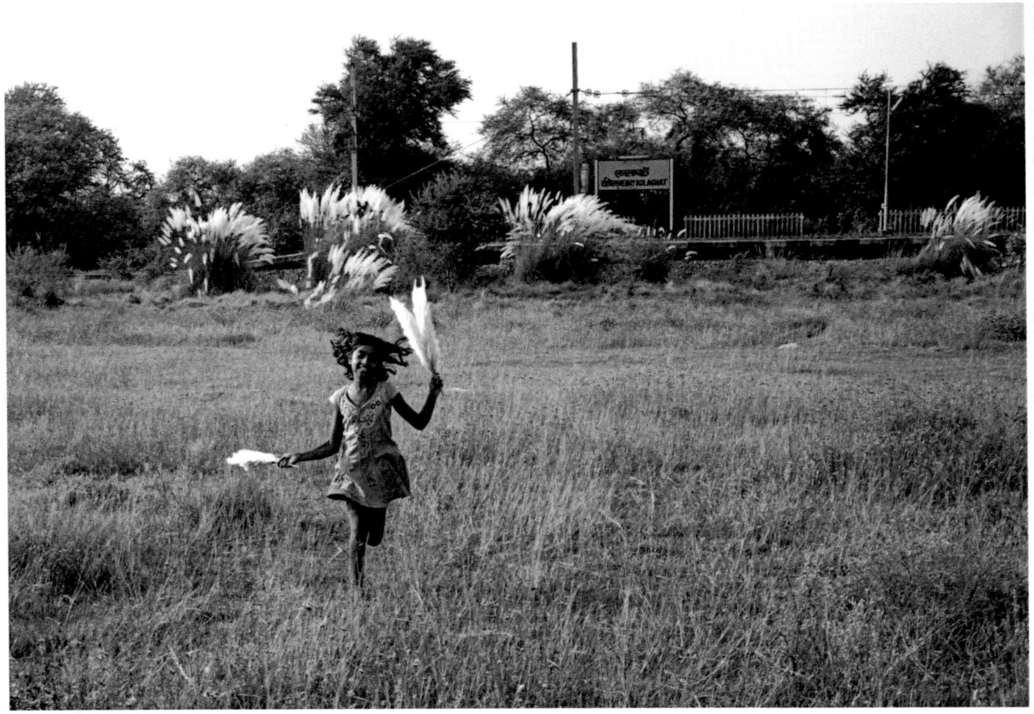

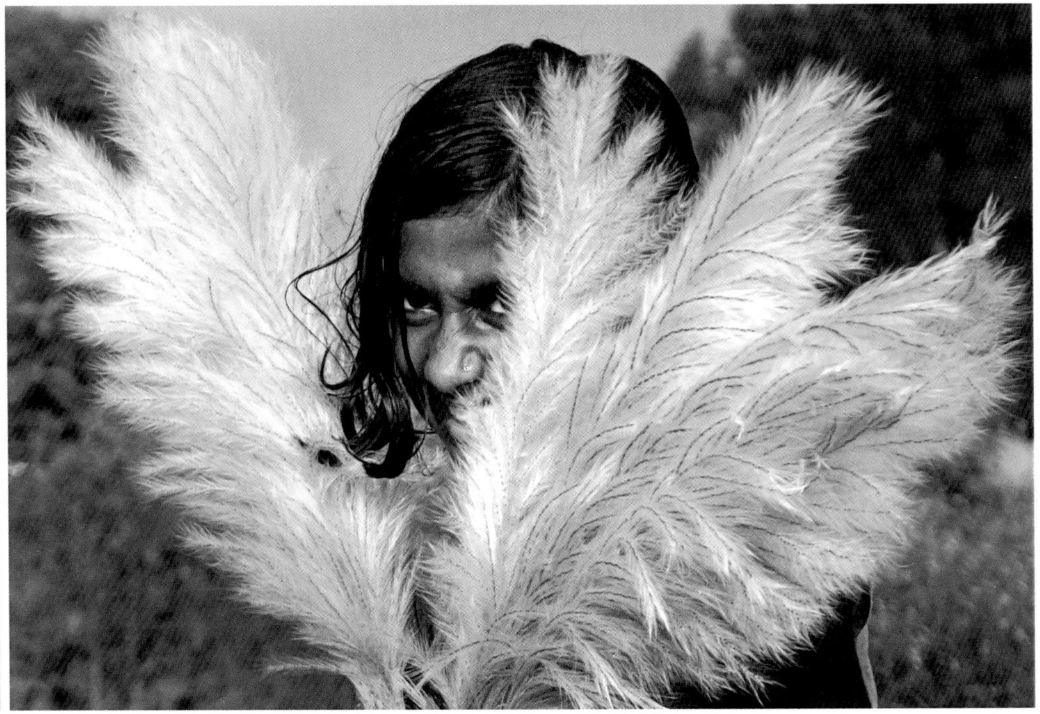

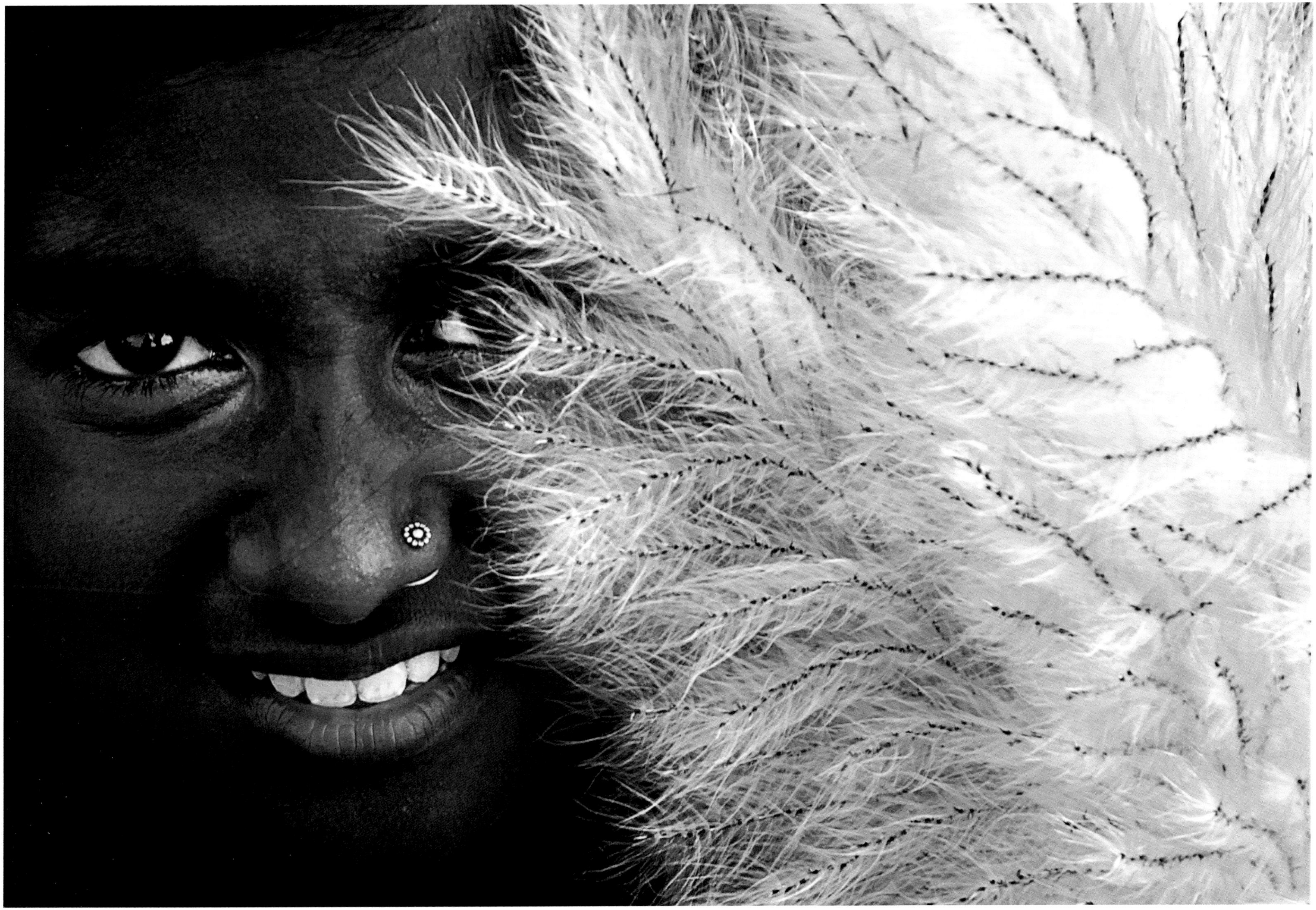

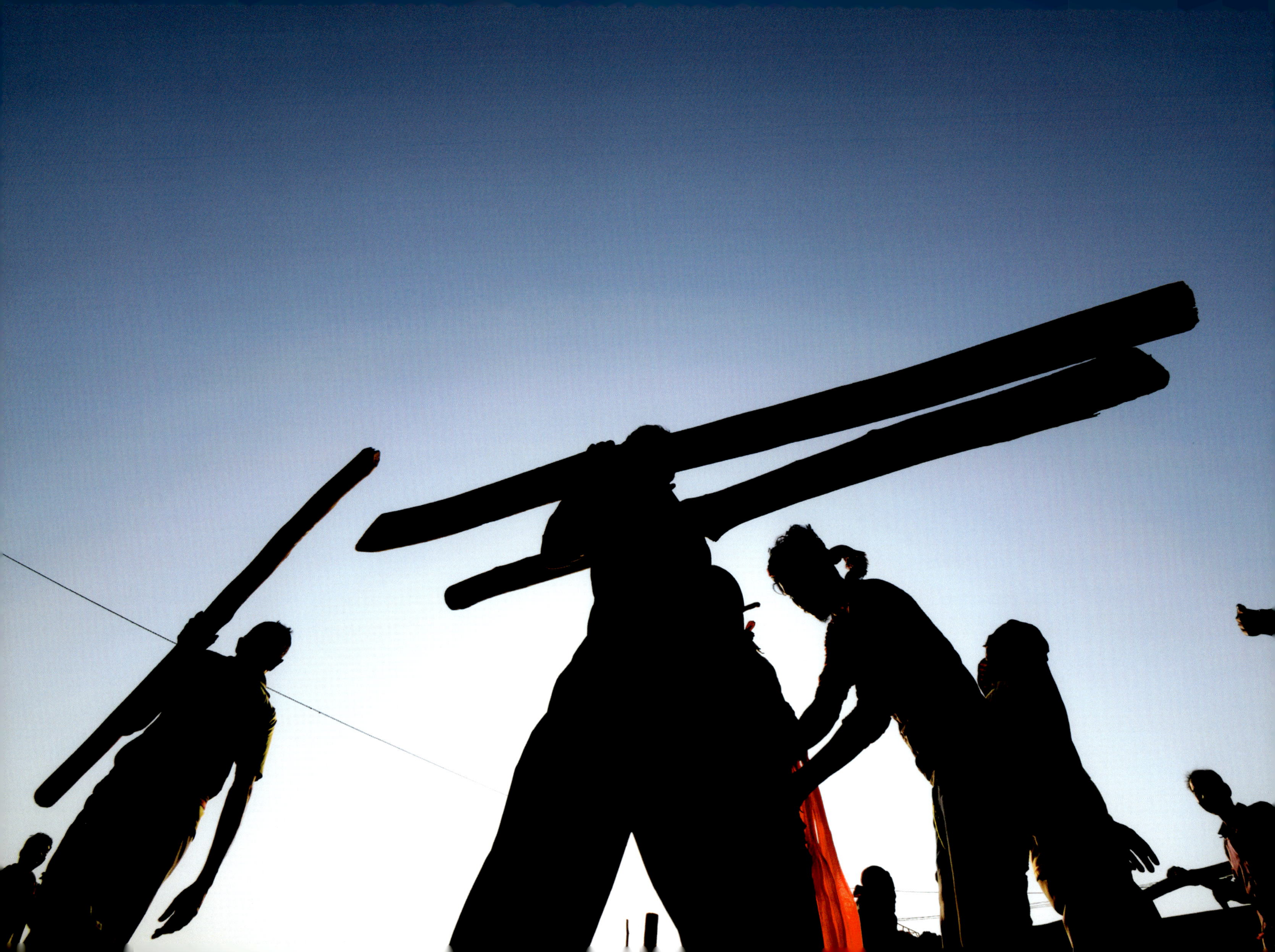

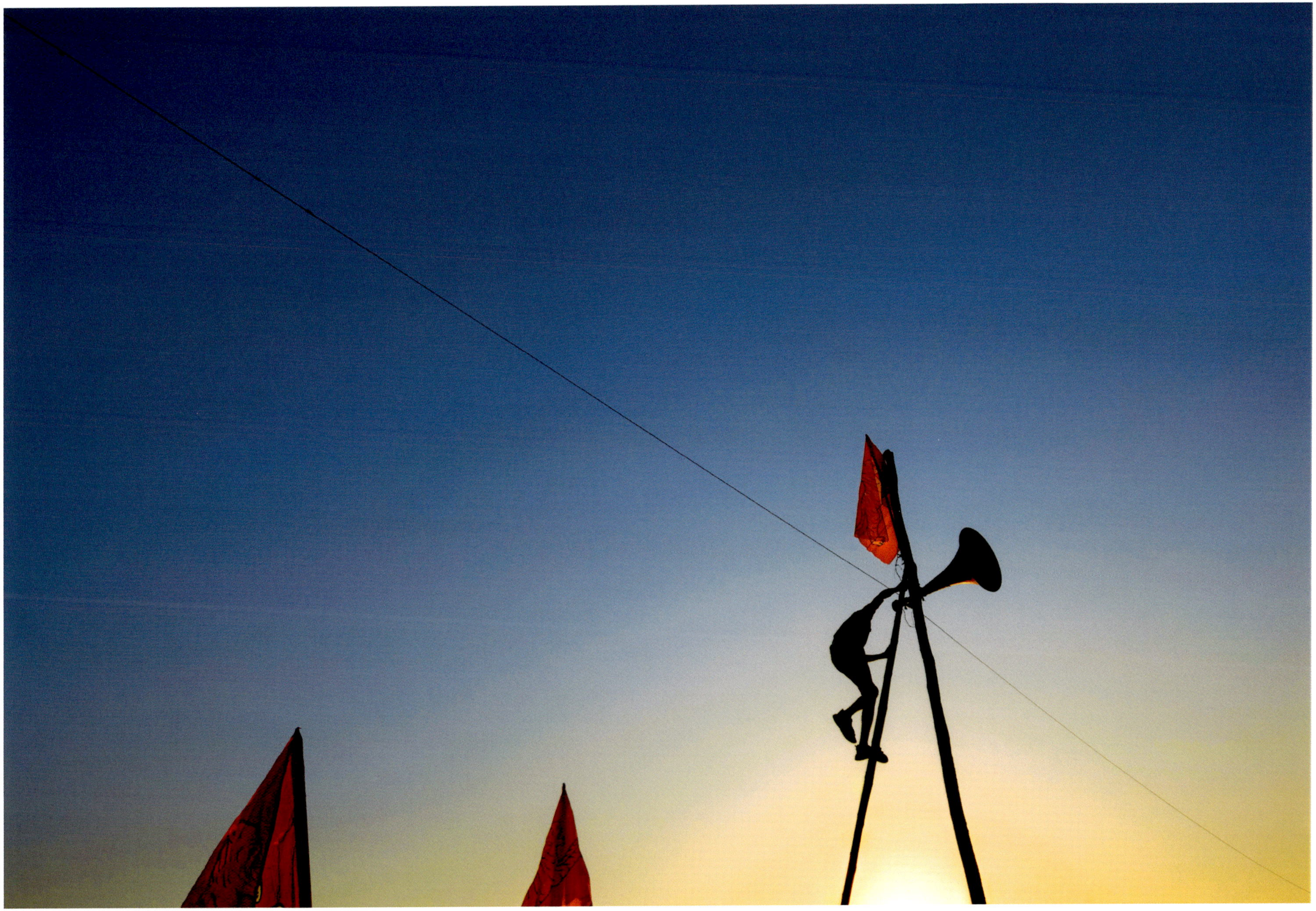

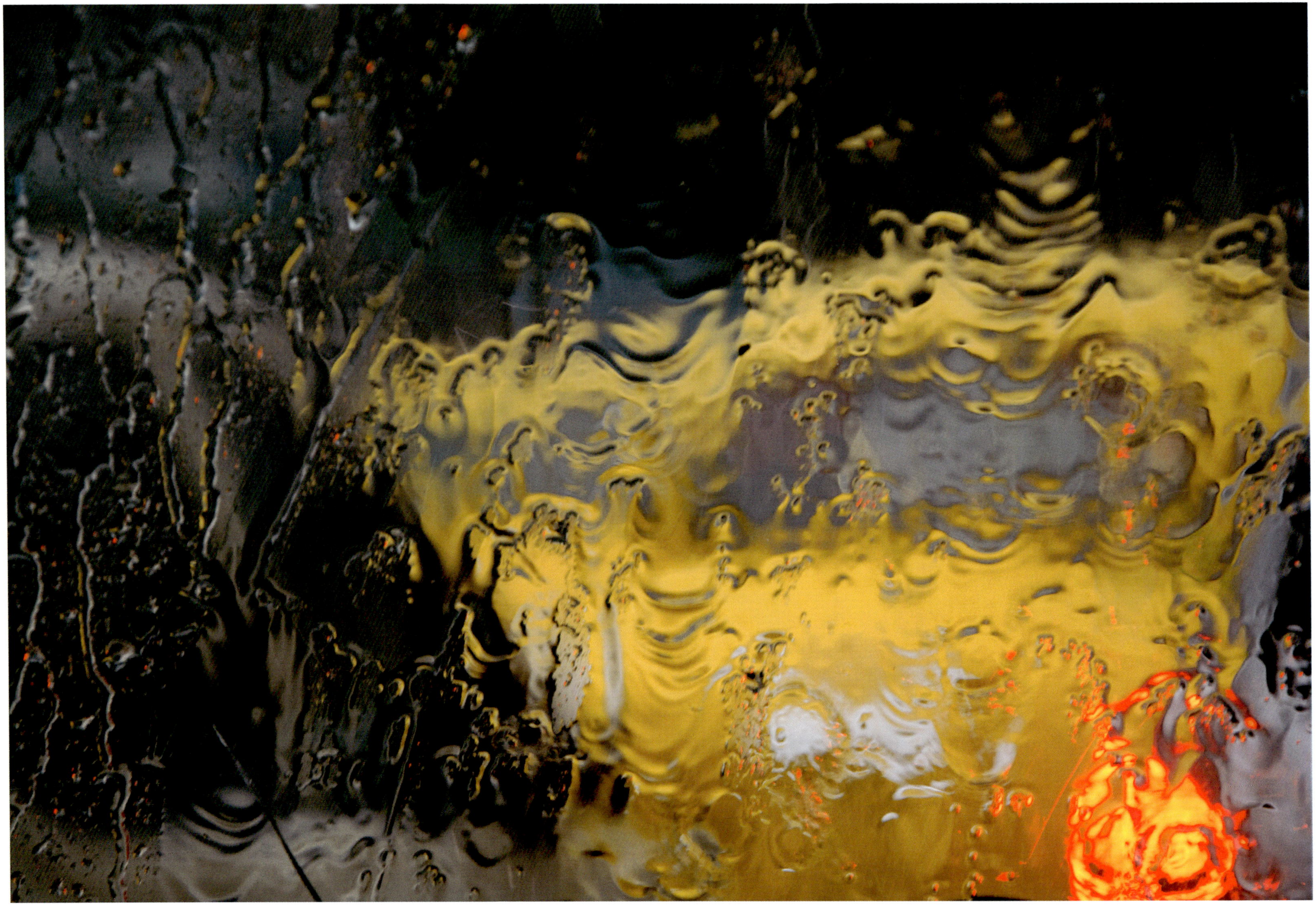

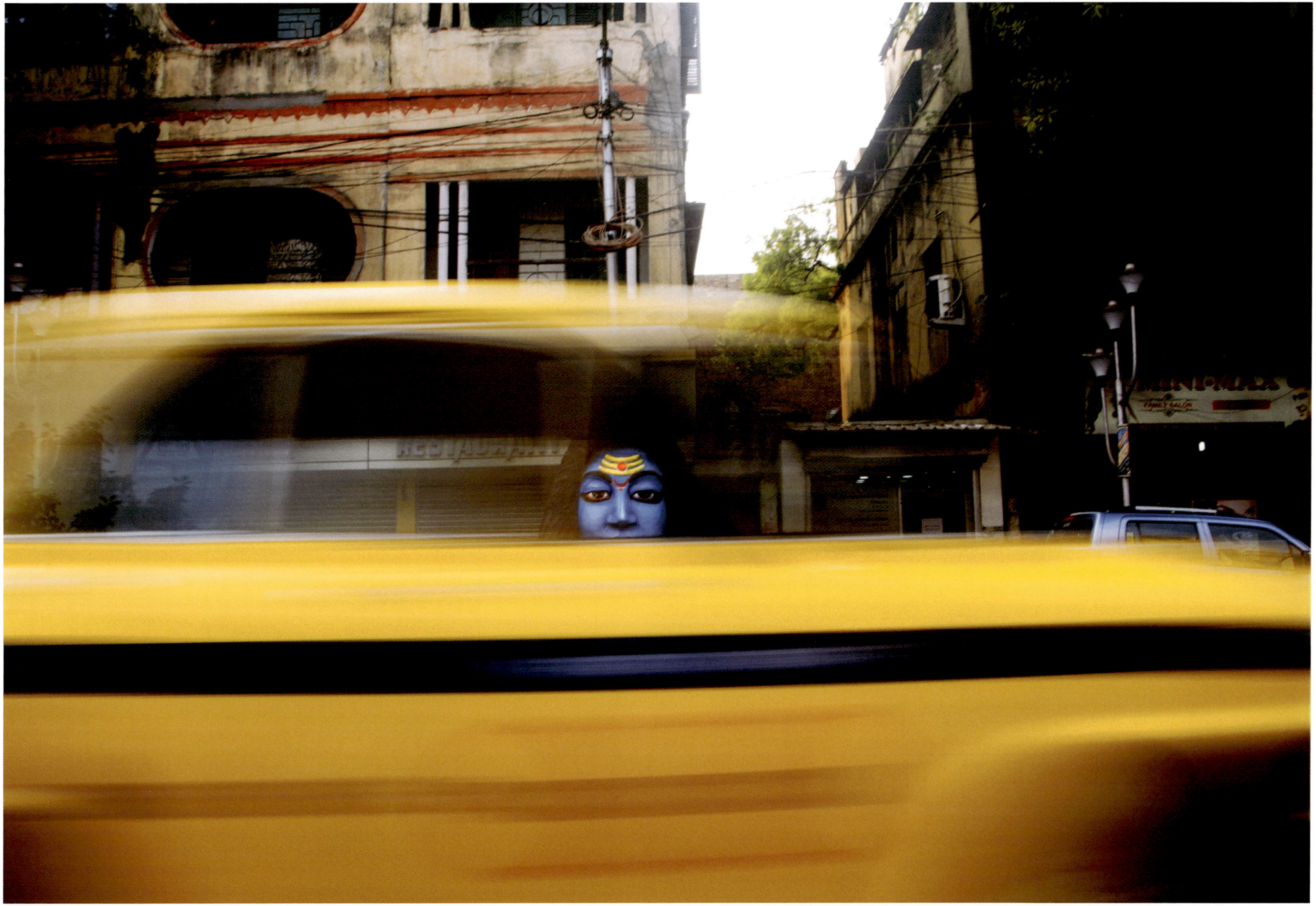

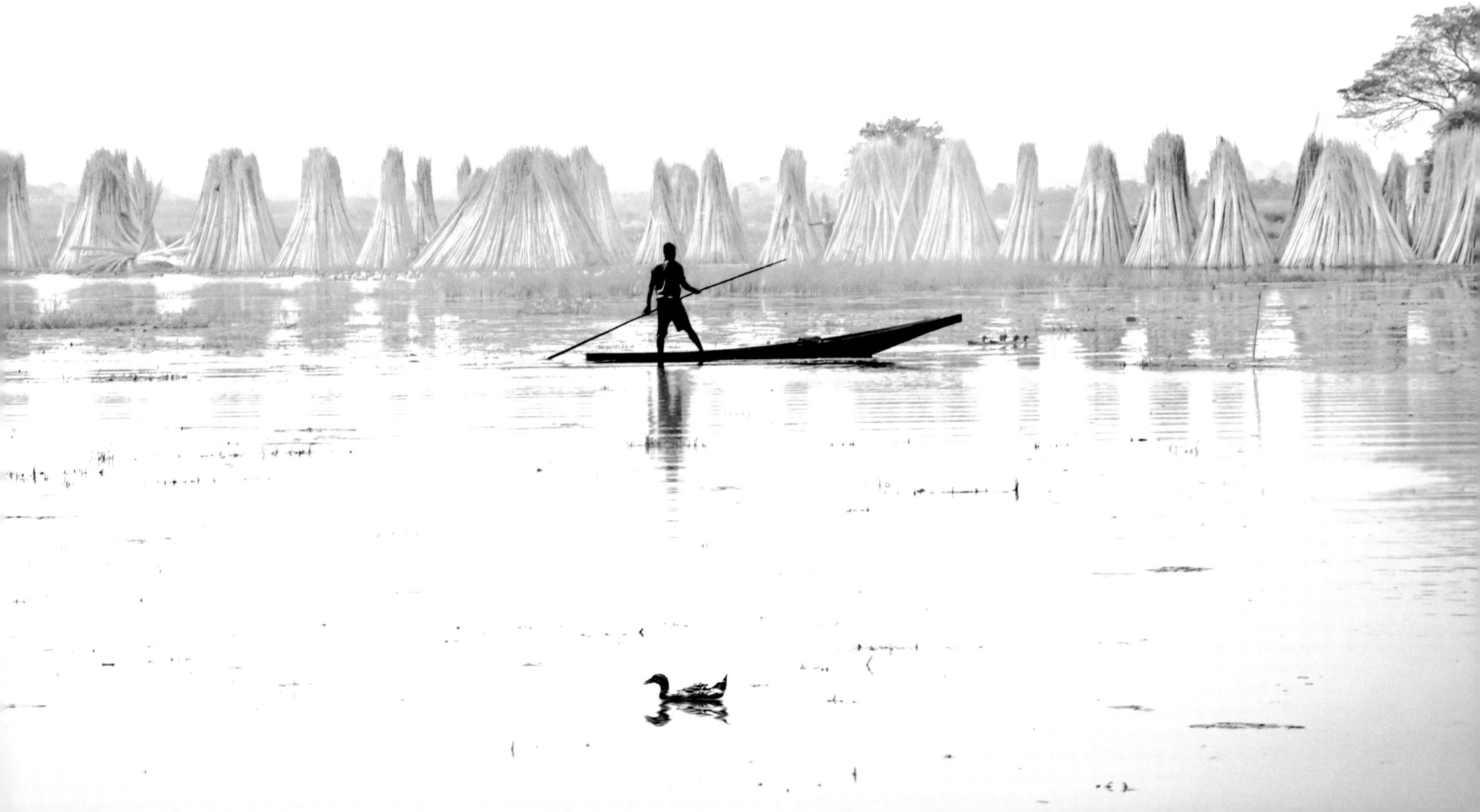

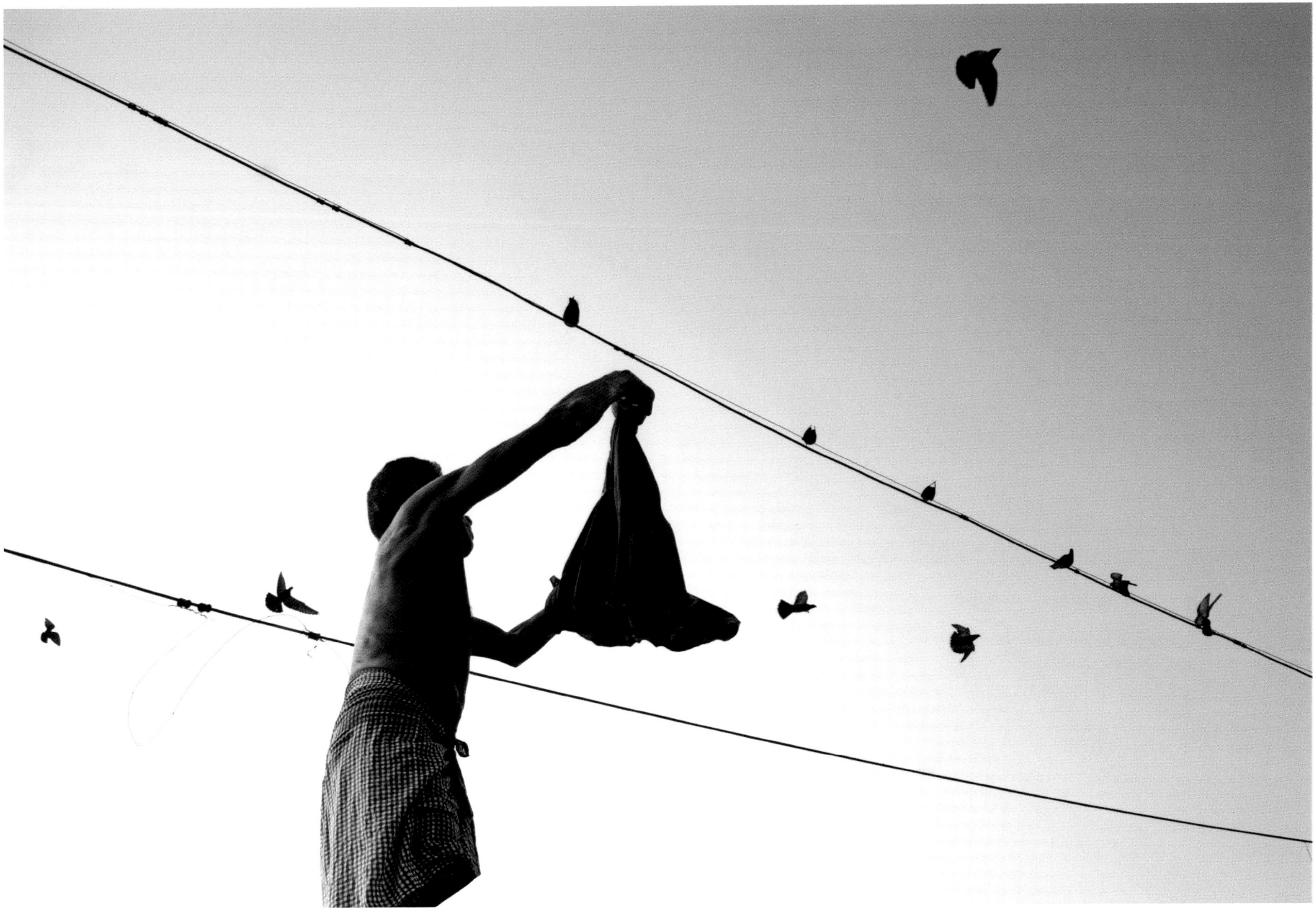

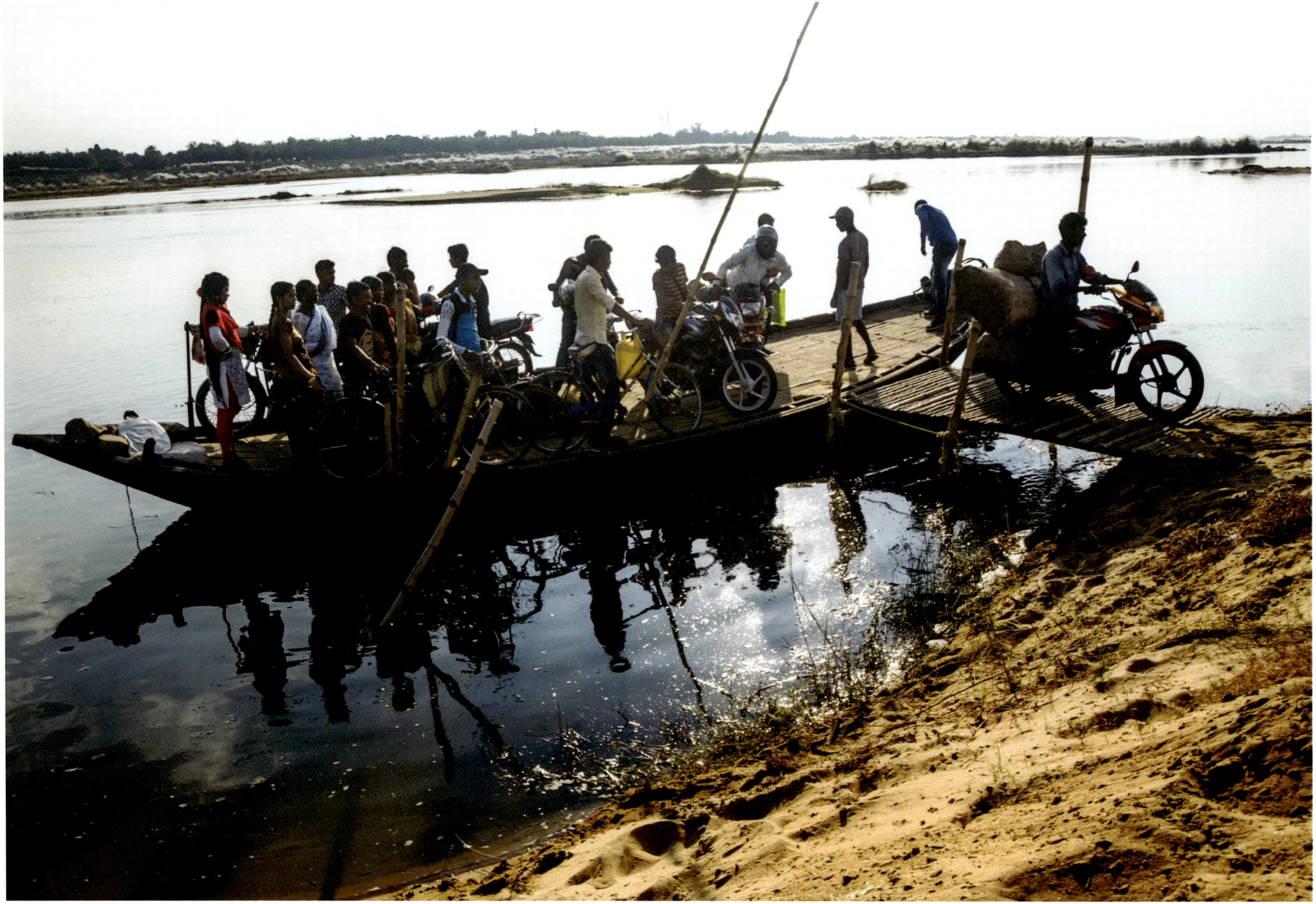

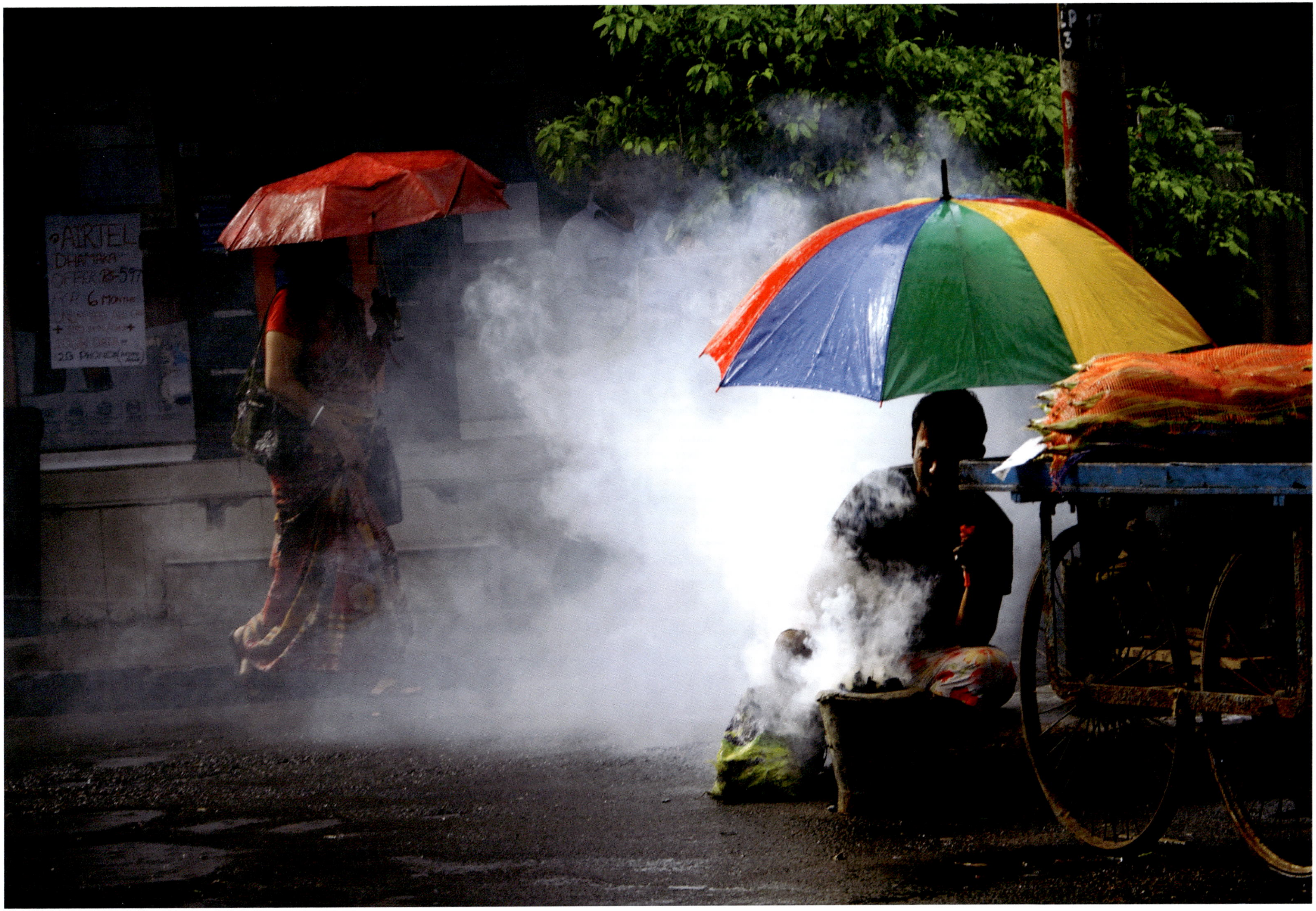
AIRTEL
DHAMAKA
OFFER
6 Months
2G PHONES

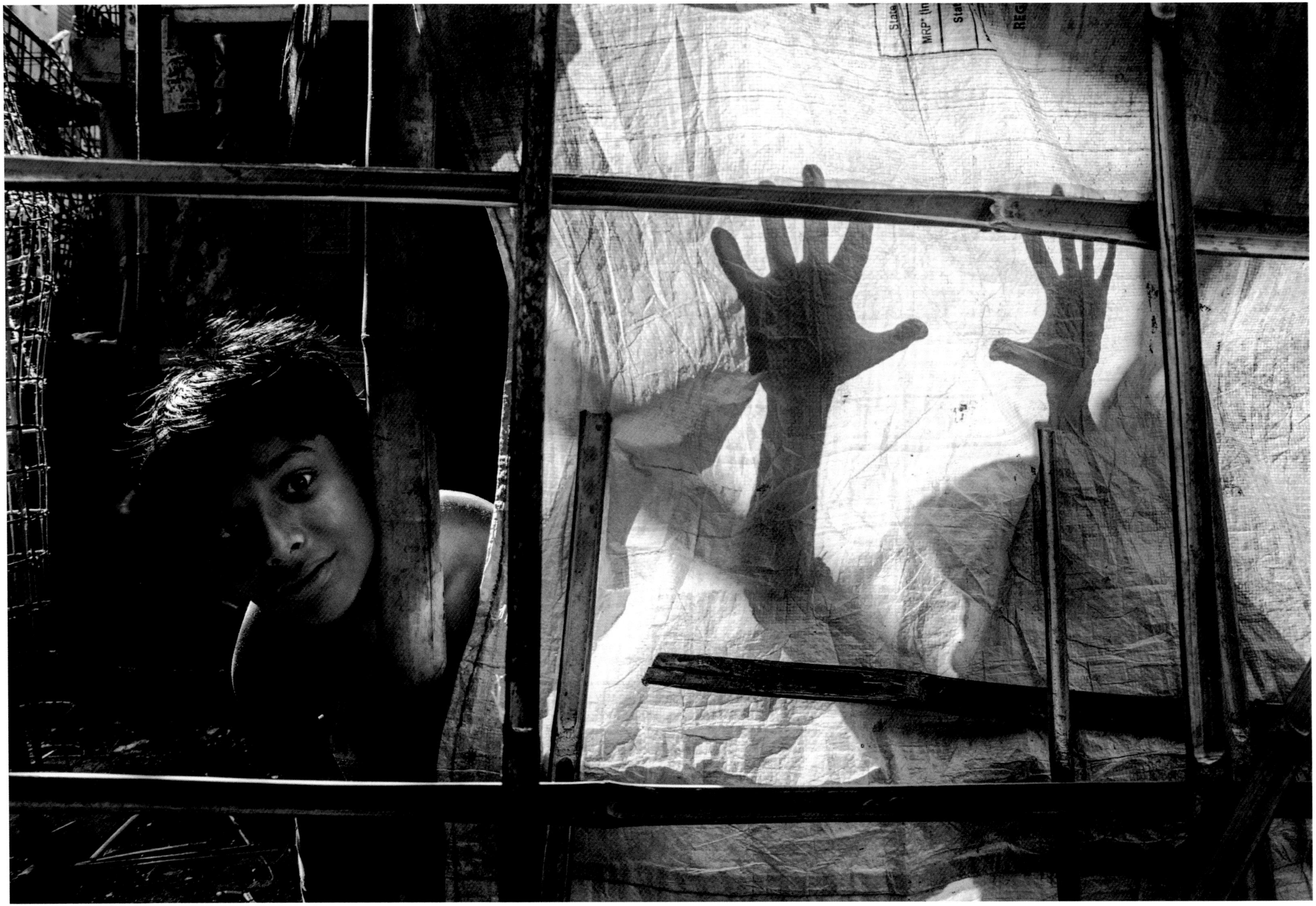

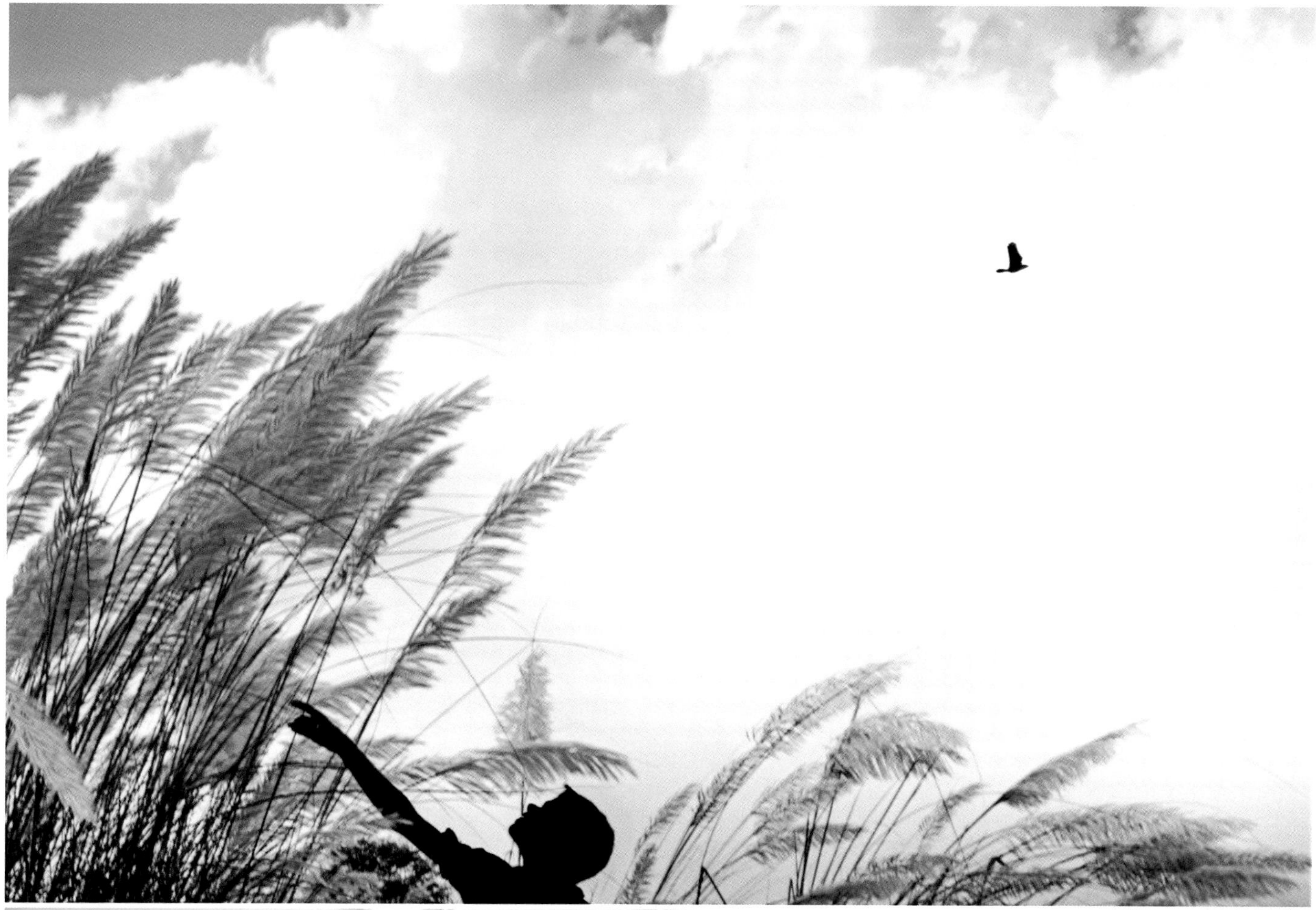

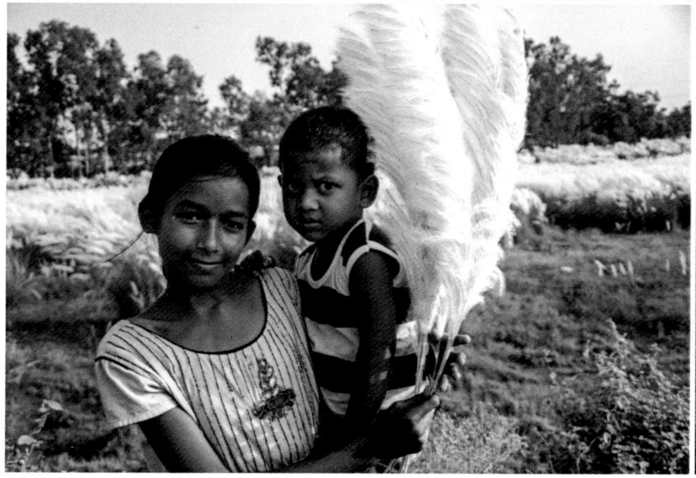

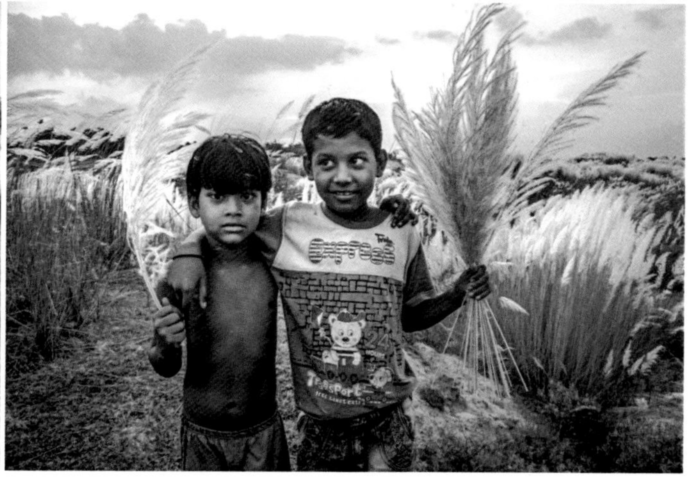

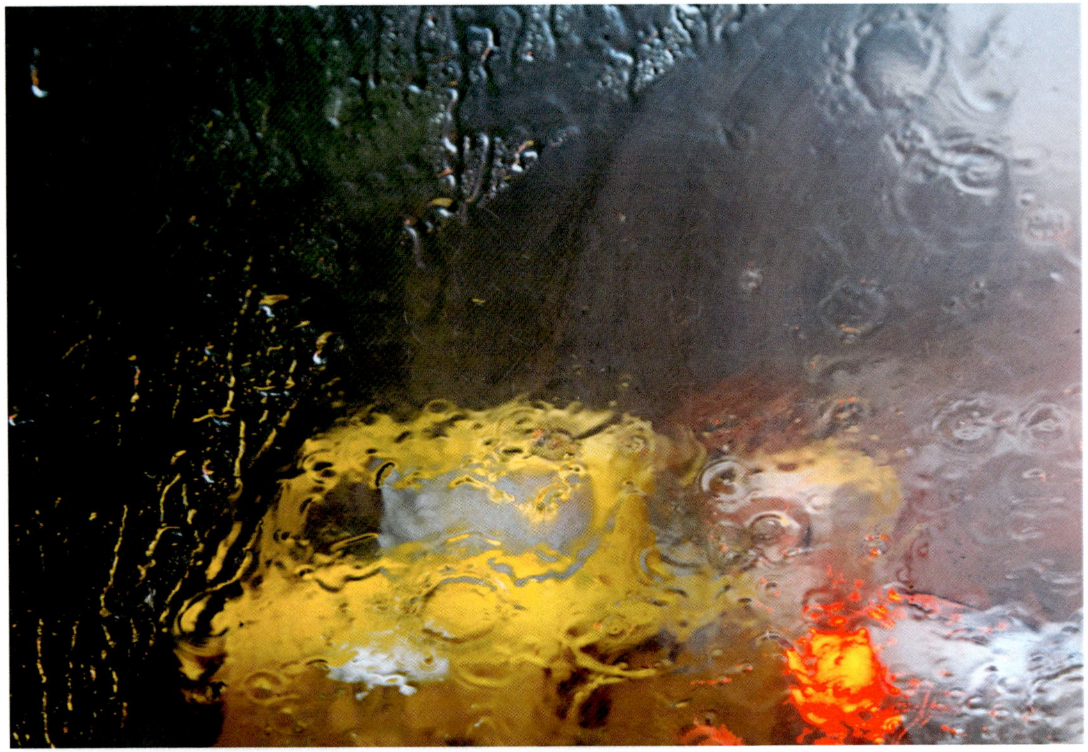
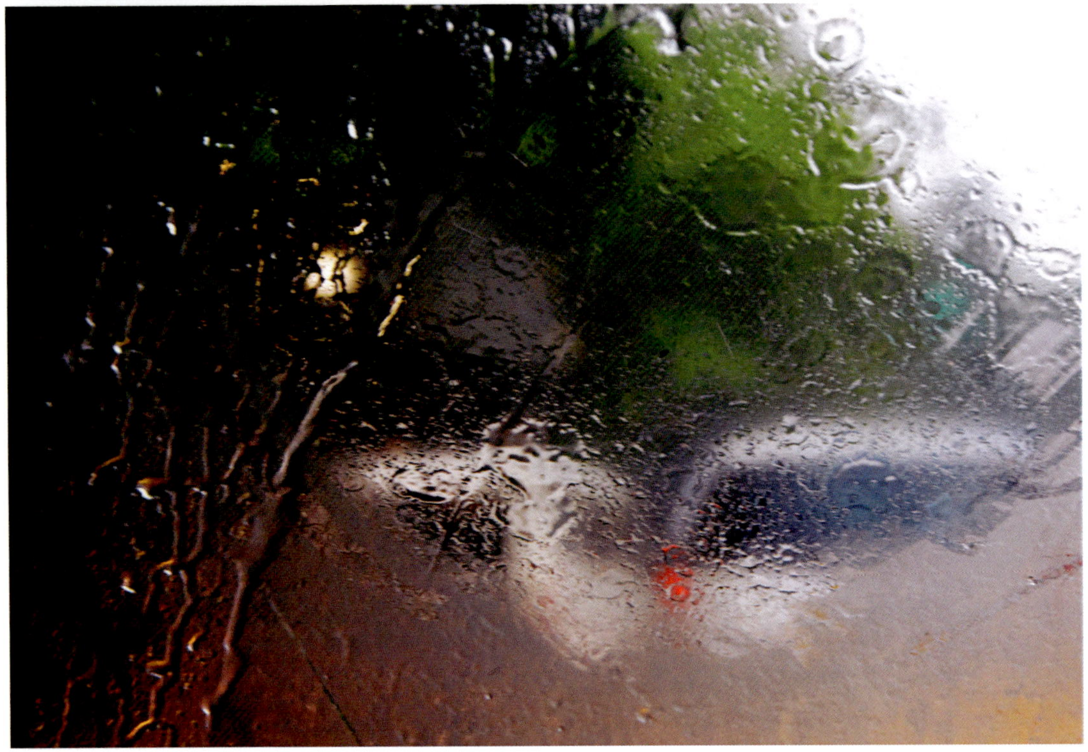

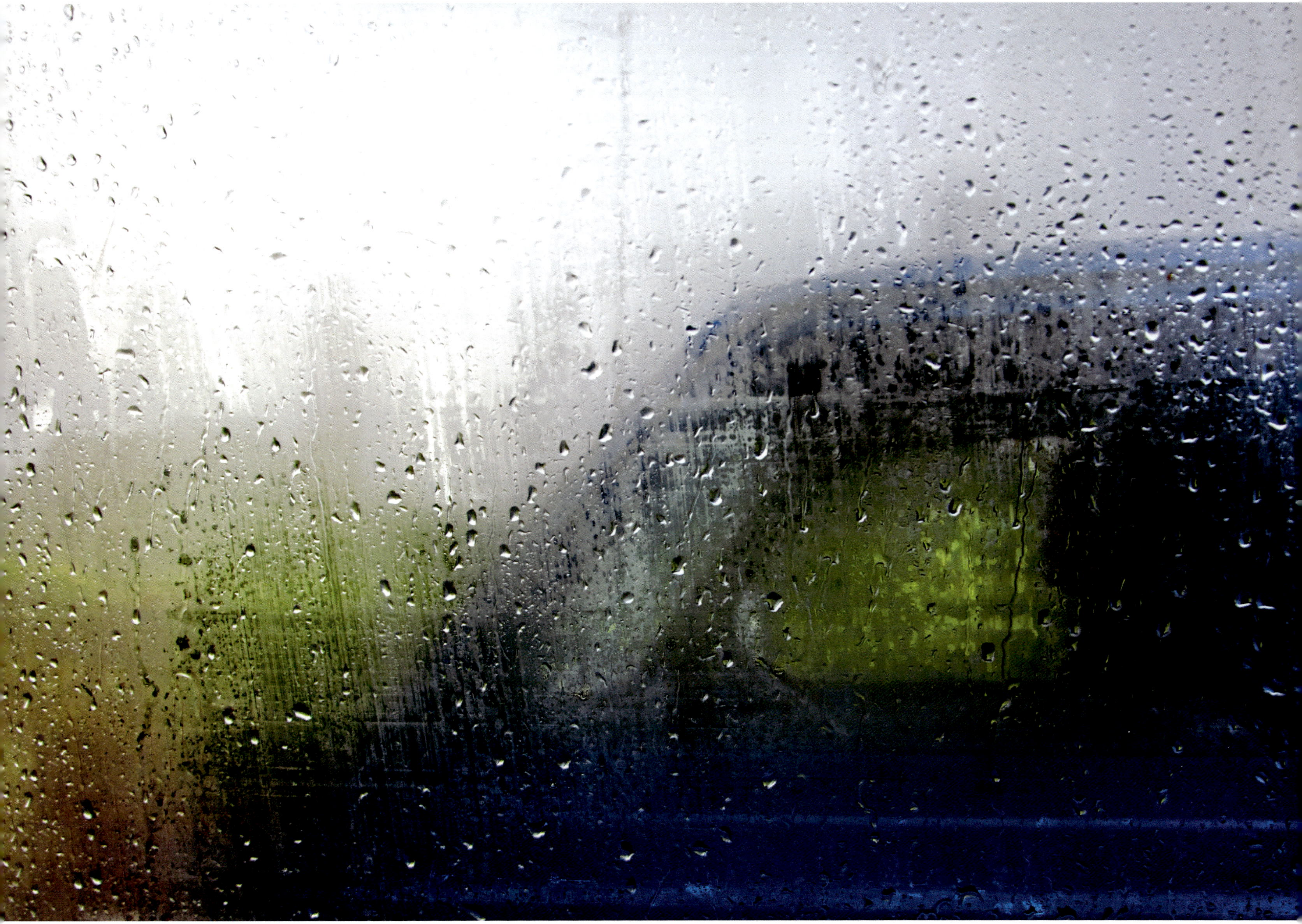

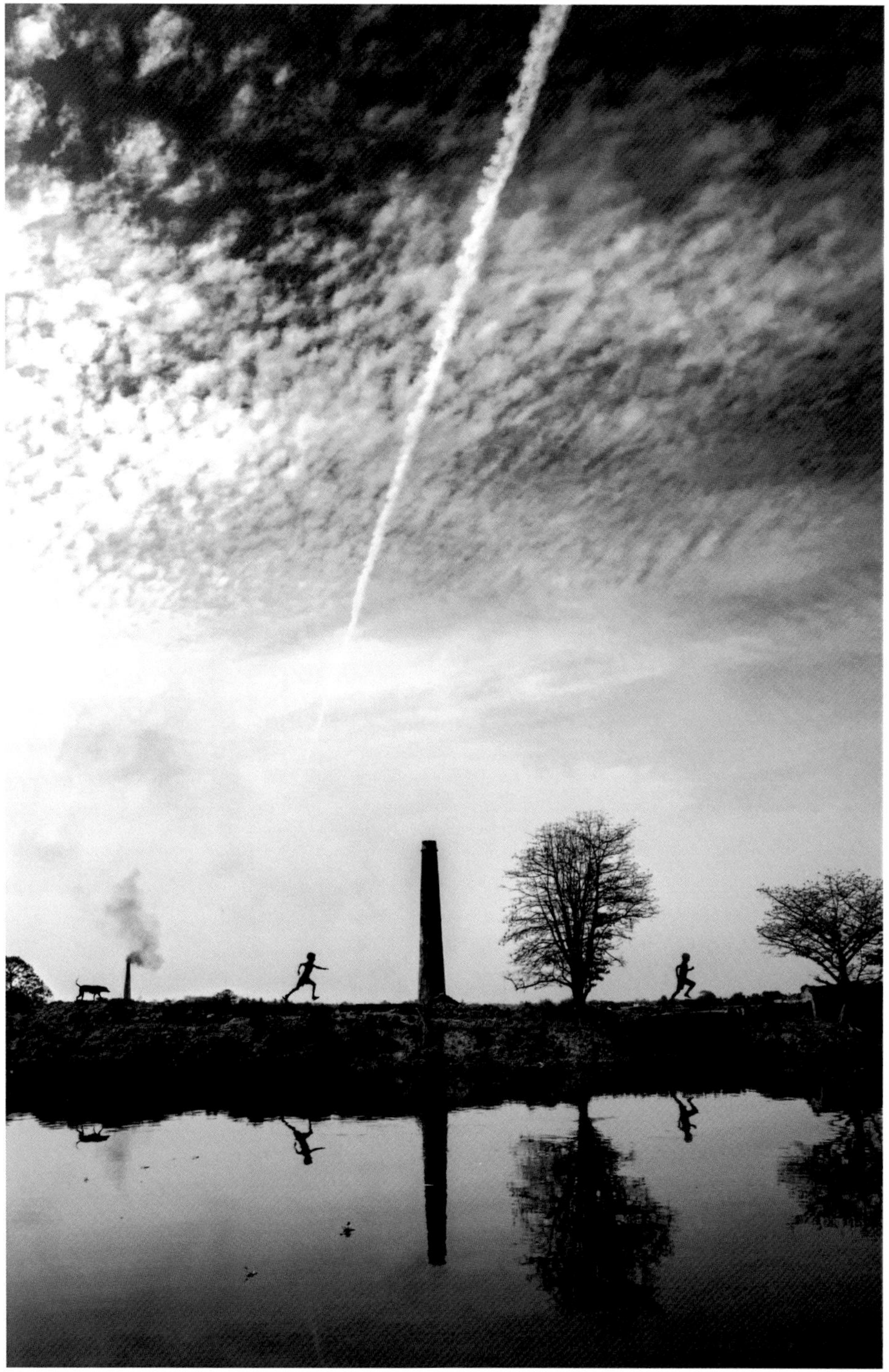

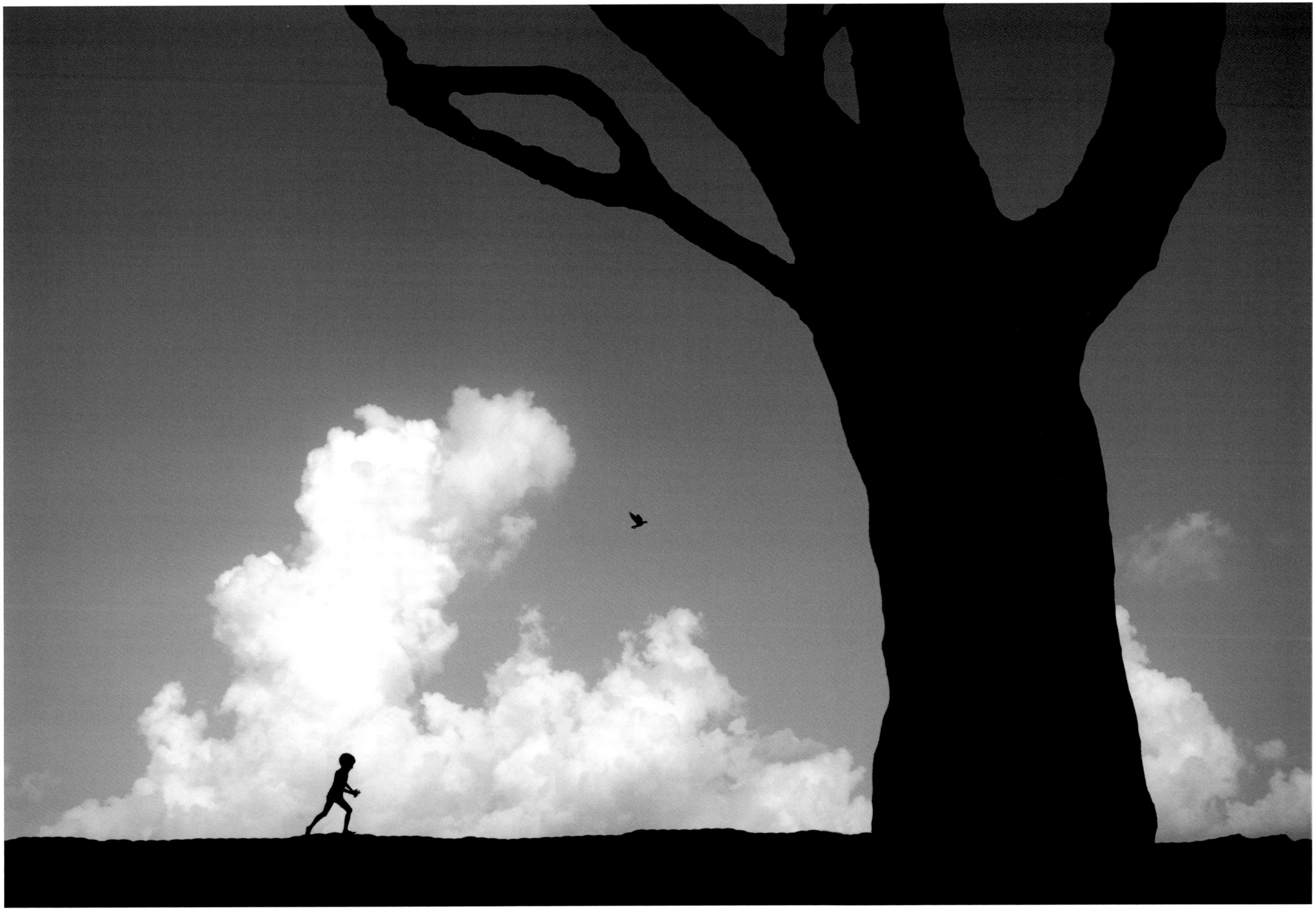

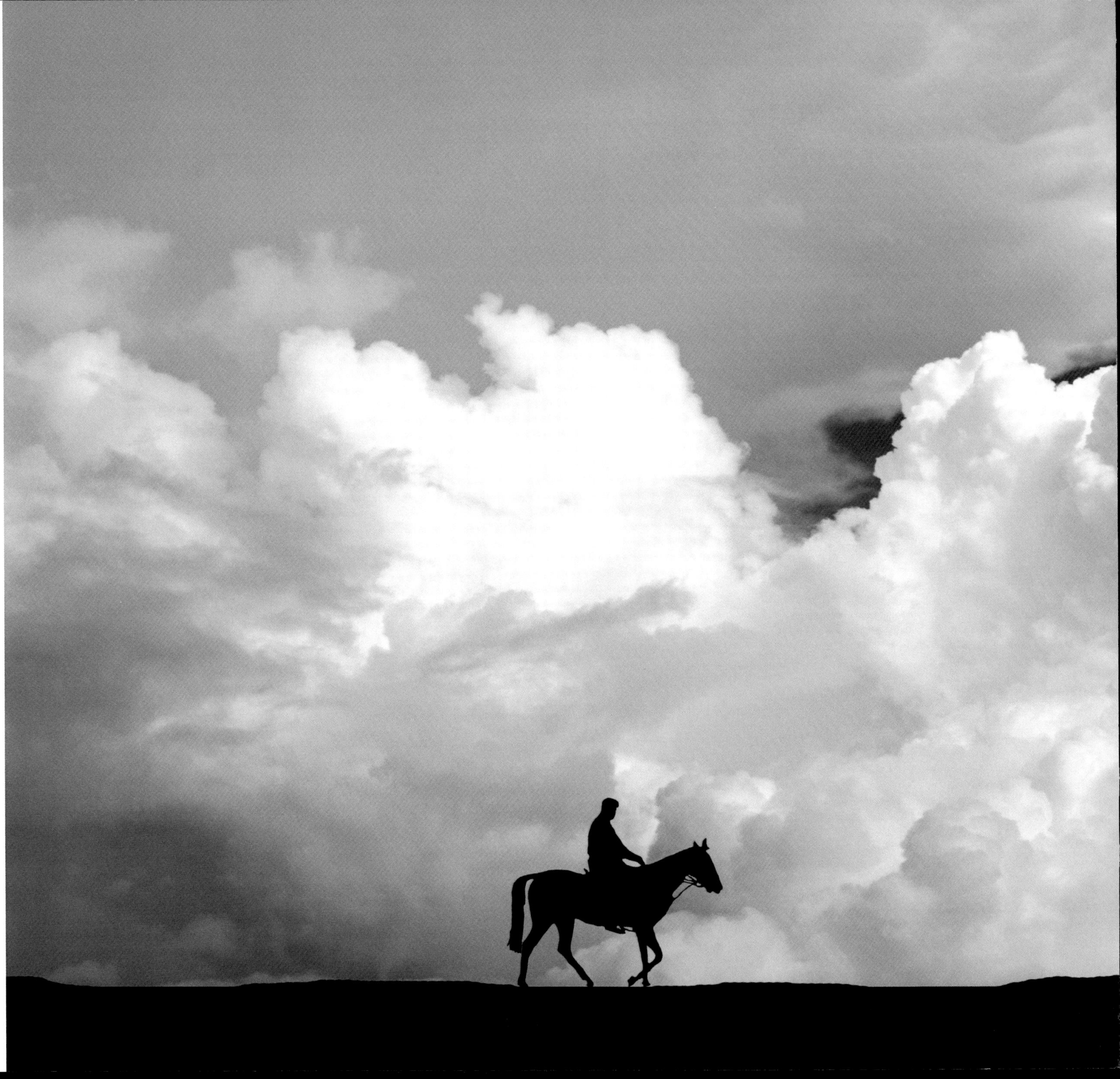

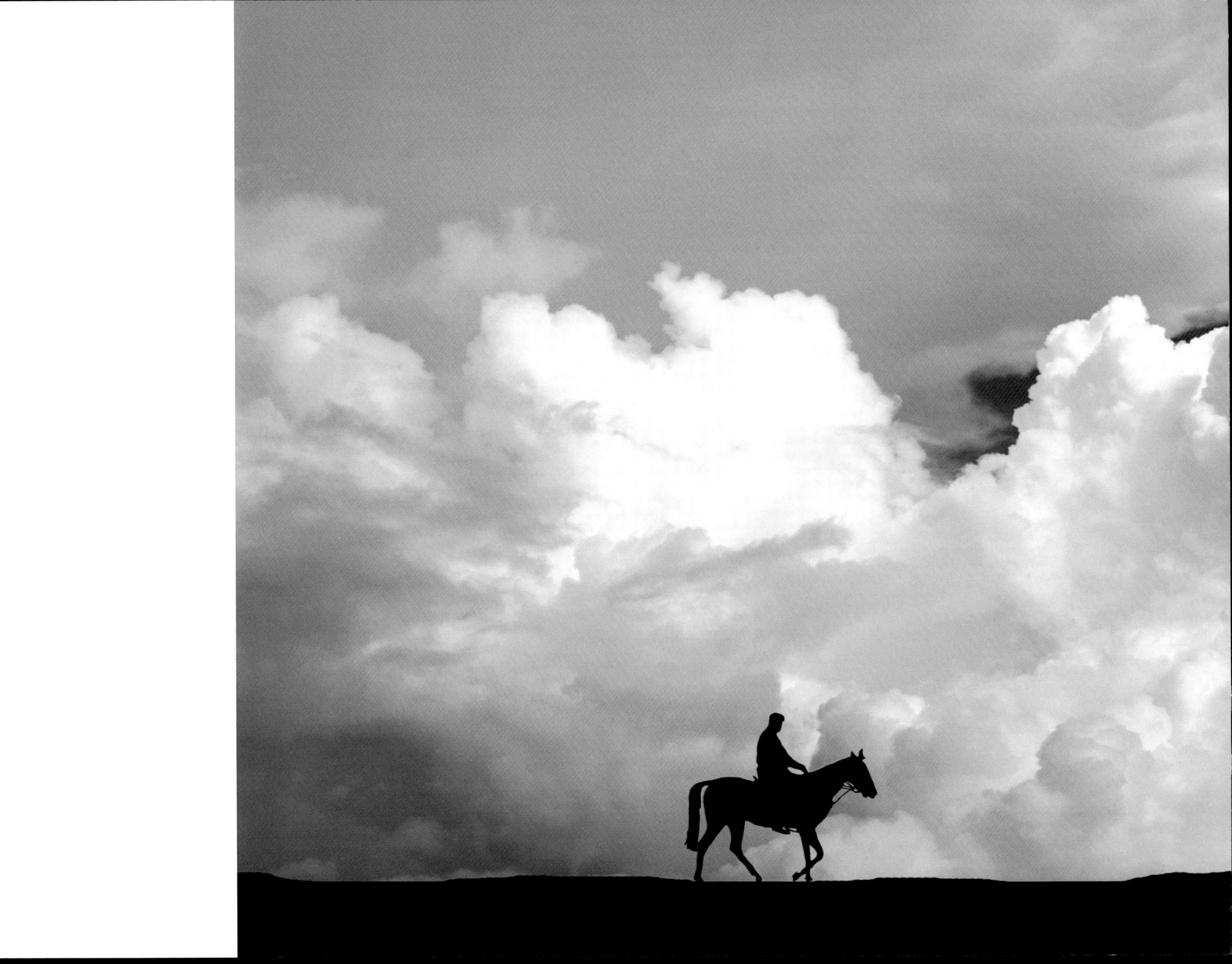

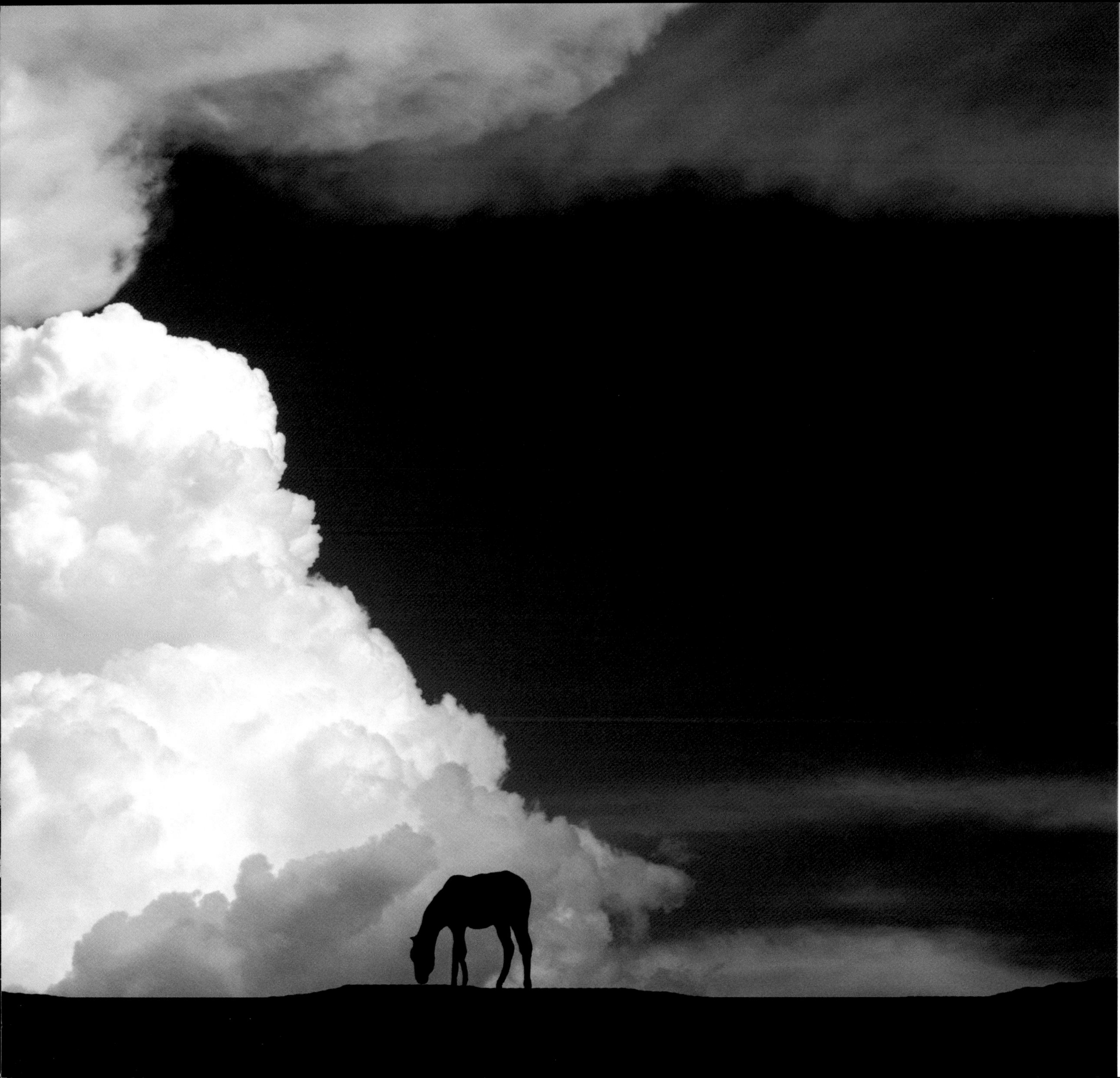

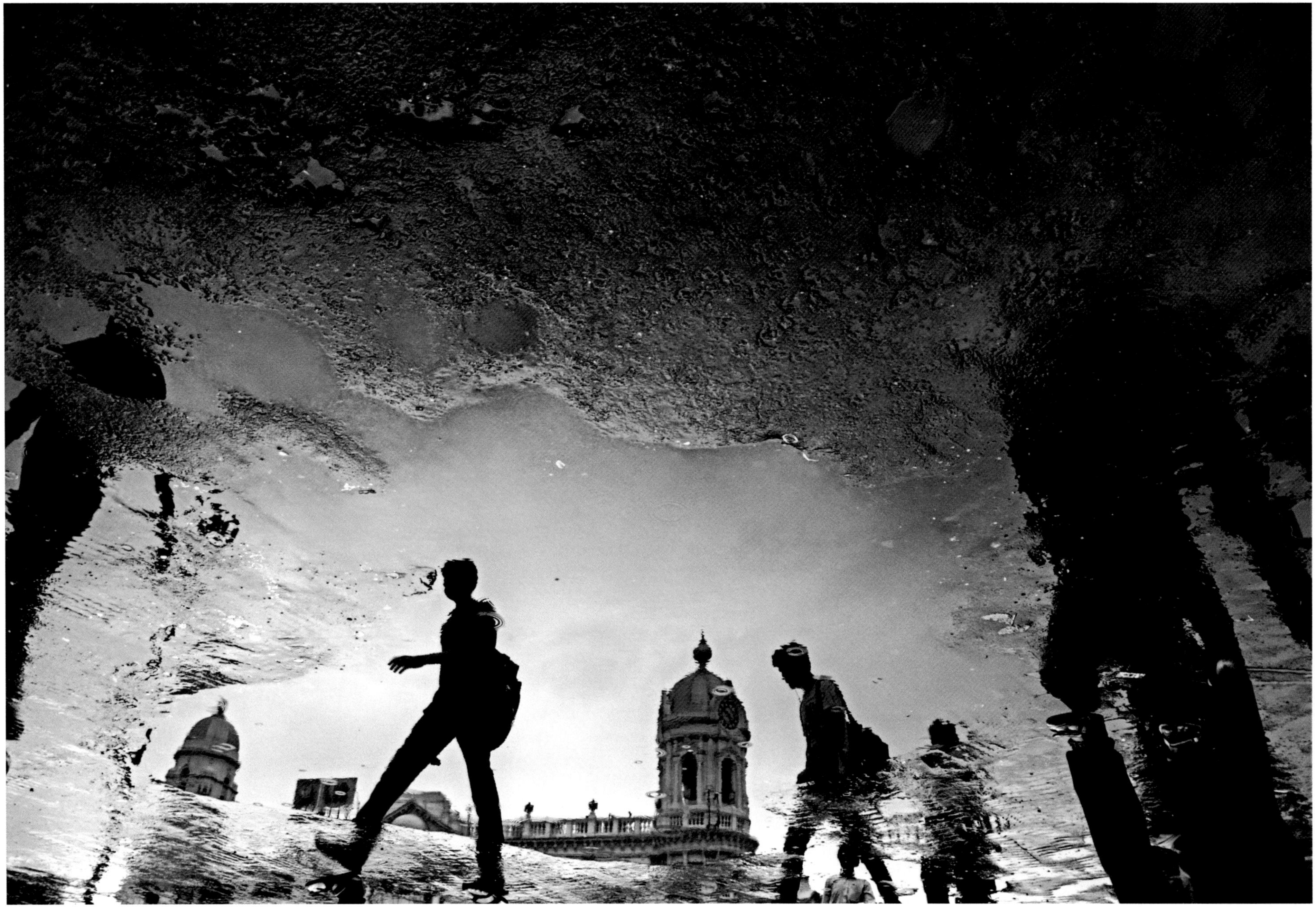

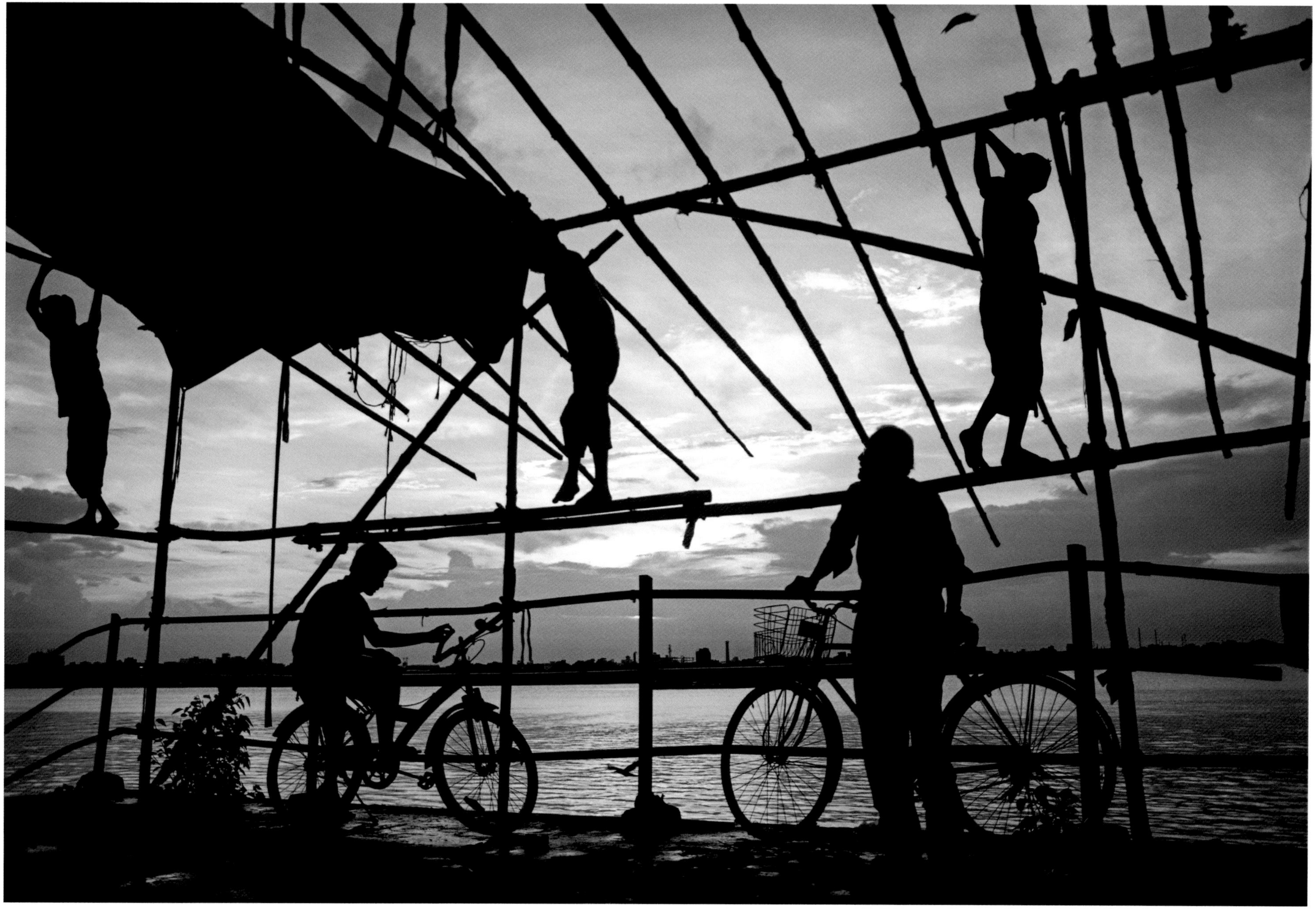

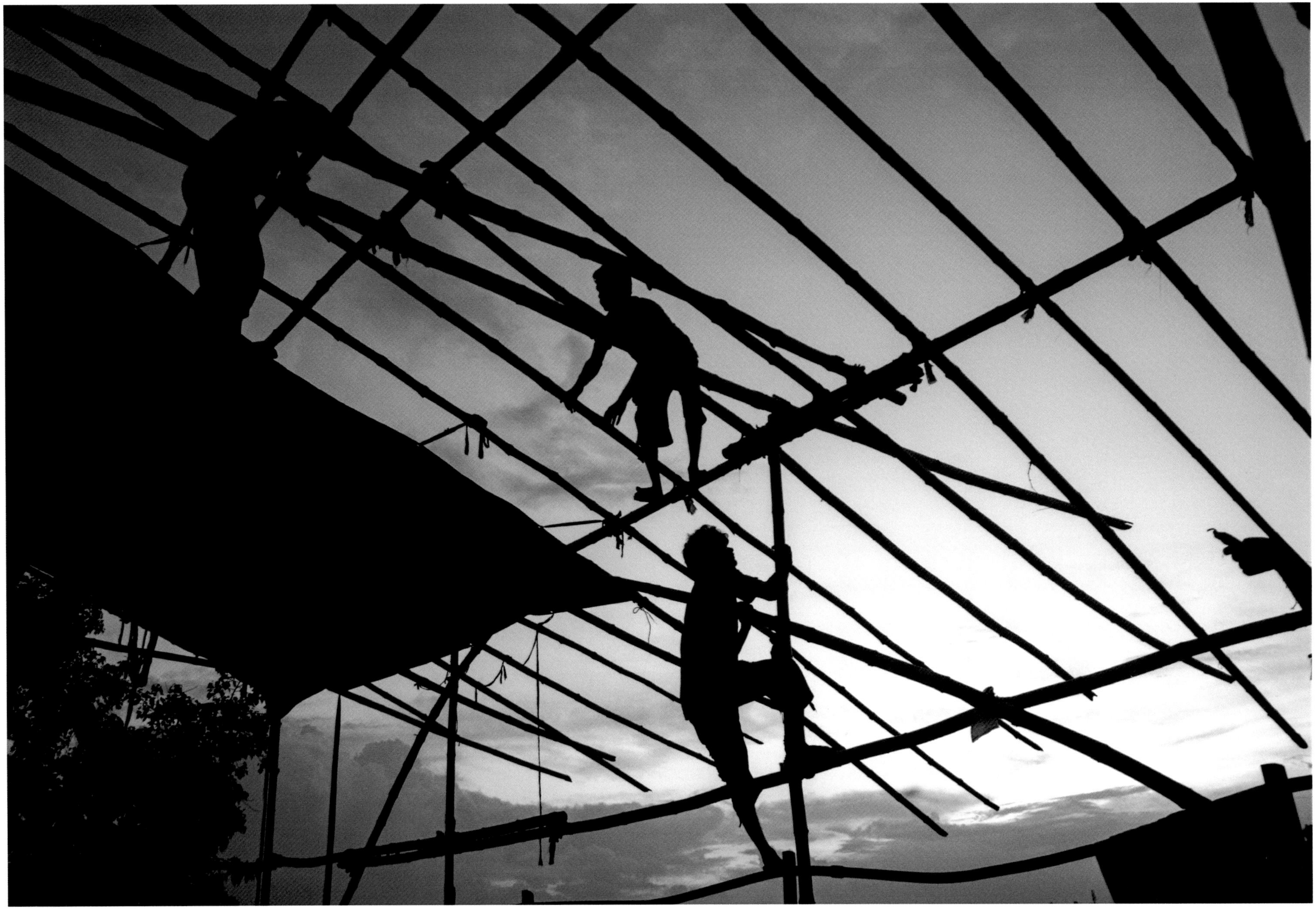

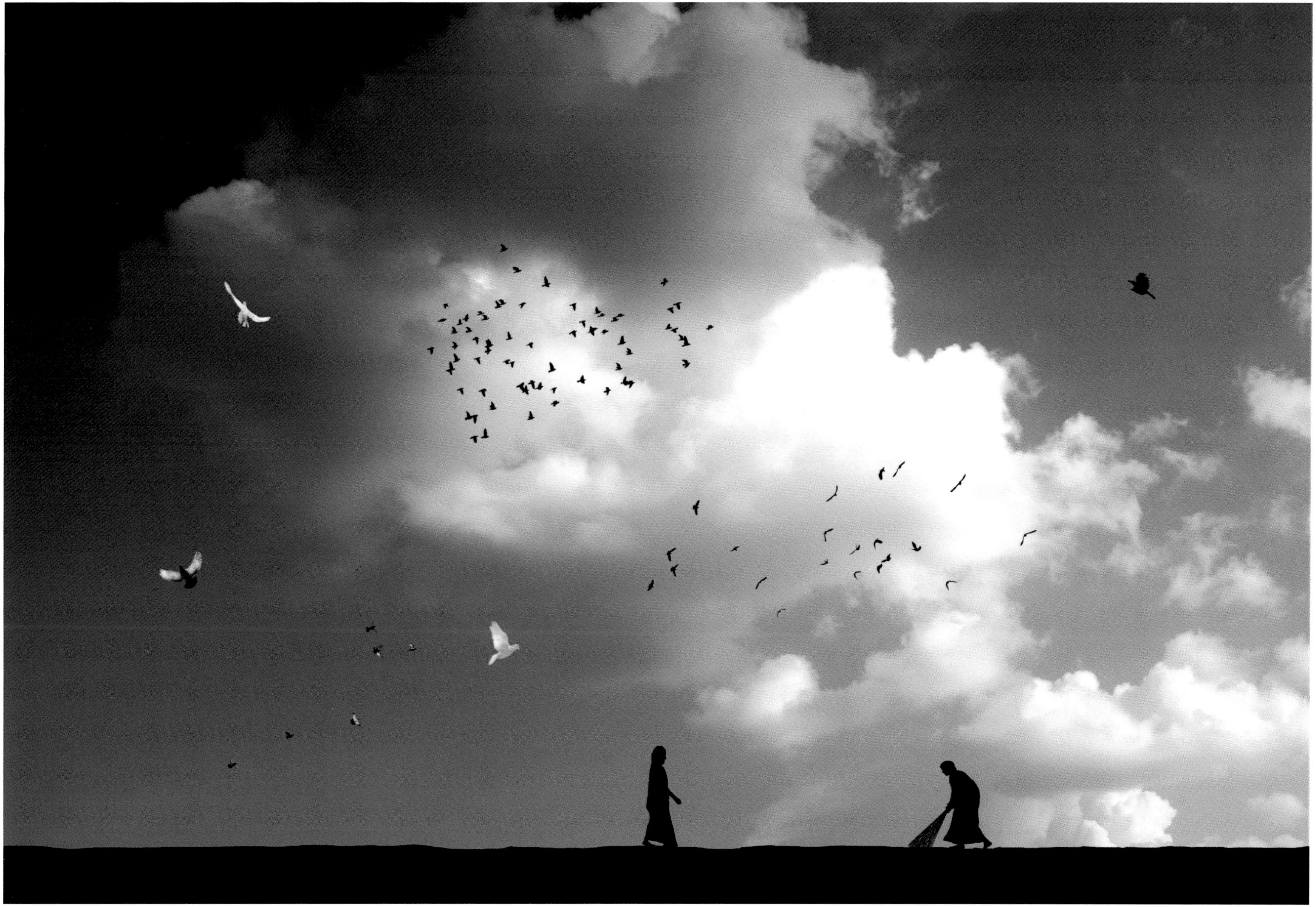

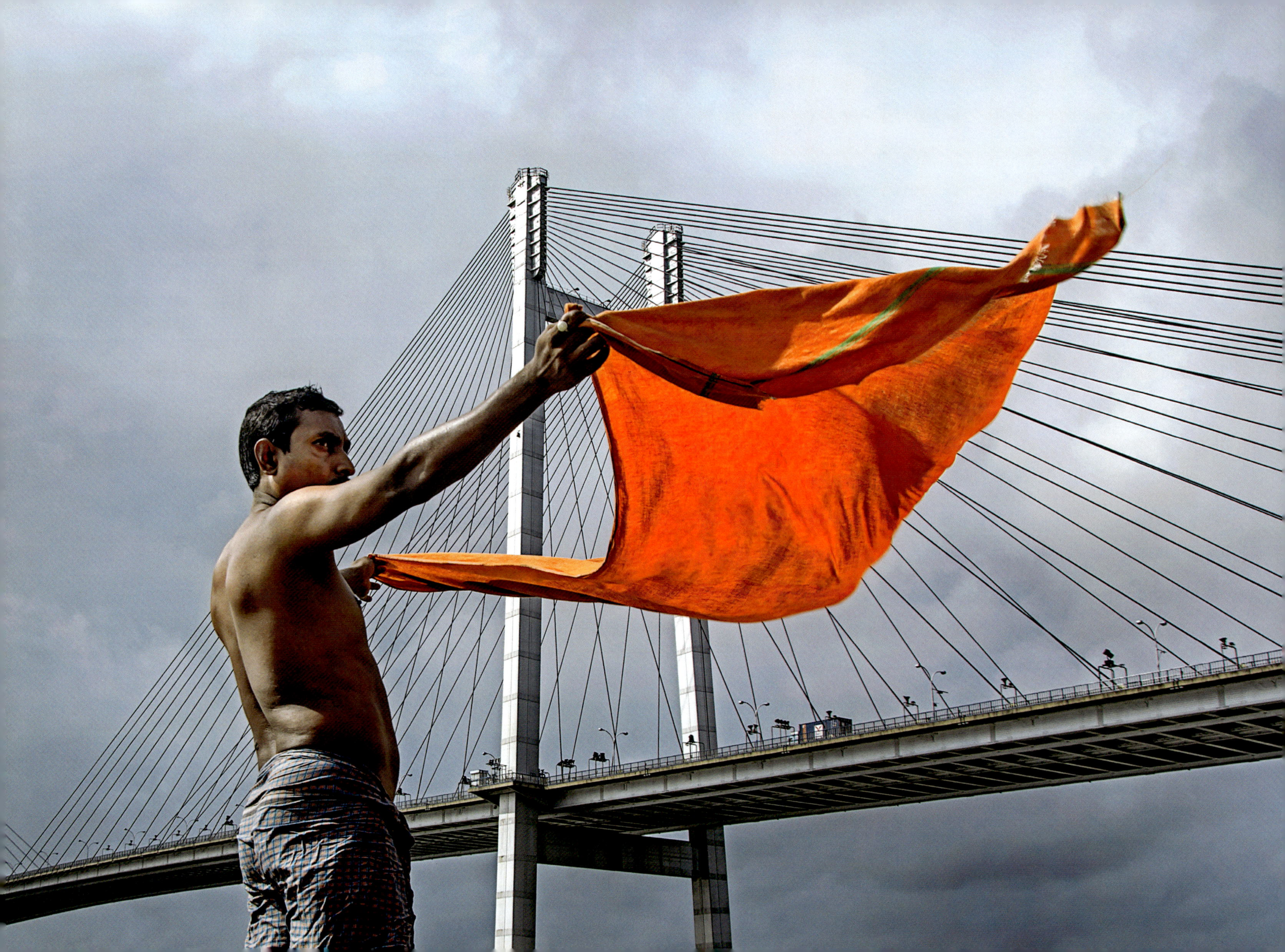

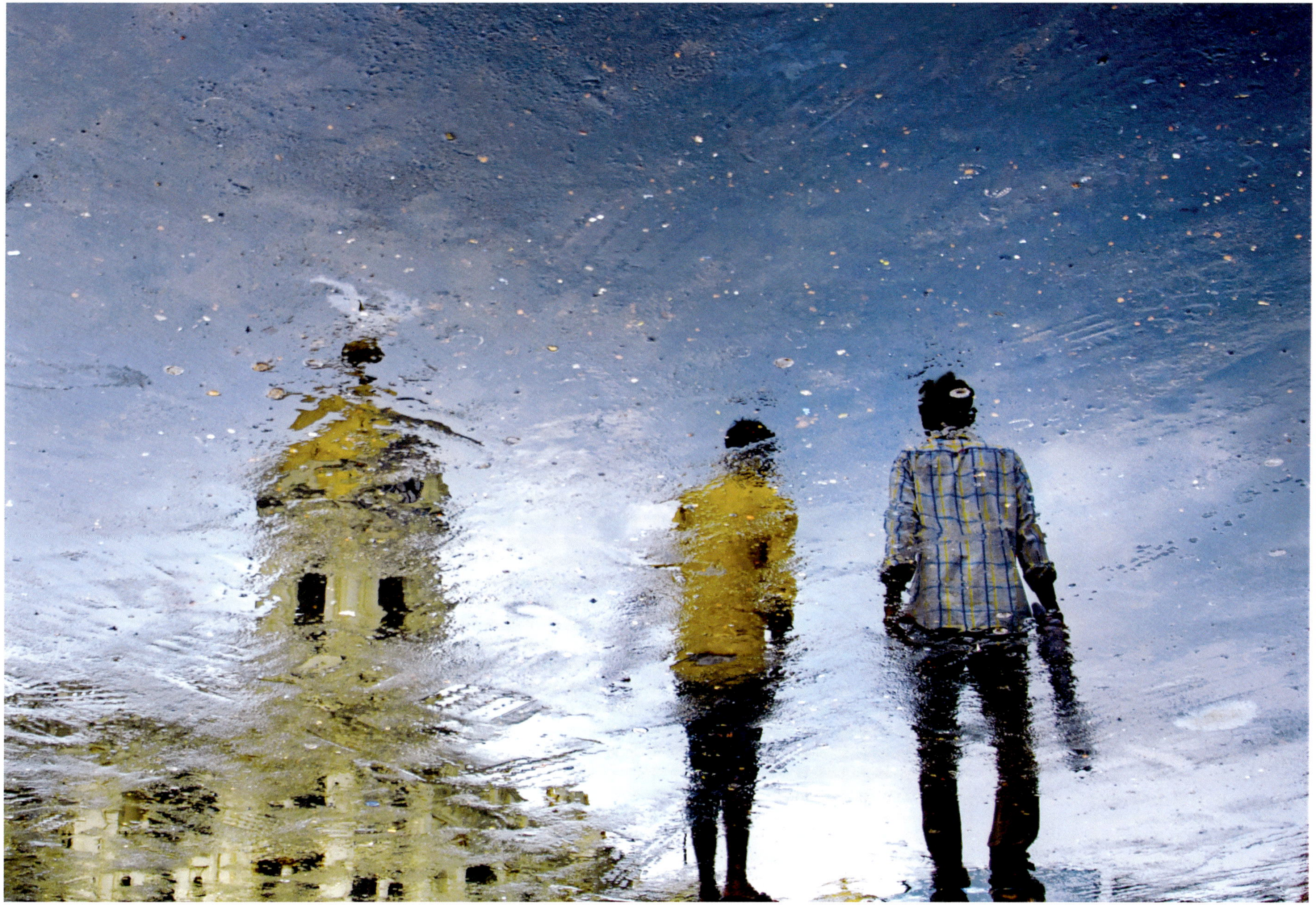

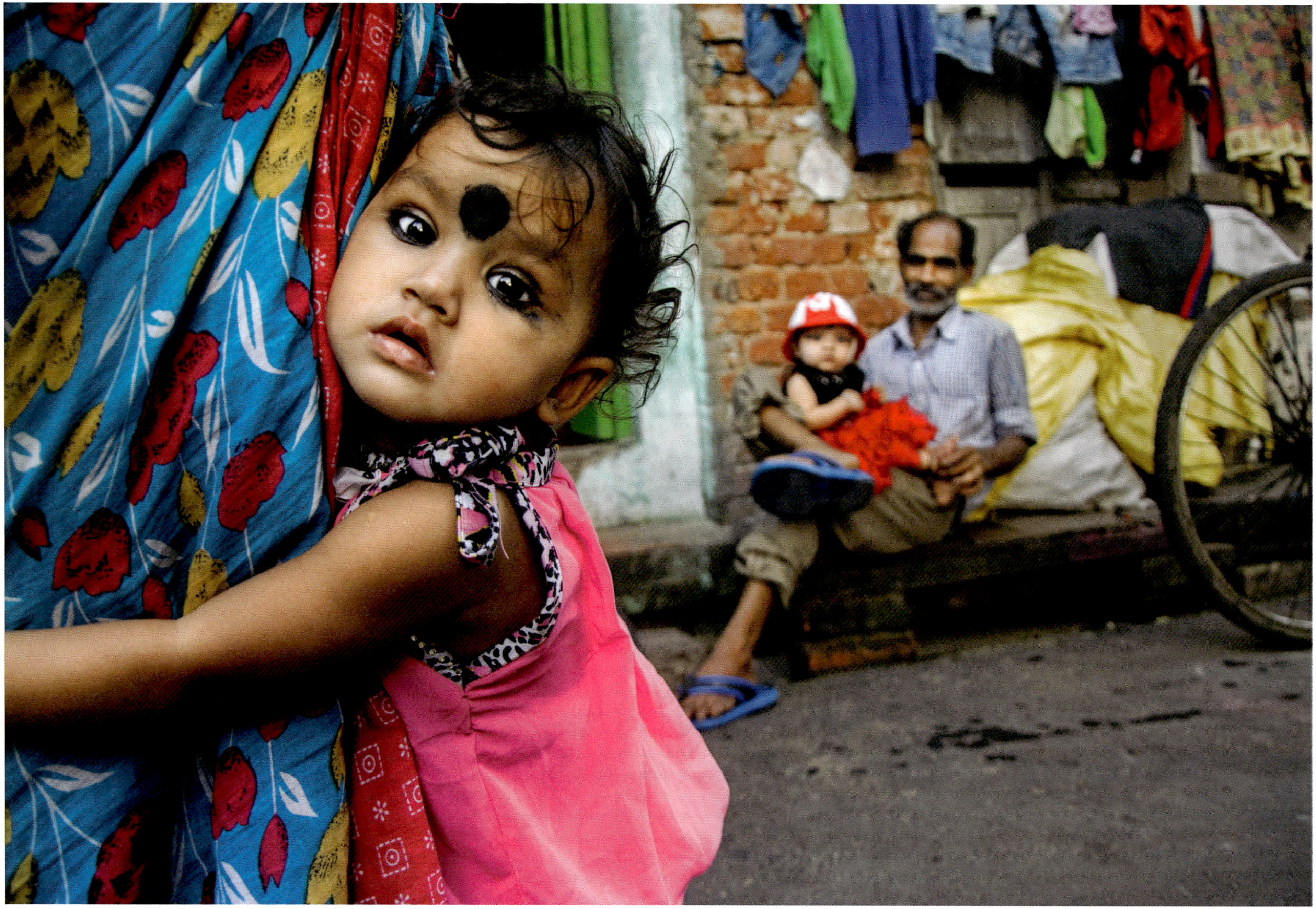

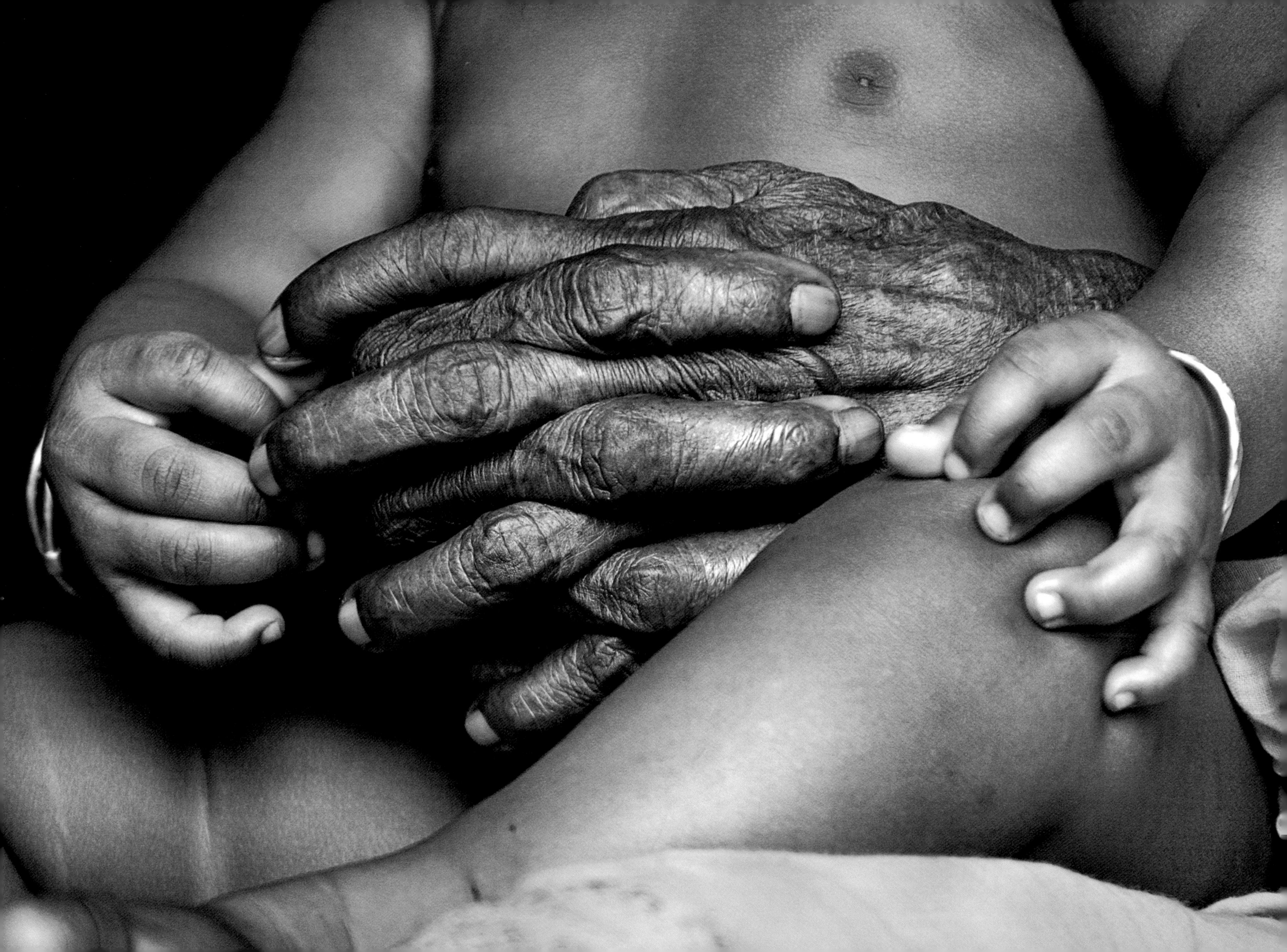

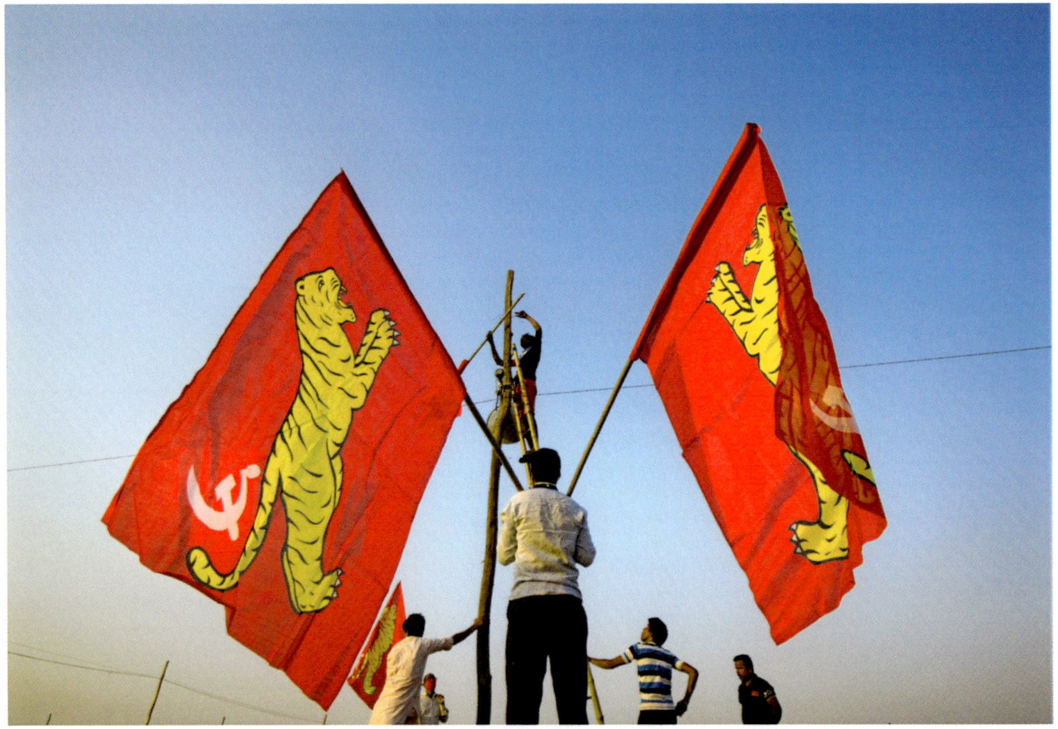
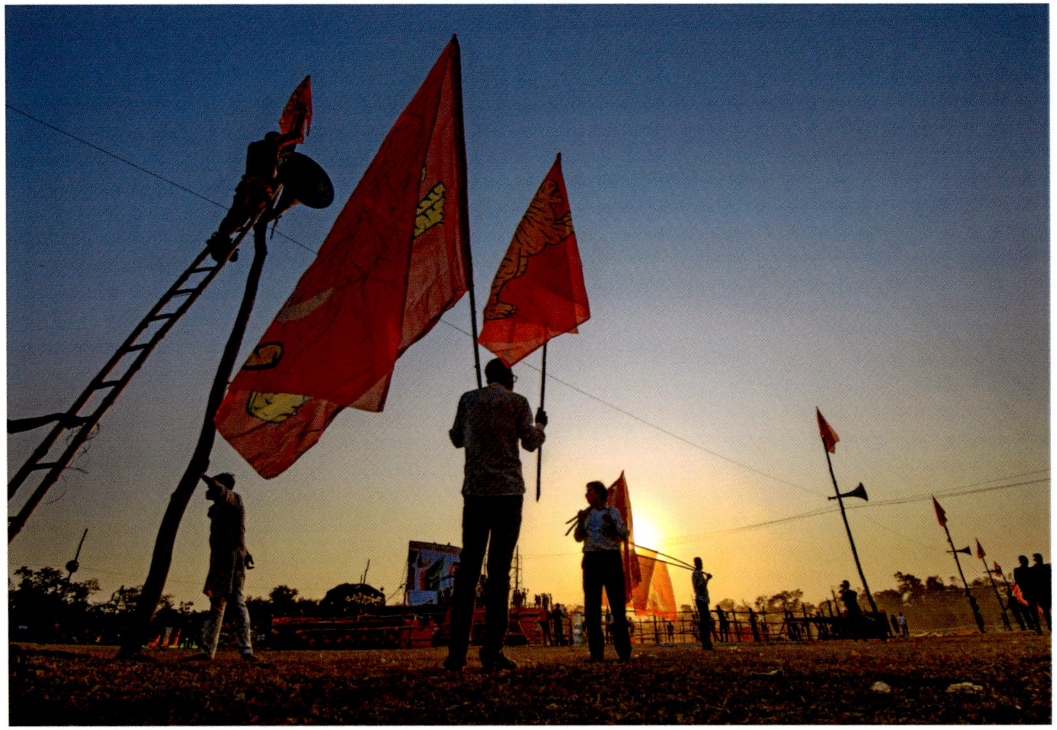

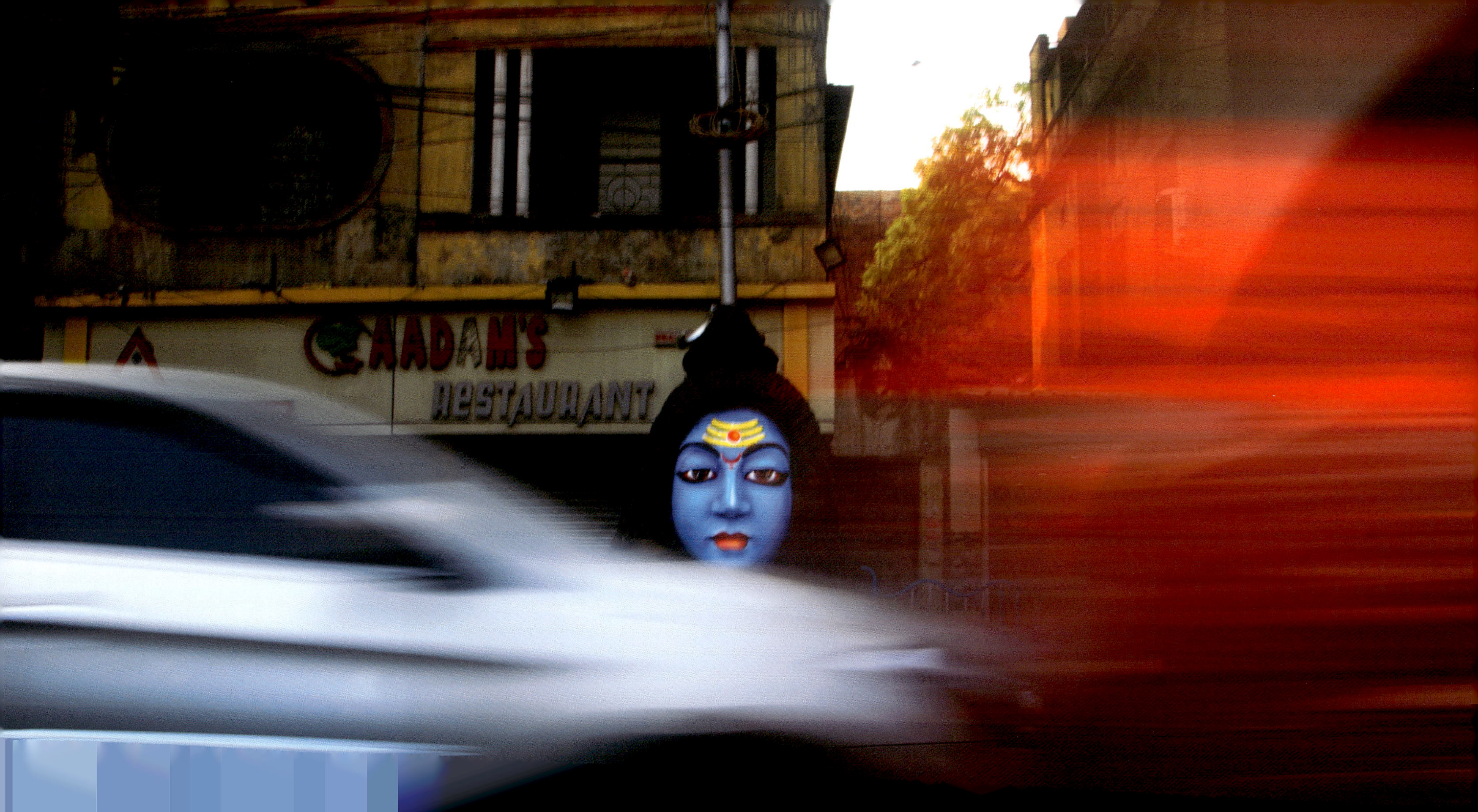
AADAM'S
RESTAURANT

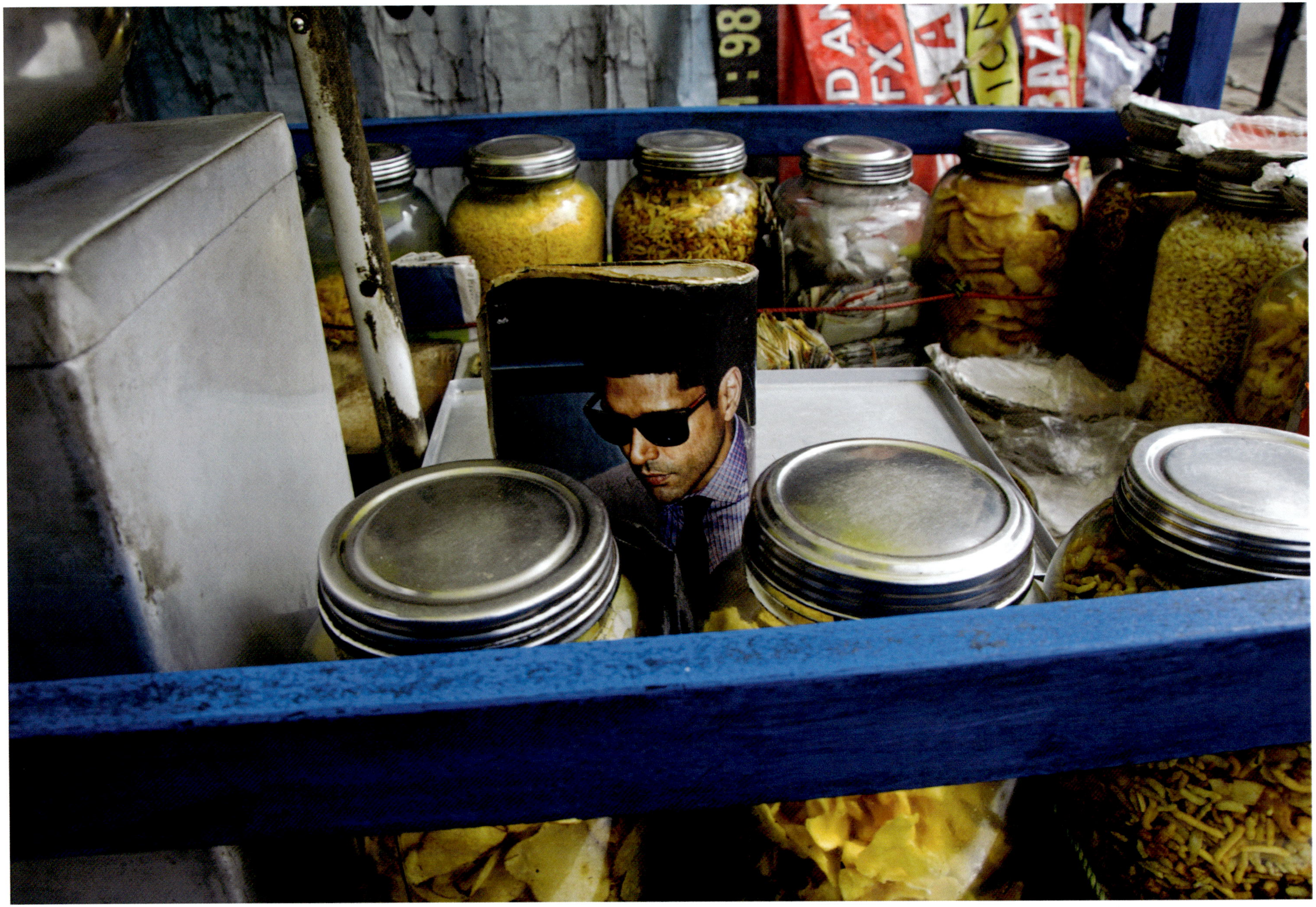

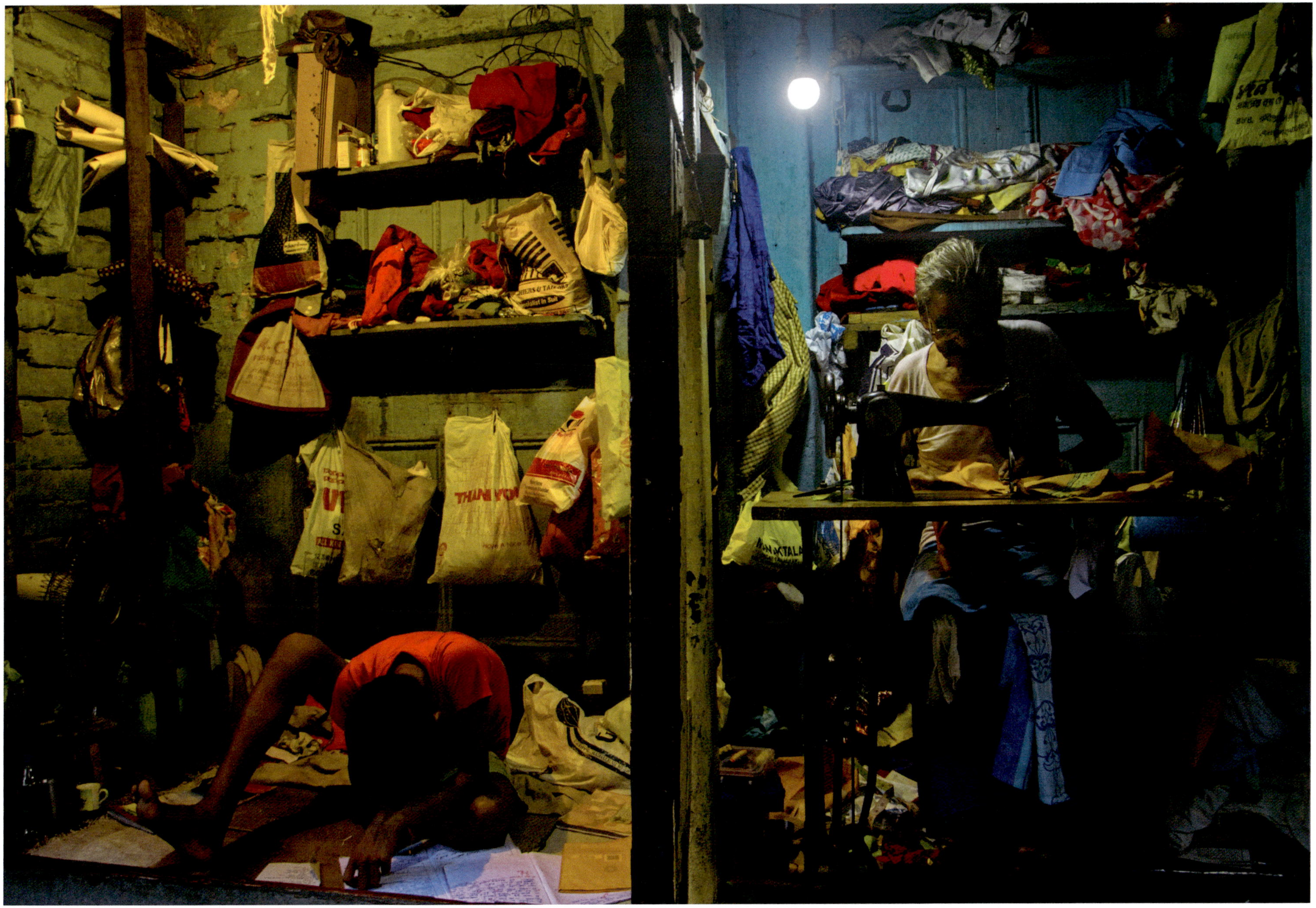

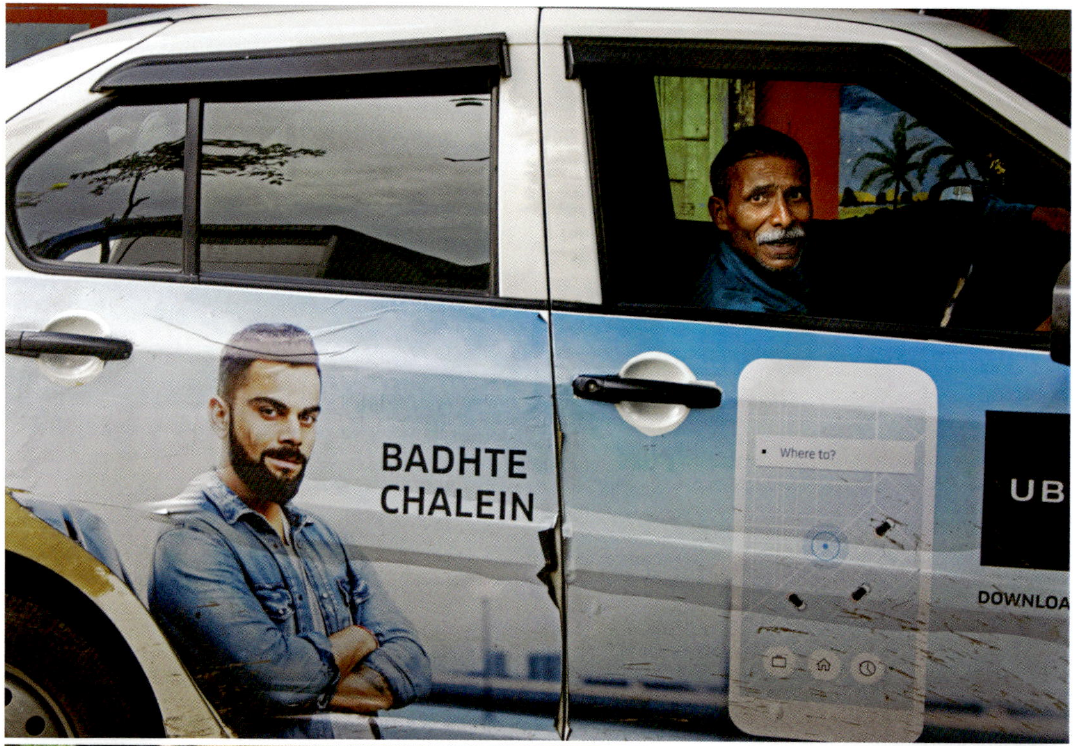
BADHTE
CHALEIN
Where to?
UB
DOWNLOA

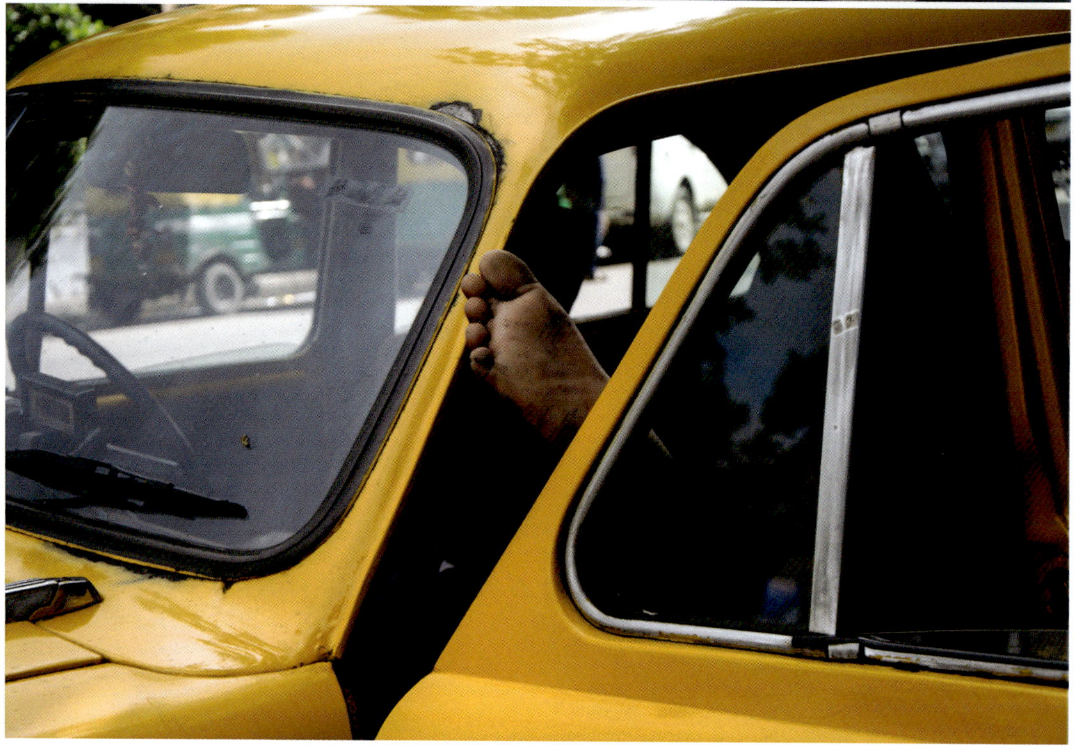

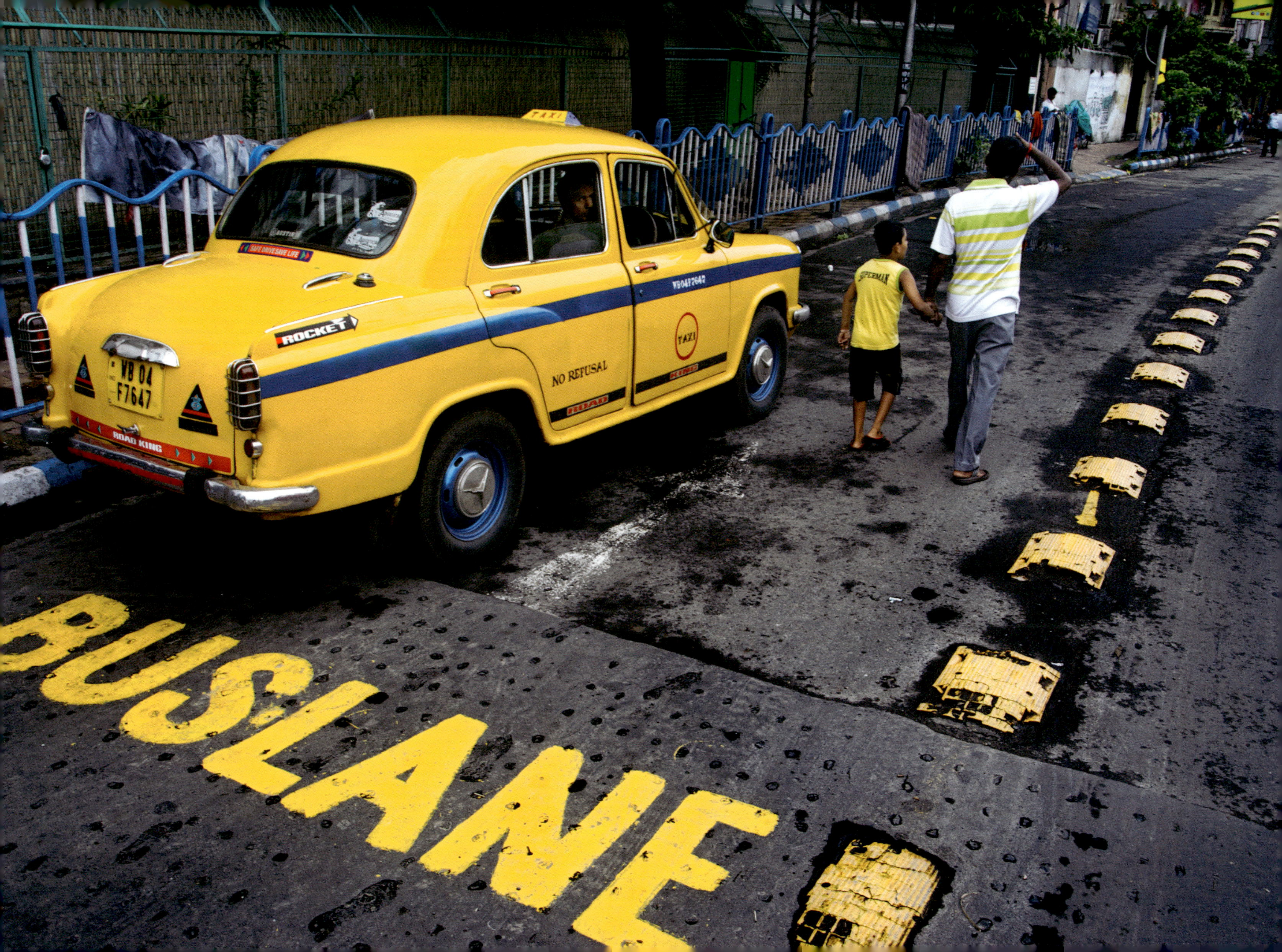
TAXI
ROCKET
WB 04
F7647
ROAD KING
NO REFUSAL
TAXI
BUSLANE

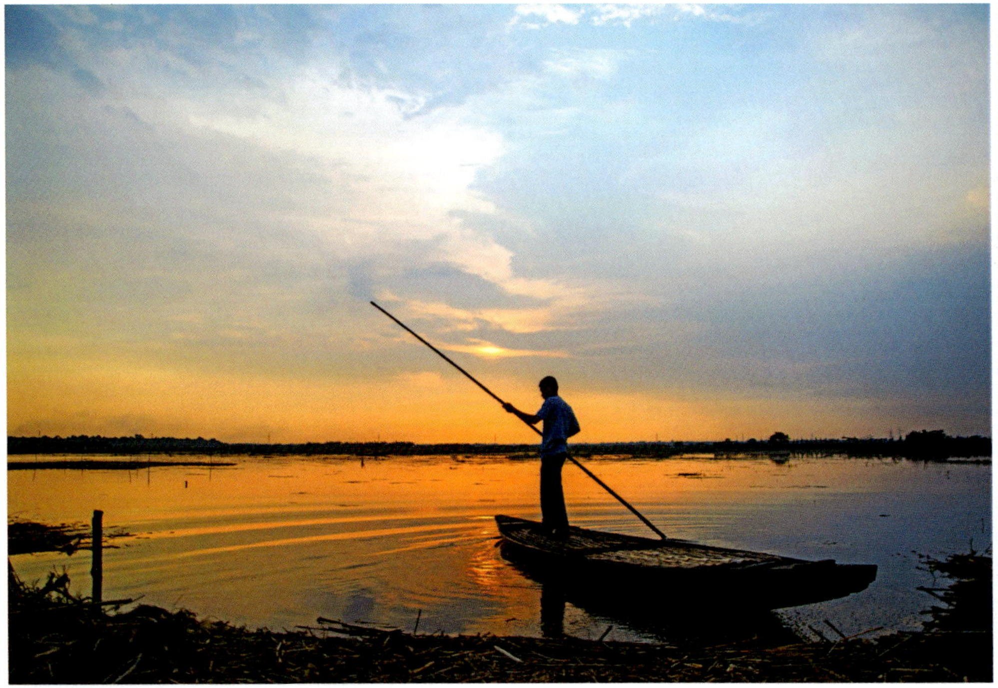
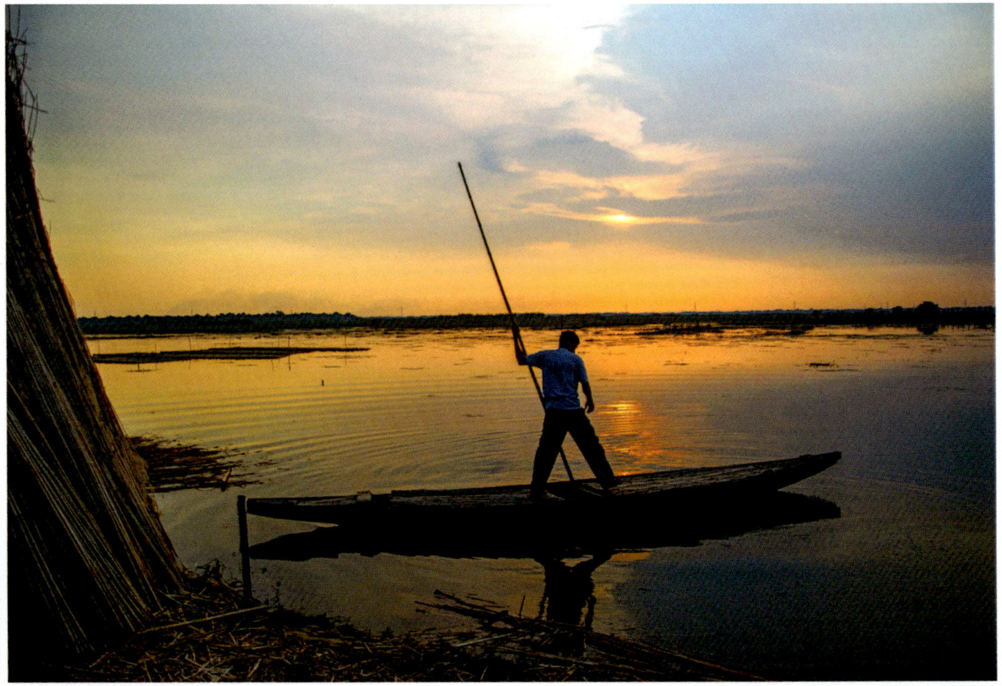
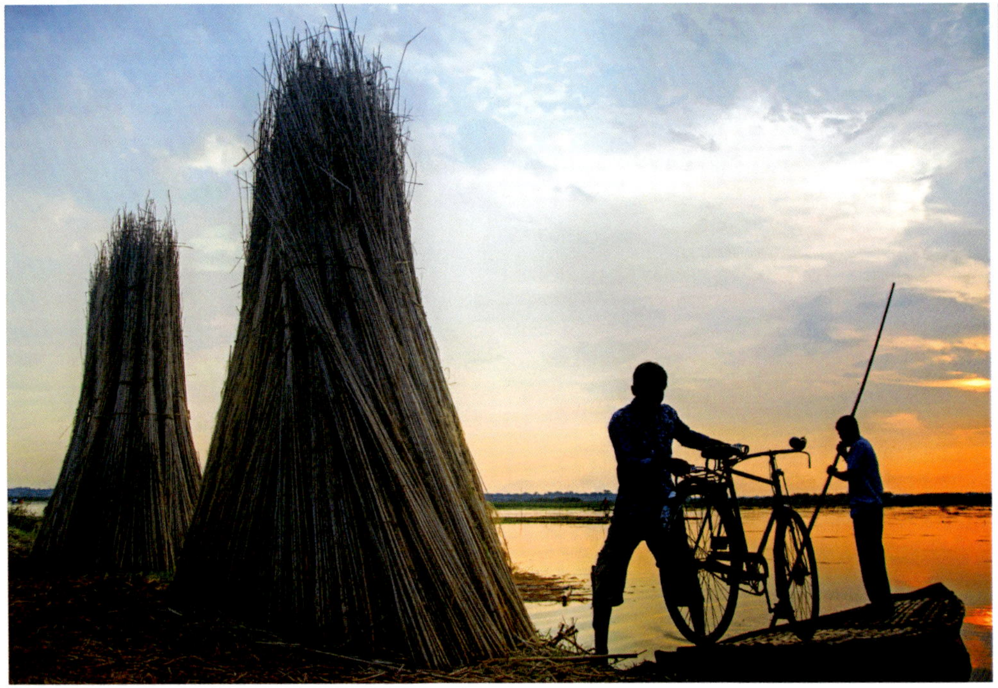
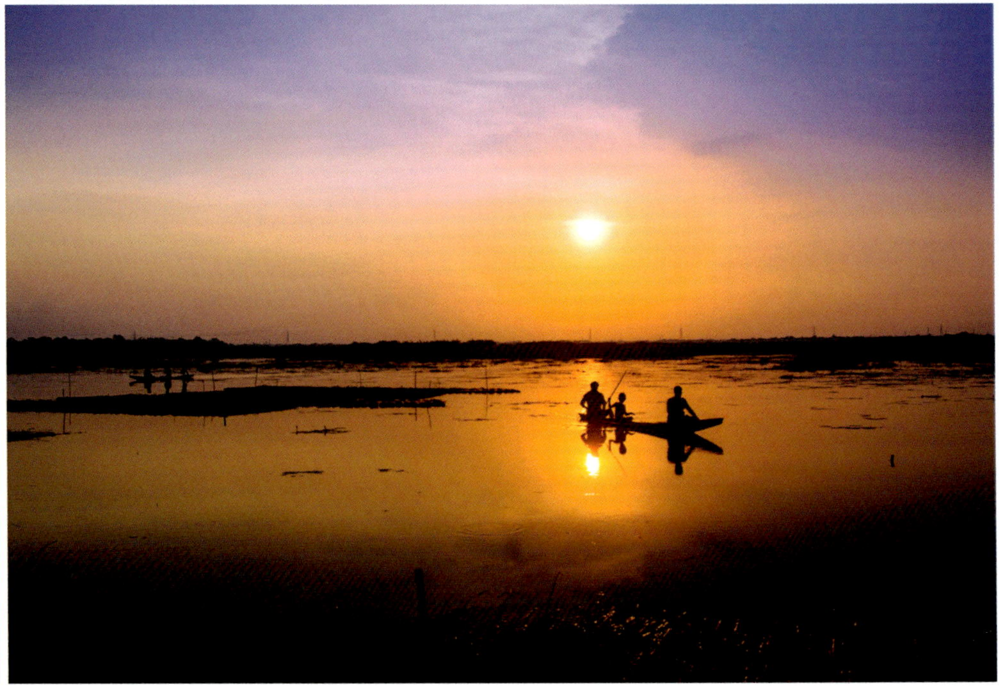

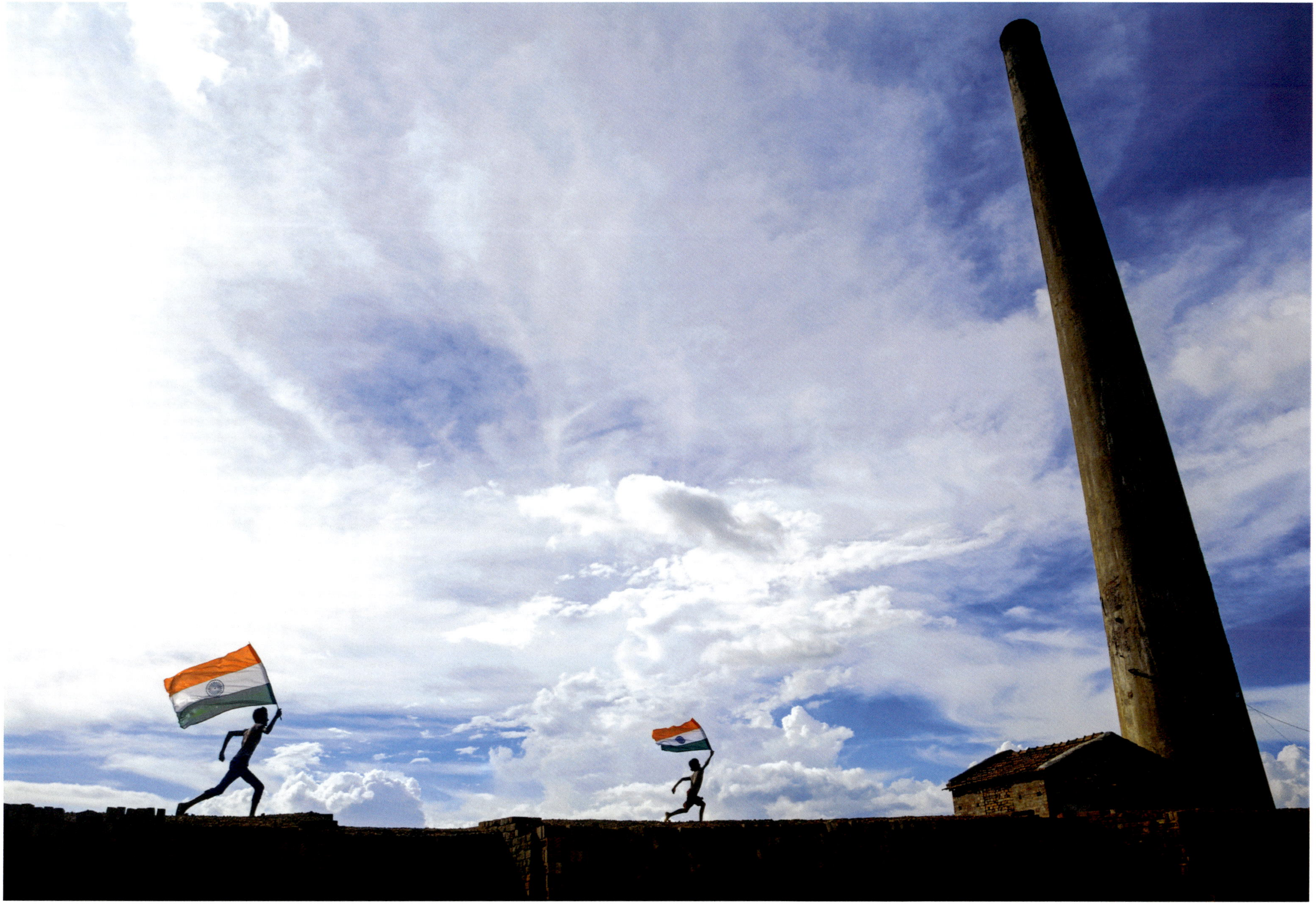

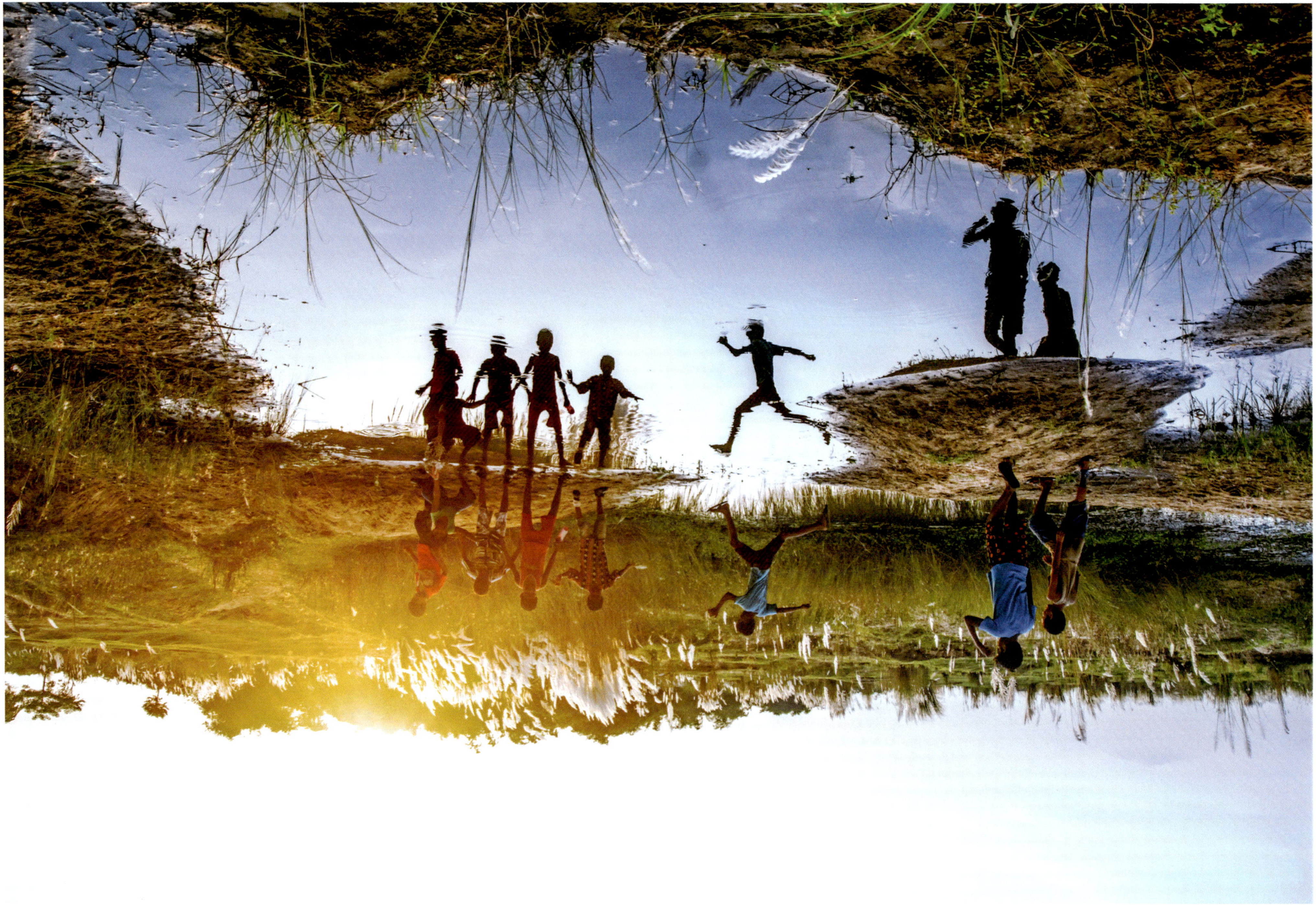

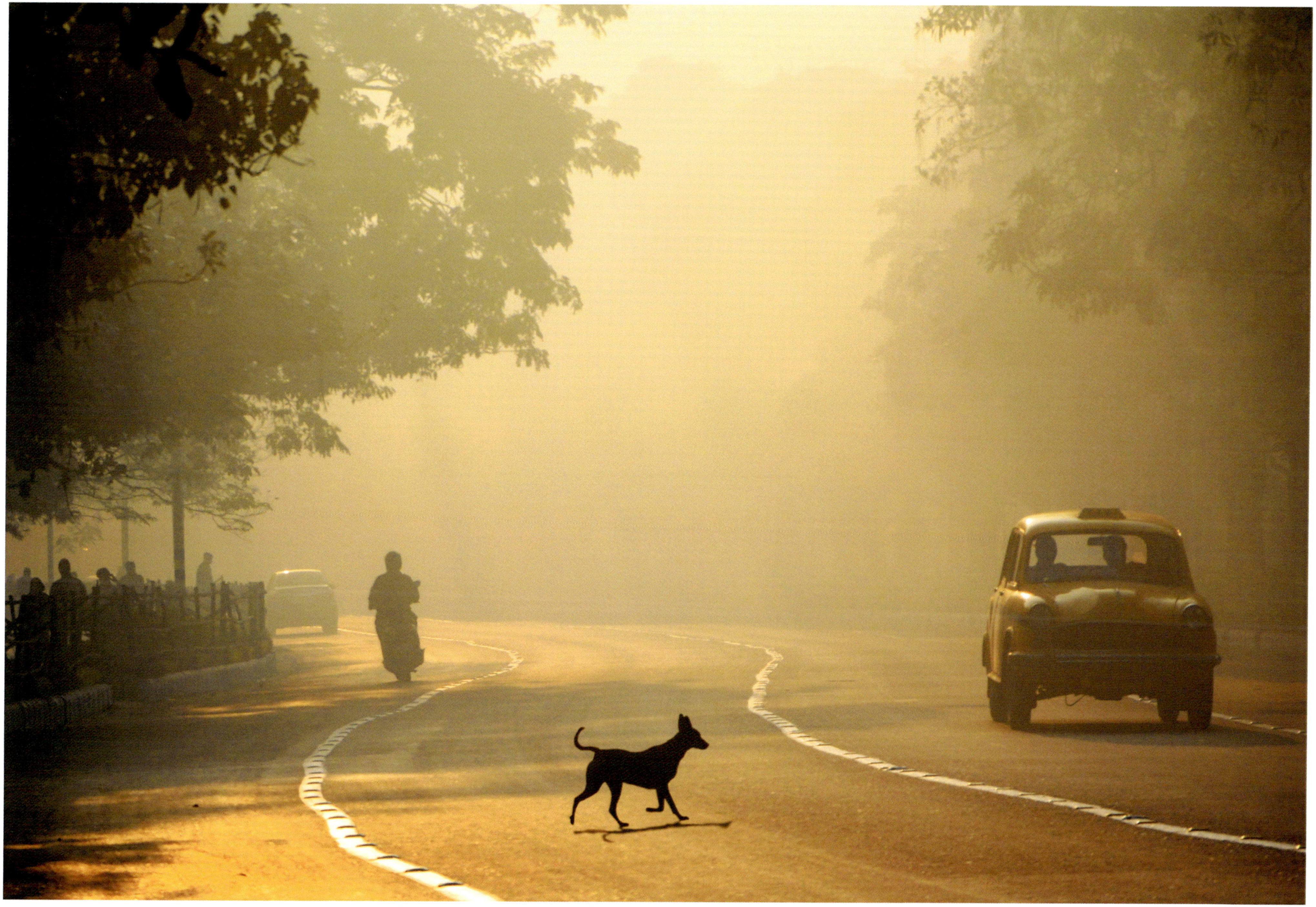

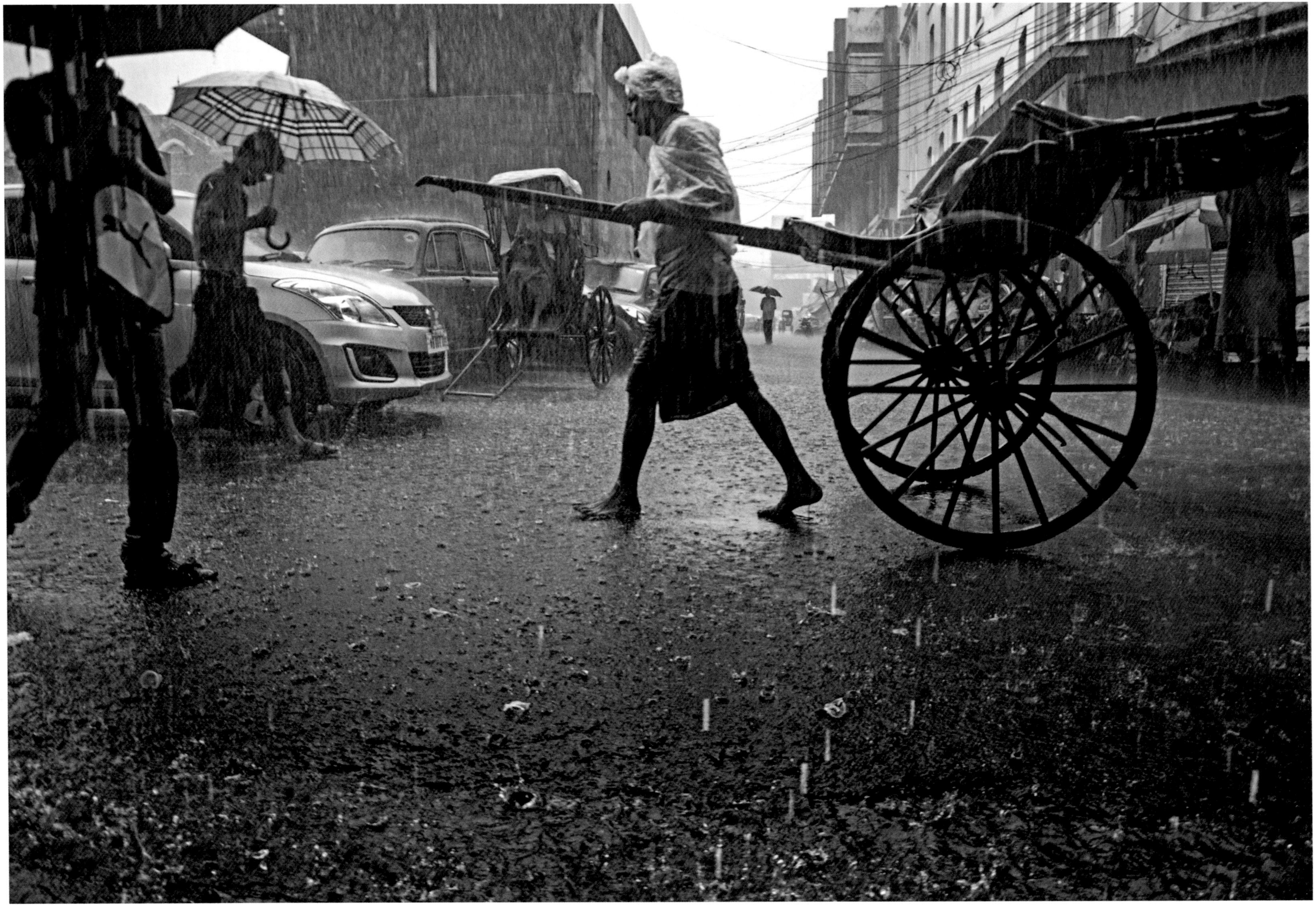

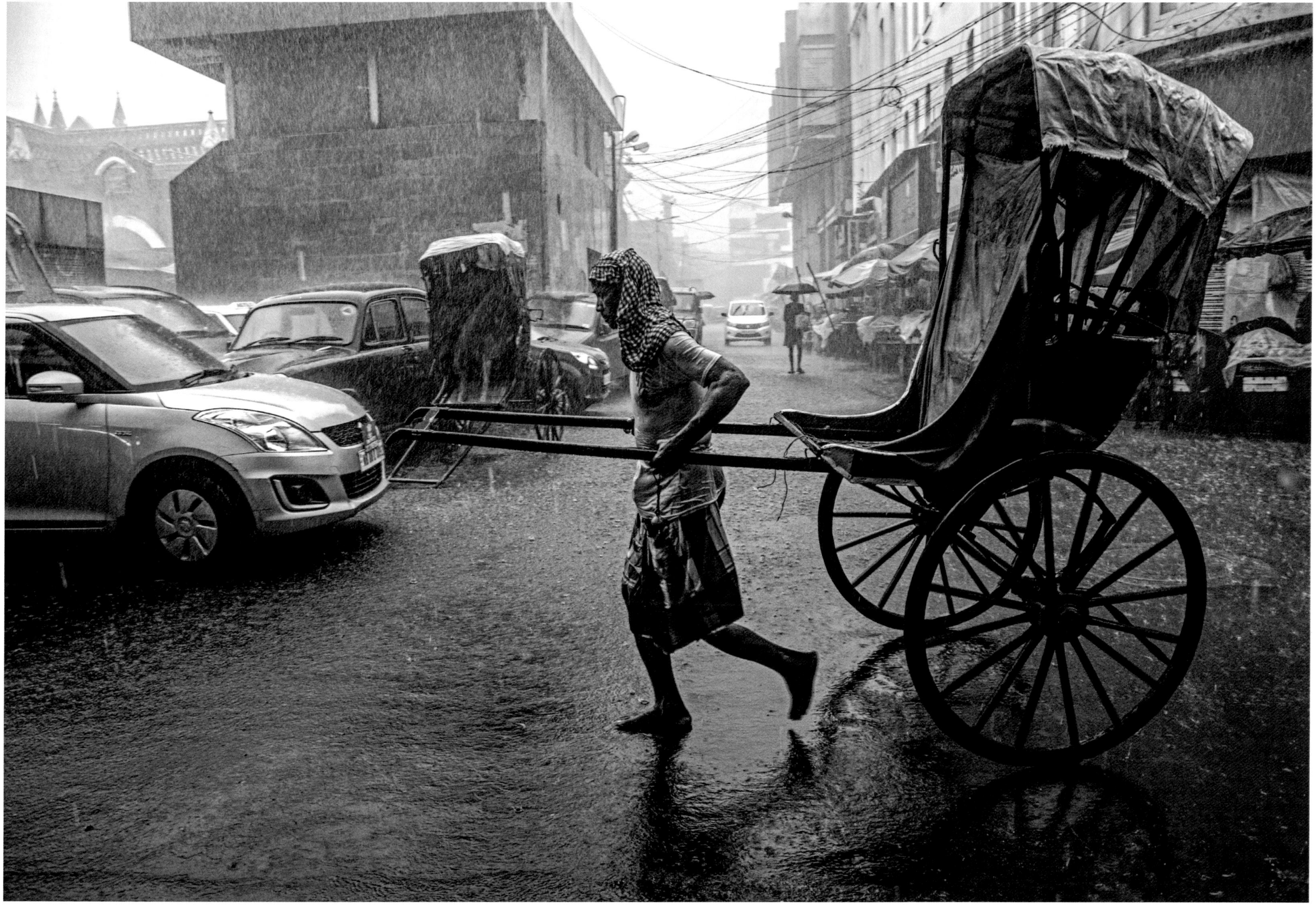

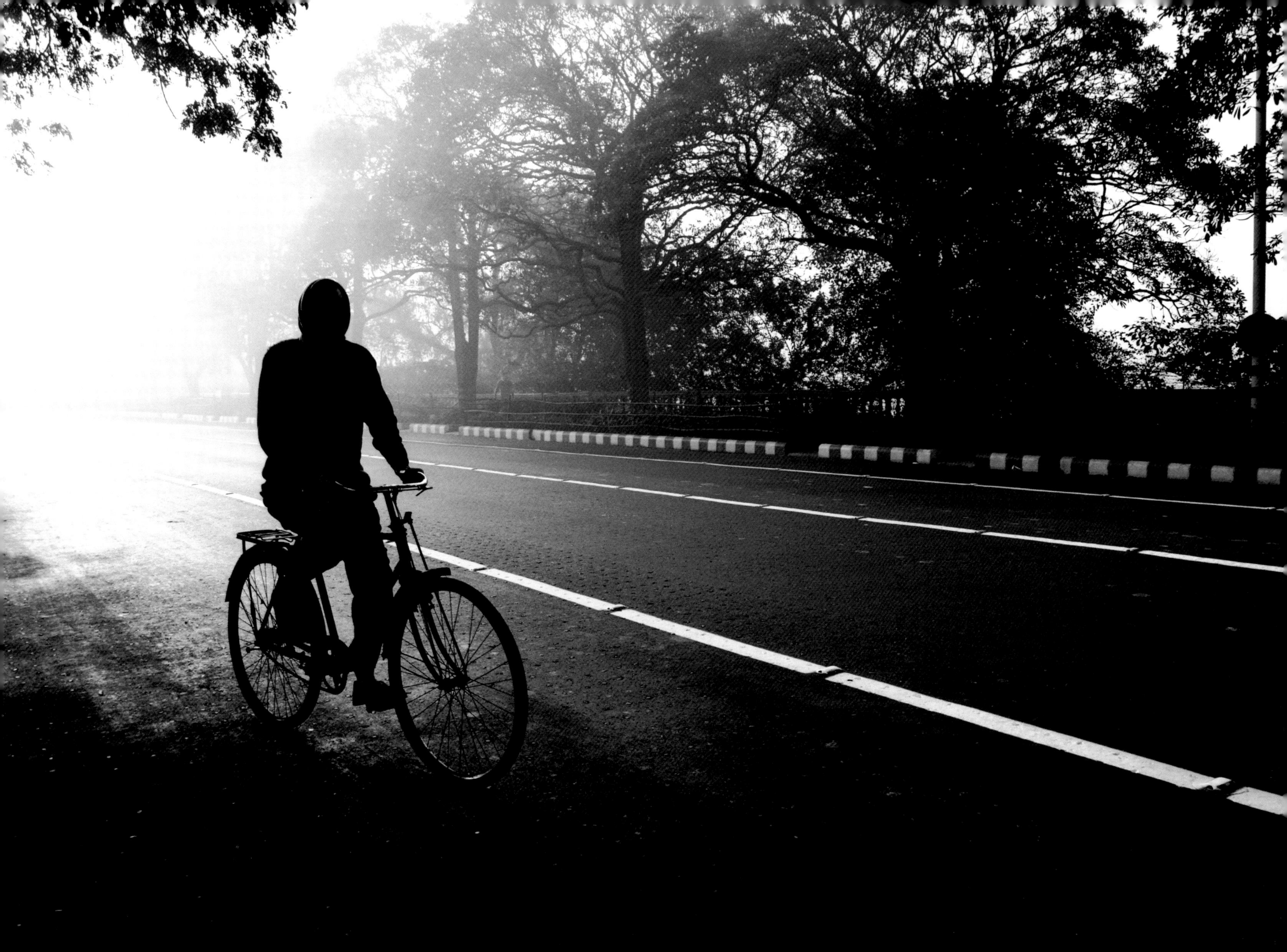

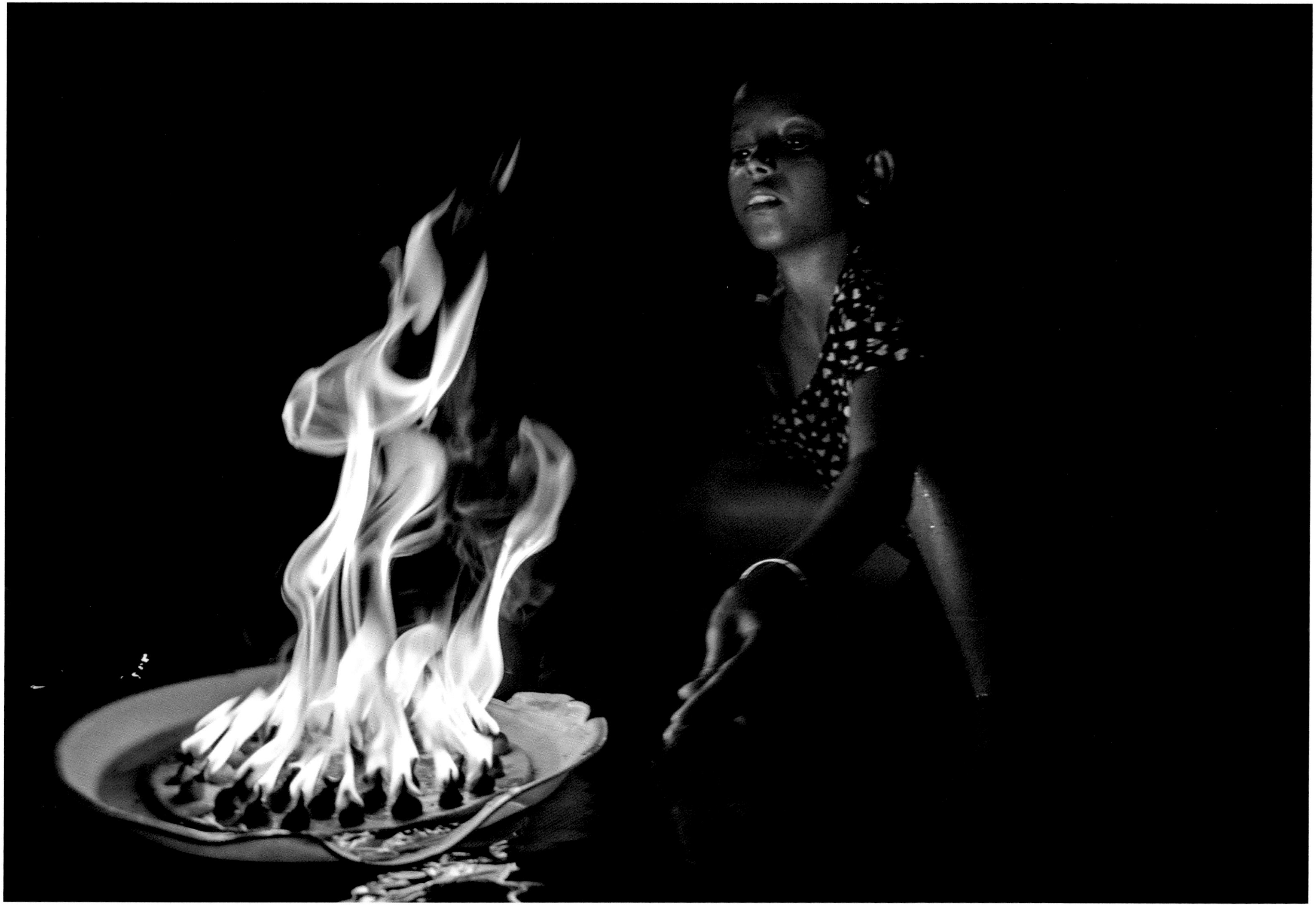

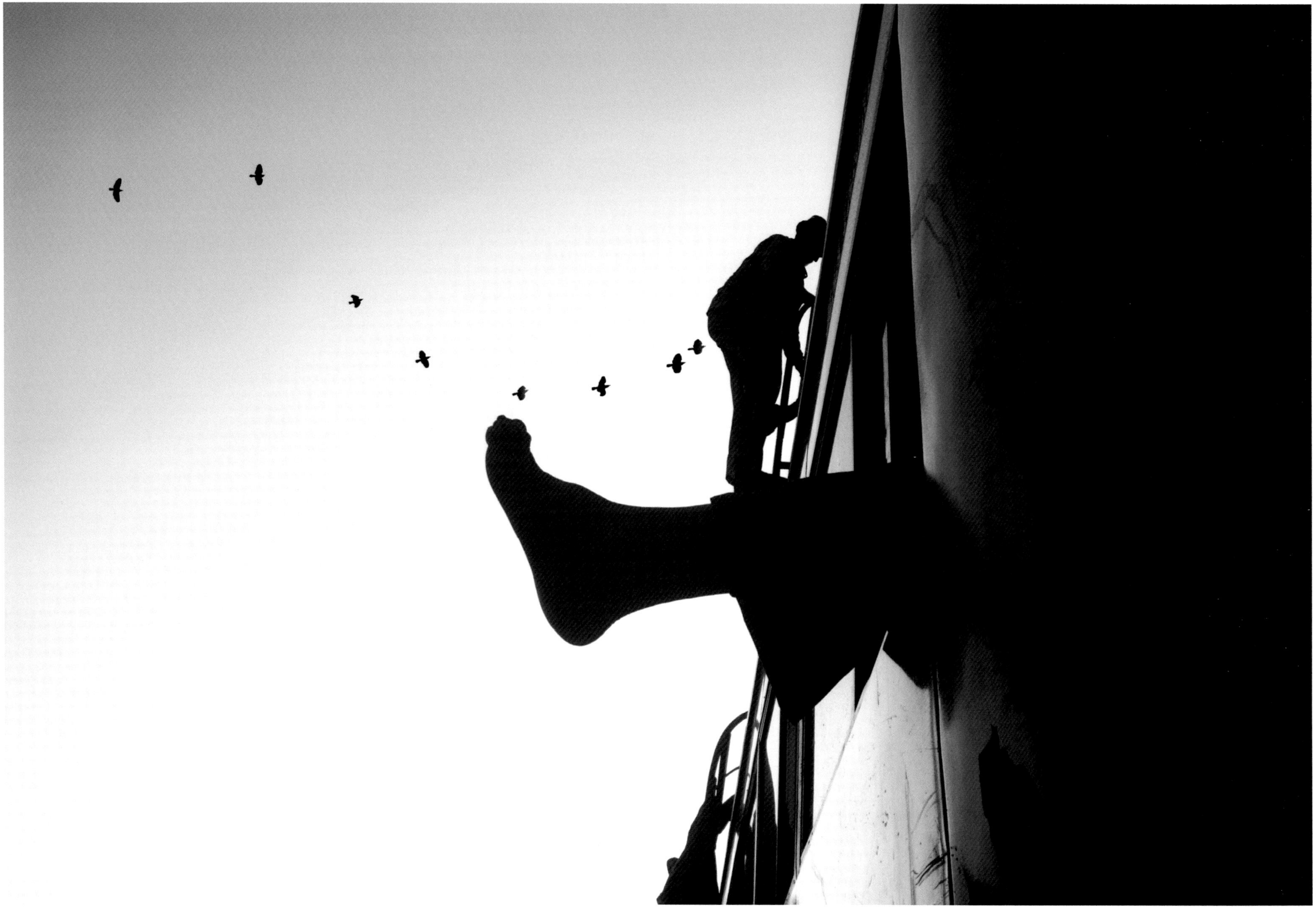

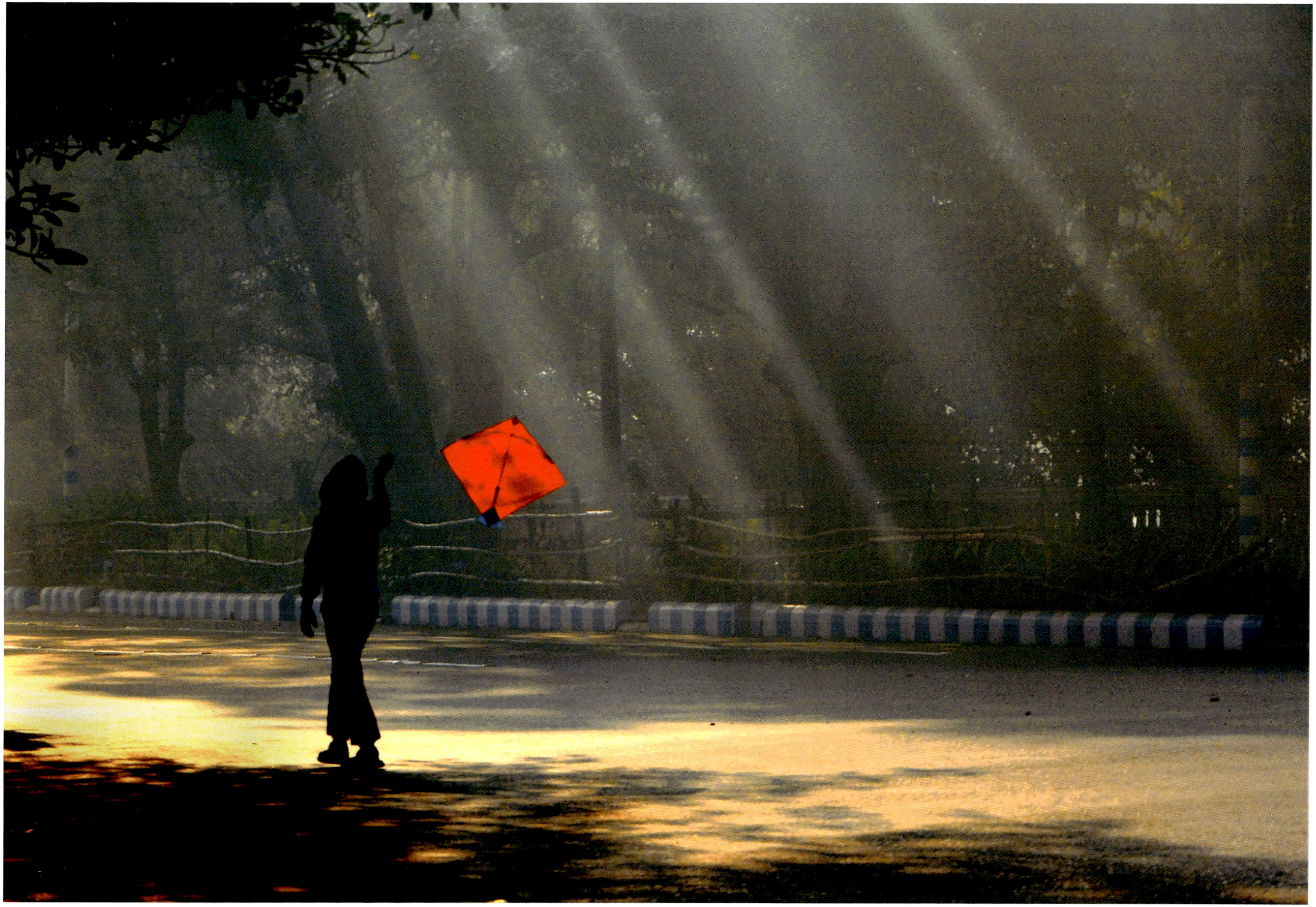

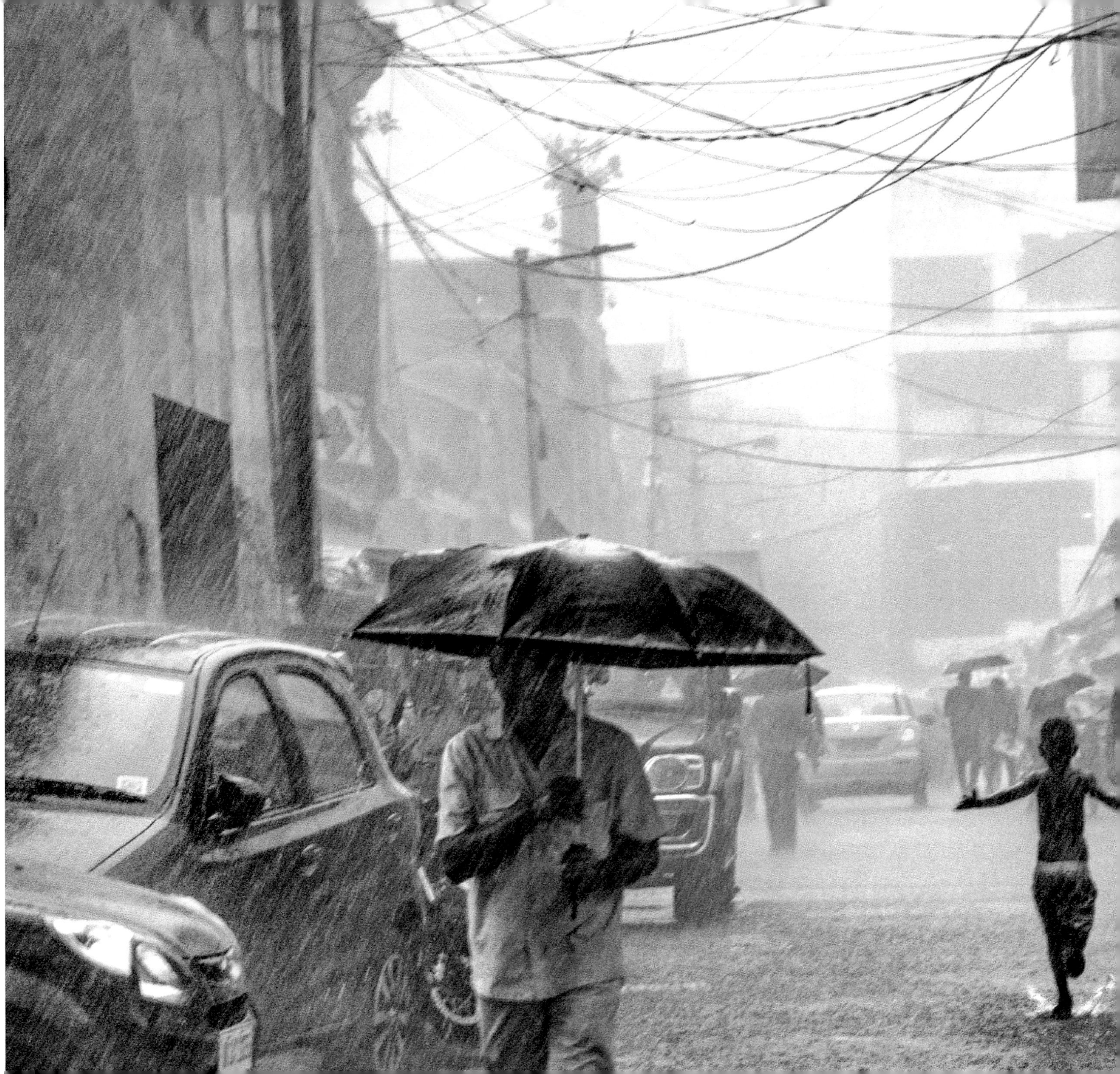

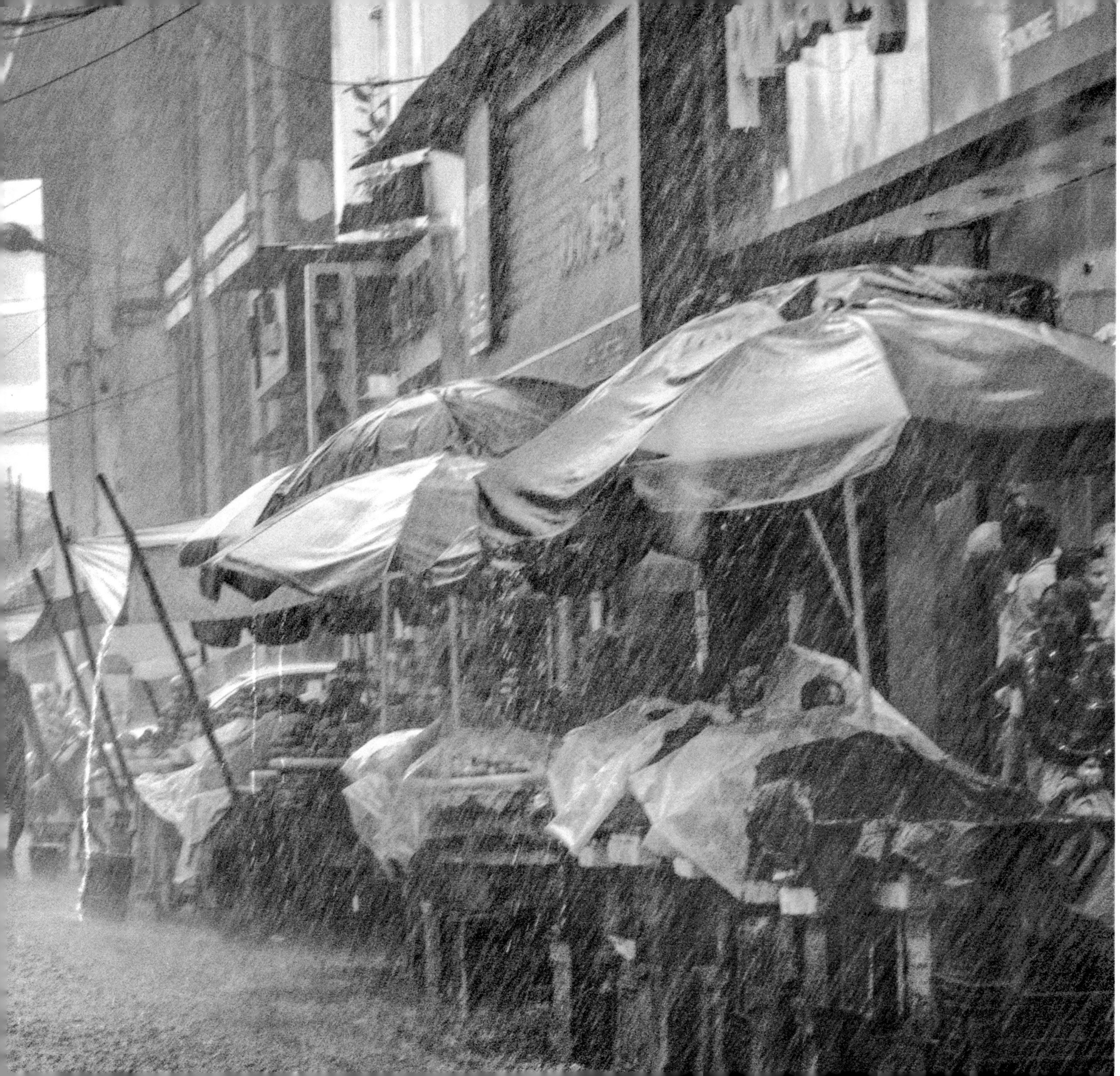

Imprint

Any brand names and product names mentioned in this book are subject to trademark, brand or patent protection and are trademarks or registered trademarks of their respective holders. The use of brand names, product names, common names, trade names, product descriptions etc. even without a particular marking in this work is no way to be construed to mean that such names may be regarded as unrestricted in respect of trademark and brand protection legislation and could thus be used by anyone.

Publisher:
Snap Collective
Is a trademark of
Rock N Books Ltd.
59 St. Martin's Lane, Suite 8, London, WC2N 4JS, UK

Printed at: EsserDruck Solutions GmbH Untere Sonnenstraße 5, 84030 Ergolding

ISBN: 978-1-914569-39-5
Design by: Tea Jagodic

Copyright © Arunabha Kundu
Copyright © 2022 Rock N Books Ltd.